Divination and Philosophy in the Letters of Paul

Edinburgh Studies in Religion in Antiquity

Series editors: Matthew V. Novenson, James B. Rives, Paula Fredriksen

Edinburgh Studies in Religion in Antiquity publishes cutting-edge research in religion in the ancient world. It provides a platform for creative studies spanning time periods (classical antiquity and late antiquity), geographical regions (the Mediterranean and West Asia), religious traditions (Greek, Roman, Jewish, Christian and more), disciplines (comparative literature, archaeology, anthropology, and more) and theoretical questions (historical, philological, comparative, redescriptive, and more). Deconstructing literary canons and confessional boundaries, the series considers and questions what we moderns call "religion" as a prominent feature of the human past and a worthy object of historical enquiry.

Advisory Board

Helen Bond, University of Edinburgh
Kimberley Czajkowski, University of Edinburgh
Benedikt Eckhardt, University of Edinburgh
Martin Goodman, University of Oxford
Oded Irshai, Hebrew University of Jerusalem
Timothy Lim, University of Edinburgh
Yii-Jan Lin, Yale University
Candida Moss, University of Birmingham
Paul Parvis, University of Edinburgh
Matthew Thiessen, McMaster University
Philippa Townsend, University of Edinburgh
Greg Woolf, University of California-Los Angeles

Books published in the series

Megan S. Nutzman, *Contested Cures: Identity and Ritual Healing in Roman and Late Antique Palestine*
Matthew T. Sharp, *Divination and Philosophy in the Letters of Paul*

Visit the series webpage: https://edinburghuniversitypress.com/series-edinburgh-studies-in-religion-in-antiquity

Divination and Philosophy in the Letters of Paul

Matthew T. Sharp

EDINBURGH
University Press

Edinburgh University Press is one of the leading university presses in the UK. We publish academic books and journals in our selected subject areas across the humanities and social sciences, combining cutting-edge scholarship with high editorial and production values to produce academic works of lasting importance. For more information visit our website: edinburghuniversitypress.com

© Matthew T. Sharp, 2023, 2024

Edinburgh University Press Ltd
The Tun – Holyrood Road
12(2f) Jackson's Entry
Edinburgh EH8 8PJ

First published in hardback by Edinburgh University Press 2023

Typeset in 11/13 Bembo Std by
IDSUK (DataConnection) Ltd

A CIP record for this book is available from the British Library

ISBN 978 1 3995 0357 0 (hardback)
ISBN 978 1 3995 0358 7 (paperback)
ISBN 978 1 3995 0359 4 (webready PDF)
ISBN 978 1 3995 0360 0 (epub)

The right of Matthew T. Sharp to be identified as the author of this work has been asserted in accordance with the Copyright, Designs and Patents Act 1988, and the Copyright and Related Rights Regulations 2003 (SI No. 2498).

Contents

Acknowledgements vi
Abbreviations viii

Introduction: On Categories and Comparisons 1

1 The Mechanics of Divination 27

2 Visions 62

3 Speech 97

4 Texts 133

5 Signs 163

Conclusion: Divination and Philosophy in Paul 197

Bibliography 205
Index 231

Acknowledgements

I am grateful to many people who have played a part in helping this book to completion. The book is based on my PhD thesis from the University of Edinburgh, and so I must thank first and foremost my supervisor, Matthew Novenson. He has been, and remains, an essential source of wisdom and encouragement. The ever-growing Novenson cohort also deserves special mention who, at various stages of the process, have been invaluable scholarly colleagues: Bernardo Cho, J. Thomas Hewitt, Benj Petroelje, Daniel Jackson, Teresa McCaskill, Sydney Tooth, Brian Bunnell, Patrick McMurray, Sofanit Abebe, Alex Muir, and Manse Rim. The COVID Collective of Isaac Soon, Grace Emmett, and Logan Williams provided feedback on a number of draft portions of this book during the depths of national lockdowns. Belonging to both the above groups are Ryan Collman and Charles Cisco who if I were to mention at every relevant point in these acknowledgements would, along with their families, appear multiple times over for both their friendship and scholarship.

Various portions of this book have been presented at different scholarly venues: the New College Biblical Studies Seminar, the Northern Universities Postgraduate Day at Durham, and the annual meetings of the British New Testament Society and the Society of Biblical Literature. My thanks go to all who offered questions and feedback at these venues. I would particularly like to thank Jennifer Eyl for providing me with early pre-publication drafts of her book, which have been enormously helpful in sharpening the questions and approach of my own work. My examiners, Philippa Townsend and George van Kooten, both provided expert feedback, and have in their own ways influenced the final form of this book, not least its title. The contributions of the two anonymous reviewers for Edinburgh University Press and the series editors, Matthew Novenson, Paula Fredriksen, and James Rives have also improved the work in both style and content. While my research has been enriched by such excellent conversation partners, any deficiencies are of course entirely my own.

I would finally like to thank the many family members who have aided the completion of this project in one way or other. My parents furnished me with an enduring love and curiosity of all things biblical and have provided the most enduring support and encouragement to all my endeavours. Special thanks go to Gan for providing study space and refreshments, and to Manny and Pippa for the many gifts, material and immaterial, that have eased the whole process of postgraduate study for our family. Thanks especially to Pippa for her proof-reading and editorial expertise. My deepest gratitude, love, and admiration go to my wife Becki who is truly the one who has made this project possible. The credit for maintaining a fully functioning and flourishing family during the long years of postgraduate research goes entirely to her. Her capacity is extraordinary, and I am so glad she is now excelling at her own studies. I dedicate this work to her.

Abbreviations

All abbreviations conform to those prescribed in *The SBL Handbook of Style: For Biblical Studies and Related Disciplines*, ed. Billie Jean Collins, Bob Buller, and John F. Kutsko, 2nd ed. (Atlanta: SBL Press, 2014). Any abbreviations not included in *The SBL Handbook of Style* are listed below.

ASE	*Annali di Storia dell'Esegesi*
HM	Heythrop Monographs
JECH	*Journal of Early Christian History*
JSJSup	Supplements to Journal for the Study of Judaism
OG	Old Greek
SCJ	Studies in Christianity and Judaism
SCJR	*Studies in Christian-Jewish Relations*
α'	Aquila
θ'	Theodotion
σ'	Symmachus

INTRODUCTION

On Categories and Comparisons

> What is hidden from mortals we should try to find out from the gods by divination for to him that is in their grace the gods grant a sign.
> (Xenophon, *Memorabilia* 1.1.9)

Throughout his letters, Paul claims to convey the words and will of his God, and of that God's Messiah, Jesus. This observation is painfully obvious, but has not generally received the attention it deserves in Pauline scholarship. For those studying his letters from a confessional perspective such an observation may be taken for granted or treated at the level of the general inspiration of scripture. For many lay readers of Paul the passages that need more explanation are those in which he claims *not* to be speaking directly for God (such as 1 Cor 7:12). For critical scholarship, the truth value of such claims is appropriately bracketed, and attention instead focuses on the development of his ideas within his cultural and religious milieu. Within this cultural and religious milieu, though, we may still ask the question: if Paul claims to convey the words and will of a deity, how does he believe he has received such knowledge? His letters suggest a variety of means through which he discerns the divine will: he has visions and revelations of the risen Jesus, he receives prophetic words and wisdom transmitted by holy *pneuma*, he interprets Jewish sacred texts and, more generally, he reads signs of divine activity in the human and natural world around him.

The aim of this study is twofold: to provide a category through which these various methods of hearing from the divine can be conceptualised in Paul's first-century context and, second, to provide a reading of Paul's letters that attends to how these various methods function in relation to each other in Paul's broader worldview.[1] Many of these aspects of Paul's letters have been

---

[1] Paul's letters for the purposes of this study are the seven virtually undisputed letters: Romans, 1 Corinthians, 2 Corinthians, Galatians, Philippians, 1 Thessalonians, and Philemon. For the text of these and other NT texts I follow Barbara Aland et al., *Novum Testamentum Graece*, 28th ed. (Stuttgart: Deutsche Bibelgesellschaft, 2012). Text critical issues will be noted where appropriate.

extensively studied in their own right, but Pauline scholarship has so far lacked an adequate analytical category through which to account for all of these methods of divine communication in Paul's historical context. The most common categories that might accomplish such a task are "revelation" or "prophecy," but both of these are limited in the evidence they allow for consideration and in the way they relate Paul to his historical and philosophical context. Studies of Paul and "revelation" have generally proceeded from a theological framework, which focuses on the event of God's saving action rather than Paul's own role in obtaining and mediating divine information. Studies of Paul as a prophet or visionary have tended to make "inspiration" a defining characteristic, and so have excluded the full range of available evidence for how people of the Graeco-Roman world solicited information from the divine world.

It is the argument of this book that Paul's various means of communication with the divine are best situated within the context of ancient divination, and that such a category provides a fruitful lens through which these practices can be compared with each other, and with similar practices in Paul's broader historical and cultural context. Some recent scholarship has begun to apply the label "divination" to a number of Paul's practices, but has not yet reckoned fully with the utility of this category for understanding Paul's thought and practice regarding divine communication. Therefore, in what follows I offer a close reading of Paul's letters through the lens of comparative divination. As will be seen, this category irreducibly connects to a number of much larger themes in Paul's letters, thereby providing fresh understandings of his anthropology, cosmology, eschatology, and theology.

In order to adequately prepare the ground for such a study I will first define what I mean by divination and how I am using it as an analytical category. I will then survey previous scholarship on revelation, prophecy, and divination in Paul. In the former two instances I show how they have not adequately accounted for the breadth of Paul's means of access to divine knowledge or how this relates to his broader historical context. In the latter instance I show how they have demonstrated the utility of the category of divination but without yet providing a thorough reading of the relevant aspects of Paul's letters in light of this category. This introductory chapter will conclude by clarifying some methodological aspects, particularly regarding how I relate Paul to his historical context.

Defining Divination

I define "divination" as the reception and interpretation of knowledge that is believed to have a divine, or superhuman, source. This is an intentionally broad

(*Cont.*) Pauline letters of disputed authorship and his literary depictions (most notably in the Acts of the Apostles) will occasionally be discussed but do not serve as primary evidence for the Apostle.

definition as it is designed to capture within its purview the wide variety of practices and phenomena that scholars of the ancient Mediterranean give the name divinatory.² Sarah Iles Johnston notes: "Some degree of variability and adaptability is characteristic of all religious phenomena, but ancient divination was particularly pliant. A relatively straightforward goal – to gain knowledge of what humans would not otherwise know – manifested itself in a variety of ways that combined and recombined themselves."³ This led to a vast array of objects and occurrences that could in various ways convey knowledge from a god: earthquakes, thunder claps, the flight of birds, animal entrails, dreams or inspired oracles among many others: all were identifiable under the single heading of divination.⁴

Paul does not describe his activities with the usual Greek words for divination, and one does not need to look too far to find a likely reason for this. In the LXX, words such as μάντις and μαντεύομαι are generally restricted to the illegitimate practices of the Gentile nations. Deuteronomy 18:9–14, for instance, forbids the Israelites from imitating a long list of practices from the nations they are about to dispossess.⁵ These nations listen to "omens and divinations" (κληδόνων καὶ μαντειῶν), but the Israelites will listen to the only legitimate spokesperson for Yahweh, the προφήτης (Deut 18:15–20).⁶ Paul's terminology, which happily

---

² For similarly broad definitions, see Peter T. Struck, *Divination and Human Nature: A Cognitive History of Intuition in Classical Antiquity* (Princeton: Princeton University Press, 2016), 3: "The art of translating information from gods into the realm of the human." Michael Attyah Flower, *The Seer in Ancient Greece* (Berkeley: University of California Press, 2008), 72: "Divination is a means of bridging the gap between gods and humans in such a way that humans may profit from the knowledge thus acquired." Martti Nissinen, *Ancient Prophecy: Near Eastern, Biblical, and Greek Perspectives* (Oxford: Oxford University Press, 2017), 13: "The function of divination is to acquire and transmit superhuman knowledge."

³ Sarah Iles Johnston, *Ancient Greek Divination* (Oxford: Wiley-Blackwell, 2008), 3–4.

⁴ The most comprehensive study of ancient divination is still Auguste Bouché-Leclercq, *Histoire de la divination dans l'antiquité*, 4 vols. (Paris: Leroux, 1879–1882). The study is primarily a collection of relevant data. In the course of the four volumes he touches on early Christian engagement with divination, but does not devote any space to Jewish evidence or the evidence of the New Testament.

⁵ The precise nuances and distinctions between all the Greek terms are uncertain and it is likely that the proliferation of terms is intended to be exhaustive: περικαθαίρων τὸν υἱὸν αὐτοῦ ἢ τὴν θυγατέρα αὐτοῦ ἐν πυρί, "one who purifies his son or daughter in fire," μαντευόμενος μαντείαν, "a diviner who practices divination," κληδονιζόμενος, "one who receives omens," καὶ οἰωνιζόμενος, "one who reads the flight of birds," φάρμακος, "sorcerer," ἐπαείδων ἐπαοιδήν, "chanter of spells/oracles," ἐγγαστρίμυθος, "belly-talker," καὶ τερατοσκόπος, "observer of omens," ἐπερωτῶν τοὺς νεκρούς, "consulter of the dead." The same applies to the Hebrew text: S. R. Driver, *A Critical and Exegetical Commentary on Deuteronomy*, 3rd ed., ICC (Edinburgh: T&T Clark, 1902), 221–22; Jeffrey H. Tigay, *Deuteronomy*, JPS Torah Commentary (Philadelphia: Jewish Publication Society of America, 1996), 464–65.

⁶ Cf. Lev 19:26; 1 Sam 15:23; 28:3; 2 Kgs 17:14–18; 21:6; Isa 3:2; Jer 27:9; 29:8; Ezek 13:6–9; 22:28; Mic 3:11; Zech 10:2.

includes προφητεία but not μαντεία, is thus likely an alignment with the taxonomic preference of Deuteronomy.[7]

We should be careful, however, not to confuse a taxonomic and linguistic preference with an eschewal of divination altogether. There are in fact a variety of legitimate means of divination in the Hebrew Bible, as can be illustrated by 1 Sam 28:6. Here, Saul "inquires of the Lord" concerning military strategy, and the text says, "the Lord did not answer him, not by dreams, nor by Urim, nor by prophets."[8] At this point in the narrative, Saul has lost favour with God and receives no answer by these methods, but the methods themselves are both legitimate and effective at numerous points within the Hebrew Bible.

Yahweh frequently communicated through dreams.[9] This was how the patriarchs received their covenants (Gen 15:12–21; 26:24; 28:10–22). Joseph and Daniel prove themselves superior to their foreign counterparts both in receiving and in interpreting dreams (Gen 41; Dan 2:1–45; 4:1–27).[10] As the example of Saul shows, dreams could also be sought as a means of inquiry. This would most likely occur through incubation at a sanctuary as in 1 Kgs 3:4–15/2 Chr 1:5–13. Here Solomon travels to Gibeon and offers sacrifices before sleeping near the altar and encountering Yahweh in a dream.[11] Dreams and visions will be discussed in greater detail in Chapter 2.

The Urim refers to one part of the Urim and Thummim, which were kept in the pouch (or breast-piece [חשן]) of the high priest (Exod 28:30; Lev 8:8) and used as a means of priestly divination (Num 27:21; cf. Ezra 2:63; Neh 7:65). The pouch attached to the high priest's ephod, which itself occasionally

---

[7] From the list of Deut 18, one word is attested by Paul (φάρμακος), included in the vice-list of Gal 5:19–20.

[8] For the phrase "inquire of the Lord," see Rannfrid I. Thelle, *Ask God: Divine Consultation in the Literature of the Hebrew Bible*, BBET 30 (Frankfurt: Lang, 2002). For the role of Greek diviners in military situations, see Flower, *Seer in Ancient Greece*, 153–87. In the Hebrew Bible, see Ann Jeffers, *Magic and Divination in Ancient Palestine and Syria*, SHCANE 8 (Leiden: Brill, 1996), 236–43.

[9] See the helpful "Table of Biblical Dreams" in Frances Flannery, *Dreamers, Scribes, and Priests: Jewish Dreams in the Hellenistic and Roman Eras*, JSJSup 90 (Leiden: Brill, 2004), 42–44, and the essays collected in Esther J. Hamori and Jonathan Stökl, eds., *Perchance to Dream: Dream Divination in the Bible and the Ancient Near East*, ANEM 21 (Atlanta: SBL Press, 2018).

[10] These figures also appear to engage in some other forms of divination. Joseph has a cup through which he divines (נחש, οἰωνίζομαι), possibly through some form of hydromancy (Gen 44:5, 15). Daniel is trained in "the writing and language of the Chaldeans" (Dan 1:4), which likely refers to Babylonian divinatory arts, although Daniel is clear that his divinatory abilities derive ultimately from his God rather than his training (Dan 2:17–28). See Jonathan Stökl, "Daniel and the 'Prophetization' of Dream Divination," in Hamori and Stökl, *Perchance to Dream*, 139–40.

[11] See C. L. Seow, "The Syro-Palestinian Context of Solomon's Dream," HTR 77 (1984): 141–52; Jeffers, *Magic and Divination*, 130, 134–37.

functioned as a means of divination, perhaps in conjunction with the Urim and Thummim (Judg 17–18; 1 Sam 14:18–19 LXX; 23:6–12; 30:7–8).[12] What exactly the Urim and Thummim were, or how they were used to discern the divine will is never clearly spelled out, though most scholars suppose they refer to a type of lot-oracle.[13]

Israelites and non-Israelites alike cast lots for a variety of divinatory purposes, such as allocating land between the different Israelite tribes (Num 26:55–56; 33:54; 34:13; 36:2; Josh 18), or assigning cities to certain priests and Levites (Josh 21). Lots are also used in appointing a king (1 Sam 10:20–22) or cultic functionary (1 Chr 24–26), as well as identifying a guilty person in certain scenarios (Josh 7:14–21; 1 Sam 14:41–42; Jonah 1:7).[14] Proverbs 16:33 expresses the belief that casting lots reveals the will of Yahweh: "The lot is cast into the lap, but the decision is the Lord's alone."

Second Temple sources tend to shift the priestly technology of divination to the breast-piece itself, which is referred to as the λόγιον, "oracle" (Josephus, *Ant.* 3.163, 217; Let. Aris. 97; Sir 45:11; Exod 28:15 LXX). Josephus describes its functioning thus:

> By means of the twelve stones, which the high-priest wore upon his breast stitched into the essên [breast-piece], God foreshowed victory to those on the eve of battle. For so brilliant a light flashed out from them, ere the army was yet in motion, that it was evident to the whole host that God had come to their aid. (*Ant.* 3.216–217 [Thackeray, LCL])

Several Dead Sea Scrolls appear to presuppose the continued use of the Urim and Thummim, and similarly associate their functioning with the shining of

---

[12] In addition to the Judges reference cited above, Hos 3:4 mentions the teraphim (probably a form of cult statue) positively in conjunction with the ephod as a means of divination (the LXX reads "Urim" [δήλων]). Most other references from the Hebrew Bible portray teraphim as an illicit and ineffectual means of divination: 1 Sam 15:23; 2 Kgs 23:24; Zech 10:2; Ezek 21:21.

[13] This is certainly how the LXX of 1 Sam 14:41–42 portrays them being used. See, Johannes Lindblom, "Lot-Casting in the Old Testament," *VT* 12 (1962): 170–78; Wayne Horowitz and Victor Avigdor Hurowitz, "Urim and Thummim in Light of a Psephomancy Ritual from Assur (LKA 137)," *JNES* 21 (1992): 95–115; Anne Marie Kitz, "The Plural Form of ʾÛrîm and Tummîm," *JBL* 116 (1997): 401–10; Victor Avigdor Hurowitz, "True Light on the Urim and Thummim," *JQR* 88 (1998): 263–74; Jeffers, *Magic and Divination*, 209–15. A significant dissenter is Cornelis Van Dam, *The Urim and Thummim: A Means of Revelation in Ancient Israel* (Winona Lake, IN: Eisenbrauns, 1997). His analysis is, however, coloured by a general theological unease with "divination."

[14] See Lindblom, "Lot-Casting," 164–66; Hanna Tervanotko and Kyle Schofield, "'Let us cast lots, so that we may know' (Jonah 1:7): Oracle of Lot as a Ritual-Like Activity in Ancient Jewish Texts," *BibInt* (2021): 5–6.

the stones on the high priest's garments.[15] By the time Josephus was writing at the end of the first century CE, however, this oracular technology had been out of use for around two hundred years (*Ant.* 3.218).[16]

Returning to 1 Sam 28:6, the inclusion of prophets as third in a list of divinatory options shows that there are ways of classifying (even legitimate) Israelite divinatory methods that do not pit prophecy against everything else.[17] Rather, prophecy takes its place as one form of divination among others. Only when these legitimate options are exhausted does Saul turn further afield to the illegitimate practice of necromancy (1 Sam 28:7–19). Even here there is some ambiguity. Esther Hamori's analysis of this passage in 1 Sam shows that the main target of the story's condemnation is not necromancy or the necromancer, but Saul, and his "constant capacity for self-defeat."[18] Due to his inability to hear from Yahweh he is forced to turn to a divinatory intermediary that he has just outlawed (1 Sam 28:3). The necromancer herself, according to Hamori, is portrayed positively as the one who "finally provides Saul with the access to Yahwistic knowledge he has been seeking, through raising the prophet of Yahweh. Necromancy may be portrayed as one step further removed from Yahweh, but this is a matter of degree, and not of kind."[19]

This is correct, but it is this degree that puts necromancy beyond the pale for much of biblical tradition. While 1 Sam 28 does not condemn the בעלת-אוב, "ghost-diviner," those who consult אבות, "ghosts," are roundly condemned in much of the rest of the Hebrew Bible.[20] Furthermore, it is only with Saul's turn to necromancy in 1 Sam 28 that the word μαντεύομαι starts to appear in the Greek translations. The earlier methods of incubation, Urim, and inquiring of a prophet are all simply described as "asking the Lord" (ἐπηρώτησεν ... διὰ κυρίου [v. 6]), whereas necromancy is "divination."[21] In the same way for Paul,

---

[15] Crispin Fletcher-Louis, *All the Glory of Adam: Liturgical Anthropology in the Dead Sea Scrolls*, STDJ 42 (Leiden: Brill, 2002), 222–51; Lisbeth S. Fried, "Did Second Temple High Priests Possess the Urim and Thummim?" *JHebS* 7 (2007): 2–25; Van Dam, *Urim and Thummim*, 16–21.

[16] Fried ("Urim and Thummim") argues that Josephus is essentially correct about this.

[17] Martti Nissinen, "The Socio-Religious Role of the Neo-Assyrian Prophets," in *Prophetic Divination: Essays in Ancient Near Eastern Prophecy*, BZAW 494 (Berlin: de Gruyter, 2019), 119–20.

[18] Esther J. Hamori, *Women's Divination in Biblical Literature: Prophecy, Necromancy, and Other Arts of Knowledge*, AYBRL (New Haven: Yale University Press, 2015), 114–17.

[19] Hamori, *Women's Divination*, 130.

[20] Lev 19:31; 20:6, 27; Deut 18:11; 2 Kgs 21:6; 23:24; 2 Chr 33:6; Isa 8:19; 19:3. In 1 Chr 10:13 Saul's act of consulting the necromancer is one of the contributing factors to Yahweh's abandonment of him.

[21] The words μάντις, μαντεία, μαντεύομαι have an almost exclusively negative sense in the LXX: Num 23:23; Deut 18:10, 14; Josh 13:22; 1 Sam 6:2; 2 Kgs 17:17; Sir 34:5. In the prophets the terms are associated with lying and "false" prophecy: Isa 16:6; 44:25; Jer 14:14; 34:9; 36:8; Ezek 12:24; 13:6–8, 23; 21:26–28, 34; 22:28. Josephus, on the other hand, is an example of a Jewish writer who is happy to use mantic terminology of himself. While the only biblical

while he does not use the terminology of "divination" for his own activities, he does use words for oracles (λόγια), dream-visions (χρηματισμός), prophecy (προφητεία), signs (σημεῖα), and omens (τέρατα) that demonstrably fit into the context of divination as Paul's contemporaries would have understood it. This suggests that the difference between his own divinatory practices and those native to his broader context are theological, cultural, and rhetorical as opposed to phenomenological or ontological.[22]

To classify Paul's access to divine knowledge as divination is thus an act of redescription. Redescription is, according to Jonathan Z. Smith, "to construe one thing in terms of another ... so that we may see things in a new, and frequently unexpected, light."[23] By construing Paul's access to divine knowledge in terms of the ways that such access was understood by the broader Hellenistic culture of which he was a part (regardless of how he categorises it himself), we may illumine both the arguments and the exegesis of his letters, and position Paul as an historical actor within his native ancient context.

To provide some further clarity to matters of definition, it is useful to separate three distinct orders of discourse in historical work.[24] The first order

---

figures he uses the terms of are Balaam (*Ant.* 4.102–130, 157–158), the necromancer of Endor (*Ant.* 6.327–342), Jotham (*Ant.* 5.253), and Babylonian diviners (*Ant.* 10.195), his own predictions are described with the words προμαντεύομαι (*B.J.* 3.405) and μαντεία (*B.J.* 4.625). Judas the Essene is also described positively as a μάντις (*B.J.* 2.112; *Ant.* 17.345). See further Rebecca Gray, *Prophetic Figures in Late Second Temple Jewish Palestine: The Evidence from Josephus* (Oxford: Oxford University Press, 1993), 107–10.

[22] Laura Nasrallah has drawn attention to the way taxonomies of dreams, ecstasies, spiritual gifts, and similar phenomena are often rhetorically constructed, and serve to delimit appropriate and inappropriate means of accessing knowledge: Laura Salah Nasrallah, *An Ecstasy of Folly: Prophecy and Authority in Early Christianity*, HTS 52 (Cambridge, MA: Harvard University Press, 2003), esp. 198–201. Cf. Jennifer Eyl, *Signs, Wonders, and Gifts: Divination in the Letters of Paul* (Oxford: Oxford University Press, 2019), 81–84.

[23] Jonathan Z. Smith, "When the Chips are Down," in *Relating Religion: Essays in the Study of Religion* (Chicago: University of Chicago Press, 2004), 29. For a more technical definition, see Ron Cameron and Merrill P. Miller, "Introducing Paul and the Corinthians," in *Redescribing Paul and the Corinthians*, ed. Ron Cameron and Merrill P. Miller, ECL 5 (Atlanta: SBL Press, 2011), 1: "a form of explanation that privileges difference and involves comparison and translation, category formation and rectification, definition and theory." Barclay offers an additional perspective that helps to clarify the value of redescription within various ways of knowing: "what happens when we use categories different to those indigenous to a tradition is not a privileged discovery of its 'real' meaning, but the addition of *another* perspective, with multiple potential benefits" (italics original). John M. G. Barclay, "'O wad some Pow'r the giftie gie us, To see oursels as others see us!': Method and Purpose in Comparing the New Testament," in *The New Testament in Comparison: Validity, Method, and Purpose in Comparing Traditions*, ed. John M. G. Barclay and Benjamin G. White, LNTS 600 (London: T&T Clark, 2020), 15–16.

[24] For orders of discourse applied to religion generally, see Gavin Flood, "Reflections on Tradition and Inquiry in the Study of Religion," *JAAR* 74 (2006): 54–57; David E. Aune, "'Magic' in Early Christianity and its Ancient Mediterranean Context: A Survey of Some Recent Scholarship," *ASE* 24 (2007): 231–34. My summary largely adapts that of Aune.

consists of what can be learned of ancient divinatory practice itself from literary descriptions, inscriptions, iconography, and other primary sources. This might take the form, for example, of inscriptions or lead tablets recording oracular questions and responses. The second order consists in the organisation and reflection upon these practices by those involved. Paul's own classification of his practices, or those of the LXX, are examples of second-order discourse, as well as the descriptions and definitions of divination given in Cicero's *De divinatione*. Both first- and second-order discourse are emic in nature as they represent an "insider" view of the subject under discussion. Third-order discourse, by way of contrast, is etic reflection on first- and second-order discourse by those who stand outside the object of study; it is by nature comparative.[25] The category of "religion," for example, is largely a modern one, which does not map neatly onto the ways most ancient people talked about relations with their gods, but it is still a useful way to categorise and compare the practices of different groups when properly defined.[26]

Michael Satlow argues that third-order categories are best viewed as utilitarian constructs that serve as tools for comparison: "They are definitions that we create in order to select data to compare."[27] In this sense, these categories need not always be limited by how ancients understood their own practice (second order) or how scholars have previously categorised these practices (third order) since the comparison exists, as Smith has famously argued, "within the space of the scholar's mind for the scholar's own intellectual reasons."[28] Once the category has served its purpose in gathering a set of data to compare, it can be dispensed with so that the actual task of comparison can take place.[29] The overall utility of the category will depend on its ability to draw interesting and fruitful comparisons.[30]

---

[25] Flood, "Tradition and Inquiry," 55.
[26] For religion as a modern category, see Brent Nongbri, *Before Religion: A History of a Modern Concept* (New Haven: Yale University Press, 2013). For its continuing utility, see Heidi Wendt, *At the Temple Gates: The Religion of Freelance Experts in the Roman Empire* (Oxford: Oxford University Press, 2016), 31–34; Larry W. Hurtado, *Destroyer of the Gods: Early Christian Distinctiveness in the Roman World* (Waco, TX: Baylor University Press, 2016), 38–44.
[27] Michael L. Satlow, "Disappearing Categories: Using Categories in the Study of Religion," *MTSR* 17 (2005): 293. Satlow actually refers to these as second-order categories as in his *schema* he only deals with first (emic) order and second (etic) order. Satlow's second order thus corresponds to Aune's and Flood's third order.
[28] Jonathan Z. Smith, *Drudgery Divine: On the Comparison of Early Christianities and the Religions of Late Antiquity* (Chicago: University of Chicago Press, 1990), 51.
[29] This is where Satlow distinguishes himself from Smith as he does not believe the category itself can say anything about the nature of human activity, Satlow, "Disappearing Categories," 290–91.
[30] See Troels Engberg-Pedersen, "The Past is a Foreign Country: On the Shape and Purposes of Comparison in New Testament Scholarship," in Barclay and White, *The New Testament in Comparison*, 60.

To a point, this is how I use the category of divination. Since it is not a category that Paul uses to frame his own activities, "divination" functions here as a third-order category that heuristically selects a body of first- and second-order data with which to bring Paul's letters into conversation. As divination can also become intertwined with other second- and third-order categories, such as magic, miracles, prophecy, or religion, the third-order categorisation is also helpful for delimiting the boundaries of what is to be compared. For this it is necessary to exercise scholarly judgement to decide when to bracket out certain types of data and when to include others, based on the definition of one's chosen category. Per my stated definition above, the most salient characteristic of divination for the purposes of this study is the reception and interpretation of knowledge believed to have a divine source.

Previous Research: In Search of a Category

There have been a number of previous studies that treat Paul's access to divine knowledge. These are usually treated under the categories of "revelation" or "prophecy." A survey of these previous studies shows that both these categories tend to skew analysis of Paul's letters towards certain types of divine communication, while ignoring or deliberately excluding others. In the case of revelation, texts and concepts that reveal pivotal aspects of salvation history are privileged, while "occasional revelations" that merely impart information are sidelined. With prophecy, interpreters focus only on practices that can be classed as "inspired," while ignoring the more interpretive tasks of understanding texts and other non-verbal signs of divine wrath or approval. With both categories interpreters also often start from problematic assumptions about the relation of Paul to his broader context. Some scholars have begun to apply the term divination to Paul's activities, but have not yet moved beyond the task of classification to further understand Paul's letters in the light of this classification.

Paul and Revelation

A comprehensive account of Paul's access to divine knowledge has most often been discussed under the heading "revelation." This category, as Nicole Belayche and Jörg Rüpke point out, tends to be reserved for discussion of the three Abrahamic religions, and entails a theological focus on divine agency.[31] As such, revelation in Paul is usually approached as a theological category (as part

---

[31] Nicole Belayche and Jörg Rüpke, "Divination et révélation dans les mondes grec et romain," *Revue de l'histoire des religions* 2 (2007): 144.

of a broader NT theology of revelation) and has therefore become caught up in the theological debates of the twentieth century.[32] It is axiomatic for much contemporary theological discourse that revelation cannot simply refer to the communication of knowledge, but rather to the act of divine self-disclosure, which is necessarily unique. Wolfhart Pannenberg sees this consensus as a legacy of German idealism, which rejected the supernaturalism of earlier dogmatic formulations.[33] So, for Rudolf Bultmann, revelation in the "religious sense" refers to "that opening up of what is hidden which is absolutely necessary and decisive for man if he is to achieve 'salvation' or authenticity."[34] For Ulrich Wilckens, revelation is "the *complete self-disclosure of God*," which is "necessarily one and to be distinguished from mere appearances of God."[35]

For both understandings there is little space for revelation as the disclosure of information from the divine realm to the human. Rather revelation is essentially synonymous with salvation, whether understood existentially or in terms of salvation history. These discussions of revelation in the NT are explicitly theological in nature, starting from a definition of revelation derived from modern theology, and then seeing what material the NT has to offer this understanding.[36] This is a perfectly legitimate procedure as the clear third-order definitions the authors create are suitable to the tasks that both set out to do in their respective works. There is a problem, however, when these definitions and assumptions determine the more exegetical and historical studies of the subject as it obfuscates a clear understanding of revelation, as both a concept and a practice in its historical context.

Albrecht Oepke's *TDNT* article on the subject, in place of a philological study of the ἀποκαλύπτω word-group, opts to trace the *idea* of revelation in religious history.[37] The prior theological understanding of revelation he adopts determines to a large extent how the evidence is evaluated. In discussing revelation in the Hellenistic world he surveys all the various forms of divination. Divination and revelation at first appear to fit in the same category until Greek religion, as a whole, is found wanting as it lacks "a unique and central act of

---

[32] For a helpful overview of the debates, see Carl E. Braaten, "The Current Controversy on Revelation: Pannenberg and His Critics," *JR* 45 (1965): 225–37.

[33] Wolfhart Pannenberg, "Introduction," in *Revelation as History*, ed. Wolfhart Pannenberg, trans. David Granskou and Edward Quinn (London: Sheed & Ward, 1969), 4–6.

[34] Rudolf Bultmann, "The Concept of Revelation in the New Testament," in *Existence and Faith: Shorter Writings of Rudolf Bultmann*, trans. Schubert M. Ogden (London: Hodder & Stoughton, 1961), 59; trans. of *Der Begriff der Offenbarung im Neuen Testament* (Tübingen: Mohr Siebeck, 1929).

[35] Ulrich Wilckens, "The Understanding of Revelation within Primitive Christianity," in Pannenberg, *Revelation as History*, 58 (italics original).

[36] In this vein, see also Ernest F. Scott, *The New Testament Idea of Revelation* (London: Nicholson & Watson, 1935); F. Gerald Downing, *Has Christianity a Revelation?* (London: SCM, 1964).

[37] Albrecht Oepke, "ἀποκαλύπτω, ἀποκάλυψις," *TDNT* 3:563–92.

revelation" (567). It has "revelations" but not "revelation." This distinction is common in much theologically inflected work on this topic, in which the multiple and trivial *revelations* of Greek religion are contrasted with the "new and unique *revelation* given to Israel" (571). The singular Israelite revelation is "not the impartation of supernatural knowledge or the excitement of numinous feelings," but rather, "in the proper sense, it is the action of Yahweh" (573). Since this action reveals not just information from God but God himself, discussion easily slides from *how* things are revealed to *what* God is revealed to be: "Yahweh reveals Himself as the Lord of history, as holy and gracious, and as the Creator of the world" (572). Focusing on putative content rather than means at this point makes it much easier to contrast the Hebrew and Greek evidence, but we have not thereby arrived at a different concept of revelation.

Paul's view of revelation, for Oepke, stands on top of this OT sense of revelation (ignoring contemporary Judaism) with the added content of the Christ-event.

> Revelation was again understood, not as an impartation of supernatural knowledge, but as the coming of God, as the disclosure of the world to come, which took place in a historical development up to the person and death and resurrection of Jesus in the last time (1 Cor 10:11; Heb 1:1f.) and which will culminate in the cosmic catastrophe at the end of history.[38]

Revelation then becomes synonymous with the events of salvation history and eschatology, which, in a neat biblical theology, grows out of the OT but bears no relation to Paul's contemporary Judaism or the broader Hellenistic world. As I will argue in the following chapters, these schemes are really dealing with the content of what is revealed to Paul, rather than Paul's means of receiving divine information, which are remarkably similar to those of his surrounding cultural context.

Dieter Lührmann, in contrast to Oepke, takes an expressly exegetical approach, seeking to determine Paul's understanding of revelation from his use of the Greek words ἀποκαλύπτειν, ἀποκάλυψις, φανεροῦν, and φανέρωσις.[39] In the course of this analysis he privileges certain Pauline passages as "central statements about revelation" (Gal 1:12, 16; 3:23; Rom 1:17; 3:21),[40] and pushes other instances of the same terminology (Gal 2:2; 1 Cor 2:10; 14:6, 26–30; 2 Cor 12:1) to the periphery, explaining them either by the vocabulary and understandings

---

[38] Oepke, "ἀποκαλύπτω," 3:582–83.
[39] In this he follows the earlier work of Hannelis Schulte, *Der Begriff der Offenbarung im Neuen Testament*, BEvT 13 (Munich: Kaiser, 1949).
[40] Dieter Lührmann, *Das Offenbarungsverständnis bei Paulus und in paulinischen Gemeinden*, WMANT 16 (Neukirchen-Vluyn: Neukirchener Verlag, 1965), 157.

of Paul's opponents, or simply asserting that they do not refer to the same thing. The religious milieu of Paul and his opponents for Lührmann is apocalypticism on the one hand and gnosticism on the other, which are both seen as the raw materials from which Paul can form his own concept of revelation which, in the end, transcends them both. Lührmann's main conclusions ultimately support Bultmann's existentialist understanding: revelation for Paul is the "salvific action of God, which appears in the 'now.'"[41] Such an analysis shows that "pure" exegesis is still being determined by the same unstated overarching theological categories, which assumes that "revelation" in Paul must mean more than simply the disclosure of information, and when Paul is involved in the mediation of divine information, this is not in itself revelation.[42]

Johannes Lindblom largely escapes a number of these issues by choosing to analyse not *Offenbarung*, but *Offenbarungen* in early Christianity (not "revelation" but "revelations").[43] He does this, however, primarily against the comparative context of the Hebrew Bible rather than the contemporary Hellenistic and Roman environments of early Christianity. The wide scope of early Christianity also means that Paul's letters come in for relatively little focused treatment. Paul comes in for most discussion under the category "Christus Internus," which Lindblom argues is a form of mystical piety unique to Paul, and one which defies categorisation.[44]

Markus Bockmuehl has made the most valuable contribution to situating Paul and revelation historically in relation to ancient Judaism. He begins with a broad working definition of revelation, which is loosely determined from the ancient evidence rather than from specific words or theological reasoning: "a) any divine disclosure communicated by visionary or prophetic means, or b) the manifestation of heavenly realities in a historical context."[45] The relationship between this idea and "mystery" is then explored through a broad range of Second Temple Jewish texts, early rabbinic literature and Pauline Christianity.[46] The wide-ranging nature of this study means that only

---

[41] Lührmann, *Offenbarungsverständnis*, 158: "Heilshandelns Gottes, das im 'jetzt' in Erscheinung tritt."
[42] This approach, which involves identifying opponents, aligning them with a particular intellectual position in Graeco-Roman or Jewish culture, and then reading Paul in way that transcends that position in a startlingly modern way, is critiqued by Stanley K. Stowers, "Kinds of Myth, Meals, and Power: Paul and the Corinthians," in Cameron and Miller, *Redescribing Paul and the Corinthians*, 106–7.
[43] Johannes Lindblom, *Gesichte und Offenbarungen: Vorstellungen von göttlichen Weisungen und übernatürlichen Erscheinungen im ältesten Christentum* (Lund: Gleerup, 1968), 13.
[44] Lindblom, *Gesichte und Offenbarungen*, 114–44.
[45] Markus N. A. Bockmuehl, *Revelation and Mystery in Ancient Judaism and Pauline Christianity*, WUNT 2/36 (Tübingen: Mohr Siebeck, 1990; repr., Eugene, OR: Wipf & Stock, 2009), 2.
[46] "Pauline Christianity" for Bockmuehl entails the evidence of Rom, 1 Cor and Col as authentic epistles (chapters 8–10) and 2 Thess, Eph, Rom 16:25–27, the pastoral epistles, the Didache, Ignatius, Justin, and the Epistle to Diognetus as "postscripts to Paul" (chapter 11).

two of the eleven chapters are specifically concerned with the undisputed letters of Paul. The parameters of the study are also restricted to a contemporary ancient Jewish context for Pauline Christianity. While Bockmuehl acknowledges the general "influence of the Hellenistic religious milieu," this is only overtly engaged in discussion of Philo.

In the chapters on Paul, Bockmuehl still primarily focuses on the *concepts* of revelation and mystery, and his treatment of these ideas, in my view, does not escape the theological privileging of a certain understanding of revelation over others. Bockmuehl's structure of revelation in Paul is reminiscent of Wilckens's, being divided into past, present, and future revelation. Past revelation consists primarily in the "Christ-event." Present revelation bespeaks the ongoing preaching of the gospel and the apostolic ministry. Future revelation denotes Christ's parousia. Further space is devoted to considering the revelation of the gospel *to* Paul, as well as the role of "occasional revelations" and the Jewish scriptures. Bockmuehl considers all of these important for Paul, but since his focus is on the *idea* of revelation, these are all (apart from Paul's "on principle unrepeatable" Damascus road experience)[47] ultimately sidelined as "not foundational or constitutive" for Paul's broader theology of revelation.[48]

The tendency to understand revelation as primarily an event dominates recent work on "apocalyptic" in Paul. For this scholarship (which traces its theological lineage to Barth), it is axiomatic that God's "apocalypse" has nothing to do with visionary experiences or the transmission of information, but refers to God stepping onto the scene of world history in the person of Jesus.[49] Now is not the time to give a full critique of such apocalyptic readings of Paul.[50] For my present purpose, the main issue is not how such readings interpret Paul, but how they tie these readings to the ἀποκάλυψις

---

[47] Bockmuehl, *Revelation and Mystery*, 137.

[48] Bockmuehl, *Revelation and Mystery*, 144, 226.

[49] Richard E. Sturm, "An Exegetical Study of the Apostle Paul's Use of the Words *Apokalyptō/Apokalypsis*: The Gospel as God's Apocalypse" (PhD diss., Union Theological Seminary, 1983); J. Louis Martyn, "Apocalyptic Antinomies in Paul's Letter to the Galatians," NTS 31 (1985): 410–24; J. Louis Martyn, *Galatians*, AB 33A (New Haven: Yale University Press, 1997); Martinus C. de Boer, "Paul, Theologian of God's Apocalypse," *Interpretation* 56 (2002): 21–33; Douglas A. Campbell, *The Deliverance of God: An Apocalyptic Rereading of Justification in Paul* (Grand Rapids: Eerdmans, 2009).

[50] See the evaluations of R. Barry Matlock, *Unveiling the Apocalyptic Paul: Paul's Interpreters and the Rhetoric of Criticism*, JSNTSup 127 (Sheffield: Sheffield Academic, 1996); J. P. Davies, *Paul Among the Apocalypses? An Evaluation of the 'Apocalyptic Paul' in the Context of Jewish and Christian Apocalyptic Literature*, LNTS 562 (London: T&T Clark, 2016); Loren T. Stuckenbruck, "Some Reflections on Apocalyptic Thought and Time in Literature from the Second Temple Period," in *Paul and the Apocalyptic Imagination*, ed. Ben C. Blackwell, John K. Goodrich, and Jason Maston (Minneapolis: Fortress, 2016), 137–55; Loren T. Stuckenbruck, "Overlapping Ages at Qumran and 'Apocalyptic' in Pauline Theology," in *The Dead Sea Scrolls and Pauline Literature*, ed. Jean-Sébastien Rey, STDJ 102 (Leiden: Brill, 2014), 309–26.

word-group, which has a varied usage in Paul that cannot be forced into a single theological concept (see Chapter 2).

Many of these studies, particularly those of Bockmuehl and Lührmann, provide much that is relevant and exegetically useful for the present study, and agreements and disagreements with these works will be further detailed at the appropriate points. In regard to the category of revelation, however, it suffices to note that this category privileges a certain type of divine disclosure over others in ways that isolate Paul from his broader cultural environment in the Greek and Roman world. It assumes that true revelation exists only in Jewish or Christian religion and is of an entirely different order to the mere revelations of Greek or Roman religion. As a result, the "mere" revelations of Paul's letters are also sidelined and marginalised.

Paul and Prophecy

Another category relevant to Paul's access to divine knowledge is "prophecy." This category shifts attention to the "occasional revelations" marginalised by studies on revelation. While scholars have often argued for an exclusively Jewish context for Paul's prophecy, since the publication of David Aune's *Prophecy in Early Christianity and the Ancient Mediterranean World*, there has been a general recognition that the phenomenon of prophecy is broadly attested in the ancient world.[51] Even those studies that strenuously deny any connection with the similar practices in Paul's cultural environment still recognise the need to conduct their studies in comparison with such practices.

How exactly these comparisons are carried out, however, depends to a large extent on how prophecy is defined, both with respect to Paul and with respect to the contemporary context with which he is being compared. Prophecy can be defined narrowly to represent a type of inspired speech, in which case it would be only one of many possible means of access to divine knowledge. On the other hand, it could be defined more broadly to represent the various things a "prophet" does. In this definition, studies of prophecy have allowed for the incorporation of various means of divine communication such as visions,

---

[51] David E. Aune, *Prophecy in Early Christianity and the Ancient Mediterranean World* (Grand Rapids: Eerdmans, 1983); e.g., Antoinette Clark Wire, *The Corinthian Women Prophets: A Reconstruction Through Paul's Rhetoric* (Minneapolis: Fortress, 1990); Christopher Forbes, *Prophecy and Inspired Speech in Early Christianity and its Hellenistic Environment*, WUNT 2/75 (Tübingen: Mohr Siebeck, 1995); Nasrallah, *Ecstasy of Folly*; Clint Tibbs, *Religious Experience of the Pneuma: Communication with the Spirit World in 1 Corinthians 12 and 14*, WUNT 2/230 (Tübingen: Mohr Siebeck, 2007; repr., Eugene, OR: Wipf & Stock, 2012); Jill E. Marshall, *Women Praying and Prophesying in Corinth: Gender and Inspired Speech in First Corinthians*, WUNT 2/448 (Tübingen: Mohr Siebeck, 2017). See further Chapter 3.

or the interpretation of sacred texts (under the label "charismatic exegesis").[52] As the label "charismatic exegesis" shows, the assumption is still that the role of a prophet must be in some way linked to inspiration.[53] Ordinary scriptural interpretation is not prophecy, but if the interpretation is said to be inspired in some sense, then it can be grouped together with visions and inspired speech as examples of prophecy. In this sense, "prophecy" is defined in opposition to the technical ("pagan") interpretation of signs, which is labelled "divination."

In the field of NT studies (and biblical studies more generally), prophecy and divination have traditionally been defined in opposition to each other. Prophecy (like revelation) is understood to refer to directly inspired revelation initiated through divine agency, while divination is the interpretation of signs, and originates in human agency.[54] A frequent assumption has also been that while ancient Jews and Christians enjoyed the direct divine revelation of prophecy, "pagan" religions had to make do with indirect and artificial means of divination.[55]

The theological judgements underpinning such categorisations are evident, but even where these are less than explicit, this historical picture has been enabled by the conflation of two different distinctions made by ancient authors. First are the various prohibitions of the idolatrous practices of the

---

[52] See e.g., Karl Olav Sandnes, *Paul – One of the Prophets? A Contribution to the Apostle's Self-Understanding*, WUNT 2/43 (Tübingen: Mohr Siebeck, 1991); Jacob Myers and Edwin Freed, "Is Paul Also Among the Prophets?" *Interpretation* 20 (1966): 40–53; Tobias Nicklas, "Paulus – der Apostel als Prophet," in *Prophets and Prophecy in Jewish and Early Christian Literature*, ed. Joseph Verheyden, Korinna Zamfir, and Tobias Nicklas, WUNT 2/286 (Tübingen: Mohr Siebeck, 2010), 77–104. These discussions are less helpful when they slide fully in the direction of mapping allusions and references to OT prophets, Jeffrey W. Aernie, *Is Paul Also Among the Prophets? An Examination of the Relationship Between Paul and the Old Testament Prophetic Tradition in 2 Corinthians*, LNTS 467 (London: T&T Clark, 2012).

[53] The same is true of categories such as "visionary," or "religious experience": Ernst Benz, *Paulus als Visionär: eine vergleichende Untersuchung der Visionsberichte des Paulus in der Apostelgeschichte und in den paulinischen Briefen*, Verlagde Akademie der Wissenschaften und der Literatur (Mainz: F. Steiner Wiesbaden, 1952); Bernhard Heininger, *Paulus als Visionär: eine religionsgeschichtliche Studie* (Freiburg: Herder, 1996); James Buchanan Wallace, *Snatched into Paradise (2 Cor 12:1–10): Paul's Heavenly Journey in the Context of Early Christian Experience*, BZNW 179 (Berlin: de Gruyter, 2011); Larry W. Hurtado, "Religious Experience and Religious Innovation in the New Testament," in *How on Earth Did Jesus Become a God? Historical Questions About Earliest Devotion to Jesus* (Grand Rapids: Eerdmans, 2005), 179–204; Larry W. Hurtado, "Revelatory Experiences and Religious Innovation in Earliest Christianity," *ExpTim* 125 (2014): 469–82.

[54] Even when the broader definition of divination is acknowledged, it is quickly discarded in favour of the more restrictive definition, Aune, *Prophecy*, 23, 339; N. C. Croy, "Religion, Personal," *DNTB*: 927.

[55] See e.g., Abraham J. Heschel, *The Prophets* (New York: Harper & Row, 1962), 459; Forbes, *Inspired Speech*, 289–302; Craig S. Keener, *Acts: An Exegetical Commentary*, vol. 1 (Grand Rapids: Baker Academic, 2012), 896–902.

nations in the Hebrew Bible and the Septuagint, which were discussed above and can include various forms of divination. The second distinction is the one drawn by writers such as Plato (*Phaedr.* 244) and Cicero (*Div.* 1.12, 34; 2.26) between natural and technical divination. The former depends on inspiration and some form of divine ecstasy, while the latter relies on the learned art (τέχνη) of interpreting signs. Once the biblical terminology is conflated with elite philosophical distinctions, the picture of inspired prophecy versus mere pagan divination results. Value judgements are blunt instruments for historical analysis. These neither represent accurately the distinctions in the texts themselves, nor do they represent the non-"denominational" reality of divinatory practices evident in our ancient sources.

On the first issue, these two streams of evidence are not in fact making the same point, and neither supports the divide of Jewish/Christian inspired prophecy versus pagan indirect divination. The Jewish texts do not disparage the various forms of divination because they are indirect or interpretive, but because they are the practices of foreign nations that do not speak for the right god. Certain technical means of divination escape this censure in the Hebrew Bible as well as in early Christian texts, such as oneiromancy (dream divination), cleromancy (lot divination), the divinatory use of the ephod, Urim, and Thummim, as well as various portents and omens.[56] Prophecy is also not inviolable by nature for the various biblical authors, as prophets may also speak in the name of other gods, or speak words in the name of Yahweh that Yahweh had not actually spoken, and such people are equally to be excluded (Deut 18:20–22; Jer 27:9; 29:8; Ezek 13:6–9; 22:28).

On the Greek and Roman side, at the level of words and categories, neither Plato nor Cicero uses the term "divination" (μαντική/*divinatio*) as technique: it is rather the broad category under which the two classes of divination fit (Cicero, *Div.* 1.12, 34). Where value judgements are concerned it is in fact the first, inspired category that is more worthy of the name "divination" (Plato, *Phaedr.* 244b–d; Cicero, *Div.* 1.5).[57] This may seem like a trivial semantic issue, but to apply the word "divination" only to the restricted category of technical divination is to both misrepresent the ancient sources and to lose an analytical category for perceiving the wider range of divine communication.

---

[56] Aune, *Prophecy*, 82–83; Nissinen, *Ancient Prophecy*, 17–18; Hamori, *Women's Divination*, 26–28; Bockmuehl, *Revelation and Mystery*, 8–9; Ritva H. Williams, "Accessing Divine Knowledge," in *Early Christian Ritual Life*, ed. Richard E. DeMaris, Jason T. Lamoreaux, and Steven C. Muir (Abingdon: Routledge, 2018), 65–68.

[57] Plutarch does link μαντική with the indirect interpretation of signs, in contrast to figures such as Socrates who could directly hear the counsel of the gods (*Gen. Socr.* 593). This comes in the midst of a discussion which also describes inspired figures as μαντικόν and μάντεις (*Gen. Socr.* 592c, 593c).

Further: many scholars have pointed out that the rigid distinction between inspiration and interpretation, although held by some in antiquity, does not correspond well to actual practices in the ancient world.[58] Dreams, for example, a widely available means of divination across the purported "Judaism/Hellenism" divide, were understood to be given through inspiration, but still mostly required interpretation, as did most prophetic oracles. An inspired figure such as the Pythia at Delphi may have also made use of lot-oracles. An interpretation itself may also be understood to be inspired, or enabled by the receipt of divine wisdom.[59] This makes many actual instances of divination difficult to categorise along the theologically inflected natural/technical or inspired/interpreted divide, and suggests that, while the distinction may be helpful in some instances, it should not be used to ontologically exclude certain practices, or to define prophecy and divination against each other.[60] It also highlights the need for third-order categories that are not restricted to the way some ancient authors defined their practices, which are not necessarily accurate or representative of the ancient world as a whole.[61]

The confusion caused when prophecy is not clearly or consistently defined is illustrated well by Christopher Forbes's detailed work *Prophecy and Inspired Speech in Early Christianity and its Hellenistic Environment*. In his comparisons, Forbes initially adopts "prophecy" as a broad category of divine communication, defined in third-order terms, which fits very closely with how I have defined divination: "the native ability or learned art of receiving and mediating information from . . . supposed supernatural sources."[62] He then lists the many forms of "inductive divination" found in the Graeco-Roman world that would rightly fit under such a definition. When he turns to the early Christian

---

[58] See especially, Flower, *Seer in Ancient Greece*, 84–91; Struck, *Divination and Human Nature*, 16–17; Iles Johnston, *Ancient Greek Divination*, 8–9, 28; Lester L. Grabbe, *Priests, Prophets, Diviners, Sages: A Socio-Historical Study of Religious Specialists in Ancient Israel* (Valley Forge, PA: Trinity, 1995), 124, 139–41; Nissinen, *Ancient Prophecy*, 14–19.

[59] Flower (*Seer in Ancient Greece*, 88) cites Calchas, whose ability to interpret bird signs was given by Apollo.

[60] The distinction does have some recent defenders: Yulia Ustinova, "Modes of Prophecy, or Modern Arguments in Support of the Ancient Approach," *Kernos* 26 (2013): 25–44. In this case, interestingly, the distinction is supported in order to argue for the uniqueness of Greek inspired prophecy.

[61] Many understand Plato's distinction to be arguing against the grain of common Greek understanding for his own rhetorical purposes, Flower, *Seer in Ancient Greece*, 84–91; Nasrallah, *Ecstasy of Folly*, 32–35. Other Greek thinkers, particularly Stoic, sought to understand both natural and technical methods as a singular unified system (see Chapter 1), Struck, *Divination and Human Nature*, 17.

[62] Forbes, *Inspired Speech*, 279.

evidence (represented by Paul and Luke), however, he immediately limits the comparison by switching to a second-order definition.

> Of all these forms of "prophecy," the one most likely to be useful for parallels with early Christian prophecy is that known as "inspiration manticism." . . . Though early Christianity also believed in revelations in spontaneous dreams and in waking visions, as well as in other forms . . . it did not describe such revelations as prophecy.[63]

Forbes at once acknowledges the variety of access to divine knowledge in early Christianity, while dismissing all *comparanda* that are not prophecy – a prophecy which no longer matches the original definition he gave. Otherwise, he would need to include dreams, visions, and the other varia, which he included in the non-Christian evidence even though they did not call it "prophecy" either. This problem highlights the need for a clear and explicit analytical category that is capable of performing non-value-laden comparisons across difference. Prophecy as a category can only account for a subset of Paul's means of divine communication, and defining it in opposition to divination only results in lopsided and misleading comparisons between Paul and his cultural matrix.

Paul and Divination

Some scholars, applying the label "divination" to Paul's activities, have begun to importantly reframe our scholarly categories. And this reframing provides the opportunity for fresh exegesis of Paul's letters.

Heidi Wendt theorises the third-order category of "freelance religious expert," under which she groups various priests, diviners, mystery initiators, astrologers, and similar figures of the Roman world who specialised in religious activities independently of institutional frameworks and hierarchies. In so doing, she is particularly concerned to transcend both emic self-designations (such as "apostle") and pejorative categorisations (such as "magician," "false prophet") that impede comparisons across the patrolled borders of "pagan," "Jewish," and "Christian" figures in antiquity.[64]

Within this framework, Wendt argues that Paul was "a kind of expert in Judean religion who had a demonstrable facility with practices and concepts generally associated with philosophers and other kinds of teachers, as well as with initiators in the mysteries of foreign gods" (189). Among this bundle of practices she describes Paul's use of the "Judean writings" as a form of "literary

---

[63] Forbes, *Inspired Speech*, 280.
[64] Wendt, *At the Temple Gates*, 20–24, 187–88.

divination," and notes that Paul resembles other first-century Judeans in the ways that he receives "messages from God through revelations, dreams, or other methods of divination" (154). She does not develop this insight any further with examples or exegesis; the only instance of divination, literary or otherwise, given a detailed treatment in a separate article is Gal 3:1.[65] It does show however that when one moves beyond rigid categorisations and dichotomies such as Judaism, Hellenism, prophecy, and magic, the similarities of divinatory practices emerge more clearly.

Jennifer Eyl has issued the fullest account of Paul's divinatory practices to date in her book *Signs, Wonders, and Gifts: Divination in the Letters of Paul*. Eyl is similarly concerned to find taxonomies and categorisations of Paul's practices that normalise him in his historical environment, and she critiques previous scholarship for perpetuating ideologically grounded classifications that favour a Paul that is unique in his historical environment. To this end, she constructs a threefold taxonomy of Paul's divinatory practices: the interpretation of non-verbal divine signs; the channelling of speech from a divine source; and the use of literary texts or written symbols. Each Pauline behaviour has useful *comparanda* in the broader Mediterranean world.

Eyl also draws on Stanley Stowers's "modes of religiosity" to identify a key factor in the scholarly resistance to a divinatory Paul.[66] Scholars are accustomed to viewing Paul as inhabiting an "intellectualist" mode of religiosity, which focuses on lofty concepts of theology and ethics, but have more resistance to seeing him in more "mundane" relationships of everyday social exchange with the divine. This is where divination most naturally finds itself, as Eyl places the reception of divine knowledge alongside the reception of divine power (evident in Paul's wonderworking and healing abilities) as (in Paul's view) gifts of God given in response to human *pistis*. While the subtitle promises a book devoted to divination in the letters of Paul, it is the rehabilitation and deployment of this "religion of everyday social exchange" for analysing Paul that drives the book. Its content is more accurately represented by its title, with *Signs* (divination), *Wonders* (miracles, wonderworking), *and Gifts* (divine-human reciprocity) being the three pillars of her (re)description.

The studies of both Wendt and Eyl have importantly recategorised Paul's practices within his ancient context. They are foundational for the argument of the present study. There are some factors to note, however, which will illustrate where this project differs from these two earlier approaches while remaining indebted to their frameworks.

---

[65] Heidi Wendt, "Galatians 3:1 as an Allusion to Textual Prophecy," *JBL* 135 (2016): 369–89.
[66] Stanley K. Stowers, "The Religion of Plant and Animal Offerings Versus the Religion of Meanings, Essences, and Textual Mysteries," in *Ancient Mediterranean Sacrifice*, ed. Jennifer Wright Knust and Zsuzsanna Várhelyi (Oxford: Oxford University Press, 2011), 35–56.

Because both Wendt and Eyl are not primarily concerned with divination as an area of study in its own right, but as an aspect of their broader categories of interest (freelance experts, or divine-human reciprocity), divination emerges primarily as a function of those broader categories rather than as a genuine means of accessing knowledge or making decisions. Both authors are careful not to deny that divination functioned this way for Paul, but this is not where their interest in divination lies.[67] For Wendt, divination emerges as another tool in Paul's belt, which forms part of a range of demonstrable expertise that helps to identify him as a freelance religious expert. For Eyl, divination sits alongside wonderworking and reciprocity as an example of the religion of everyday social exchange. Eyl devotes comparatively more space to understanding the general shape of Paul's divinatory practices in his ancient context, but only to the extent that *comparanda* can be established, and a taxonomy formed. By treating divination as a subset of broader categories that include wonderworking, mystery initiations, and so on, divination as an enterprise and goal in itself, and the logic behind it, are sidelined and subsumed within these broader interests.[68] This is not a criticism of these works as such, rather an acknowledgement of their scope and purpose, which leave room for a more detailed examination of the precise shape of Paul's divinatory practices, informed by this new comparative context.

This difference of approach can be illustrated by contrasting the ways in which Eyl and I treat the topic of glossolalia in Paul. Since Eyl is interested primarily in the polythetic categorisation of Paul's practices, glossolalia sits alongside prophecy as an example of "channelling divine speech." Eyl critiques other scholars who would create separate taxonomic categories for prophecy and glossolalia merely based on the intelligibility of the speech. Since I am interested in understanding the role of different methods within Paul's divinatory repertoire, however, I cannot ignore that glossolalia, as Paul presents it, is not a method of divination at all since it conveys no information. There is an analytical utility to keeping divination tightly defined in this manner. The concept and goal of divination can become diluted when it is too readily combined with other wonderworking practices that are not aimed at gaining knowledge from the divine. While glossolalia can certainly be categorised along with prophecy

---

[67] The same can be said for Graham Twelftree's study of the "miraculous" in Paul, which includes a wide range of "revelatory experiences" but is not primarily concerned with the issue of divine communication: Graham H. Twelftree, *Paul and the Miraculous: A Historical Reconstruction* (Grand Rapids: Baker Academic, 2013).

[68] This is noted by Federico Santangelo, review of *At the Temple Gates*, by Heidi Wendt, *HR* 58 (2019): 353: "We actually get to hear fairly little about the religion of the experts that are placed at the center of this study. Most of what is discussed revolves around the nature of their expertise, the strategies through which it was asserted, and the grounds on which it was contested."

as an example of divine speech, this does not help us understand how divination functions for Paul as a means of knowledge (see further Chapter 3).

Another result of these approaches is that divination emerges as a primarily performative phenomenon. Both Wendt and Eyl are careful to remain ambivalent and detached from trying to discern Paul's own intentions and motivations, and instead focus on the categorisation of his practices. Again, this is an appropriate methodological rule for the aims of their projects, and Eyl is right to caution against those who claim to discern Paul's thoughts, which end up looking suspiciously like those of the interpreter. This can lead to some distortion, though, as Eyl separates her taxonomy of divinatory practices (which include signs, glossolalia, and written prophecies) from "discursive claims to divine authority" (which are treated in a separate chapter, and include claims to epiphanies, visions, and the revelation of mysteries). There is an important point being made here: religious practices are open to analysis in a way that religious experiences are not, so it is possible she is being cautious about the nature of the evidence at our disposal. This will be further discussed in the chapter on visions, but inasmuch as these epiphanies and revelations are said to communicate knowledge from the divine, it seems artificial to me to separate these from the taxonomy of divinatory practices itself. If our goal is to understand the broad range of means of access to divine knowledge as Paul presents them, then such visionary and revelatory experiences do not just legitimate Paul's divinatory practices but are themselves a further means of divination.

Peter Struck categorises the history of scholarship on divination into two main groups. The first treats divination primarily as a tool of social and political power. It is "a means to invoke the ultimate authority of the divine in order to construct and maintain social orders by building consensus and managing conflict."[69] The second treats it as a subset of the underworld of occult "magical" practices in antiquity, as illustrated by the frequency of the pairing "magic and divination" in scholarly work. Both perspectives have a fair amount of truth to them. It should be axiomatic that any claim to communication from the divine is a claim for the authority of what is supposedly being communicated. This results in a certain amount of symbolic capital for the one privileged to receive and able to interpret that information. In the period most directly relevant for Paul the freelance religious expert could also more indiscriminately merge what might be called "divinatory" and "magical" expertise. Paul himself, in his list of *charismata*, includes side-by-side divinatory practices such as prophecy and interpretation of languages, and "magical" practices, such as works of power and gifts of healing (1 Cor 12:8–10).

---

[69] Struck, *Divination and Human Nature*, 5.

Both approaches though, according to Struck, proceed from an "irrationalist premise," which assumes that divination in and of itself does not make sense. Therefore, scholars seek to understand it within the more comprehensible realms of social capital, or the psychologising of an "ancient mind-set, groping to find effective means of dealing with a sometimes brutal world."[70] In contrast to these positions Struck argues that divination, at all levels of ancient society, was thought to work, and was thought to make sense as a means of knowledge, both by those who practiced it, and by those who reflected on it.[71]

This is the approach adopted in this book, in which I seek to understand how divination (by which I mean divine-to-human communication) functioned as a means of knowledge for Paul, which both made sense within his broader world view, and also played a role in shaping that world view. In this sense this study treads a middle path between previous scholarship on "Paul and revelation" and "Paul and divination." In contrast to the studies of Paul and revelation, I do not treat divination simply as an ahistorical theological category, about which Paul formed thoughts and taught others, but as something that Paul was actively engaged in, even while he sought to understand it. In contrast to the studies of Paul and divination, however, I am not only interested in the categorisation of Paul's practices, but how he understands them in ways similar to other figures of the ancient Mediterranean world, as well as how the information he claims to have received through divinatory methods shapes the arguments and discourse of his letters.

In doing this, I do not claim unfiltered access to Paul's mind, nor do I deny the occasional nature of his letters or the rhetorical situations that shape his responses. I do, however, approach the evidence of his letters with the assumption that they are intended to communicate ideas, the logic of which can be followed, and which make sense in his historical context independently of the rhetorical power that they wield.[72]

---

[70] Struck, *Divination and Human Nature*, 9. For a similar critique, see Flower, *Seer in Ancient Greece*, 4.

[71] Struck, *Divination and Human Nature*, 9–14. The remainder of Struck's book is dedicated to precisely understanding how ancient philosophers theorised divination, and understood it as a type of non-discursive means of knowledge, akin to modern notions of intuition. Cf. Walter Burkert, "Signs, Commands, and Knowledge: Ancient Divination Between Enigma and Epiphany" in *Mantikê: Studies in Ancient Divination*, ed. Sarah Iles Johnston and Peter T. Struck, RGRW 155 (Leiden: Brill, 2005), 30.

[72] Engberg-Pedersen presents strong arguments for the various ways in which Paul can be seen as "philosophical," including his "systematic urge," Troels Engberg-Pedersen, "Paul the Philosopher," in *The Oxford Handbook of Pauline Studies*, ed. Matthew V. Novenson and R. Barry Matlock (Oxford: Oxford University Press, 2022).

Contexts and Comparisons

The category of divination functions (as outlined above) as a redescriptive category, with which to select a heuristic set of data to compare with Paul's practices. The nature of the comparisons being made depends on the purposes to which they are put. In this study, I do not seek to compare two or more parallel systems of thought so as to bring out all the structural similarities and differences between them. Rather, the comparisons I employ primarily serve the purpose of contextualisation. This is because, while divination is not a Pauline term, it is an ancient one, and one that can encompass a broad range of phenomena in antiquity, some of which Paul self-consciously engages in (e.g., visions, oracles, signs). This makes the task of relating Paul to his context one of "situating in" rather than "comparing with."[73]

Paul, as a historical figure, does not stand apart from his context, but should be understood fully as a part of it. The comparisons I undertake are analogical rather than genealogical, as I am not interested in positing particular lines of dependence between ancient sources.[74] They are analogical, however, within a particular historical and cultural context.[75] This context is, broadly speaking, the Hellenistic culture of the early Roman Empire, and the comparative material I draw on comes primarily from the Hellenistic and early Roman periods.[76] I also occasionally refer to earlier texts such as Homer, Hesiod, and Plato due to their influence upon these later periods.

By situating Paul within the context of Roman Hellenism, I consciously avoid two distinctions common to much previous scholarship on prophecy and revelation in Paul. One is the anachronistic distinction between Judaism

---

[73] For the difference between "comparing" and "situating," see Troels Engberg-Pedersen, foreword to *Paul and the Greco-Roman Philosophical Tradition*, ed. Joseph R. Dodson and Andrew W. Pitts, LNTS 527 (London: T&T Clark, 2017), xvii. More generally, see L. Michael White and John T. Fitzgerald, "Quod Est Comparandum: The Problem of Parallels," in *Early Christianity and Classical Culture: Comparative Studies in Honor of Abraham J. Malherbe*, ed. John T. Fitzgerald, Thomas H. Olbricht, and L. Michael White, NovTSup 110 (Leiden: Brill, 2003), 13–39.

[74] On this distinction, see Adolf Deissmann, *Light from the Ancient East: The New Testament Illustrated by Recently Discovered Texts of the Graeco-Roman World*, trans. Lionel R. M. Strachan (New York: Hodder & Stoughton, 1910), 262–63; Smith, *Drudgery Divine*, 47–53.

[75] M. David Litwa (*Iesus Deus: The Early Christian Depiction of Jesus as a Mediterranean God* [Minneapolis: Fortress, 2014], 28–32) draws attention to a shared "culture" as a historical basis for comparison, drawing on Jonathan Z. Smith ("In Comparison a Magic Dwells," in *Imagining Religion: From Babylon to Jonestown* [Chicago: University of Chicago Press, 1982], 19–35).

[76] I most often refer to this cultural mix as "Graeco-Roman." This should not be taken to imply a single homogeneous culture, but precisely a cultural mix. There were regional or diachronic differences and I will often use the more specific terms "Greek" or "Roman" when referring to evidence that relates specifically to one of these societies. I also, as I detail below, do not use the term in a way that excludes Judaism from this cultural mix.

and Christianity in the mid-first century CE. Whether or not one wants to describe Paul as a Christian,[77] his convictions about Jesus as Christ are never, for him, at the expense of his Jewishness.[78] Indeed, Paul's demand that Gentiles turn from idols and serve the true and living God (1 Thess 1:9) is itself a form of Judaising within a first-century Hellenistic context.[79]

This points towards the second dichotomy I avoid, which is that between Judaism and Hellenism.[80] Undoubtedly, many Jews of the first century maintained certain cultural and theological distinctives in relation to their "pagan" neighbours (such as exclusive allegiance to the Jewish God).[81] But by the time of Paul, Jews were working these distinctives out from fully within the dominant Hellenistic culture rather than outside of it, or in opposition to it.[82] Walter Burkert notes that when it comes to divination "there clearly was a Near Eastern-Mediterranean *koinē* of forms and traditions – with local variants, intercultural infiltrations, and some continuous change of trends or fashions."[83] The Jewish matrix of Paul's day represents a particular inflection of this broader cultural *koinē*, and this makes it fruitless to argue for an exclusively Jewish or Hellenistic context for Paul's thought and practice.[84] In the words of Troels Engberg-Pedersen:

[77] From a second-order perspective, this is not a term or concept Paul ever applies to himself. From a third-order perspective, Paul clearly fits within a discernible category of authors who centred their activities and religious devotion on the figure of Jesus as a uniquely divine being.

[78] See Matthew V. Novenson, "Did Paul Abandon either Judaism or Monotheism?" in *The New Cambridge Companion to St Paul*, ed. Bruce W. Longenecker (Cambridge: Cambridge University Press, 2020), 239–59; and the diverse perspectives represented in Mark D. Nanos and Magnus Zetterholm, eds., *Paul Within Judaism: Restoring the First-Century Context to the Apostle* (Minneapolis: Fortress, 2015).

[79] Paula Fredriksen, "Judaizing the Nations: The Ritual Demands of Paul's Gospel," *NTS* 56 (2010): 232–52.

[80] I use the terms "Judaism," "Jew," and "Jewish" to refer to the ethnic and cultural group denoted by the Greek Ἰουδαῖος and Latin *Iudaeus*, which includes, but is not limited to, aspects we would call "religious."

[81] See John M. G. Barclay, *Jews in the Mediterranean Diaspora: From Alexander to Trajan (323 BCE– 117 CE)* (Berkeley: University of California Press, 1999); John J. Collins, *Between Athens and Jerusalem: Jewish Identity in the Hellenistic Diaspora*, 2nd ed. (Grand Rapids: Eerdmans, 2000).

[82] See Martin Hengel, *Judaism and Hellenism: Studies in their Encounter in Palestine during the Early Hellenistic Period*, trans. John Bowden (London: SCM, 1974); Carol Bakhos, ed., *Ancient Judaism in its Hellenistic Context*, JSJSup 95 (Leiden: Brill, 2004); Troels Engberg-Pedersen, ed., *Paul Beyond the Judaism/Hellenism Divide* (Louisville: Westminster John Knox, 2001).

[83] Burkert, "Signs, Commands, and Knowledge," 29.

[84] The turn to interpreting oracular texts is a particular feature of Jewish divination in this period, which will be discussed in more detail in Chapter 4. See further Alex P. Jassen, *Mediating the Divine: Prophecy and Revelation in the Dead Sea Scrolls and Second Temple Judaism*, STDJ 68 (Leiden: Brill, 2007); Hanna Tervanotko, "Reading God's Will? Function and Status of Oracle Interpreters in Ancient Jewish and Greek Texts," *DSD* 24 (2017): 424–46; Hanna Tervanotko, "Searching the Book of Law: Jewish Divination in 1 Maccabees 3:48," in *The Early Reception of Torah*, ed. Kristin de Troyer et al., DCLS 39 (Berlin: de Gruyter, 2020), 121–37.

Instead, one must look entirely open-mindedly at the facts: the actual use of comparable ideas and practices in the cultural context no matter where and irrespective of their roots. Only by going beyond the Judaism/Hellenism divide . . . will scholars be able to see Paul in the broad cultural context to which he belonged and to use that insight fruitfully for the comparative elucidation of his own ideas and practices.[85]

Indeed. The last sentence of the above quotation is especially important for my own approach in this book. The goal of my contextualisation is not redescription or taxonomy for its own sake, but to better understand the precise shape of Paul's own practices and ideas in the light of these *comparanda*.[86] The *comparanda* are brought in for the express purpose of illuminating Paul's letters from the vantage point of this new comparative context. In doing so I hope that Paul can function as a case study, which contributes beyond the area of Pauline studies to the broader study of divination in the ancient world and Graeco-Roman religion. I do this, however, by focusing on Paul as one such divinatory actor and thinker, fully engaged in his ancient context.

Outline

This study is organised thematically with each chapter covering a particular aspect of divination in Paul's letters, drawing in contextual material for comparison in the course of the analysis. Chapter 1 treats the "mechanics" of divination in Paul, examining how Paul conceptualises the transmission of knowledge from the divine to the human level in conversation with contemporary philosophical reflections on the same topic. Chapter 2 treats the role of visions in providing divine information, while Chapter 3 deals with instances of divine or inspired speech. Chapter 4 examines Paul's divinatory use of texts in comparison with the use of oracle collections and textual divination in the ancient world. Chapter 5 considers the role of signs and omens from which Paul draws inferences about divine activity and disposition. Finally, in the conclusion, I bring these methods together, drawing some synthetic conclusions about the functioning of divine communication for Paul.

By analysing Paul's claims to divine knowledge from the perspective of divination we are able to bring together a collection of related practices and ideas in Paul's letters that existing scholarly categories usually keep apart.

---

[85] Troels Engberg-Pedersen, "Introduction: Paul Beyond the Judaism/Hellenism Divide," in Engberg-Pedersen, *Paul Beyond the Judaism/Hellenism Divide*, 3–4.
[86] This is what Engberg-Pedersen elsewhere calls "heuristic comparison," Engberg-Pedersen, "Past is a Foreign Country," 57–61.

By shelving categorical distinctions such as "prophecy versus divination," "inspiration versus interpretation," or "Judaism versus Hellenism" we can also gain a much fuller and clearer picture of Paul's access to divine knowledge in his first-century context.

CHAPTER I

The Mechanics of Divination

The Stoic philosopher Posidonius is said to have enumerated three different ways that the divine could communicate with humans in dreams.

> First, the soul is clairvoyant of itself because of its kinship with the gods; second, the air is full of immortal souls, already clearly stamped, as it were, with the marks of truth; and third, the gods in person converse with men when they are asleep. (Cicero, *Div.* 1.64 [Falconer, LCL])

Since divination concerns communication between divine and human realms, in order for this communication to take place there must be some way in which the divine and human realms can connect and interact. In the mythical world of epic, gods and humans could more or less straightforwardly appear to each other and talk, but in the systems of the philosophers these interactions needed to be worked out in ways that fitted into their cosmological and anthropological frameworks. The quote from Posidonius outlines three ways in which these connections could be made, which Cicero expands beyond dreams to include other moments of divine inspiration.

In what follows, I will sketch a general picture of various ways in which divinatory signs and messages were thought to be able to traverse the gap between human and divine in the ancient world, before examining how Paul's statements about divine knowledge fit within these possibilities. Scholars have long recognised that Paul's letters demonstrate a certain facility in the philosophical terms and concepts of his day.[1] Attention has often focused on the affinities he shares with ancient rhetoric and moral philosophy.[2] More recently however scholars

---

[1] For a recent survey see Engberg-Pedersen, "Paul the Philosopher."
[2] E.g., Abraham J. Malherbe, *Paul and the Popular Philosophers* (Minneapolis: Fortress, 1989); Edwin Judge, "St Paul and Socrates," in *The First Christians in the Roman World: Augustan and New Testament Essays*, ed. James R. Harrison, WUNT 229 (Tübingen: Mohr Siebeck, 2008), 670–83;

have directed energy towards understanding the philosophical contours of Paul's physics, which includes his cosmology and anthropology.[3]

Stowers, in particular, has sought to locate Paul with some precision in the intellectual climate of the late Roman Republic and early Empire.[4] Before the first century BCE, Hellenistic philosophy had been characterised by the rival schools of Stoicism, Epicureanism, and the sceptical Academy. But after the closing of the Academy in Athens in 86 BCE, philosophy was no longer centralised in Athens and witnessed a renewed interest in interpreting the texts of Plato and Aristotle, and recovering the doctrines of Pythagoras.[5] While the Hellenistic schools generally retained their character as "total ways of thought and life that were largely exclusive of other systems," the renewed interest in Plato and Pythagoras was marked by a greater openness and flexibility to other traditions.[6] This involved interpreting Plato in the light of Stoic, Peripatetic, and Pythagorean ideas, amongst others.[7]

In addition to the creative fusing of philosophical doctrines, this philosophising was often put to practical religious ends, which often went hand in hand with divination. The philosophy of Eudorus of Alexandria, for example, appears to have consisted of a critical blend of Platonism, Aristotelianism, and Pythagoreanism, the *telos* of which was "assimilation to God."[8] P. Nigidius

---

Troels Engberg-Pedersen, ed., *Paul in his Hellenistic Context* (Minneapolis: Fortress, 1995); Troels Engberg-Pedersen, *Paul and the Stoics* (Edinburgh: T&T Clark, 2000); Emma Wasserman, *The Death of the Soul in Romans 7: Sin, Death, and the Law in Light of Hellenistic Moral Psychology*, WUNT 2/256 (Tübingen: Mohr Siebeck, 2008).

[3] George van Kooten, *Cosmic Christology in Paul and the Pauline School: Colossians and Ephesians in the Context of Graeco-Roman Cosmology, with a New Synopsis of the Greek Texts*, WUNT 2/171 (Tübingen: Mohr Siebeck, 2003); George van Kooten, *Paul's Anthropology in Context: The Image of God, Assimilation to God, and Tripartite Man in Ancient Judaism, Ancient Philosophy, and Early Christianity*, WUNT 232 (Tübingen: Mohr Siebeck, 2008); Troels Engberg-Pedersen, *Cosmology and Self in the Apostle Paul: The Material Spirit* (Oxford: Oxford University Press, 2010); Stanley K. Stowers, "Paul and the Terrain of Philosophy," EC 6 (2015): 141–56; Stanley K. Stowers, "The Dilemma of Paul's Physics: Features Stoic-Platonist or Platonist-Stoic?" in *From Stoicism to Platonism: The Development of Philosophy, 100 BCE–100 CE*, ed. Troels Engberg-Pedersen (Cambridge: Cambridge University Press, 2017), 231–53.

[4] Stowers, "Terrain"; Stowers, "Paul's Physics."

[5] On this development, see the essays collected in Malcolm Schofield, ed. *Aristotle, Plato and Pythagoreanism in the First Century BC: New Directions for Philosophy* (Cambridge: Cambridge University Press, 2013); Engberg Pedersen, *From Stoicism to Platonism*.

[6] Stowers, "Terrain," 145.

[7] Mauro Bonazzi and Jan Opsomer, eds., *The Origins of the Platonic System: Platonisms of the Early Empire and their Philosophical Contexts* (Leuven: Peeters, 2009).

[8] John Dillon, *The Middle Platonists: A Study of Platonism 80 BC to AD 220*, rev. ed. (London: Duckworth, 1996), 115–35; Mauro Bonazzi, "Pythagoreanising Aristotle: Eudorus and the Systematisation of Platonism," in Schofield, *Aristotle, Plato and Pythagoreanism*, 160–86.

Figulus, to whom Cicero credited the contemporary revival of Pythagoreanism (*Tim.* 1.1), was also keenly interested in divination and principally remembered as an astrologer (Lucan 1.639–72; Suetonius, *Aug.* 94.2). The same combination of Platonic-Pythagorean philosophy and astrology is also present in Thrasyllus, the court philosopher of Tiberius.[9]

This mixture of philosophical doctrines and practical religious ends evidently proved attractive to a number of Jewish intellectuals of the first centuries BCE/CE. Philo of Alexandria, most famously, claims to have derived his own brand of Stoicised Platonism from Moses via Pythagoras. Other texts, such as the Wisdom of Solomon and Fourth Maccabees, do not openly claim Plato or any other Greek philosopher as a source but betray the same intellectual milieu as they merge biblical exegesis with their own distinctive blends of Stoic and Platonic cosmology and physics.[10] Paul fits in this context, not as a professional philosopher, but as one, like other figures of his day, who could make creative and flexible use of these intellectual currents for his own practical ends. As will be seen, Paul's statements about the mechanics of divination are all comprehensible within these broader philosophical discourses in Graeco-Roman antiquity, even as he treats some familiar concepts in distinctive ways and turns them towards his own ends.

Different philosophers and philosophical schools harboured differing opinions about the efficacy and value of divination. Epicureans, unsurprisingly, rejected the possibility of divination altogether, while Platonists (as we have seen) and some Peripatetics distinguished between "true" divination of the inspired variety and the inductive reading of signs, which they rejected. The Stoic school on the other hand defended both types of divination and understood them to function through the same mechanisms, although Roman Stoics such as Epictetus and Marcus Aurelius tended to criticise people's overreliance on divination.[11]

The two most prominent sources I shall use to represent the Graeco-Roman discussions are Cicero's *De divinatione* and Plutarch's Delphic dialogues, as well as his work *De genio Socratis*. Three factors make these particularly valuable sources for both the practice of divination and the theoretical reflection on its working at the time of Paul.[12] First, they are chronologically located relatively close together on either side of Paul. Cicero wrote *De divinatione* near the end

---

[9] On these figures see Wendt, *At the Temple Gates*, 119–29; Dillon, *Middle Platonists*, 117–18, 184–85.
[10] Engberg-Pedersen, *Cosmology and Self*, 22–26; Stowers, "Terrain," 146–48.
[11] Robert Parker, "Divination, Greek," *OCD*: 470; A. A. Long, "Astrology: Arguments Pro and Contra," in *From Epicurus to Epictetus: Studies in Hellenistic and Roman Philosophy* (Oxford: Oxford University Press, 2006), 133–34.
[12] Levison presents similar reasons for their relevance to other Jewish authors of the same time period. John R. Levison, *The Spirit in First-Century Judaism*, AGJU 29 (Leiden: Brill, 1997), 13–17.

of his life, between 45 and 44 BCE,[13] and Plutarch's Delphic dialogues were composed around the beginning of the second century CE.[14] The common themes and perspectives preserved in both make it very likely that such views remained fairly consistent and formed part of Paul's immediate environment.

Second, neither author argues a single case, but rather presents a variety of perspectives on the issues that concern them. Cicero's philosophical allegiance is to Academic scepticism, and so the *De divinatione* is structured as a debate/dialogue between Cicero and his brother Quintus on the nature and efficacy of divination. In Book 1, Quintus presents positive arguments for the truth of divination, which Cicero then dismantles in Book 2. The positive case for divination is explicitly characterised as a Stoic perspective (*Div.* 2.8), but the text cites two main sources for the philosophical sections in 1.60–71 and 1.109–131: the Stoic Posidonius and the Peripatetic philosopher Cratippus.[15] The two perspectives cannot always be easily reconciled with each other, and Cicero does not seem particularly concerned with doing so, but instead presents both perspectives. Plutarch himself represents the philosophy of "Middle-Platonism," which exemplifies the creative but critical fusing of various philosophical perspectives I have outlined above. His works also take the form of dialogues among people of varying philosophical perspectives, and he is often content to let different perspectives sit side by side. Consequently, both Cicero and Plutarch bear witness to an impressive range of ideas about divination, and in what follows I am less concerned to determine the exact personal views of each author and more concerned with the various possibilities of thought to which they attest.

Finally, Cicero and Plutarch's own involvement with divination, and the practical religious ends of their philosophical projects make them valuable points of comparison and contrast with Paul. Cicero was a member of the college of augurs at Rome and writes his dialogues *De natura deorum* and *De divinatione* for the purpose of moderating Roman *religio* with philosophy

---

[13] For dating and introductory issues, see David Wardle, *Cicero: On Divination, Book 1, translated with introduction and commentary* (Oxford: Clarendon, 2006), 37–44; Federico Santangelo, *Divination, Prediction and the End of the Roman Republic* (Cambridge: Cambridge University Press, 2013), 10.

[14] The precise dating is uncertain, see Christopher P. Jones, "Towards a Chronology of Plutarch's Works," *JRS* 56 (1966): 61–74.

[15] For a balanced, recent treatment of Cicero's sources, see Wardle (*On Divination*, 28–36), who ultimately affirms the earlier views of Karl Reinhardt (*Poseidonios* [Munich: Beck, 1921], 422–64) that 1.109–116 represent the views of Cratippus and 1.117–131 represent those of Posidonius. The shorter section 1.60–71 contains material attributed explicitly to Posidonius (1.64) and Cratippus (1.70–71), but the Platonic material in 1.60–63 could plausibly have come through either of them. See Friedrich Pfeffer, *Studien zur Mantik in der Philosophie der Antike* (Meisenheim am Glan: Hain, 1976), 76.

(*Nat. d.* 1.1).[16] Plutarch was a priest at Delphi and his Delphic dialogues are largely taken up with understanding, interpreting, and defending the workings of the god at that oracle.[17] Both authors, therefore, share with Paul a practical, not just a theoretical, interest in divination. Their elite social status and connections to official divinatory institutions, however, differentiate them from Paul's more freelance expertise and impinge in various ways on the religious ends to which each author puts his philosophical resources.

These two authors form the richest points for comparison, but other sources will also be brought in to provide some further context when required, particularly the works of Plato, which are influential for both Stoic and Middle-Platonic thought.

The Mechanics of Divination in Antiquity

Direct Involvement of the God

Returning to the Posidonius quote with which this chapter began, his third option is the relatively simple idea that "the gods in person converse with men when they are asleep." According to I. G. Kidd, this may refer specifically to dream-oracles and incubation, but ancient sources are full of gods appearing and conversing with humans in a variety of contexts, both in sleep and awake.[18] There is little reason to believe this was not the majority belief and that most people did not feel the need to work through how exactly this was possible. Elsewhere in *De divinatione*, however, Quintus effectively denies the truth of epiphanies, and uses their falsity as a foil for more subtle explanations of divination (Cicero, *Div.* 1.79; cf. *Har. resp.* 62).

A related idea is that the god could be directly involved in possessing and speaking through a human medium. Although acting as a mediator between the god and humanity, the human medium is still coming into direct contact with the god. Speaking of Delphi, Iles Johnston writes that "there was little doubt in antiquity that Apollo spoke from within the Pythia."[19] She spoke her oracles in the first-person singular as from Apollo himself, and the verbs used

---

[16] On the moderation of religion as the central question in these dialogues, see J. P. F. Wynne, *Cicero on the Philosophy of Religion: On the Nature of the Gods and On Divination* (Cambridge: Cambridge University Press, 2019).

[17] See Elsa Giovanna Simonetti, *A Perfect Medium? Oracular Divination in the Thought of Plutarch* (Leuven: Leuven University Press, 2017); Dillon, *Middle Platonists*, 185–89.

[18] L. Edelstein and I. G. Kidd, eds., *Posidonius* (Cambridge: Cambridge University Press, 1988), 2:432. On epiphanies, see Chapter 2 below.

[19] Iles Johnston, *Ancient Greek Divination*, 44; so also E. R. Dodds, *The Greeks and the Irrational*, Sather Classical Lectures 25 (Berkeley: University of California Press, 1959), 70–71.

to describe the process imply the presence of Apollo within her: ἐνθουσιάζειν, literally "to have a god inside," and κατέχειν, "possess" or "occupy."[20] Plutarch's dialogues both witness to this belief, and also ridicule it, suggesting that if a god were to enter into a medium's body and use the medium's mouth as an instrument, he would be "prodigal with his majesty," and would not "observe the dignity and greatness of his preeminence" (*Def. orac.* 414e). Platonists such as Plutarch also faced larger problems of how the immaterial interacts with the material. This denial of the straightforward presence and action of the god leads to the need for other theories to explain the god's contact with mortality, but the theories need not be mutually exclusive. In the case of Posidonius, the three theories were evidently held together as alternative means of communication that could be employed at different times, and were perhaps relevant to different divinatory experiences.

Daimons as Intermediaries

The second way Posidonius supposed gods could communicate with humans invokes the presence of daimons and heroes: "the air is full of immortal souls, already clearly stamped, as it were, with the marks of truth."[21] Plato, in his *Symposium*, had already posited τὸ δαιμόνιον as a mid-way point between divine and mortal realms, responsible for "interpreting and transporting human things to the gods and divine things to humans" (*Symp.* 202e). This encompasses all forms of "divination (ἡ μαντική) and priestcraft concerning sacrifice and ritual and incantations, and all soothsaying (τὴν μαντείαν) and sorcery" (*Symp.* 202e). The person who has skill in these areas can be labelled a δαιμόνιος ἀνήρ. In Plato's vocabulary, τὸ δαιμόνιον refers to the intermediate realm between divine and mortal, which is populated by individual δαίμονες.[22] Expounding these views in the second century CE, Apuleius takes this role into account for both natural and technical forms of divination.

> For particular members of their company are appointed, according to the area assigned to each, to see that dreams are formed, entrails are cloven, that birds are guided to fly propitiously and made to sing prophetically, that thunderbolts are hurled, clouds made to flash, and all the other signs by which we foretell the future. We must believe that all

---

[20] Iles Johnston, *Ancient Greek Divination*, 44–45; Fritz Graf, *Apollo* (Abingdon: Routledge, 2009), 63.

[21] The description of souls as *immortales* is unlikely to have come from Posidonius, and may have been Cicero's own addition, Edelstein and Kidd, *Posidonius*, 431–32.

[22] Cf. Plato, *Tim.* 40d.

such things occur through the will, power and authority of the heavenly gods, but also by the compliance, service and agency of the demons. (Apuleius, *De deo Socr.* 6.4–5 [Jones, LCL])

These daimons can be divided into two broad classes, being either the souls of deceased humans (sometimes distinguished as "heroes"), or a higher class of divine beings of non-human origin.[23] In either case, they are generally thought of as psychic beings, formed of the same substance as the soul. It is to this latter class that Apuleius assigns the infamous daimon of Socrates, who, upon receiving sufficient worship and recognition,

Alerts you in uncertainty, forewarns you in doubt, protects you in danger, supports you in need; by dreams or omens, or perhaps in person if the situation demands, he can sweep away what is evil and promote what is good, raise up what is cast down, steady what is tottering, illuminate what is dark, guide success and undo failure. (Apuleius, *De deo Socr.* 16.8–9 [Jones, LCL])

As an intermediate divine being, this daimon can send dreams or omens, but also speak and appear in person. Apuleius makes clear that these are the sorts of signs that Socrates could apprehend with both his ears and eyes, sometimes being able to see the appearance of the daimon itself, albeit in a way that was only visible to him (*De deo Socr.* 20.4–7). In terms of mechanics, then, there is little difference between this view and the first view, which posits the direct involvement of the god. The only difference lies in what sort of being is communicating.

Plutarch, in tackling the same question of Socrates's daimon, puts forward a number of explanations that foreground the idea of daimons as souls (ψυχαί), which have a different way of communicating with human souls, without the need for aural or visual contact.[24] Socrates was not guided by spoken

---

[23] Some ancient sources may prefer one of these views over the other, or they may list them side by side as separate classes. For the latter, see Apuleius, *De deo Socr.* 15–16; for the former, Brenk has argued that Plutarch consistently favours the idea of daimons as the souls of deceased humans, see Frederick E. Brenk, "Genuine Greek Demons, 'In Mist Apparelled'? Hesiod and Plutarch," in *Relighting the Souls: Studies in Plutarch, in Greek Literature, Religion, and Philosophy, and in the New Testament Background* (Stuttgart: Franz Steiner Verlag, 1998), 170–81; Frederick E. Brenk, "In the Light of the Moon: Demonology in the Early Imperial Period," *ANRW* 16.3:2117–30.

[24] On the coherence and significance of Plutarch's daimonology in general and in *De genio Socratis*, see the differing views of Dillon, *The Middle Platonists*, 223–24; Daniel Babut, "La doctrine démonologique dans le *De genio Socratis* de Plutarque: cohérence et fonction," *L'information littéraire* 35 (1983): 201–205; Frederick E. Brenk, *In Mist Apparelled: Religious Themes in Plutarch's Moralia and Lives*, Mnemosyne 48 (Leiden: Brill, 1977), 85–144; Brenk, "Demonology," 2128–30.

language, "but the unuttered words of a daimon, making voiceless contact with his intelligence by their sense alone (τῷ δηλουμένῳ τοῦ νοοῦντος [*Gen. Socr.* 588e])." Ammonius in *De defectu oraculorum* suggests a similar explanation for how daimons inspire oracles.[25] Since daimons are disembodied souls, they can communicate directly with human souls by creating in them images of the future (φαντασίας ἐμποιοῦσι τοῦ μέλλοντος [*Def. orac.* 431c]).[26] Ammonius situated this with other forms of non-verbal communication between humans such as a touch or a glance, made possible in this instance because of their shared psychic nature.

Stoic thought also accommodated daimons of both human and non-human origin, and understood both as psychic entities, composed of the same material as the soul.[27] Thus Posidonius could speak of souls (*animi*) which fill the air and communicate divine knowledge to humans through a kinship with their own soul. Another passage in *De divinatione* makes this clearer: "Since the universe is wholly filled with the Eternal Intelligence and the Divine Mind (*aeterno sensu et mente divina*), it must be that human souls are influenced by their sympathy[28] with divine souls (*divinorum animorum* [*Div.* 1.110])." This, like in Plutarch's formulation, also happens without the use of the bodily senses, but through intelligence and the mind.

The Innate Capacity of the Soul

Souls In and Outside the Body

The view that daimons are disembodied souls who can communicate with human souls, leads logically to Posidonius's first means of divination, in which "the soul (*animus*) foresees all by itself because of the relationship with the gods it possesses (Cicero, *Div.* 1.63)." Lamprias, in *De defectu oraculorum*, notes the logical connection between these two ideas: "For if the souls (ψυχαί) which have been severed from a body, or have had no part with one at all, are

---

[25] Simonetti (*Perfect Medium*, 85) links Ammonius's description to individual divination (as in *Gen. Socr.*), in opposition to institutional oracular divination. This may be true of Plutarch's broader thought, but at this point in the dialogue it enters the discussion as a solution to the functioning of the oracle, *Def. orac.* 431b.
[26] Drawing on Hesiod, *Op.* 125, for his description of daimons as souls.
[27] Keimpe Algra, "Stoics on Souls and Demons," in *Body and Soul in Ancient Philosophy*, ed. Dorothea Frede and Burkhard Reis (Berlin: de Gruyter, 2009), 372.
[28] The correct reading of this word is debated. The manuscripts read *cognitione*, which is widely regarded as a corruption. The alternative readings are either *cognatione*, "relationship," adopted by Wardle (*On Divination*, 374) and Arthur Stanley Pease (*De divinatione*, vol. 1 [Urbana: University of Illinois Press, 1920]) or *contagione*, translated by Wardle as "corruption" and thus dismissed for its negative connotations, but rendered by Struck (*Divination and Human Nature*, 210, n. 67) as "sympathy," understanding it as Cicero's Latin translation of συμπάθεια.

daimons . . . why deprive souls in bodies of that power by virtue of which the daimons possess the natural faculty of knowing and revealing future events?" (Plutarch, *Def. orac.* 431e [Babbitt, LCL]). Most philosophers believed that the human soul, or part of it at least, was drawn from the divine.[29] In Plato's *Timaeus*, the highest part of the soul (περὶ τοῦ κυριωτάτου . . . ψυχῆς), is itself called δαίμων. It was given to each person by God and housed in the top of the body, which draws the person up to the heavens and keeps him upright (Plato, *Tim.* 90a). The idea of an internal daimon which can (to varying degrees) be identified with the human soul became particularly prominent in Roman Stoicism, where it can even be called the "God within" (Epictetus, *Diatr.* 1.14.14 [δαίμων]; Seneca, *Ep.* 41.2 [*spiritus*]; Marcus Aurelius, *Med.* 3.3 [νοῦς καὶ δαίμων]).[30]

Souls and the Constraints of the Body

If souls in bodies have the same divine potential for knowledge as daimonic souls outside the body, then there must be something about the conditions of the body itself which hinders people from having a constant access to this knowledge. There must also be certain conditions in which the bodily influence recedes and allows the soul to access this information. These conditions remain constant through all discussions of the role of the soul in divination: in sleep, at the point of death, and in moments of inspiration. A fourth state which sometimes appears is a particular purity of soul.

Plato's *Timaeus* offers much of the framework for these views, although he differs in many important respects from the discussions which follow him. For Plato, divination is comprehended in the lower, appetitive part of the soul, which speaks the language of εἴδωλα and φαντάσματα, both common words for divinatory visions. Divinatory knowledge is much lower on Plato's epistemological scale of value than rational, discursive reasoning, but it is still a divine gift, given by God as compensation to the lower part of the soul so that it may attain some measure of truth (ἵνα ἀληθείας πη προσάπτοιτο [*Tim.* 71e]).[31] It can only do this, however, by being in the right state to receive this truth, which involves both being free of rationality (asleep, ill, enthused) and also being

---

[29] See Wardle (*On Divination*, 373) for references. Pease called this view a philosophical and religious commonplace, Pease, *De divinatione*, 208.

[30] According to Algra ("Stoics on Souls and Demons," 363), this notion of an internal daimon may have originated as "offering an implicit critique of, and an internalizing alternative to, the kind of traditional conceptions of external helping demons," although by our period they often appear side by side in the same author.

[31] On Plato's estimation of divination, see Francis M. Cornford, *Plato's Cosmology: The Timaeus of Plato translated with a running commentary* (London: Kegan Paul, Trench, Trubner & Company, 1937).

tamed and ordered by a breath (ἐπίπνοια) from the divine part of the soul; the part that is made of the same stuff as the world's soul and later described as δαίμων. The term ἐπίπνοια is Plato's term for divine inspiration, used in the *Phaedrus* to speak of divination as a breath from Apollo (μαντικὴν μὲν ἐπίπνοιαν Ἀπόλλωνος θέντες [*Phaedr.* 265b]).[32]

This inspiration happens through a physical process, involving the physical organ of the liver. The liver translates messages from the divine to the appetitive part of the soul, by changing colour and shape depending on the information the rational soul sends it.[33] The mind sends out thoughts (διανοήματα), which are received by the liver as impressions (τύποι) and reflected back as images (εἴδωλα) which the appetitive part can understand. Negatively, the mind can send threats, which, using the liver's bitterness, scare the soul into submission.[34] Positively, it can breathe upon, or inspire (ἐπίπνοια), gentle images, which use the liver's sweetness to put the appetitive soul into an ordered and measured state. In this state, this part of the soul can spend the night experiencing divination in its sleep (μαντείᾳ χρωμένην καθ' ὕπνον). This process is purely internal to the soul and body itself in its various parts and does not require the mediating influence of external daimons. It is also specific to natural forms of divination, such as dreams, visions, and prophecies, as opposed to the interpretation of signs, which, for Plato, is a purely rational activity. Reason will be required again to interpret the significance of the things seen and heard in these states, but this is an entirely separate process which should be performed by someone other than the one who received the divination itself (Plato, *Tim.* 71e).

In later sources, the hindrances to the divinatory power of the soul become less focused on rationality and more on the impurities and imperfections of the bodily senses. Lamprias, in *De defectu oraculorum*, agrees with Plato that the correct temperament for the soul to receive divination is one in which "the reasoning and thinking (λογιστικὸν καὶ φροντιστικόν) faculty of the souls is relaxed and released from their present state as they range amid the irrational and imaginative (τῷ ἀλόγῳ καὶ φαντασιαστικῷ) realms of the future" (Plutarch, *Def. orac.* 432c). But this is part of a broader problem, in which the power of

---

[32] See also *Resp.* 499c; *Leg.* 738c, 747e, 811c; *Crat.* 399a; *Symp.* 181c; Struck, *Divination and Human Nature*, 83.

[33] The use of the liver in this system reflects the role of the liver in traditional hepatoscopy, on which see Derek Collins, "Mapping the Entrails: The Practice of Greek Hepatoscopy," *AJP* 129 (2008): 319–45. Plato appears to be offering an explanation of this form of divination that removes it further from the direct involvement of the god, Struck, *Divination and Human Nature*, 83–84.

[34] These are conveyed through the liver's bitterness, which causes it to become wrinkled, rough and bilious in colour. For Plato's indirect engagement with hepatoscopy in this section, see Struck, *Divination and Human Nature*, 81–82.

the soul is dampened by being conjoined to the body and its mortal nature (τὸ θνητόν [*Def. orac.* 431f–432a]). Cratippus, Cicero's Peripatetic source in *De divinatione*, reverses Plato's system, so that the rational part of the soul receives divine knowledge when free from the body, as the appetitive part is "inseparable from bodily influence" (*Div.* 1.70). For Posidonius, in line with Stoic thought, the soul cannot be divided into rational and appetitive parts, but as a whole is hampered by being chained to the bodily senses (*corporis sensibus*). When released from these chains by the usual methods (sleep, illness, inspiration), the soul can see things "without the intervention of eyes, ears or tongue" in the same way as the gods communicate with each other (*Div.* 1.129). Thus, what for Plato was a matter of interior exhalations between differing parts of one human soul via the liver, is put on a larger scale of human souls being freed from the hindrances of bodily senses in order to communicate with the divine realm. In some discussions, the soul appears to be freed from its bodily restrictions in order to communicate with other daimonic souls in the air, as shown in the previous section. At other points, though, the innate capabilities of the soul can almost dispense with the need for intermediary daimons altogether. This is certainly true for Lamprias's discussion of Delphic inspiration, in which daimons as intermediary beings are given quite a different role as general overseers and guardians of the oracular process (*Def. orac.* 436f). The fact that daimons are still retained in this system at all may very well be purely a concession to Cleombrotus's position in the dialogue, and does not seem necessary to Lamprias's own position.[35]

Souls, Minds, and Daimons in De genio Socratis

The myth of Timarchus in Plutarch's *De genio Socratis* provides another example of how ancient authors can combine and redefine a common set of concepts (souls, minds, daimons, rationality) in different and creative ways. The myth tells of Timarchus, who consults the chthonic oracle of Trophonius for an answer to the puzzle of Socrates's daimon. In the oracle, his soul is transported out of his body, and he experiences visions of the cosmos and the daimonic souls that inhabit it. The voice of a daimonic guide explains to him what he is seeing.

> Every soul (ψυχή) partakes of understanding (νοῦ); none is irrational or unintelligent. But the portion of the soul that mingles with flesh and passions (σαρκὶ μιχθῇ καὶ πάθεσιν) suffers alteration and becomes in the pleasures and pains it undergoes irrational (τὸ ἄλογον). Not every

[35] Brenk, *In Mist Apparelled*, 119.

soul mingles to the same extent: some sink entirely into the body, and becoming disordered throughout, are during their life wholly distracted by passions; others mingle in part, but leave outside what is purest in them.... Now the part carried submerged in the body is called the soul (ψυχή), whereas the part left free from corruption is called by the multitude the understanding (νοῦν), who take it to be within themselves ... but those who conceive the matter rightly call it a daimon (δαίμονα), as being external. (Plutarch, *Gen. Socr.* 591d–e [De Lacy, LCL])

Taking his cue from Plato, Plutarch identifies the highest, rational part of the soul with a daimon. The myth though is not a purely internal account of anthropology but uses the daimonic soul to bridge the gap in some way between the individual soul and the cosmic world soul. Souls can submit in varying degrees to their outer daimons. Some need to be chastened and cajoled and eventually made responsive by symbols and signs (ὑπὸ συμβόλων ... καὶ σημείων), while others are responsive from birth. The responsive souls, according to the daimonic guide, form the race of seers and inspired men (τὸ μαντικόν ... καὶ θεοκλυτούμενον γένος) among whom Socrates may be counted (*Gen. Socr.* 592c).[36] These souls are not removed from rationality as in the *Timaeus*, but fully guided by it, rather they are removed from the flesh and the passions. Socrates was one of a blessed few who are privy to the conversations of the gods themselves, in contrast to the majority of the population who have to make do with signs. Plutarch thus explains individual divination, like institutional divination in the Delphic dialogues, by a mixture of the innate capacity of souls, freed from bodily, fleshly influence, and the mediating influence of daimons, which are combined in this account to represent two sides of the same coin. In this combination, the *nous* comes to exercise a far greater role than at Delphi, where the Pythia's passive reception of divine signs was seen by some as a prerequisite for effective divine communication. Both institutional and individual divination, however, Plutarch distinguishes from the technical interpretation of signs, which does not rely on the same mechanisms.

Pneuma

Marie Isaacs, in her study of *pneuma* in Hellenistic Judaism and the NT, notes that "although Greek writers certainly had a concept of inspiration, they did

---

[36] The similarities with the *Timaeus* are evident, but the modifications are equally significant. For a fuller discussion of the influence of the *Timaeus* on Plutarch's theories of divination, see Simonetti, *Perfect Medium*, 192–203, esp. 198–201.

not usually associate πνεῦμα with the process."³⁷ Aune agrees and concludes that "among Graeco-Roman authors the term has no theological significance and is marginal for their understanding of divine inspiration."³⁸ It is true that among the works surveyed, the operative terms have been νοῦς, ψυχή, and δαίμων, and their Latin equivalents *mens*, *animus*, *daemon*. These are the anthropological and cosmological elements that make divination possible. Plato does also make use of a divine breath in divination, but uses the related word ἐπίπνοια. When we take a broader look at the cosmologies underpinning such discussions, however, we can see that the concept and the substance of πνεῦμα does in fact play a much larger role, even when it is not explicitly mentioned.

This is particularly true for the Stoic sources for whom *pneuma* was a "vital physiological and cosmological substance that was active in varying amounts in all areas of the cosmos."³⁹ As a particularly refined, rarified form of matter, it was understood as the air the cosmos breathes and present in all levels of the cosmos, from rocks and metals to the heavenly bodies. At various levels it provided structure and cohesion to all of nature, and gave rise to intelligence and perception in animate beings.⁴⁰ Posidonius and earlier Stoics defined the soul itself as πνεῦμα ἔνθερμον, "hot *pneuma*," as it provides life, agency, and movement to the body.⁴¹ Human souls are fragments of the divine soul, and according to Posidonius, daimons are also, as psychic beings, "created and partitioned from the substance of *aether*."⁴² Thus, when Posidonius speaks of the air being filled with divine souls which communicate information to human souls (Cicero, *Div.* 1.64, 110), he is speaking about communication between differentiated fragments of the cosmic *pneuma*, in what Struck calls a "direct *pneuma-pneuma* transfer of information."⁴³ Philo, who among other Hellenistic Jews represents a "unique blend of Platonist metaphysics, Stoic physics and Jewish biblical exegesis," describes the substance (οὐσία) of angels

---

[37] Marie E. Isaacs, *The Concept of Spirit: A Study of Pneuma in Hellenistic Judaism and its Bearing on the New Testament*, HM 1 (London: Heythrop College, 1976), 15.

[38] Aune, *Prophecy*, 34.

[39] Paul M. Robertson, "De-Spiritualizing 'Pneuma': Modernity, Religion, and Anachronism in the Study of Paul," *MTSR* 26 (2014): 368. See also Dale B. Martin, *The Corinthian Body* (New Haven: Yale University Press, 1995), 21–25; Troy W. Martin, "Paul's Pneumatological Statements and Ancient Medical Texts," in *The New Testament and Early Christian Literature in Greco-Roman Context: Studies in Honor of David E. Aune*, ed. John Fotopoulos, NovTSup 122 (Leiden: Brill, 2006), 105–26.

[40] See, particularly, A. A. Long and D. N. Sedley, *The Hellenistic Philosophers*, vol. 1 (Cambridge: Cambridge University Press, 1987), 281–89; R. J. Hankinson, "Stoicism and Medicine," in *The Cambridge Companion to the Stoics*, ed. Brad Inwood (Cambridge: Cambridge University Press, 2003), 298–301.

[41] Diogenes Laertius, *Lives* 7.1 Zeno (157).

[42] Edelstein and Kidd, *Posidonius*, fr. 24; Algra, "Stoics on Souls and Demons," 372.

[43] Struck, *Divination and Human Nature*, 210.

as pneumatic (πνευματική [QG 1.92]).[44] Tatian, a century later, similarly describes daimons as being without flesh, rather "their structure is pneumatic (πνευματική) like fire or air" (Or. Graec. 15 [ANF 2:71; PG 6:840]). Jewish authors around the first century CE could occasionally refer to mediating divine beings as *pneumata*, who were capable of inspiring prophetic speech.[45] The Greek Magical Papyri[46] also attest to the term πνεῦμα being used in a way that is synonymous with δαίμων, although this is very unusual in Greek usage before the second century CE.[47]

The same pneumatic logic is present in discussions of the innate divinatory capacity of the soul. Sleep and severe illness are natural states in which souls can be freed from bodily influence, but times of inspiration or frenzy require an external divine stimulus to bring the soul out of its bodily constraints (Cicero, *Div.* 1.66; cf. Plutarch, *Def. orac.* 432d). This can happen in a number of different ways, according to Quintus in *De divinatione*, but all derive from the gods diffusing their power (*vis*) throughout the earth, "sometimes enclosing it in caverns of the earth and sometimes imparting it to human beings" (*Div.* 1.79). Commentators on Cicero link this *vis* with Stoic notions of *pneuma*, which also pervades the world.[48] The Pythia's inspiration came from the *terrae vis*, "power of the earth," which was transmitted through subterranean vapours or exhalations (*anhelitus*), and the Sibyl's came from the *naturae* [*vis*], "power of nature."[49] In the case of Delphi this *pneuma* or vapour was widely held to have risen from a chasm in the ground in the aduton directly underneath the Pythia's tripod (Cassius Dio, 63.14.2; Strabo, 9.3.5).[50] *Pneuma*, in the sense of a vapour,

---

[44] Phillip Sidney Horky, "Cosmic Spiritualism among the Pythagoreans, Stoics, Jews and Early Christians," in *Cosmos in the Ancient World*, ed. Phillip Sidney Horky (Cambridge: Cambridge University Press, 2019), 292. For further comments on the mix of Stoicism and Platonism in Philo, see Levison, *Spirit*, 144–51; Engberg-Pedersen, *Cosmology and Self*, 24–26.

[45] Josephus, *A.J.* 4.108; Philo, *Vit. Mos.* 1.274–77. See the discussion in Levison (*Spirit*, 28–30, 34–55), who links this understanding with Cleombrotus's understanding of daimons in *De defectu oraculorum*.

[46] The Greek Magical Papyri is the name given by scholars to a collection of papyri assembled from Egypt, which contain a mixture of spells, rituals, and hymns, and whose contents date from between the second century BCE and the fifth century CE. See Hans Dieter Betz, ed., *The Greek Magical Papyri in Translation Including the Demotic Spells* (Chicago: University of Chicago Press, 1986).

[47] Richard Reitzenstein, *Hellenistic Mystery-Religions: Their Basic Ideas and Significance*, trans. John E. Steely (Pittsburgh: Pickwick, 1978), 391–93; Gérard Verbeke, *L'évolution de la doctrine du pneuma du stoïcisme à S. Augustin* (Paris: Descleé de Brouwer, 1945), 323–24; Terence Paige, "Who Believes in 'Spirit'? Πνεῦμα in Pagan Usage and Implications for the Gentile Christian Mission," *HTR* 95 (2002): 431–33.

[48] Wardle, *On Divination*, 301. Struck describes Cicero's use of *vis* as specifically denoting a power of *pneuma*, *Divination and Human Nature*, 192 n. 46.

[49] For the Pythia, cf. Cicero, *Div.* 1.38, 115.

[50] For ancient and modern explanations of the *pneuma*, see Iles Johnston, *Ancient Greek Divination*, 45–50; Graf, *Apollo*, 70–71.

was not the only way souls could be kindled to ecstasy. Certain tones of voice or music, groves, forests, and rivers had similar effect but these are all in some way conduits for the transmission of divine *vis* (Cicero, *Div.* 1.80, 114). This is a decidedly naturalistic explanation, dependent as it is on specific locations and climates, but it is no less theological, as it is precisely the power and *pneuma* of the gods that are spread through these different locations.[51]

This view of the cosmos as held together and animated by *pneuma* also provides an explanation, in Stoic thought, for "artificial" forms of divination such as the observance and interpretation of signs (Cicero, *Div.* 1.130). The cosmos as a single body is deterministically linked by a series of interlocking causes, so that some of the impulses transmitted by *pneuma* concern the causes and signs of events still to happen in the future. A soul, suitably freed from the necessities of waking life, is able to discern the causal structures built into the *pneuma* with which it is in contact, and so correctly interpret the signs of future events. This way both inspiration and interpretation of natural events occur at the level of *pneuma*, through the impulses it sends out.[52]

This idea of pneumatic "sympathy" was particularly Stoic, but one did not need to be a thoroughgoing Stoic to share the basic understanding of *pneuma* as a type of substance that can interact with the body in different ways. Before the Stoics, other philosophers and medical writers were discussing the role of *pneuma* as "air in motion" responsible for many of the vital functions of the body.[53] Plutarch, whom scholars generally locate within Middle Platonism, frequently polemicised against the hyper-materialism of the Stoics. He is also unlikely to have fully identified *pneuma* with the substance of the soul, but he still held the μαντικὸν πνεῦμα at Delphi to be a physical vapour, which was somehow able to interact with an immaterial soul with which it shared an affinity (συγγενές [*Def. orac.* 433a]).[54] According to Lamprias in the dialogue, the *pneuma* first mixes in with the body (καταμειγνύμενον ... εἰς τὸ σῶμα), being carried either through the air or in running water, from which it then produces in the soul the correct temperament or mixture (κρᾶσις) to unleash its innate divinatory capability. Lamprias tries out a number of physical analogies to describe how exactly the *pneuma* effects this change in souls, but his favoured option is that the soul needs *pneuma* in order to divine like the

---

[51] It is only Delphi that was associated with a vaporous *pneuma*. Most other oracular sanctuaries were associated with spring water as a means of inspiration, which would presumably act as a carrier of the god's power. Fritz Graf, "Apollo, Possession, and Prophecy," in *Apolline Politics and Poetics: International Symposium*, ed. Lucia Athanassaki, Richard P. Martin, and John F. Miller (Athens: European Cultural Centre of Delphi, 2009), 599.
[52] See Struck, *Divination and Human Nature*, 201–213.
[53] Hankinson, "Stoicism and Medicine," 299–301. On predecessors to the cosmic function of *pneuma*, see Horky, "Cosmic Spiritualism," 272–75.
[54] For Plutarch's relationship to Stoicism, see Jan Opsomer, "Plutarch and the Stoics," in *A Companion to Plutarch*, ed. Mark Beck (Oxford: Blackwell, 2014), 88–103.

eye needs light to see. Thus, while the soul has an innate power of divination, which can occasionally be unleashed in sleep or illness, it functions best when it is complemented with divine *pneuma* from the earth. The material (ὕλη) of divination is the human soul; the *pneuma* is the active instrument or plectrum that plays it (*Def. orac.* 436f). Scholars have debated to what extent the ideas put forth by Lamprias reflect Plutarch's own views. Some have simply labelled Lamprias as representing the Stoic view, which Plutarch himself would reject.[55] Lamprias himself, however, is not a consistently "Stoic" character, as he also displays some Platonic tendencies earlier in the dialogue in his views on daimons (*Def. orac.* 414e). In other dialogues he critiques Stoic views and often appears as the mouthpiece for Plutarch's own perspective.[56] Others then have sought to integrate this perspective more fully into Plutarch's own divinatory account, leading them to speak of a more "ambivalent, hybrid and fluid conception of 'matter.'"[57]

The early Christian philosopher Origen is often cited to demonstrate the gulf between Stoic and Christian understandings of *pneuma*.[58] Origen certainly refutes a Stoic understanding of the claim "God is *pneuma*," but in doing so, he shows that his default understanding of the term itself is still materialistic and substantial.

> Nor is the Spirit, in our opinion, a "body," any more than fire is a "body," which God is said to be in the passage, "Our God is a consuming fire." For all these are figurative expressions, employed to denote the nature of "intelligent beings" by means of familiar and corporeal terms.
>
> Οὐδὲ γὰρ σῶμα τὸ καθ' ἡμᾶς πνεῦμα, ὡς οὐδὲ σῶμα τὸ πῦρ, ὅπερ εἶναι λέγεται θεὸς ἐν τῷ· ὁ θεὸς ἡμῶν πῦρ καταναλίσκον. Πάντα γὰρ ταῦτα τροπικῶς λέγεται εἰς παράστασιν τὴν ἀπὸ τῶν συνήθων καὶ σωματικῶν ὀνομάτων τῆς νοητῆς φύσεως. (*Cels.* 6.70 [ANF 4:605])[59]

---

[55] Pierre Amandry, *La mantique Apollinienne à Delphes: essai sur le fonctionnement de l'oracle* (Paris: de Boccard, 1950), 220–221; Levison, *Spirit*, 15–16.

[56] Dillon, *Middle Platonists*, 209–11.

[57] Simonetti, *Perfect Medium*, 114; Verbeke, *Doctrine du pneuma*, 267; Will concluded from this passage that "C'est qu'en réalité il n'y a pas de différence de nature véritable entre le pneuma et l'âme ... la notion de matière est floue," Ernest Will, "Sur la nature du pneuma delphique," *BCH* 66 (1942): 172.

[58] Paige, "Who Believes in 'Spirit'?" 426; John M. G. Barclay, "Πνευματικός in the Social Dialect of Pauline Christianity," in *The Holy Spirit and Christian Origins: Essays in Honor of James D. G. Dunn*, ed. Graham N. Stanton, Bruce W. Longenecker, and Stephen C. Barton (Grand Rapids: Eerdmans, 2004), 163 n. 20.

[59] Text from Marcel Borret, ed., *Origène: Contre Celse, Livres 5 et 6*, SC 147 (Paris: Cerf, 1969).

While God is immaterial for Origen, *pneuma*, like fire, denotes something material, which can only be applied to God metaphorically and not literally. Thus to say that *pneuma* is immaterial for Origen, is really to say that it is not strictly *pneuma* at all. Actual *pneuma* is material and acts on the body in material ways. When discussing the *pneuma* at Delphi, Origen argues it was not divine, but profane and impure. This is not because it was material as opposed to immaterial, but because it entered the Pythia through her genitals and not "through the more becoming medium of the bodily pores" (*Cels.* 7.3 [*ANF* 4:612]).

Summary

Many, if not most, people of the Graeco-Roman world were content to believe that gods communicated with humans by straightforwardly appearing in dreams or inhabiting the bodies of prophets. Those with a more philosophical bent however sought ways to understand the interaction of the divine and human realms in ways that were understandable within their philosophical and cosmological systems. These frequently involve the mediation of lower divinities or daimons as well as the elements of mind, soul, or *pneuma*, which operate on both anthropological and cosmological levels. None of these terms have entirely fixed meanings or roles, but can be variously defined and combined by different authors operating in different philosophical systems and different literary contexts.

The Mechanics of Divination in Paul

Reading Paul in the context sketched above, it is clear that he, like Posidonius, envisioned a number of different ways the divine realm could communicate with the human. These ways also make use of anthropological and cosmological elements such as minds, hearts, *pneuma*, and various intermediate divine beings. In analysing Paul's letters I will follow a parallel structure to that used for the Graeco-Roman discussions, in order to clearly highlight the points of contact and contrast.

Direct Involvement

On at least two occasions Paul claims to have received information from a simple appearance of a divine being, whom he identifies as the resurrected Jesus. The straightforward verbs of seeing (ἑόρακα: 1 Cor 9:1; ὤφθη: 1 Cor 15:8) hint at no further reflection on the mechanics of these appearances. At the same time, he does not seem to have simply seen a resuscitated human body as his subsequent discussion suggests Jesus's resurrected body is pneumatic (1 Cor 15:42–49), and not composed of flesh and blood (1 Cor 15:50). The divinatory function of these appearances will be discussed in detail in Chapter 2, but, for now, it is noteworthy that Paul never claims to have seen God (ὁ θεός). The closest he comes is in 2 Cor 3:18–4:6. I quote here only the most relevant sections.

> And we all, with unveiled face, beholding the glory of the Lord, are being transformed into the same image from one degree of glory to another. For this comes from the Lord who is *pneuma* . . . and even if our good news is veiled it is veiled only to those who are perishing. In their case, the god of this age has blinded the thoughts of the unbelievers to keep them from seeing the light of the good news of the glory of Christ, who is the image of God. . . . For the God who said, "let light shine out of darkness," has shone in our hearts with the light of the knowledge of the glory of God in the face of Jesus Christ. (2 Cor 3:18–4:6)

The term τὴν δόξαν κυρίου, "the glory of the Lord," (3:18) or τῆς δόξης τοῦ θεοῦ, "the glory of God," (4:6) can be taken to refer to the כבוד יהוה of biblical prophetic visions.[60] This glory represents the substance of Yahweh's body, and Paul's claim that they have all beheld this with unveiled face is thus a striking claim.[61] It is clear from the rest of the discussion, though, that this is nothing like the direct appearance of a deity in a dream or vision. Instead it is mediated through Jesus, who is described as the εἰκὼν τοῦ θεοῦ, "image of God," involves the operation of *pneuma*, and the illumination of the heart, which provides knowledge and affects people's thoughts (τὰ νοήματα [4:4]). Now is not the time to dive into the troubled waters of Pauline Christology, but the tortured language of this passage shows that any appearance of God for Paul must be mediated by Jesus, who is himself never straightforwardly

---

[60] Alan F. Segal, *Paul the Convert: The Apostolate and Apostasy of Saul the Pharisee* (New Haven: Yale University Press, 1990), 60, see further 52–53; M. David Litwa, *We Are Being Transformed: Deification in Paul's Soteriology*, BZNW 187 (Berlin: de Gruyter, 2012), 123–26.

[61] James Buchanan Wallace (*Snatched into Paradise*, 180) cautions that the language of the biblical visions themselves pushes against an overly literal reading of Yahweh's form, claiming only to see "the likeness of the glory of the Lord" (Ez 1:28). See, though, Litwa, *We Are Being Transformed*, 123: "Although the prophet's language is highly qualified, the picture of what he saw is relatively clear . . . this is not an invisible, incorporeal God, but an anthropomorphic deity moving about in a super body . . . it would not be off the mark to call this divine body a 'body of glory.'" Cf. Benjamin D. Sommer, *The Bodies of God and the World of Ancient Israel* (Cambridge: Cambridge University Press, 2009), 68–74; Mark S. Smith, "The Three Bodies of God in the Hebrew Bible," *JBL* 134 (2015): 471–88.

called ὁ θεός.⁶² Paul does not expect God to "present himself in person" (Cicero, *Div.* 1.79) or to "enter into the bodies of his prophets" (Plutarch, *Def. orac.* 414e), instead he gestures towards more anthropological and cosmological explanations with terms such as hearts, thoughts, and *pneuma*.

Intermediary Beings

If the resurrected Jesus mediates God's will in a unique way for Paul, there is a panoply of other divine beings who at least have the potential to transmit knowledge to humans. They do not often come in for focused discussion, but appear on the periphery of a number of passages in Paul's letters.

Daimons

Daimons only appear in Paul's letters in 1 Cor 10:20–21, where he identifies them as the recipients of Gentile sacrifices. In this he echoes a common Jewish polemic against Gentile idolatry – that Gentile gods are only lower divine beings, subordinate to the God of Israel.⁶³ This perspective also puts him in agreement with the Platonic stream of thinking, which saw daimons as responsible for transporting sacrifices from humans to gods and divination from gods to humans (Plato, *Symp.* 202e). If Paul saw daimons as the true recipients of Gentile sacrifice, it is possible he would have also agreed with the second half of this Platonic equation and explained Gentile divination by means of daimons too. This is how many later Christian writers such as Origen and Eusebius would explain pagan divination, although by this time daimons are understood not simply as lower divine beings, but specifically evil beings.⁶⁴

For Paul daimons evidently exist and may have been able to communicate with humans, but such fellowship with them would not have been an option for Paul or his Christ-followers (1 Cor 10:20). For the early Christian writers, "demons" were deliberately deceptive, and so any communication that originates with them is not to be trusted as it is designed to lead the believer into error. This fits Paul's description of the "god of this age" in 2 Cor 4:4 who blinds the thoughts of unbelievers. Like the many so-called gods of 1 Cor 8:5

---

[62] For Jesus as the outward heavenly "form of God," see Markus N. A. Bockmuehl, "'The Form of God' (Phil 2:6): Variations on a Theme of Jewish Mysticism," *JTS* 48 (1997): 1–23.

[63] Paul's language most closely mirrors the song of Moses in Deut 32:17 LXX. See further Emma Wasserman, *Apocalypse as Holy War: Divine Politics and Polemics in the Letters of Paul*, AYBRL (New Haven: Yale University Press, 2018), 155–60.

[64] Origen, *Cels.* 7.3; Eusebius, *Praep. ev.* 4.3.16; cf. Bouché-Leclercq, *Histoire de la divination*, 1:97–98; Richard Stoneman, *The Ancient Oracles: Making the Gods Speak* (New Haven: Yale University Press, 2011), 201, 206, 210.

this "god" likely also represents a daimonic being for Paul that is a hindrance to real divine knowledge.⁶⁵

Daimons may be deceptive, but they may also just be ignorant. In 1 Cor 2:6–8 Paul stresses the utter unknowability of God's eschatological plan by ordinary human means, a plan that was unknown even to τῶν ἀρχόντων τοῦ αἰῶνος τούτου, "the rulers of this age." This phrase has occasioned considerable debate as to whether Paul is referring to human political powers or "supernatural" beings.⁶⁶ The only other use of ἄρχων in the undisputed letters is in Rom 13:3, also in the plural, which refers to the governing authorities to whom one pays taxes.⁶⁷ The related term ἀρχή in Rom 8:38 is paired with "angels" as one of the many elements in creation that cannot separate the believer from God's love. In 1 Cor 15:24 it also features in the triad of πᾶσαν ἀρχὴν καὶ πᾶσαν ἐξουσίαν καὶ δύναμιν, "every principle and every authority and power," whom Christ will defeat before handing the kingdom to God. In these contexts Paul is most likely referring to the principles and forces that govern the present constitution of the cosmos, the foremost of which is death (1 Cor 15:26). While they may be given a divine or semi-divine status, they are principally the changeable and corruptible elements of the present cosmos to which humans are enslaved (cf. Gal 4:8–10).⁶⁸

---

⁶⁵ The reference to "this age" may suggest a specific reference to the deified Augustus as recently argued by Frederick J. Long, "'The God of This Age' (2 Cor 4:4) and Paul's Empire-Resisting Gospel at Corinth," in *The First Urban Churches 2: Roman Corinth*, ed. James R. Harrison and L. L. Welborn, WGRWSup 8 (Atlanta: SBL Press, 2016), 219–69. This would not be at odds with understanding it as a daimonic being, but fits within the many gods and lords "whether in heaven or on earth" who are really daimons (1 Cor 8:5).

⁶⁶ See Martin Dibelius, *Die Geisterwelt im Glauben des Paulus* (Göttingen: Vandenhoeck & Ruprecht, 1909); Wesley A. Carr, "The Rulers of this Age: 1 Cor 2:6–8," NTS 23 (1976): 20–35; Gene Miller, ΑΡΧΟΝΤΩΝ ΤΟΥ ΑΙΩΝΟΣ ΤΟΥΤΟΥ: A New Look at 1 Corinthians 2:6–8," JBL 91 (1972): 522–28; Guy Williams, *The Spirit World in the Letters of Paul the Apostle: A Critical Examination of the Role of Spiritual Beings in the Authentic Pauline Epistles*, FRLANT 231 (Göttingen: Vandenhoeck & Ruprecht, 2009), 232–39. Amidst this debate, many stress the irrelevance of the choice as daimonic powers could be seen to stand behind and be represented by earthly authorities, Oscar Cullman, *Christ and Time: The Primitive Christian Conception of Time and History*, trans. Floyd V. Filson (London: SCM, 1951), 191–201; George B. Caird, *Principalities and Powers: A Study in Pauline Theology* (Oxford: Clarendon, 1956); Martin, *Corinthian Body*, 62.

⁶⁷ Although Wasserman sees even this passage as an example of the "cosmic political order," leaving the exact status of the ἄρχοντες unclear, *Apocalypse as Holy War*, 127. Ephesians 2:2 has a more clearly cosmic use of the word: "the ἄρχοντα of the authority of the air, the *pneuma* which is now at work in the sons of disobedience."

⁶⁸ See van Kooten, *Cosmic Christology*, 100–103. Wasserman correctly identifies a cosmic battle motif with lower rank divinities, but is more intent to establish their low rank than to give the terms any more specific content, Emma Wasserman, "Gentile Gods at the Eschaton: A Reconsideration of Paul's 'Principalities and Powers' in 1 Corinthians 15," JBL 136 (2017): 727–46; Wasserman, *Apocalypse as Holy War*, 122–28. Forbes emphasises the potential overlap

In the case of 1 Cor 2:6–8, I am inclined to the view that Paul is specifically referring to the human authorities who were directly responsible for Jesus's crucifixion (v. 8), and his contrast concerns the difference between human and divine wisdom.[69] This contrast becomes murky, though, where lower divine ranks are concerned, and if Paul does have the wider cosmic perspective in mind at this point, he would appear to express the view that lower ranks of divinity, while intermediate between God and humans in some respects and possessed of a certain wisdom (v. 6), are not successful mediators of God's wisdom, as they do not have privileged access to τὰ βάθη τοῦ θεοῦ, "the depths of God" (1 Cor 2:10).

Angels

Angels are also ambiguous creatures in Paul's letters. In 1 Cor 11:10, immediately after discussing the presence of daimons at Gentile sacrifices, he mentions the presence of angels in the worship of the *ekklēsia*. The specific activities for which they are present are praying and prophesying (11:4–5), which suggests a similar mediatory role to that of daimons in the Platonic scheme, transporting prayers to God and prophecies from God.[70] The name ἄγγελος itself would, of course, suggest that their primary function should be as messengers and intermediaries, and Philo makes this exact connection with the daimons of the philosophical tradition, "for they both convey the biddings of the Father to His children and report the children's need to their Father" (Philo, *Somn.* 1.141 [Colson and Whitaker, LCL]).[71] But, on the two occasions Paul mentions angels explicitly in this role, he downplays their value.

---

with demonological and cosmological language in Paul's context, Christopher Forbes, "Pauline Demonology and/or Cosmology? Principalities, Powers and the Elements of the World in their Hellenistic Context," *JSNT* 85 (2002): 51–73.

[69] I see no evidence elsewhere in Paul that Jesus's crucifixion was directly attributable to cosmic or "daimonic" powers. First Corinthians 11:23 is sometimes cited as evidence that Jesus was handed over by God to "the powers," reading παρεδίδετο as a divine passive. This requires reading into the passage a certain interpretation of 1 Cor 2:8 to fill in the blanks. It could just as easily refer to his arrest and "handing over" to human authorities. First Thessalonians 2:15, which I take to be authentic, attributes Jesus's death to certain Judeans. Cf. Carr, "The Rulers of this Age," 25–27; Dale C. Allison, *Constructing Jesus: Memory, Imagination, and History* (Grand Rapids: Baker Academic, 2010), 396–403.

[70] Peter Lampe, "Die dämonologischen Implikationen von 1 Korinther 8 und 10 vor dem Hintergrund paganer Zeugnisse," in *Die Dämonen: Die Dämonologie der israelitisch-jüdischen und frühchristlichen Literatur im Kontext ihrer Umwelt*, ed. Armin Lange, Hermann Lichtenberger, and K. F. Diethard Römheld (Tübingen: Mohr Siebeck, 2003), 597.

[71] Cf. Tob 12:12 for angels transporting prayers to God. Philo explicitly identifies angels with the daimons of the philosophers in *Gig.* 6, 16.

In Gal 3:19 he attributes the giving of Torah to the mediating role of angels (διαταγεὶς δι' ἀγγέλων ἐν χειρὶ μεσίτου). The μεσίτης, "mediator" in the second half of the clause is almost unanimously understood by scholars to refer to Moses, thus setting up a chain of mediation, first through angels and then through Moses.[72] The multiplicity of mediators is contrasted with the oneness of God, who gave the promise of a single seed directly to Abraham.[73] Paul does not take issue with the concept of mediation in general, but argues in this case that the multiplicity of mediating angels are unable to fulfil the promise of one seed of Abraham, and thus represent an inferior revelation.[74] In Gal 1:8 Paul also entertains the possibility that an angel might disclose a different good news to the one that he was proclaiming himself: "Even if we, or an angel from heaven proclaim a good news different from the good news we proclaimed to you, let him be cursed." This may be pure hyperbole, in which case the effect of the hyperbole is to suggest that angels are normally expected to be reliable communicators of God's will. In this case, however, and in comparison with the message he had received from and about Christ, Paul does not hesitate in saying the angel would be wrong.[75]

Pneumata

When Paul mentions angels in the above passages he mentions them in a simple matter-of-fact manner, more akin to Apuleius – where daimons can be seen and heard by the senses – than Plutarch's more nuanced theories. They can proclaim things (εὐαγγελίζηται [Gal 1:8]) in the same manner as Paul and his associates can. He comes closer to Plutarch's various daimonological perspectives when he speaks of πνεύματα in the plural, as present and active when the Corinthians are prophesying and engaging in ecstatic speech. He says the Corinthians are

---

[72] Gaston objects, maintaining that this verse does not reference Sinai at all, but the 70 angels of the nations who administered the law to Gentiles. This reading has much to commend it, but the clear chronological reference in Gal 3:17 ties this verse inextricably to the giving of Torah at Sinai, Lloyd Gaston, "Angels and Gentiles in Early Judaism and in Paul," *SR* 11 (1982): 65–75. Wasserman accepts the Sinai reference but dispenses with Moses, *Apocalypse as Holy War*, 139. More objectionable still are those readings which see Paul claiming not just an angelic *mediation*, but an angelic *origin* for the law, Rudolf Bultmann, *Theology of the New Testament*, trans. Kendrick Grobel (London: SCM, 1952), 1:174, 268; Martyn, *Galatians*, 367–68.
[73] Francis Watson, *Paul and the Hermeneutics of Faith*, 2nd ed. (London: T&T Clark, 2016), 257–58.
[74] Pace Hans Dieter Betz, *Galatians*, Hermeneia (Philadelphia: Fortress, 1979), 171. This basic point is argued, with considerable variation, by Gaston, "Angels and Gentiles," 74; N.T.Wright, *The Climax of the Covenant: Christ and the Law in Pauline Theology* (London: T&T Clark, 1991), 169–71. Cf. Linda L. Belleville, "The Sinai-Μεσίτης Tradition in Galatians 3:19–20," in *Paul and Scripture*, ed. Stanley E. Porter and Christopher D. Land, Pauline Studies 10 (Leiden: Brill, 2019), 325–34.
[75] Forbes notes that these passages in Paul "tell us more about what angels do not (or cannot) do than what they actually might do," Christopher Forbes, "Paul's Principalities and Powers: Demythologizing Apocalyptic?" *JSNT* 82 (2001): 64.

"enthusiastic about spirits" (ζηλωταί ἐστε πνευμάτων [1 Cor 14:12]), and that they should excel in this (περισσεύητε) in a way that edifies the *ekklēsia*, which in context means through prophecy. Some Corinthians have the gift of being able to distinguish (or perhaps interpret) *pneumata* (1 Cor 12:10), and Paul provides a catch-all criterion for distinguishing whether or not it is God's *pneuma* by whom someone is speaking (12:3). This has led some scholars to posit angels or, more broadly defined, "spiritual beings" as the primary source of prophetic inspiration in these passages.[76] As we have seen, the link between ἄγγελοι and πνεύματα was an easy one, particularly if we take Philo's line that the substance (οὐσία) of angels is pneumatic (πνευματική [QG 1.92]). The main difficulty with this position for Paul has always been how to reconcile it with his repeated insistence on the single *pneuma* which supplies all the gifts of 1 Cor 12:4–11.[77]

Clint Tibbs has attempted to overcome this by reading the articular τὸ πνεῦμα not as "the spirit," but as "the spirit world." Anarthrous uses of the word can then refer to "a spirit," which speaks through human mediums and forms one member of a larger, singular spirit world.[78] This could be a plausible reading if understood against the Stoic notion of an all-pervasive *pneuma*, of which daimons and human souls are detached portions. Adopting this perspective may help understand Paul's various references to "the one *pneuma*" (1 Cor 12:11), which distinguishes and distributes particular gifts, "my *pneuma*," which produces unintelligible speech and could be identified in some way with the soul (1 Cor 14:13), and the many other *pneumas*, which could be identified with angelic or daimonic beings (1 Cor 12:10), but are all derived from the single *pneuma*. A closer examination, however, suggests that the one *pneuma* should be identified not with the "spirit world" of God, but specifically with the *pneuma* of Christ.

A number of scholars have noticed that the role Stoics gave *pneuma* in relation to the cosmos, Paul narrows and specifies in relation to the *ekklēsia*.[79] For the Stoics, the cosmos was a living organism, within which the *pneuma*

---

[76] The most recent and thorough statement of this case is by Tibbs, *Religious Experience*, but see, before him, E. Earle Ellis, *Prophecy and Hermeneutic in Early Christianity: New Testament Essays*, WUNT 18 (Tübingen: Mohr Siebeck, 1978), 24–38; Morton Smith, "Pauline Worship as Seen by Pagans," *HTR* 73 (1980): 244. They also draw for support on 1 Cor 14:32: "the *pneumata* of the prophets are subject to the prophets."

[77] Shantz sees this as sufficient reason for reading 1 Cor 14:32, at least as not referring to a host of inspiring spirits, Colleen Shantz, *Paul in Ecstasy: The Neurobiology of the Apostle's Life and Thought* (Cambridge: Cambridge University Press, 2009), 191.

[78] Tibbs, *Religious Experience*; Clint Tibbs, "Πνεῦμα as 'Spirit World' in Translation in the New Testament," *BT* 62 (2011): 172–84. E. Earle Ellis (*Prophecy and Hermeneutic*, 32) pointed to a similar (non-Pauline) oscillation in 1 John 4:1–3 between τὸ πνεῦμα τοῦ θεοῦ, "the spirit of God," and πᾶν πνεῦμα ... ἐκ τοῦ θεοῦ, "every spirit ... from God," without attempting to explain it.

[79] Michelle V. Lee, *Paul, the Stoics, and the Body of Christ*, SNTSMS 137 (Cambridge, Cambridge University Press, 2006), 131, 198; Horky, "Cosmic Spiritualism," 290–91; Engberg-Pedersen, *Cosmology and Self*, 169–71.

both unites the various bodies of the cosmos together and also differentiates them from each other through different degrees of tension.[80] For Paul, the Corinthians were also a body, constituted by a single *pneuma* at baptism (1 Cor 12:13), which also differentiated (διαιροῦν) different gifts (12:8–10) and roles (12:28–30) within the body.[81] This single *pneuma* is expressly Christ's *pneuma*, which forms the Corinthian believers into Christ's body (12:12, 27; cf. 2 Cor 3:17–18). This is more specific and limited than a generic "spirit world" and is also more limited than an all-pervasive cosmic *pneuma*.

There is more to say about the relationship of Christ's *pneuma* to these other *pneumata*, but for the present discussion Morton Smith's solution is, in my view, the most likely: that the experience of multiple mediating *pneumata* was the norm and reality perceived by Paul and the Corinthians, and Paul's insistence on the one *pneuma* of Christ is a theological and normative projection that he wished to impose on the Corinthian practice.[82] Indeed, Paul is elsewhere suspicious of any other *pneumata* with which the Corinthians may be engaging (2 Cor 11:4). As with Paul's view of angels more generally in his letters, he assumes there are multiple "spirits" who mediate communication between God and humans, both through epiphanies and inspiration, but they cannot always be trusted, and certainly not in comparison with revelations of Christ received through his own *pneuma*. This *pneuma* of Christ shares some features with an angel or daimon. As the *pneuma* of a resurrected Jewish prophet it is a personally identifiable entity. But by indwelling believers and forming them into a structured and unified body it operates more like the cosmic *pneuma* of Stoicism on a restricted scale. It will only become universal for Paul when creation itself is transformed and "God will be all in all" (1 Cor 15:28; cf. Rom 8:19–23).[83]

The (Lack of) Innate Capacity and the *Pneuma* of God

Paul details the role of *pneuma* in providing access to divine knowledge most fully in 1 Cor 2:6–16, and so this passage merits sustained attention.[84] Against

---

[80] Horky, "Cosmic Spiritualism," 276–77; Teun Tieleman, "The Spirit of Stoicism," in *The Holy Spirit, Inspiration, and the Cultures of Antiquity: Multidisciplinary Perspectives*, ed. Jörg Frey and John R. Levison, Ekstasis 5 (Berlin: de Gruyter, 2014), 42–43.

[81] Lee, *Paul*, 124–25; Horky, "Cosmic Spiritualism," 291.

[82] Smith, "Pauline Worship," 245–46.

[83] On Paul's use of the phrase "God will be all in all" in comparison with the Stoics, see van Kooten, *Cosmic Christology*, 106–7.

[84] In the history of scholarship this passage has frequently been taken to represent views and concepts that are in one way or another un-Pauline, and indebted to the language and frame of reference of Paul's opponents. See, particularly, Ulrich Wilckens, *Weisheit und Torheit: Eine exegetisch-religionsgeschichtliche Untersuchung zu 1 Kor. 1 und 2*, BHT 26 (Tübingen: Mohr Siebeck,

those whom he took to be valuing human wisdom and rhetorical performance, Paul stresses the utter unknowability of God's plans by ordinary human means, including the place of crucifixion within them (1 Cor 1:18–24). Paul quotes an oracle from an unknown source to the effect that God's plan cannot be known by the normal sensory perception of the eyes, ears, or even heart.[85] Instead of the mediating role of angels or other intermediary beings, in this passage Paul appeals to the concept of God's *pneuma* as the vehicle through which God has revealed his plans.

Pneuma and the Reception of Divine Wisdom (1 Corinthians 2:10–12)

But God revealed [these things] to us through the *pneuma*. For the *pneuma* searches everything, even the depths of God. For what person knows the things of a person except the *pneuma* of the person; in the same way no one has known the things of God except the *pneuma* of God. Now we have not received the *pneuma* of the cosmos, but the *pneuma* that is from God, in order that we might know the things given to us by God.

ἡμῖν δὲ ἀπεκάλυψεν ὁ θεὸς διὰ τοῦ πνεύματος· τὸ γὰρ πνεῦμα πάντα ἐραυνᾷ, καὶ τὰ βάθη τοῦ θεοῦ. Τίς γὰρ οἶδεν ἀνθρώπων τὰ τοῦ ἀνθρώπου εἰ μὴ τὸ πνεῦμα τοῦ ἀνθρώπου τὸ ἐν αὐτῷ; οὕτως καὶ τὰ τοῦ θεοῦ οὐδεὶς ἔγνωκεν εἰ μὴ τὸ πνεῦμα τοῦ θεοῦ. ἡμεῖς δὲ οὐ τὸ πνεῦμα τοῦ κόσμου ἐλάβομεν ἀλλὰ τὸ πνεῦμα τὸ ἐκ τοῦ θεοῦ, ἵνα εἰδῶμεν τὰ ὑπὸ τοῦ θεοῦ χαρισθέντα ἡμῖν. (1 Cor 2:10–12)

1959), 52–98; Lührmann, *Offenbarungsverständnis*, 113; Robert Jewett, *Paul's Anthropological Terms: A Study of their Use in Conflict Settings*, AGJU 10 (Leiden: Brill, 1971), 186–89. Some have gone so far as to suggest an interpolation here, William O. Walker Jr., *Interpolations in the Pauline Letters*, JSNTSup 213 (Sheffield: Sheffield Academic, 2001), 127–46; Martin Widmann, "1 Kor 2:6–16: ein Einspruch gegen Paulus," *ZNW* 70 (1979): 44–53. I am more persuaded by the readings of Bockmuehl (*Revelation and Mystery*, 158 n. 5) and Judith Kovaks ("The Archons, the Spirit and the Death of Christ: Do We Need the Hypothesis of Gnostic Opponents to Explain 1 Cor 2:6–16?" in *Apocalyptic and the New Testament: Essays in Honor of J. Louis Martyn*, ed. Joel Marcus and Marion L. Soards, JSNTSup 24 [Sheffield: Sheffield Academic, 1989], 217–36), who show the continuity in thought both with the immediate context and Paul's broader discourse in his letters. For the view that 1 Cor 2:6–16 deals specifically with the mechanism of divination and prophetic speech, see Gerhard Dautzenberg, "Botschaft und Bedeutung der urchristlichen Prophetie nach dem ersten Korintherbrief (2:6–16; 12–14)," in *Prophetic Vocation in the New Testament and Today*, ed. J. Panagopoulos, NovTSup 45 (Leiden: Brill, 1977), 142.

[85] On the source of the quotation, see Klaus Berger, "Zur Diskussion über die Herkunft von 1 Kor 2:9," *NTS* 24 (1978): 271–83; now supplemented by Claire Clivaz and Sara Schulthess, "On the Source and Rewriting of 1 Corinthians 2:9 in Christian, Jewish and Islamic Traditions," *NTS* 61 (2015): 183–200.

Paul introduces *pneuma* into the discussion in 1 Cor 2:10 as a mobile, intelligent substance that searches everything, even τὰ βάθη τοῦ θεοῦ, "the depths of God." This description of *pneuma* is reminiscent of descriptions of the soul in Cicero and Plutarch that "sees everything in nature" when unencumbered by the body and even "ranges amid the irrational and imaginative realms of the future" (Plutarch, *Def. orac.* 432c). It is also similar to Diogenes Laertius's statement that "*nous* permeates every part of [the universe]" (*Lives* 7.1 Zeno 139).[86] *Pneuma*, by nature, can bridge the gap between the highest and lowest forms of matter in the universe, connecting the divine and human spheres.[87] In 2:11–12 Paul appears to distinguish different levels or types of *pneuma* which are appropriate to different spheres. There is the *pneuma* of a person, the *pneuma* of the cosmos, and the *pneuma* of God (or the *pneuma* from God).

Philosophers and medical writers also divided *pneuma* into different species depending on its role in different types of bodies. Galen writes:

> There are two kinds of innate *pneuma*, the physical kind (τὸ φυσικόν) and the animate kind (τὸ ψυχικόν). Some people [i.e. the Stoics] also posit a third, the tenor kind (τὸ ἑκτικόν). The *pneuma* which sustains stones is of tenor kind, the one which nurtures animals and plants the physical, and the animate is that which, in animate beings, makes animals (ζῷα) capable of sensation and of moving in every way (*SVF* 2.716).[88]

The "*pneuma* of a person that is in him" appears to correspond to the type of *pneuma* that is in every person and is necessary for life and thought, akin to Galen's animate *pneuma*.[89] Contemporary Jewish sources often related this *pneuma* that is inside every person to the breath that God breathed into Adam in Gen 2:7: καὶ ἐνεφύσησεν εἰς τὸ πρόσωπον αὐτοῦ πνοὴν ζωῆς, καὶ ἐγένετο ὁ ἄνθρωπος εἰς ψυχὴν ζῶσαν, "and [God] breathed into his face a breath of life, and the human became a living soul."[90] For Philo this breath imparted *pneuma* which makes up the substance (οὐσία) of the higher part of the soul, the *nous*, while the lower part of the soul consists of blood, in harmony with Lev 17:11.[91] This higher part of the soul, also called the rational soul (λογικῇ ψυχῇ), represents the highest species of *pneuma*, which separates humans from animals

---

[86] Engberg-Pedersen, *Cosmology and Self,* 228 n. 42.
[87] Robertson, "De-Spiritualizing 'Pneuma'," 368; Stanley K. Stowers, "What is 'Pauline Participation in Christ'?" in *Redefining First-Century Jewish and Christian Identities: Essays in Honor of Ed Parish Sanders,* ed. Fabian E. Udoh (Notre Dame, IN: University of Notre Dame Press, 2008), 357–60.
[88] Translation modified from Long and Sedley, *Hellenistic Philosophers,* 47N.
[89] On *pneuma* as the cause of thought and rationality in a person, see Martin, "Paul's Pneumatological Statements," 113–14, 120–21.
[90] See Wis 15:11; Josephus, *A.J.* 1.34; on Philo, see note 94 below.
[91] *Her.* 55–56; see van Kooten, *Paul's Anthropology,* 279, 282–83.

and enables humans to have a conception (ἔννοια, ἐνόησεν) of God (*Deus* 35; *Leg.* 1.37–38).⁹²

Paul most probably shared the notion that human *pneuma* derives ultimately from God, and perhaps can be equated with the substance of the soul. First Corinthians 15:45 shows that Paul also worked with Gen 2:7 for his anthropology. Here God's breath created Adam as a living soul, which Paul equates with a σῶμα ψυχικόν, "animate body" (15:44). Paul contrasts this with Christ, who became not only a living but a life-giving (ζῳοποιοῦν) *pneuma* with a σῶμα πνευματικόν, "pneumatic body."⁹³ The same contrast between different types of "breath" is present in 1 Cor 2:11, specifically in the area of knowledge. Contrary to Philo, and any of the other authors discussed, Paul's contrast denies any innate capacity of divination to the natural human soul. Paul supposes that knowledge of human things (τὰ τοῦ ἀνθρώπου) is impossible without *pneuma*, but the scope of the knowledge of human (or ψυχικόν) *pneuma* is limited to the human realm. Knowledge of divine things (τὰ τοῦ θεοῦ) instead requires God's *pneuma*.⁹⁴ At this stage Paul is only establishing his point by comparison: just as the *pneuma* within is the cause of rationality and has access to the human mind, so the *pneuma* of God has the same access and relationship to divine things. The correlation of the two is more than just a linguistic coincidence though, as the comparison depends on the shared capacities and characteristics of the same type of substance across both human and divine realms.⁹⁵

In v. 12, the contrast between human and divine *pneuma* changes to a contrast between the *pneuma* of the cosmos and *pneuma* that is from God. It is unclear whether human *pneuma* and cosmic *pneuma* are meant to represent the

---

⁹² Horky, "Cosmic Spiritualism," 281–285.

⁹³ Some commentators assume such passages imply that Paul believed humans to be entirely without *pneuma* until Christ bestowed it on them, Engberg-Pedersen, *Cosmology and Self*, 103–104; Jewett, *Paul's Anthropological Terms*, 185. As 1 Cor 2:11 shows, there is *pneuma* in every person that is distinguishable from the gift of God's *pneuma*. Van Kooten (*Paul's Anthropology*, 295, 303–4) prefers to speak of "the reconstitution of man's own *pneuma*" that occurs with the gift of divine *pneuma*. This runs the risk of downplaying the seemingly novel character Paul gives the *pneuma* granted by Christ – the second Adam is not just a restoration of, but an improvement upon the first Adam – but it does accurately recognise that Paul assumes *pneuma* of some sort to always be present in humans.

⁹⁴ Philo can also at times downplay the initial *pneuma* received in Gen 2:7 referring to it as πνοή in line with the LXX translation, which he says is lighter and less substantial than *pneuma* (*Leg.* 1.42). As van Kooten notes, this generates rather than solves problems for Philo as it is inconsistent with his usage elsewhere, *Paul's Anthropology*, 281.

⁹⁵ *Pace* Anthony C. Thiselton, *The First Epistle to the Corinthians*, NIGTC (Grand Rapids: Eerdmans, 2000), 257–59; Gordon D. Fee, *The First Epistle to the Corinthians*, rev. ed., NICNT (Grand Rapids: Eerdmans, 2014), 119, who both deny that Paul is making any sort of anthropological statement or correlation, and the *pneuma* of a person is simply taken to mean a person's inner life.

same thing, perhaps understood as *pneuma* inside and outside of human bodies. It is clear from the logic of his argument, though, that they are both limited in their knowledge to their respective realms. Paul, then, does posit a break in the hierarchy of substances between God and cosmos, making it clear that it is only God's *pneuma* that can in fact extend to τὰ βάθη τοῦ θεοῦ, "the depths of God." While Lamprias was happy to identify the earth itself which gave forth *pneuma* as divine, and Quintus described the gods diffusing their *vis* throughout the earth, Paul maintains a separation between God and cosmos such that divine knowledge can only come directly from God himself. It is mediated through his own *pneuma*, which is separate from the vapours and exhalations of the earth.[96] Paul is possibly making a specific polemical point here against the standard explanations for Delphic inspiration and Stoic notions of divination.[97]

This *pneuma* from God that "we have received" does not refer to the *pneuma* that all humans have received, but to a special holy *pneuma* given by God (1 Thess 4:8; Gal 3:5) and received by Paul's assemblies (Rom 8:15; Gal 3:2; 2 Cor 11:4) so that Paul can say it lives in believers (Rom 8:9, 11; 1 Cor 3:16) and they can call it their possession (1 Cor 7:40). As *pneuma* that comes somehow from outside the cosmos it represents something new. It is the *pneuma* that raised Christ from the dead, the first fruits of the general resurrection, which will also give immortal life to those it currently inhabits (Rom 8:11; cf. 1 Cor 15:20–22, 45).[98] At the same time, it still behaves in the ways one would expect of *pneuma*. While there are significant differences in cosmology between Paul and his philosophical contemporaries, there is a basic similarity in physics. As noted earlier, the *pneuma* gives structure and unity to the "new

---

[96] Most definitions of the cosmos included the gods within it, or identified the substance of God with the cosmos. See Edelstein and Kidd, *Posidonius*, fr. 14, 20, and the definitions of ps.-Aristotle and Chrysippus discussed by Monte Ransome Johnson, "Aristotle on Kosmos and Kosmoi," in Horky, *Cosmos in the Ancient World*, 76–78.

[97] Matthew Thiessen (*Paul and the Gentile Problem* [Oxford: Oxford University Press, 2016], 114) argues that Stoic categories would be the general default for understanding *pneuma* in Paul's context, so had Paul taken issue with any element of this understanding "he presumably would have gone out of his way to correct any such misunderstandings." In general I agree, but this would appear to be one such point at which Paul does go out of his way to impose a distinction that would be foreign to Stoic thought. Cf. John M. G. Barclay, "Stoic Physics and the Christ-Event: A Review of Troels Engberg-Pedersen, *Cosmology and Self in the Apostle Paul: The Material Spirit* (Oxford: Oxford University Press, 2010)," *JSNT* 33 (2011): 411–12; Edward Adams, *Constructing the World: A Study in Paul's Cosmological Language*, SNTW (Edinburgh: T&T Clark, 2000), 117. This does not mean that Paul must therefore reject everything about a Stoic view of *pneuma* and how it operates but it does highlight one important point of departure.

[98] Barclay, "Stoic Physics," 411; Joel White, "Paul's Cosmology: The Witness of Romans, 1 and 2 Corinthians, and Galatians," in *Cosmology and New Testament Theology*, ed. Jonathan T. Pennington and Sean M. Mcdonough, LNTS 355 (London: T&T Clark, 2008), 103–104.

creation" which it constitutes (1 Cor 12:4–28), and transmits knowledge and wisdom between God and humans.

For Plutarch, the soul receives *pneuma* into the body, from which it forms a κρᾶσις with the soul and enables the receipt of divine knowledge (*Def. orac.* 432e). For Paul, *pneuma* is most often received into the heart (Gal 4:6; 2 Cor 1:22).[99] From there it is reasonable to suppose a form of κρᾶσις taking place between God's *pneuma* and the *pneuma* already inside a person. Paul does not explicitly state so much in this passage, but Matthew Thiessen has recently argued that ancient discussions of mixtures and κρᾶσις provide the best lens for understanding the reception of *pneuma* in Paul's thought more generally. In κρᾶσις, "complete interpenetration of all the components takes place, and any volume of the mixture, down to the smallest parts, is jointly occupied by all the components in the same proportion, each preserving its own properties under any circumstances."[100] In this blending, the two parts are fully mixed, while still retaining their individual distinctiveness, a view which goes a long way towards explaining the relationship between human and divine *pneuma* in certain Pauline statements.

The total interpenetration of substances means that believers are ἐν πνεύματι, precisely because God's *pneuma* is also ἐν ὑμῖν.[101] Visible manifestations (φανέρωσις) of *pneuma* such as prophecy and the speaking and interpretation of different languages are both given by the one *pneuma* (1 Cor 12:4–11) and operated through the *pneumata* of the individuals in the assembly, and it is not always easy to distinguish the two. Paul says it is his *pneuma* that prays when he prays in a language (1 Cor 14:14), and prophets need to be able to control their own *pneuma* when they prophesy so as to keep order in the assembly (1 Cor 14:32). In Rom 8:16 the *pneuma* of the believers and the *pneuma* that they have received are both joined and distinguished as they bear witness together (συμμαρτυρεῖ) that they are children of God by producing the ecstatic cry *abba*.[102] Human *pneuma* on its own is not able to do any of these things, but when joined and interpenetrated with God's *pneuma* it has the power to know and speak divine things. John Chrysostom,

---

[99] Cf. Rom 5:5 in which God's love is poured into the heart διὰ πνεύματος ἁγίου, "by holy *pneuma*." Troy Martin notes that there was disagreement between ancient medical writers over whether *pneuma* was dispersed to the body from the brain or the heart, "Paul's Pneumatological Statements," 108–11; cf. Hankinson, "Stoicism and Medicine," 296–98.

[100] Samuel Sambursky, *Physics of the Stoics* (London: Routledge & Kegan Paul, 1959), 13, quoted in Thiessen, *Gentile Problem*, 112. On mixtures in Stoic and Aristotelian perspectives, see further Long and Sedley, *Hellenistic Philosophers*, 1.290–94.

[101] Rom 8:9: Ὑμεῖς δὲ οὐκ ἐστὲ ἐν σαρκὶ ἀλλ' ἐν πνεύματι, εἴπερ πνεῦμα θεοῦ οἰκεῖ ἐν ὑμῖν.

[102] For those who see *pneuma* as referring only to God's *pneuma* in Paul, these verses cause intractable theological problems, Robert Jewett, "The Question of the 'Apportioned Spirit' in Paul's Letters: Romans as a Case Study," in Stanton, Longenecker, and Barton, *The Holy Spirit and Christian Origins*, 199–200; Samuel Vollenweider, "Der Geist Gottes als Selbst der Glaubenden," *ZThK* 93 (1996): 176–79.

in his homily on this passage of 1 Corinthians, explained Paul's words with exactly the same analogy as Lamprias used in Plutarch to explain the need the soul has of *pneuma* to see divine things: "For eyes are beautiful and useful, but should they choose to see without light, their beauty profits them nothing. . . . So if you mark it, any soul also, if it choose to see without the Spirit, becomes even an impediment unto itself" (*Hom. 1 Cor* 7.9 [*NPNF* 12:38]).[103]

Pneuma and the Interpretation of Divination (1 Corinthians 2:13–16)

Paul transitions in v. 13 from how divine knowledge is initially received to how it is proclaimed and interpreted.[104]

> Things which we also speak, not in words taught by human wisdom, but taught by *pneuma*, interpreting pneumatic things to pneumatic people. Now, the [merely] animate person does not accept the things of God's *pneuma*, for it is folly to him and he is not able to know, because it is discerned pneumatically. But the pneumatic discerns all things, but he is discerned by no one. "For who has known the mind of the Lord so as to instruct him?" But we have the mind of Christ.
>
> ἃ καὶ λαλοῦμεν οὐκ ἐν διδακτοῖς ἀνθρωπίνης σοφίας λόγοις ἀλλ' ἐν διδακτοῖς πνεύματος, πνευματικοῖς πνευματικὰ συγκρίνοντες. ψυχικὸς δὲ ἄνθρωπος οὐ δέχεται τὰ τοῦ πνεύματος τοῦ θεοῦ· μωρία γὰρ αὐτῷ ἐστιν καὶ οὐ δύναται γνῶναι, ὅτι πνευματικῶς ἀνακρίνεται. ὁ δὲ πνευματικὸς ἀνακρίνει [τὰ] πάντα, αὐτὸς δὲ ὑπ' οὐδενὸς ἀνακρίνεται. τίς γὰρ ἔγνω νοῦν κυρίου, ὃς συμβιβάσει αὐτόν; ἡμεῖς δὲ νοῦν Χριστοῦ ἔχομεν. (1 Cor 2:13–16)

The knowledge that was received and taught by divine *pneuma* is the same message that Paul and the other apostles then spoke to the Corinthians. Here it emerges that divine *pneuma* is required not only for the initial reception of knowledge in the "divinatory moment," but also for its subsequent interpretation. The statement πνευματικοῖς πνευματικὰ συγκρίνοντες is terse, and leaves open a number of grammatical and lexicographical possibilities for translation.[105]

---

[103] Wicker also notices Paul's similarity with Plutarch in very general terms, in which "cooperation is required between the spirit of God and the person or person's spirit," Kathleen O'Brien Wicker, "De defectu oraculorum (Moralia 409E–438E)," in *Plutarch's Theological Writings and Early Christian Literature*, ed. Hans Dieter Betz, SCHNT (Leiden: Brill, 1975), 134.

[104] Hans Conzelmann, *1 Corinthians: A Commentary on the First Epistle to the Corinthians*, trans. James W. Leitch, Hermeneia (Philadelphia: Fortress, 1975), 67.

[105] See the overviews in Archibald Robertson and Alfred Plummer, *A Critical and Exegetical Commentary on the First Epistle of St Paul to the Corinthians*, 2nd ed., ICC (Edinburgh: T&T Clark, 1914), 46–48; Thiselton, *First Corinthians*, 264–65. Paul's only other extant use of the

The verb συγκρίνειν and the corresponding nouns σύγκριμα/σύγκρισις are used in the Greek Bible predominantly to speak of the interpretation of dreams (Gen 40:8, 16, 22; 41:12–13; Judges 7:15; θ' Dan 7:16) and omens, such as the writing on the wall in Daniel 5.[106] This meaning fits most naturally into Paul's current context where he speaks about the interpretation of πνευματικά, that is, the things God has pneumatically revealed. He interprets these things to pneumatic people.[107] Paul's previous categories of human and divine *pneuma* have now been exchanged for the adjectives ψυχικός and πνευματικός to describe different types of people. Just as Plutarch could describe the soul as that part of the mind submerged in the body (*Gen. Socr.* 591e), so for Paul the "soulish" (ψυχικός) person is the person who only possesses natural human *pneuma*, while the person whose *pneuma* has blended with and been transformed by divine *pneuma* is properly called πνευματικός.[108] That pneumatic things are folly (μωρία) to the merely animate person mirrors 1 Cor 1:23 in which μωρία was the general Gentile estimation of the message of a crucified Messiah. The ψυχικός person cannot perceive the correct interpretation of such a message because it is discerned pneumatically (πνευματικῶς ἀνακρίνεται).

This puts Paul at odds with the Platonic stream of thinking on divination, in which divination itself is an irrational activity, but the process of interpretation (κρίνειν, κριτὰς ἐπικαθιστάναι, ὑποκριταί) must be handled by some other right-minded person through a process of logical reasoning (λογισμῷ διελέσθαι [Plato, *Tim.* 71e]). This distinction between inspiration and interpretation is also responsible for the divide between natural and technical divination. The interpretation of signs and omens is a purely rational, deductive process, which theoretically anyone could engage in, in contrast to the rarer instances of inspiration connected to sacred places (such as Delphi) and special people (such as Socrates). Stoic thinking, as we have seen, differed in this regard, as

---

verb is in 2 Cor 10:12: "We do not dare to classify or compare (συγκρῖναι) ourselves with some of those who commend themselves. But when they measure themselves by one another, and compare (συγκρίνοντες) themselves with one another, they do not show good sense."

[106] The writing on the wall is called a σημεῖον in OG Daniel 5:9. The expression τὸ σύγκριμα τῆς γραφῆς, "the interpretation of the writing," appears repeatedly in v. 7 of the OG to refer to the interpretation that the king seeks. The Theodotion text similarly says the Babylonian diviners were unable τὴν σύγκρισιν γνωρίσαι, "to make the interpretation known" [5:8].

[107] Taking πνευματικοῖς as masculine. The neuter reading ("by pneumatic things") could admit of a number of possible interpretations, the most feasible being "by pneumatic means/faculties," see Robertson and Plummer, *First Corinthians*, 47. In this case, though, one might more readily expect the adverb πνευματικῶς, which is supplied by some MSS (B, 33).

[108] Cf. 1 Cor 15:44–49 in which ψυχικός and πνευματικός describe different kinds of body, pre- and post-resurrection. Isaacs concluded that "in his anthropology Paul did not make a rigid distinction between πνεῦμα and ψυχή," so that natural human *pneuma* and *psyche* could be viewed as the same, Isaacs, *Concept of Spirit*, 73.

it attempted to explain both natural and technical divination by the same means of *sympatheia*. Paul does not hold to a view of the cosmos that allows for a full-blown notion of *sympatheia*,[109] but his thought does come closer to Stoic reasoning than Platonic here as it combines all reception of divination, both interpretative and direct, into the single operation of *pneuma*. Like the hypothetical Stoic wise man whose soul would be able to "discern the links that join each cause with every other cause" (Cicero, *Div.* 1.127), the pneumatic person can examine and discern everything (πάντα) while remaining inscrutable to everyone else (1 Cor 2:15). The variety of gifts that *pneuma* can bestow include special gifts of interpretation and discernment, such as the διακρίσεις πνευμάτων, "discernment of *pneumata*," and the ἑρμηνεία γλωσσῶν, "interpretation of languages."

Divination and Flesh (1 Corinthians 3:1–4)

Such "elevated language" about the abilities of πνευματικοί does make one wonder whether it is all too good to be true. Did Paul really think he and his fellow Christ-followers had unrestricted access to Christ's own mind and a perfect understanding of all of God's plans?[110] Even the parallel example of the Stoic wise man, if not entirely hypothetical, is assumed to be an extremely rare occurrence; certainly not an ability common to all Stoics.[111] Elsewhere, Paul is more circumspect about the scope of divinatory knowledge, but in this context he presents the flesh as a mitigating factor in receiving and understanding divine knowledge.[112]

For Plato, it was predominantly rationality that needed to be removed, so that the appetitive part of the soul (ἐπιθυμητικὸν τῆς ψυχῆς), when peaceful, could receive divinatory images. This is expanded in the later works of Cicero and Plutarch so that the natural impulses of the soul are impeded by the general influence of the body and the bodily senses (Cicero, *Div.* 1.70, 129). In Plutarch's discussion of Socrates, it is the extent to which the soul mingles with flesh and passions (σαρκὶ μιχθῇ καὶ πάθεσιν) that hinders its appreciation of divine truth. Socrates could listen to his prompting daimon because he was

---

[109] Cf. Barclay, "Stoic Physics," 411–12.

[110] T. J. Lang notices the same, and suggests the language should be tempered by the content of the message that is revealed, which is "that of an executed messiah," T. J. Lang, *Mystery and the Making of a Christian Historical Consciousness: From Paul to the Second Century*, BZNW 219 (Berlin: de Gruyter, 2015), 64.

[111] See René Brouwer, *The Stoic Sage: The Early Stoics on Wisdom, Sagehood and Socrates*, Cambridge Classical Studies (Cambridge: Cambridge University Press, 2014), 92–135.

[112] Cf. 1 Cor 13, which is discussed in Chapter 3, and Rom 11:34, where Paul quotes the same words from Isa 40:13 with the opposite implication – no one has known the mind of the Lord.

pure and free from passion (καθαρὸς ὢν καὶ ἀπαθής), only mingling with the body when necessary (*Gen. Socr.* 588e).

Paul exhibits something similar when, in 1 Cor 3:1, he tells the Corinthians that they were not able to receive or understand the solid food (βρῶμα) of divine instruction from him because they were still σαρκικοί, "fleshy."[113] The evidence of this is their jealousy and strife (ζῆλος καὶ ἔρις) and the fact that they are still dividing into factions. Paul does not speak as if the Corinthians lack God's *pneuma* altogether, he assumes they do possess it (1 Cor 3:16; 12:13), and so the adjectives σάρκινος/σαρκικός do not describe people lacking in *pneuma*.[114] Rather the dominance of fleshly concerns hampers their ability to use the innate powers of knowledge and understanding this *pneuma* gives.[115]

Focusing on the food imagery of this passage, John Penniman identifies the milk that Paul said he initially had given to the Corinthians (in contrast to solid food) with the *pneuma* that was conveyed in his teaching; thus "Paul sees his pupils ... as moldable mounds of flesh (*sarkikoi*) needing a proper regimen for the ongoing formation of body and mind. That regimen begins with his milk and the divine *pneuma* contained within it."[116] In this sense, Paul is seeing the pneumatic milk that he is feeding the Corinthians as enabling their own *pneumata* to break free of the fleshly bonds that are preventing them from receiving solid food.

Conclusion

From this contextualisation of Paul within philosophical discussions of divination we may first attempt a summary of Paul's own position. For Paul, the primary means of attaining knowledge from God is through the agency of the

---

[113] Note that in Paul's case, he says his own excess of revelations (τῇ ὑπερβολῇ τῶν ἀποκαλύψεων) was tempered by a fleshy impediment given by God (2 Cor 12:7).

[114] John David Penniman, *Raised on Christian Milk: Food and the Formation of the Soul in Early Christianity*, Synkrisis (New Haven: Yale University Press, 2017), 72 n. 68; Lang, *Mystery*, 65 n. 141.

[115] It is often argued that Paul's *sarx/pneuma* dichotomies represent an ethical duality as opposed to an anthropological duality (Isaacs, *Concept of Spirit*, 76–78). I am not sure such a strong contrast need exist, as the use of anthropological terms points to an anthropological basis for the ethical statements. There is also a strong sense in Paul that *pneuma* is able to transform believers ethically so that through it they can overcome the desires of the flesh. See Engberg-Pedersen, *Cosmology and Self*, 172–205; from a different perspective, Volker Rabens, *The Holy Spirit and Ethics in Paul: Transformation and Empowering for Religious-Ethical Life*, 2nd rev. ed. (Minneapolis: Fortress, 2014); Nélida Naveros Córdova, *To Live in the Spirit: Paul and the Spirit of God* (Minneapolis: Fortress, 2018).

[116] Penniman, *Raised on Christian Milk*, 73.

resurrected Jesus, in his role as a life-giving *pneuma*. Other "spirits," angels, and daimons exist who are capable of communicating information. Sometimes these may be reliable, sometimes they may be ignorant, and sometimes they may be deliberately deceptive, but none are as reliable or important as the *pneuma* of Christ. This Jesus had appeared to him, but also now lives in him and other Christ-followers who have been baptised into the same *pneuma* by the physical intermingling of Christ's *pneuma* with their own *pneuma*. If the clouding influence of the flesh can be overcome, the reconstituted soul and mind of a believer is capable of access to Christ's own mind, which can reach to the deepest places of God and the cosmos to provide insight and the ability to interpret unknown aspects of God's plans and purposes.

A number of individual points of connection with the philosophical discussions of divination have been brought out in the course of the analysis, but there are also a few broader points to mention at this stage. First, Paul does make sense in his ancient context, and presents a reasonably coherent and thought-out system for how humans can receive and make sense of divinatory information. He does not, of course, map perfectly onto a particular Stoic or middle-Platonic perspective on divination (Stoic or middle-Platonic authors themselves rarely adhere perfectly to the strictures of their own system), but he makes use of the same set of concepts of souls, minds, daimons, and *pneuma* to articulate his position. Paul is not, like most of the comparative texts studied in this chapter, setting out to solve a philosophical problem or presenting a full philosophical explanation and defence of his solution. His overall purpose in his letters remains focused on achieving certain outcomes in specific situations he deems problematic; in the case of 1 Cor 2 he is responding to the existence of factions gathering around certain apostles. In addressing this issue, however, he partially spells out, and more often hints at, underlying suppositions and frameworks in which his statements make sense. Often Pauline scholars have tended towards denying any particular coherence to Paul's thought because of eschatological urgency or rhetorical and situational expediency, but my reading above demonstrates that when Paul is in "philosophical mode" he can be quite specific and coherent with the concepts he engages.[117]

Second, Greek philosophical thinking about divination, from Plato to the Stoics, has recently been characterised as "psychophysiological systems embedded in an organism." That is, they are embedded in the natural faculties of "the human animal and the living animal that is the cosmos."[118] Paul takes an interesting position alongside this perspective. On the one hand, the insistence on a *pneuma* that is not of the cosmos posits a sharp break between natural

---

[117] See Engberg-Pedersen, "Paul the Philosopher"; Stowers, "Paul's Physics."
[118] Struck, *Divination and Human Nature*, 215.

psychophysiological systems and knowledge from the divine realm, more in line with later Neoplatonic thought. On the other hand, this *pneuma* appears not simply as an alien intrusion into the world of matter, but as the power of resurrection that will, very soon for Paul, renew and transform the nature of all creation (Rom 8:19–23). It is a new type of pneumatic cosmogony which, in a sense, represents the physics of "new creation."[119] All of this takes him very far from some of the basic presuppositions of Greek philosophy, but he nevertheless uses philosophical concepts to describe it, and thus imagines a different sort of psychophysiological system through which knowledge is conveyed.[120] Within this context, the scope of divinatory knowledge, or perhaps all knowledge in general, is expansive and includes the wisdom of God and the mind of Christ himself. These give insights into God's broad eschatological plan of salvation, which is only understandable through the help of *pneuma*.

With this broad perspective in place, it remains in the following chapters to examine the various ways that this knowledge is received and interpreted in practice: through visions, inspired speech, the interpretation of written oracles, and the interpretation of signs and omens.

---

[119] See Horky, "Cosmic Spiritualism," 292–94.
[120] For the basic incompatibility with Greek philosophy, see Barclay, "Stoic Physics," 411 n. 9.

CHAPTER 2

Visions

In the last chapter, I discussed the three means of divine communication enumerated by Posidonius: the personal appearance of a god, the mediation of daimons, and the innate capacity of the soul. Of these, the most direct way that a god can communicate is by appearing in person to a human being, either in a dream or a waking vision. Paul claims to have received knowledge through such means on at least two specific occasions (Gal 1:11–12; 2 Cor 12:1–10), and displays a certain ambivalence about how these fit into the mechanics he works out elsewhere (2 Cor 12:2–3).

Scholarship is divided over how to view the place of visionary experiences in Paul's life. Some fully embrace the image of Paul as mystic and visionary.[1] A more common approach is to sharply distinguish Paul's initial encounter with the risen Christ from any subsequent visionary experiences – the former being a pivotal moment of objective revelation and the latter being private and subjective spiritual experiences to which he attaches little importance.[2] Among those who compare Paul's claims to visionary experience with his broader Graeco-Roman environment, the tendency is to view Paul's visions not as a method of divination – a means through which to acquire divine knowledge – but as a means through which to assert divine authority. Such experiences are important for his rhetoric, but less so for his thought and practice.[3]

---

[1] Benz, *Paulus als Visionär*; Segal, *Paul the Convert*; John Ashton, *The Religion of Paul the Apostle* (New Haven: Yale University Press, 2000); Shantz, *Paul in Ecstasy*; Christopher Rowland, "Paul as an Apocalyptist," in *The Jewish Apocalyptic Tradition and the Shaping of New Testament Thought*, ed. Benjamin E. Reynolds and Loren T. Stuckenbruck (Minneapolis: Fortress, 2017), 131–53.

[2] William Baird, "Visions, Revelations, and Ministry: Reflections on 2 Cor 12:1–5 and Gal 1:11–17," *JBL* 104 (1985): 651–62; James D. G. Dunn, *Jesus and the Spirit: A Study of the Religious and Charismatic Experience of Jesus and the First Christians as Reflected in the New Testament* (Grand Rapids: Eerdmans, 1975), 104–114; Bockmuehl, *Revelation and Mystery*, 137, 144–45.

[3] Eyl, *Signs, Wonders, and Gifts*; Sarah E. Rollens, "The God Came to Me in a Dream: Epiphanies in Voluntary Associations as a Context for Paul's Vision of Christ," *HTR* 111 (2018): 41–65;

In this chapter, I will assess the nature and functions of Paul's visionary experiences in comparison with the divinatory functions of dreams and visions in the Graeco-Roman world. Such visions did indeed play a pivotal role in establishing Paul's authority as an apostle, but this is inextricably intertwined with their role as conveyors of divine knowledge, and they thus form an important part of Paul's divinatory repertoire.

Dreams, Visions, and Experience: Preliminary Issues

The mode of divination in which "the gods in person converse with men" (Cicero, *Div.* 1.64) at first sight appears the most straightforward, but it presents particular challenges to historical analysis and classification. Before proceeding, two particular questions must be dealt with. First is how to distinguish and classify dreams, epiphanies, and waking visions in the context of divination. Second is how to treat the relation of dream and vision reports to actual experience.

Dreams

Dreams are a ubiquitous source of divine communication in ancient literature. Everyone dreams, and thus everyone has the potential to receive a divinely sent dream in their own bedroom.[4] The divinatory potential of dreams was a popular topic for ancient authors, with Aristotle, Demetrius of Phalerum, Antiphon, Chrysippus, Galen, Artemidorus, Philo, and Tertullian being only some of the figures known to have written books on dreams which acknowledge and analyse their role in divination.[5] Divinatory dreams take two main forms, although as with all classifications there are plentiful examples that do not neatly fit into either category.[6] First is the epiphany or message dream, in which a divine (or otherwise notable) figure appears and relays a message or instruction to the recipient.[7] To be counted as notable, the figure would

---

James C. Hanges, *Paul, Founder of Churches: A Study in Light of the Evidence for the Role of "Founder-Figures" in the Hellenistic-Roman Period*, WUNT 292 (Tübingen: Mohr Siebeck, 2012).

[4] Gil H. Renberg, *Where Dreams May Come: Incubation Sanctuaries in the Greco-Roman World*, RGRW 184 (Leiden: Brill, 2017), 1:4; Stoneman, *Ancient Oracles*, 104.

[5] Few of these survive, Stoneman, *Ancient Oracles*, 106–9. Aristotle is often thought to represent a purely rationalist approach to dreams, but see the more subtle analysis by Struck, *Divination and Human Nature*, 91–170.

[6] This influential classification was given by A. Leo Oppenheim, "The Interpretation of Dreams in the Ancient Near East, with a Translation of an Assyrian Dream-Book," TAPS 46 (1956): 185, 190. On the problems with scholarly categorisation as well as the general usefulness of Oppenheim's division, see Juliette Harrisson, *Dreams and Dreaming in the Roman Empire: Cultural Memory and Imagination* (London: Bloomsbury, 2013), 57–68.

[7] See, especially, William V. Harris, *Dreams and Experience in Classical Antiquity* (Cambridge, MA: Harvard University Press, 2009), 23–90.

normally have to be of a sort that one would not have encountered in ordinary life. Often gods or goddesses themselves would deliver a message, as would other divine beings such as nymphs or daimons. The dead were also frequently encountered in dreams. At other times, the dream may simply be of a figure separated by distance, such as Paul's night-vision (ὅραμα διὰ νυκτός) of the Macedonian man in Acts 16:9–10.[8] Such a figure is not a god or divine being himself, but God is understood to have sent the vision, so Paul can conclude that it was God who was calling Paul and his companions through the vision.[9]

From this category of "divinely sent vision," one can slide easily into the second category, that of symbolic dreams. Here, rather than an explicit message from a figure in the vision, the dreamer or visionary experiences an image or series of events that convey a message symbolically. Pharaoh's dream of seven fat cows representing seven years of plenty in Gen 41 is an example of a symbolic dream. Another example is a dream recorded by Chrysippus, in which a man saw an egg suspended above his bed. This was interpreted to mean there was treasure buried under his bed, the yolk representing gold, the white representing silver (Cicero, *Div.* 2.134).[10] These dreams differ from epiphany dreams in how the divinely sent information is received. Symbolic visions are non-discursive, and there is a more obvious need for interpretation by the seer. Artemidorus's second-century CE book *The Interpretation of Dreams* is primarily devoted to decoding symbolic dreams.

Visions

Both of these dream forms could also occur in waking visions, and the Greek and Latin terminology often does not care to specify or distinguish between the two.[11] While a number of terms specifically refer to dreams (ἐνύπνιον, ὄναρ, ὄνειρος/ὄνειρον, *somnium, insomnium*), the terms for vision (ὅραμα, ὄψις, ὀπτασία, *visus/visum*) focus on the visual apprehension of something that could be seen either in a dream or while awake, and are thus ambiguous. Terms that refer to

---

[8] Jipp calls this episode an "epiphany," further demonstrating the elasticity of the term, Joshua Jipp, *Divine Visitations and Hospitality to Strangers in Luke-Acts: An Interpretation of the Malta Episode in Acts 28:1–10*, NovTSup 153 (Leiden: Brill, 2013), 241.

[9] Keener (*Acts*, 3:2345) cites a number of parallel texts in which individual figures in visions might be seen as representing the spirit of a location or people-group.

[10] Numerous examples of both types of dream are given by Cicero, *Div.* 1.39–59.

[11] It is a scholarly commonplace to note the range and ambiguity of the terminology, John S. Hanson, "Dreams and Visions in the Graeco-Roman World and Early Christianity," *ANRW* 23.1:1408–9; Gil H. Renberg, "'Commanded by the Gods': An Epigraphical Study of Dreams and Visions in Greek and Roman Religious Life" (PhD diss., Duke University, 2003), 18–19; Harrisson, *Dreams and Dreaming*, 34–35; Henk S.Versnel, "What Did Ancient Man See When He Saw a God? Some Reflections on Greco-Roman Epiphany," in *Effigies Dei: Essays on the History of Religions*, ed. Dirk van der Plas, SHR 51 (Leiden: Brill, 1987), 48.

the appearance of a god or other figure (ἐπιφάνεια, φάσμα) could also occur in either sleeping or waking contexts. These can also, in a much broader sense, refer to manifestations of a god's power in miracles, or of his intentions in omens and portents.[12] Some authors use the terms for dreams and visions interchangeably, or side-by-side in the same context (Arrian, *Peripl. M. Eux.*, 23; Philo, *Joseph*, 22.125–6; Joel 2:28; cf. Acts 2:17), and on other occasions recipients of visions seem unaware whether they are awake or asleep (Plutarch, *Gen. Socr.* 590b; Aelius Aristides, *Or.* 48.32; 51.31).[13] At other times, however, authors can be clear and purposeful about the bodily state of the recipient, usually with the effect of heightening the reality and reliability of a waking vision compared with a dream (Polybius 10.5; Pausanias 10.38.13; Statius, *Thebaid*, 10.205–206; Maximus of Tyre 9.7; Aelius Aristides, *Or.* 47.3).[14] The magical papyri record a number of spells and initiations that a person could undergo as a prelude to a visionary encounter with a god for the purposes of receiving divinatory information.[15]

The distinction between dreams and waking visions appears to have been one of degree rather than kind. By and large, the visions took the same form, and the source was judged to be equally divine in both instances. The difference lies purely in the bodily state of the recipient when receiving the vision, with waking visions seen as rarer, and concurrently more reliable.[16] As Juliette Harrisson notes, "Ancient writers ... were willing and able to draw the distinction when they needed to, but were unconcerned with such a distinction if they felt it to be unimportant."[17] As we saw in Chapter 1, sleep was a comparable state to inspiration, as in both states the soul is less hindered by the body and more capable of receiving divine knowledge.

Vision Reports and Experience

The analysis of the language and narrative patterns used to report visions raises an important question about the relation of vision reports to actual experience. Other forms of divination such as ecstatic speech and the interpretation of texts and omens are more or less observable practices. With dreams and visions,

---

[12] The classic study of F. Pfister is still foundational for this topic ("Epiphanie," PWSup 4:277–323), but see now Georgia Petridou, *Divine Epiphany in Greek Literature and Culture* (Oxford: Oxford University Press, 2015).

[13] On the difficulty of knowing whether one is awake or dreaming in general, see Plato, *Theaet.* 158b–c; Aristotle, *Insomn.* 462a.

[14] Harrisson, *Dreams and Dreaming*, 34.

[15] Iles Johnston, *Ancient Greek Divination*, 155–58.

[16] Frances Flannery, "Dreams and Visions in Early Jewish and Early Christian Apocalypses and Apocalypticism," in *The Oxford Handbook of Apocalyptic Literature*, ed. John J. Collins (Oxford: Oxford University Press, 2014), 106.

[17] Harrisson, *Dreams and Dreaming*, 35.

however, one is in the realm of experience, for which the only evidence is the testimony of those involved. As has often been pointed out, this testimony provides no access to a dream or vision itself, but only to the ways they have been interpreted and reported.[18] How much information, then, can be gained from Paul's letters about the nature and content of his visions? Can one presume that any sort of visionary experience lies behind the reports at all, or are they merely performances and constructions to serve various ends? In this case there would be no divination to speak of, as the texts speak only of the way Paul legitimated his actions, rather than how he received and interpreted what he perceived as information from the divine realm.[19]

This is not simply an enlightened modern position. Ancient authors, too, wondered whether claims to divine visions and revelations were not merely invented in order to legitimate new innovations. Plutarch mentions rulers such as Zaleucus, Minos, Zoroaster, Numa, and Lycurgus, who claimed divine visitations and advice as the source of the wisdom with which they governed their people (*Numa* 4.8). Dionysius of Halicarnassus indicates that, in the case of Numa, his contemporaries were equally unconvinced by his claims to divine visitations so that he had to convince them through various contrivances. Dionysius does not wish to wade into the debate himself, but notes that many saw Numa's claims, along with the other examples also mentioned by Plutarch, as fabrications for the sake of social and political power (Dionysius of Halicarnassus, *Ant. Rom.* 2.60.4–61.3).

It is right to hold a healthy level of scepticism towards individual cases, and undoubtedly there were people whose claims to divine visitations were consciously fabricated. On the other hand, it is also empirically observable that human beings, both ancient and modern, have experiences that they perceive as coming from the divine and that such experiences can be productive in terms of religious content.[20] How one may distinguish such cases is unclear.

---

[18] Hanson, "Dreams and Visions," 1400–1401; Harrisson, *Dreams and Dreaming*, 49; Rollens, "The God Came to Me," 46.

[19] Joshua Garroway insists that "a critical historian cannot accept that [Paul's message] resulted from an actual revelation," but instead speculates on some "this-worldly explanations" for how Paul formulated his message. James Hanges allows Paul a vague "personal experience of divine commission," but treats Paul's own account of it as nothing more than his "conversion tale" which is better dispensed with for historical purposes. Joshua D. Garroway, *The Beginning of the Gospel: Paul, Philippi, and the Origins of Christianity* (Cham: Palgrave Macmillan, 2018), 72; Hanges, *Paul, Founder of Churches*, 17, 383–84 n. 22; cf. Terence L. Donaldson, "Israelite, Convert, Apostle to the Gentiles: The Origin of Paul's Gentile Mission" in *The Road from Damascus: The Impact of Paul's Conversion on his Life, Thought, and Ministry*, ed. Richard N. Longenecker (Grand Rapids: Eerdmans, 1997), 63.

[20] For the neurobiology of altered states of consciousness, see Shantz, *Paul in Ecstasy*; cf. Hurtado, "Revelatory Experiences," 470–73; Benz, *Paulus als Visionär*.

The presence of obvious social advantages for the recipient is not necessarily a reliable criterion, as the rhetorical use of an experience says nothing about the reality of the experience itself.[21] If rhetorical value is all one can say about claims to divine visions, then we are left with a rather one-dimensional picture of human activity and experience.

In studying the testimonies to visionary experiences, one should carefully delineate the elements involved in any such experience, which are: first, the experience itself, second, the way that experience is interpreted and reported, and third, the rhetorical use to which the interpreted experience is put. The third element is what is most readily available to historians on the surface of their sources, but its presence does not negate the presence of the first and second elements.[22] It is therefore admissible to probe behind the third element to ask the question with regard to the second: how did Paul understand and interpret these experiences, and how would his Gentile audiences in Galatia, Corinth, Rome or Philippi have understood them?[23] The cultural context for making sense of such experiences and the form in which they are told – for both Paul and his audiences – is not just the culture of Second Temple Judaism, but also the wider Hellenistic and Mediterranean assumptions about visions, epiphanies, and divination, of which the Jewish culture was a part. This still does not get us back to the first element, the experience itself, which cannot and never did exist in uninterpreted form, whether it is the interpretation of the critical historian, the interested "pagan" on the streets of Corinth, or Paul himself.[24] The perspective of the interested "pagan" is particularly useful, as it can be used to think within the same cultural world as Paul, but can also provide some comparative angles he would perhaps have eschewed himself.

---

[21] *Pace* Harrison, *Dreams and Dreaming*, 216.

[22] "Just because [Paul's] reference to his own religious experiences serves certain functions and that the experiences themselves always came in interpreted form, we should not conclude that there was nothing to be interpreted and to serve those functions. That would be a fallacy of philosophical 'idealism'," Troels Engberg-Pedersen, "The Construction of Religious Experience in Paul," in *Experientia, Volume 1: Inquiry into Religious Experience in Early Judaism and Christianity*, ed. Frances Flannery, Colleen Shantz, and Rodney A. Werline, SymS 40 (Atlanta: SBL, 2008), 150.

[23] There is some overlap here with the third element, as Paul's audiences also only have access to the way he has rhetorically shaped his experience. I include it under the second element here as it concerns their interpretation of the experience itself, rather than their interpretation of Paul's social and rhetorical goals. Rollens ("The God Came to Me") also chooses to focus on the ways Paul's Gentile audience would have categorised his claim, but these Gentiles seem to think only in terms of sociological function, rather than with a more "realist" categorisation of the vision itself in terms of experience.

[24] "Paul's religious experiences did in fact come in interpreted form.... He did use the reference to his own religious experience for the various rhetorical purposes suggested.... Still, he did have them," Engberg-Pedersen, "Religious Experience," 150.

Paul's Initial Vision of Jesus

The image of Paul being "converted" by a vision on the road to Damascus is familiar to most.[25] The accounts in Acts largely guide the popular imagination, and these certainly conform to many of the expectations of a Greek epiphany.[26] Here Paul sees Jesus in the form of a lightning epiphany (Acts 9:3; 22:6) at midday (Acts 22:6; 26:13)[27] and hears a voice with which he can have a conversation (Acts 9:4–6; 22:7–9).[28] Paul's letters do not provide this level of detail, but do bear witness to a foundational moment for him that involved a vision of the risen Jesus. This is primarily attested by three texts: 1 Cor 9:1; 15:8; and Gal 1:10–17.[29]

Visions of the Dead and the Raised (1 Corinthians 9:1; 15:8)

In both 1 Cor 9:1 and later in 1 Cor 15:8, Paul claims simply to have seen Jesus, using forms of the verb ὁράω (1 Cor 9:1: οὐχὶ Ἰησοῦν τὸν κύριον ἡμῶν ἑόρακα; 15:8: ὤφθη κἀμοί). The perfect tense form (ἑόρακα) in 1 Cor 9:1 suggests a definite point in the past, on which he bases his claim to be an apostle.[30] In 1 Cor 15 it is clear that this sighting is of Jesus in his resurrected state, coming at the end of a sequence of death (ἀπέθανεν), burial (ἐτάφη), resurrection (ἐγήγερται), and appearance (ὤφθη). Paul includes himself as the last and least in a sequence of witnesses to whom Jesus had also appeared. The significance of

---

[25] The dichotomy between "conversion" and "call" which Stendahl posed was a vital corrective to his scholarly context, but the term conversion has since been appropriately nuanced so that it is entirely appropriate to speak of Paul's experience as both call and conversion, as long as one is clear that the conversion is not from "Judaism" to "Christianity." See Krister Stendahl, "Paul Among Jews and Gentiles," in *Paul Among Jews and Gentiles and Other Essays* (Philadelphia: Fortress, 1976), 7–23; Segal, *Paul the Convert*; Beverly Roberts Gaventa, *From Darkness to Light: Aspects of Conversion in the New Testament*, OBT 20 (Philadelphia: Fortress, 1986), 4–14.

[26] Frederick E. Brenk, "Greek Epiphanies and Paul on the Road to Damaskos," in *The Notion of 'Religion' in Comparative Research: Selected Proceedings of the XVIth Congress of the International Association for the History of Religions*, ed. Ugo Bianchi (Rome: Bretschneider, 1994), 415–24.

[27] On the link between epiphanies and midday, particularly in a travel context, see Petridou, *Divine Epiphany*, 210–14.

[28] Both these aspects are somewhat transformed by the second retelling in Acts 26:12–20. The flashing (περιαστράψαι) light has become a shining (περιλάμψαν) light, "brighter than the sun." The voice also provides much more detailed content than in the previous two accounts. See Ronald D. Witherup, "'Functional Redundancy' in the Acts of the Apostles: A Case Study," *JSNT* 48 (1992): 75–77.

[29] Scholars often add to these texts 2 Cor 4:6, which speaks of inner illumination but cannot be convincingly traced to this initial event, and Phil 3:4–12, which speaks of a drastic change in Paul's priorities, but not of visionary experience.

[30] Porter, as far as I am aware, is alone among recent interpreters in suggesting that 1 Cor 9:1 refers to seeing and meeting Jesus before his crucifixion, and not to a visionary experience, Stanley E. Porter, *When Paul Met Jesus: How an Idea Got Lost in History* (Cambridge: Cambridge University Press, 2016), 94–105. This possibility was accepted, but not argued by Christopher N. Johnston, *St Paul and His Mission to the Roman Empire* (London: A&C Black, 1911), 16 n. 2.

Jesus's resurrection was, for Paul, something that was unique to Jesus. As the resurrected Messiah, his resurrection heralded and set into motion the general resurrection of the dead, the renewal of creation, and the ultimate defeat of death itself.[31] This does not, however, make certain aspects of Paul's experience incomparable on a broader level, particularly as we consider the function of visions as a means of communication.

The dead frequently appeared in dreams and visions, and the significance and implications of these appearances vary greatly. The "restless dead" often appeared with instructions or information that would help them pass over fully into the realm of the dead. Those who did not have a proper burial might request one, or those who were murdered might return to disclose the identity of the murderer and demand vengeance.[32] Ghosts could also be the source of omens and advice, and were sometimes consulted at a *nekuomanteion* or summoned by ritual experts, although the evidence here is patchy and in general it seems Greeks were more at ease with consulting gods than ghosts.[33]

Paul's view of Jesus does not fit easily into any of these categories, since the primary significance of his appearance in 1 Cor 15:8 lies precisely in the fact that Jesus had been raised. In Paul's estimation this makes Jesus much more god than ghost, and puts Paul's experience closer to accounts of figures who have appeared after attaining an elevated post-mortem status.[34] In these cases

---

[31] See Paula Fredriksen, *Paul: The Pagans' Apostle* (New Haven: Yale University Press, 2017), 133–36.

[32] For visions of the restless dead, see Sarah Iles Johnston, *Restless Dead: Encounters Between the Living and the Dead in Ancient Greece* (Berkeley: University of California Press, 1999); Harrisson, *Dreams and Dreaming*, 136–46; and the sources collected in Daniel Ogden, *Magic, Witchcraft, and Ghosts in the Greek and Roman Worlds: A Sourcebook* (Oxford: Oxford University Press, 2002), 146–66. For the dead appearing to request burial rites on inscriptions, see Renberg, "Commanded by the Gods," 310–15.

[33] On the *nekuomanteion*: Iles Johnston, *Restless Dead*, 84–85, 119–24; Jan N. Bremmer, *The Rise and Fall of the Afterlife* (London: Routledge, 2002), 71–83. Iles Johnston later concludes, however, "in spite of the fact that the Greeks and Romans liked to *think* about necromancy, they seldom or never practiced it" (italics original), *Ancient Greek Divination*, 97–98; cf. Sarah Iles Johnston, "Delphi and the Dead," in Iles Johnston and Struck, *Mantikē*, 283–306.

[34] These texts are well known, and are often compared to the resurrection appearances in the Gospels, but are very rarely introduced into the discussion of Paul's visions of Jesus, perhaps because Paul offers so little detail to compare, see Eugene Boring, Carsten Colpe, and Klaus Berger, eds., *Hellenistic Commentary to the New Testament* (Nashville: Abingdon, 1995), 161–68; Wendy Cotter, "Greco-Roman Apotheosis Traditions and the Resurrection Appearances in Matthew," in *The Gospel of Matthew in Current Study*, ed. David Aune (Grand Rapids: Eerdmans, 2001), 127–53; Adela Yarbro Collins, "Apotheosis and Resurrection," in *The New Testament and Hellenistic Judaism*, ed. Peder Borgen and Søren Giversen (Aarhus: Aarhus University Press, 1995), 88–100; Adela Yarbro Collins, "Ancient Notions of Transferal and Apotheosis in Relation to the Empty Tomb Story in Mark," in *Metamorphoses: Resurrection, Body and Transformative Practices in Early Christianity*, ed. Turid Karlsen Seim and Jorunn Økland, Ekstasis 1 (Berlin: de Gruyter, 2009), 41–58; Litwa, *Iesus Deus*, 141–79. The fullest recent treatment is by John Granger Cook, *Empty Tomb, Resurrection, Apotheosis*, WUNT 410 (Tübingen: Mohr Siebeck, 2018).

the appearance serves to inform people of the figure's new status and prompt cultic action in accordance with that status. Aristeas, for example, was reported to have died in a fuller's shop, but his body had later disappeared. He was then seen once on the road by a man who said he had spoken with him, once again seven years later, and once more 240 years later in Metapontum in southern Italy (Herodotus 4.14–15). On this occasion he is said to have appeared (φανέντα) to the Metapontines and commanded them to set up an altar to Apollo with a statue of himself next to it, for Apollo had graced the Metapontines with a visit, accompanied by Aristeas himself in the form of a raven. Apollonius in his *Mirabilia* also relates the death and subsequent appearance of Aristeas in Sicily where many saw him teaching letters (γράμματα διδάσκοντα). In this version it is the frequency of his teaching appearances (φανταζομένου) that lead to the Sicilians dedicating a shrine and sacrifices to him as a hero (Apollonius, *Hist. mir.* 2.1–2 [FGH 4:1672]).[35]

In the case of Romulus, there is no death to speak of, only his inexplicable disappearance after being enveloped in a storm cloud.[36] While some believed he had been murdered and dismembered by his senators, the senators and noblemen themselves promoted the idea that he had been taken up to heaven and "added to the number of the gods" (Cicero, *Rep.* 2.18). In this state he could now be prayed to for the protection of the city. While the disappearance alone was enough to prompt the suggestion that he had been taken to heaven, this interpretation was significantly bolstered by the report of one Julius Proculus, who reported in the Forum that he had seen Romulus after his disappearance. In Livy's account Romulus descends from heaven to appear to Julius and ascends once more after delivering his message (Livy, 1.16.8). In other accounts Julius appears to meet him on the road before he has been taken up, but Romulus still bears some epiphanic attributes. Plutarch's account (*Rom.* 28.1–3) mentions beauty (καλός), size (μέγας), and bright, shining clothing (ὅπλοις δὲ λαμπροῖς καὶ φλέγουσι κεκοσμημένος).[37] In all accounts this encounter serves to confirm Romulus's divine status. Some versions also include the further command to build a shrine to the new deity (Cicero, *Rep.* 2.20) and predictions

---

[35] Not all sources include this sequence of death/disappearance, appearance, and deification/ heroisation. According to Diodorus Siculus, it was Aristeas's contact with nymphs earlier in life, and the knowledge and skills which he passed on from them, that resulted in him receiving divine honours from the people of Cyrene (Diodorus Siculus 4.81.2–3). He later travelled to Sicily where he also received divine honours on account of his teaching, but there is no mention of a death or subsequent appearances. The only disappearance comes many years later, and there are no appearances recorded after this (Diodorus Siculus 4.82.5–6).

[36] Cicero, *Rep.* 2.17–20; Livy 1.16.1–8; Dionysius of Halicarnassus, *Ant. rom.* 2.56.1–6; 63.3; Plutarch, *Rom.* 27–28.

[37] For these features as epiphanic, see Versnel, "Ancient Man," 43–44; Petridou, *Divine Epiphany*, 35–39.

about the fate of Rome, which Julius Proculus is instructed to communicate to the Roman people (Livy, 1.16.8; Plutarch, *Rom.* 28.1–3).[38] A graffito from Pompeii corroborates the notion that Romulus, in his new position in heaven, can now communicate the will of the gods and give predictions: *Romu/lu[s] in c(a)e(lo) / nunc omentor*, "Romulus is in heaven, now one who gives omens" (*CIL* 4:7353).

Paul's vision of Jesus in 1 Cor 15:8 also serves the primary purpose of convincing him that Jesus has in fact been raised and holds a special status in relation to God. In the immediate context of the letter, the significance of the appearances is to confirm that Paul's Christ-followers will also come to enjoy a similar resurrection (1 Cor 15:12–34), a conclusion that witnesses of Aristeas or Romulus did not make. It is clear from Paul's letters more generally that cultic worship of Christ was another corollary of the experience, which is common to all the examples cited above.[39] From Paul's compact account it is tempting to think that sight alone was enough to convince him of Christ's resurrected status. In the context of the above examples, and epiphany accounts in general, it is more likely that Paul's audience would have understood a fuller interaction which also involved discursive content, including an explanation of Jesus's divine status and further instructions or predictions.[40]

Visions of a glorified end to earthly existence may also prompt reflection on beginnings. When Paul narrates Christ's exaltation in Phil 2:6–11 he includes the belief that Christ enjoyed a divine pre-existence before taking human form (cf. 1 Cor 10:4). This is not a feature of most of the examples discussed above, and Paul does not link it specifically to his vision of Christ. In Plutarch's account of Romulus, however, Plutarch does have his hero tell Julius Proculus that he is "from the gods" (ἐκεῖθεν ὄντας) and was ordained to be with humans for a set time and for a specific purpose before ascending to heaven (*Rom.* 28.2). I include this example with caution as it is not entirely clear what is meant. On the common reading (facilitated by the LCL translation), Romulus comes

---

[38] In Dionysius of Halicarnassus (*Ant. rom.* 2.63.3–4), Julius's vision prompts Numa to found a temple and sacrifices, without Romulus explicitly commanding it.

[39] Hurtado ("Revelatory Experiences," 475–79) correctly notes that Paul's visions only convinced him of the truth of what other Christ-followers had already been believing and doing, and which Paul had previously opposed. He does suggest similar experiences played a similar role for other early Christ-followers too, though. He also notes how the decision to give cultic veneration to Jesus would not have been quite so easy or obvious from within Paul's Jewish matrix, Larry W. Hurtado, *Lord Jesus Christ: Devotion to Jesus in Earliest Christianity* (Grand Rapids: Eerdmans, 2003), 32–42.

[40] Betz, *Galatians*, 64: "Ample evidence from the religious literature shows that the visionary experience and the verbal revelation do not exclude each other. ... It is probably only the modern reader who finds these statements difficult to relate."

from heaven (ἐκεῖθεν ὄντας) and is returning to dwell there again (αὖθις οἰκεῖν οὐρανόν). It is equally possible, though, that Romulus's existence from the gods (ἐκεῖθεν ὄντας) simply refers to his being fathered by Mars (*Rom.* 4.2), and αὖθις, rather than "again," could mean "hereafter." On this reading, Romulus is now moving on to his new and rightful home. Romulus also speaks in the first person plural, suggesting he is one of a class of similar beings who do such things.[41] Plutarch himself understands this story in terms of the soul, which "alone is from the gods" and to the gods it returns when it is separated from the body and can ascend the ranks of divinity (*Rom.* 28.7). However this specific example is to be understood, it shows that reports of deification can also be linked to divine beginnings.

To what extent do any of these examples fit into the context of divination? Both the examples of Aristeas and Romulus relate exceptional, even legendary, occurrences and to some extent stand outside the usual, everyday practice of divination.[42] This is certainly not how one would normally expect to obtain divine knowledge, but the difference here may be one of degree rather than kind. In the similar story of the hero Cleomedes, there were no appearances after his disappearance to inform people of his heroisation, instead the Delphic oracle is the source that reveals this information (Plutarch, *Rom.* 28.5). Julius Caesar's apotheosis was said to have been inferred from the sighting of a star or comet in the sky. The sources suggest that some took the sighting as a sign that he had joined the company of the gods, while others saw the star as the soul of Caesar himself in the heavens (Suetonius, *Jul.* 88; Cassius Dio 45.6.4–7.1; Pliny, *Nat.* 2.93–94). Such information was not available by ordinary human means, but always required some form of communication from the heavenly realm to disclose it. Waking visions are merely the most vivid and direct form of communication, and therefore also one of the rarest.

The interaction of divinatory media in such a context can also be seen by a first-century CE inscription known as "The Testament of Epicrates." This inscription records a father establishing a funerary monument and hero shrine to his deceased son Diophantos on the basis of repeated dreams and visions in which his son had visited him.

> (I want my inheritors and successors after me to know that) all these things have been set apart and devoted and consecrated together to the

---

[41] Litwa adopts the LCL translation that simply translates the first-person plurals as first-person singulars, but also provides examples of some other souls that were said to be sent into human bodies for specific tasks. M. David Litwa, *Posthuman Transformation in Ancient Mediterranean Thought: Becoming Angels and Demons* (Cambridge: Cambridge University Press, 2021), 62, 79.

[42] For the possible origins of the Romulus myth, see Jan N. Bremmer, "Romulus, Remus and the Foundation of Rome," in *Roman Myth and Mythography*, ed. Jan N. Bremmer and Nicholas Horsfall (London: Institute of Classical Studies, 1987), 45–46.

funerary monument and hero Diophantos, and that I was impelled to set apart for him what was previously written, not only for the purpose of the love of my child, but also by dreams and signs and apparitions of the hero himself visiting me visibly and repeatedly to set apart for himself a portion.

… ταῦτα / πάντα ἀφώρισται καὶ ἀνεῖται καὶ συνκαθωσίωται τῷ μνημείῳ καὶ ἥρωι Διοφάν / τῳ, καὶ ὅτι τοῦτο οὐ μόνον κατὰ τὴν φιλότεκνόν μου προαίρεσιν, ἀλλὰ / καὶ ὀνείροις καὶ σημείοις καὶ φαντάσμασιν αὐτοῦ μοι τοῦ ἥρωος / ἐναργῶς πολλάκις ἐπιφοιτῶντος ἀφορισθῆναι αὐτῷ μέρη προετράπην ἀφο / ρίσαι αὐτῷ τὰ προγεγραμμένα.[43]

A variety of divinatory media prompt the impulse to set up a hero shrine. The signs (σημεία) could refer to any number of signs or portents that one might interpret as a message from the hero, but the listing of dreams (ὄνειροι) as well as apparitions (φαντάσμα) imply that the hero himself also appeared in both sleeping and waking states.[44] Like Paul, there is no explicit record of a direct command or conversation that takes place to convey the purpose of the appearances. An infinitive of purpose (ἀφορισθῆναι) establishes the reason for the visits, but not the specific way this reason was communicated (cf. Gal 1:16: ἵνα εὐαγγελίζωμαι). Sara Campanelli adds the bracketed gloss *chiedendo che* to her Italian translation to suggest that Diophantos specifically asked for the establishment of the shrine during his visitations, and given the usual narrative form of visions this is not unlikely.[45] The context of the Graeco-Roman family is much more modest in scope than the worldwide ambitions of Jesus or Romulus, and the cultic action prescribed was limited to an annual decoration of the sepulchre.[46] The visions continue to function in similar ways though, as they convey information about the state the person has attained beyond death and prompt, or more likely command, action on earth in keeping with that status.[47]

[43] Text from Renberg, "Commanded by the Gods," 483 (Cat. no. 401).
[44] Renberg, "Commanded by the Gods," 49.
[45] Sara Campanelli, "Eroizzazione e proprietà terriera nel 'Testamento di *Epikrates*': Per una proposta di lettura delle fondazioni cultuali di carattere familiare," *Hormos: Ricerche di storia antica* 4 (2012): 77.
[46] Campanelli, "Eroizzazione e proprietà terriera," 77.
[47] There is some debate over how much weight should be given to the term ἥρως in such private funerary contexts as these. Some influential classicists in the past have suggested that at this stage and in these contexts "the application of the term *herōs* to the recently dead was often a meaningless compliment" in much the same way as we might call a personal acquaintance a "saint" or an "angel." See Ulrich von Wilamowitz-Moellendorff, *Der Glaube der Hellenen* (Berlin: Weidmannsche, 1932), 2:19; Arthur Darby Nock, "Deification and Julian," in *Essays on Religion and the Ancient World*, ed. Zeph Stewart (Oxford: Clarendon, 1972), 2:842. In such a case the visions mentioned could fit into the context of ghosts returning to demand a proper burial. It is more probable, however, that the multiple divinatory signs and visions signified

Revelation and Commission (Galatians 1:10–17)

In addition to communicating the risen status of Jesus, Paul's vision also bestowed on him the title and commission of apostle. This connection always comes with a fair amount of rhetorical backpedalling in the Corinthian correspondence. In 1 Cor 9:1 Paul mentions the vision of Jesus and his apostolic status in the same breath, but only for the sake of then listing the theoretical privileges of this role that he willingly foregoes. Similarly, in 1 Cor 15 Paul's inclusion of himself in the list of witnesses to the risen Jesus also includes him in the number of apostles, but only as the last and least of them. He is not in fact worthy of the name because of his previous status as a persecutor of Christ-followers.

No such reticence is evident in the first chapter of Galatians, in which his apostolic call comes to the fore. The letter opening is strident: "Paul, an apostle not from humans nor through a human but through Jesus Christ and God the father who raised him from the dead" (Gal 1:1). The rest of chapters 1 and 2 defend this claim by stressing the independence of Paul's commission from human authority, and the independent reception of his message δι' ἀποκαλύψεως Ἰησοῦ Χριστοῦ, "through a revelation of Jesus Christ" (Gal 1:12). Several factors suggest that this is the same event Paul refers to in 1 Cor 9:1 and 15:8. In both Gal 1 and 1 Cor 15 Paul speaks of the experience occurring in the context of his previous opposition to Christ-groups, and consequently describes it as a result of God's favour (χάρις Gal 1:15; 1 Cor 15:10). All three accounts, as just noted, are also linked to his apostleship in a special way.[48] But rather than the straightforward language of "seeing," Paul here describes the experience as a "revelation." Is this merely another way of saying the same thing? Or does the different terminology suggest a different type of event?

Revelation

Scholars sometimes include the term ἀποκάλυψις in lists of technical dream and vision terminology, although Paul is the earliest, and often the only, cited example.[49] The verb ἀποκαλύπτειν together with its cognates means "to

---

a greater continuing significance for the deceased. More recent scholarship that emphasises a stronger sense to the term includes Fritz Graf, *Nordionische Kulte: Religionsgeschichtlich und Epigraphische Untersuchungen zu den Kulten von Chios, Erythrai, Klazomenai und Phokaia* (Rome: Schweizerisches Institut in Rom, 1985), 127–35; Christopher P. Jones, *New Heroes in Antiquity: From Achilles to Antinoos* (Cambridge, MA: Harvard University Press, 2010), 48–65.

[48] The "visions and revelations" of 2 Cor 12:1 are also connected in a way to Paul's status as apostle, but not in such a direct and foundational way as in these passages.

[49] In addition to Paul, Hanson ("Dreams and Visions," 1408) tentatively includes the Shepherd of Hermas, Vis. 3.13.4 (21.4); 4.1.3 (22.3). Gregor Weber (*Kaiser, Träume und Visionen in Prinzipat und Spätantike* [Stuttgart: Steiner, 2000], 32 n. 26) cites secondary discussions of apocalyptic literature but these rarely use the word itself as a technical term.

uncover" and could be used literally (to uncover the grisly contents of a basket for example [Herodotus 1.119]) or figuratively (to disclose one's thoughts [Plato, *Prot.* 352a]).[50] The LXX occasionally attests the verb in the context of divine revelation and dream visions, but still in the literal sense in which God or an angel uncovers one's eyes (Num 22:31; 24:6, 16) or ears (1 Kgdms 9:15; 2 Kgdms 7:27) so that one can see or hear him.[51] This idiom is also used of purely human communication (1 Kgdms 20:2, 13; 22:8, 17; Ruth 4:4). It is not until the Theodotion text of Daniel that the term denotes the revelation of mysteries by God or an angel in dreams and visions (ἐν ὁράματι τῆς νυκτός [Dan 2:19, 22, 28, 29, 30, 47; 10:1]). Here the word appears consistently where the OG text uses a variety of verbs for the same thing (δηλόω, ἀνακαλύπτω, φωτίζω, ἐκφαίνω, δείκνυμι).[52] The word itself then does not unambiguously refer to a visionary experience but to any of the variety of ways that something might be revealed.

Paul's letters present the same variety. Unsurprisingly, a number of things will be revealed at Christ's future coming when God makes all things new: God's righteous judgement (Rom 2:5), the future glory of the sons of God (Rom 8:18–19), each person's work (1 Cor 3:13), and Jesus Christ himself (1 Cor 1:7). Equally, a number of other things, more clearly related to knowledge, are also revealed in the present through various visionary, prophetic, or divinatory means (1 Cor 14:6, 26, 30; 2 Cor 12:1, 7; Gal 1:12, 16; 2:2; 3:23; Rom 1:17–18; 1 Cor 2:10; Phil 3:15).

A number of scholars have sought to add a great deal more content to Paul's use of the terms ἀποκάλυψις and ἀποκαλύπτειν by making the "eschatological" use determinative and all-encompassing. This serves to distance Paul's use of the terms from notions of visionary or divinatory experience and instead ties "revelation" to the event of God sending Jesus into human history.[53] There is a certain tension in these readings, which have to hold together revelation as an objective event, entirely independent of Paul, but also the personal way in which Paul speaks of it in Gal 1. So for Lührmann, the revelation of God's son in Gal 1:12 is parallel to the "sending" of the son in Gal 4:4 and the revelation

---

[50] Oepke, "ἀποκαλύπτω," 3:570–71; Morton Smith, "On the History of ΑΠΟΚΑΛΥΠΤΩ and ΑΠΟΚΑΛΥΨΙΣ," in *Apocalypticism in the Mediterranean World and the Near East: Proceedings of the International Colloquium on Apocalypticism, Uppsala, August 12–17, 1979*, ed. David Hellholm, 2nd ed. (Tübingen: Mohr Siebeck, 1989), 10–12.

[51] Num 22:31: ἐν ὕπνῳ ἀποκεκαλυμμένοι οἱ ὀφθαλμοὶ αὐτοῦ.

[52] On the knotty question of the influence of Greek Daniel on Paul, see Lang, *Mystery*, 13 n. 44; Smith, *Drudgery Divine*, 73. It would seem best to consider this text as contemporary to Paul rather than a direct influence on him.

[53] Martyn, *Galatians*, 98–99; Karl Kertelge, "Apokalypsis Jesou Christou (Gal 1,12)," in *Grundthemen paulinischer Theologie* (Freiburg: Herder, 1991), 55–56; Gaventa, *From Darkness to Light*, 23; Martinus C. de Boer, *Galatians: A Commentary*, NTL (Louisville: Westminster John Knox, 2011), 79–82; de Boer, "Paul," 21–33.

of "faith" in Gal 3:23, and so represents nothing less than "the eschatological turning point."[54] At the same time, for Lührmann, it only truly becomes "revelation" when this particular event is received and interpreted by a person: "Offenbarung ist nicht das Christusgeschehen als solches, sondern eine auf den Menschen bezogene Interpretation dieses Geschehens als den Menschen angehend durch ein neu einsetzendes Handeln Gottes."[55] Similarly, for J. L. Martyn, "Apocalypse is the *invasive* act that was carried out by God when he sent Christ and Christ's Spirit into the world and into human hearts."[56] The revelation to Paul, then, refers to Paul's own reception of this bigger cosmic event in miniature, "in a word, the gospel *happened* to Paul when God stepped on the scene, invading his life in Christ."[57] This, in my view, loads too much theological freight into a single word and is a basic confusion of *content* with *concept*. I do not dispute that as a result of this revelation Paul understood Jesus to represent an eschatological turning point, or that he understood this as God doing a new thing in the cosmos. But this is the content of Paul's revelation in this instance, and not Paul's concept of what revelation itself is. Paul uses the word ἀποκαλύψις in Gal 1:12 to describe how he came to know the good news that he proclaims, and in comparison with 1 Cor 15:8 we may surmise that this happened through a vision of Jesus himself.[58]

The terse statement of Gal 1:11–12 is more fully elaborated in 1:15–16, in which God appears as the revealer and Jesus the content of the revelation. According to Paul, Jesus was revealed ἐν ἐμοί, "in me." This could be read as the equivalent of a simple dative, "to me," and this is probably the simplest solution.[59] This would cohere grammatically with the statement that immediately follows, in which Paul proclaims Jesus ἐν τοῖς ἔθνεσιν, "to the Gentiles," and in meaning would be roughly equivalent to 1 Cor 15:8: ὤφθη κἀμοί, "he was seen by me."[60] It is also possible that Paul may be more attentive

---

[54] Lührmann, *Offenbarungsverständnis*, 75.

[55] Lührmann, *Offenbarungsverständnis*, 79.

[56] Martyn, *Galatians*, 144 (italics original).

[57] Martyn, *Galatians*, 144 (italics original).

[58] Martinus de Boer admits this, but still works particularly hard to try to distance Paul's use of ἀποκαλύψις language in Galatians from other instances in 1 Cor 14:26 and 2 Cor 12:1 where the word obviously refers to the disclosure of divine information, but he can only do so by setting up unnecessary and unconvincing contrasts, e.g., revelation to people who are "already believers" versus life-changing event, private revelations versus revelations of communal significance. None of these distinctions affect the basic sense of the word, or the experience involved, de Boer, "Paul," 30–32; de Boer, *Galatians*, 80–81. For the classic account of apocalyptic that understands it as the revelation of divine knowledge (against which de Boer is reacting), see Christopher Rowland, *The Open Heaven: A Study of Apocalyptic in Judaism and Early Christianity* (London: SPCK, 1982).

[59] Martyn, *Galatians*, 158; Lührmann, *Offenbarungsverständnis*, 79 n. 1.

[60] Bockmuehl, *Revelation and Mystery*, 136 n. 19; Gaventa, *From Darkness to Light*, 27.

to the mechanics of a visionary experience in this passage and brings the focus on the pneumatic perception of Christ and his presence within him. In 1 Cor 2:10, as we saw in Chapter 1, divine knowledge is revealed through *pneuma* (ἀπεκάλυψεν … διὰ τοῦ πνεύματος), and the pneumatic body of the risen Jesus (1 Cor 15:44) would presumably also need to be perceived at the level of *pneuma*. In 2 Cor 12:2–3, Paul expresses ambivalence about whether his visionary experience was in or out of the body, but in the rest of Galatians Paul's emphasis is on the subsequent presence of Christ within believers, as in Gal 2:18, "I no longer live, but Christ lives in me (ἐν ἐμοί)," and Gal 4:6, "God sent the *pneuma* of his son into our hearts."[61] So Paul, here, may prepare the way for this by claiming that Jesus was not just revealed to him (as in 1 Cor), but was also revealed to be in him. This is not to opt for a subjective rather than an objective experience as that is not a distinction Paul ever seems to draw.[62] Nor is it to say that Paul here refers to an experience of pneumatic possession and not a vision.[63] Rather, Paul is identifying the physics through which such a visionary experience is possible.[64]

Commission and Divine Authority

The purpose of this revelation, Paul says, was "in order that I might proclaim (εὐαγγελίζομαι) him among the Gentiles" (Gal 1:16). The link between epiphany and authority for a new commission was a natural one in the ancient world. In this connection there are at least 1,300 inscriptions surviving from across the Greek East and Latin West, dating from the fifth century BCE to the fourth century CE, that record a dedication at the command of a god.[65] Sometimes this is no more than the dedication of a small altar or statue, but it can extend to much broader and more ambitious activities. Georgia Petridou

---

[61] Heininger, *Paulus*, 200; Smith, "History," 15; Betz, *Galatians*, 71.
[62] Betz, *Galatians*, 71; cf. Lindblom, *Gesichte und Offenbarungen*, 37.
[63] Smith, "History," 15. Eyl points out that "if he were referring to intellectual or mental perception, he would not provide his restricted list of those who had seen the god [1 Cor 15:5–8]; the mental 'perception' of Christ could certainly be claimed by more people than those on his list, including Paul's own followers," *Signs, Wonders, and Gifts*, 146.
[64] Other readings of ἐν ἐμοί include the revelation of Christ to others through Paul, J. B. Lightfoot, *Saint Paul's Epistle to the Galatians*, 10th ed. (London: Macmillan, 1890), 83. This certainly finds support elsewhere in Paul but is not the focus here, where proclaiming Jesus to the Gentiles is the purpose and result of the prior revelation rather than its simple equivalent. De Boer suggests reading "in my former manner of life," which is a further attempt to emphasise the invasive and transformative character of the revelation, but not a convincing translation, *Galatians*, 92–93.
[65] Gil Renberg catalogued and analysed these inscriptions in his 2003 thesis "Commanded by the Gods." He stresses the ambiguity of much of the terminology so that it is hard to know exactly how the gods would have communicated this information, but many imply or directly narrate visual epiphanies.

writes that "all around the Greek-speaking world, epiphanies triggered the establishment of shrines, temples, altars (and other sacred buildings of all sorts), sacrifices, festivals, athletic contests, new cults, and even new cities."[66] Seeing a god always tended to prompt something new.

The presence of epiphanies in some of these narratives and inscriptions could relate to the need to provide an explanation for long-standing cults and traditions, but they can also provide the necessary authority for innovation. With every claim of divine commission necessarily comes a claim for status and legitimation. This function of visions and epiphanies has been emphasised in recent scholarship,[67] and is equally applicable to Paul as the opening of Galatians attests.[68] James Hanges has fruitfully analysed Paul in the context of founder figures in the ancient world, all of whom claimed a particular revelation, through either a dream, vision, or oracle as impetus and justification for the founding of new colonies and cults.[69] In addition to founding a cult, however, Paul also maintains a strong focus on the delivering of a message, in which he acts as a spokesperson for God, and his Messiah.

Paul's own presentation of his calling in Gal 1 has long been recognised as evocative of the call of prophets from the Hebrew Bible.[70] In Isaiah 6:1–9 and Ezekiel 1:1–28, visions of God precede their prophetic commissions. Ezekiel's vision of the כבוד יהוה, "glory/form of Yahweh," is at once detailed and restrained in its depiction. Isaiah, like Paul, is more direct, and almost as sparse in the details he offers: "I saw the Lord" (Isa 6:1). In both instances these visions precede an audible conversation in which Yahweh commissions the prophet for his task as messenger to the people of Israel. Jeremiah's call narrative does not explicitly feature a vision, instead it is only the דבר יהוה, "word of Yahweh," that comes to him.[71] His commission is then followed by a series

---

[66] Petridou, *Divine Epiphany*, 320.

[67] Petridou lists the bestowal of divine authority as one of three functions of epiphanies, the others being to provide an explanation or *aition* for something, and to act as a crisis management tool, *Divine Epiphany*, 329–43. This theme is also emphasised in Harrisson, *Dreams and Dreaming*, 49–50, 216–21; Weber, *Kaiser, Träume und Visionen*.

[68] Rollens concentrates on the sociological functions of dreams and visions in voluntary associations and Paul. Foremost of these is a claim to authority, alongside the creation of a sense of group belonging and the provision of temporal connections beyond the present, "The God Came to Me," 41–65. Eyl treats Paul's visions almost entirely as "discursive claims to divine authority," *Signs, Wonders, and Gifts*, 144–52.

[69] Hanges, *Paul, Founder of Churches*.

[70] Johannes Munck, *Paul and the Salvation of Mankind* (London: SCM, 1959), 25–29; Stendahl, "Paul Among Jews and Gentiles," 7–8; Nicklas, "Paulus—der Apostel als Prophet," 79–80; Aune, *Prophecy*, 202, 248.

[71] Although cf. 1 Sam 3:1 where the "word of the Lord" (דבר יהוה/ῥῆμα κυρίου) and "vision" (חזון/ὅρασις) appear to qualify each other. Also Isa 2:1: "The *word* (הדבר/ὁ λόγος) that Isaiah the son of Amoz *saw*."

of symbolic visions that confirm the commission.[72] Despite this difference, it is Jeremiah, as well as the servant figure of Isaiah 49, that Paul most directly evokes with the claim that he was set apart from his mother's womb to proclaim God's message to the Gentiles (Jer 1:5; Isa 49:1, 6).

The call of a prophet entails not just the initial reception and delivering of a message, but an ongoing role as mediator of divine information. The Acts accounts certainly portray Paul's commission in this way. In Acts 22, Ananias interprets Paul's vision as evidence that he has been chosen for privileged, multi-sensory access to divine knowledge, which it is his duty to communicate. He stresses knowledge, sight, and audition of God when he says Paul was chosen "to know his will and to see the righteous one and to hear a voice from his mouth" (Acts 22:14). In this account Paul immediately goes to Jerusalem and receives further visions in an ecstatic state (ἐν ἐκστάσει), and it is in this second vision that he receives his specific commission to Jews and Gentiles (Acts 22:17–21). The third account of Paul's commission in Acts 26 condenses the various stages of the previous narratives into a single speech from Jesus himself. Here the stated purpose of his vision is to be Jesus's agent and witness, both to Paul's current vision of Jesus, as well as to future visions he will have (ὧν τε εἶδές με ὧν τε ὀφθήσομαί σοι).[73]

In the Greek world epiphanies also often led to the ability to know and communicate special divine information. The paradigmatic example is from Hesiod's *Theogony* (22–34). Hesiod says he was taught (ἐδίδαξαν) beautiful song by the Muses, whom he encountered whilst pasturing lambs under Helicon.[74] They breathed a divine voice into him (ἐνέπνευσαν δέ μοι αὐδὴν θέσπιν) so

---

[72] Cf. Amos's symbolic visions which feature Yahweh as a character in the visions, 7:1–9. Visions of Yahweh seem part of the normal process of revelation for Amos as in 1:1; 9:1. On prophetic call narratives, see Burke O. Long, "Prophetic Call Traditions and Reports of Visions," *ZAW* 84 (1972): 494–500; Elizabeth R. Hayes, "The Role of Visionary Experiences for Establishing Prophetic Authority in Isaiah, Jeremiah and Ezekiel: Same, Similar, or Different?" in *'I Lifted my Eyes and Saw': Reading Dream and Vision Reports in the Hebrew Bible*, ed. Elizabeth R. Hayes and Lena-Sofia Tiemeyer, LHBOTS 584 (London: T&T Clark, 2014), 59–70.

[73] The accusative με is missing from 𝔓74, ℵ, A, E, and others, in which case the reference would be to visions in general, rather than specifically visions of Jesus. The textual evidence is very balanced and it is hard to make a decision either way, see Bruce M. Metzger, *A Textual Commentary on the Greek New Testament*, 2nd ed. (Stuttgart: Deutsche Bibelgesellschaft, 1994), 438. In either case the text expects Paul's vision of Jesus to be the first of many visionary experiences, the contents of which he has a duty to communicate to others.

[74] There is some debate over the nature of the epiphany narrated here. E. R. Dodds (*Greeks and the Irrational*, 117 n. 86) argues that Hesiod nowhere claims to have seen the Muses, but only to have heard their voices. This depends to some extent on a textual variant. Instead of reading δρέψασαι in v. 31, Dodds prefers some MSS that read δρέψασθαι. The former reading would imply the corporeal presence of the Muses as they pluck a branch of laurel themselves. The latter, understood as "they granted me to pluck for myself," might allow for a more elusive presence.

that he might glorify both past and future events in song and sing about the gods. These songs were more than just artistic accomplishments, they were also sources of divine knowledge. Herodotus would later claim all Greek knowledge of their pantheon ultimately went back to Hesiod and Homer (Herodotus 2.53). This scene became the archetype for understanding and narrating most poetic commissions. Pindar, for example, is said to have started writing poetry after experiencing a bees epiphany, bees being an epiphanic metonym for the Muses. He then enjoyed subsequent encounters with various gods commissioning works from him.[75]

Poetry and prophecy were closely linked, as both were generally thought to be divinely inspired. The link between divine epiphany and the gift of divination, however, was surprisingly not exploited as much in Greek culture as that between epiphany and poetry. Teiresias, for example, was blinded when he witnessed Athena bathing, but was granted the gift of augury as a concession owing to Athena's friendship with his mother (Callimachus, *Hymn* 5.70–130). Divination follows epiphany, but it appears as an unrelated concession to the true consequence of seeing Athena, which is blindness (*Hymn* 5.105–20).[76] Such examples show that the gods often granted divinatory abilities as a gift, which mirrors Paul's recognition that it was only by God's favour (χάρις) that he was granted his vision.[77] They do not, however, attest a particularly strong link between visions of a god and a subsequent social role as a seer. As Eyl puts it, "Paul's claim to have seen a resurrected god does not specifically identify him as a divinatory specialist, so much as it renders his divinatory authority inviolable."[78]

Content and Interpretation

If Paul's vision of Jesus granted him authority to proclaim a message, it did so by providing him with the content of that message as well. It was through his

---

[75] Petridou, *Divine Epiphany*, 222–23.
[76] Similar problems exist with most of the examples cited by Petridou (*Divine Epiphany*, 214–16), which present a common constellation of poetry, blindness, divination, and epiphany, but no direct line between epiphany and divination. Epiphany, temporary blindness, and prophecy are all present in the accounts of Paul's commission in Acts 9:1–19 and Acts 22:6–16 (the prophetic element is more pronounced in Acts 22). Here the blindness and prophetic powers are both linked to the epiphany, but are not directly related to each other.
[77] Paul's state at the time of his commission can be contrasted with Plutarch who maintains the gods only choose to hold audiences with "men of superlative goodness" who are "wise and holy" (*Numa* 4). For different ways of configuring divine "gifts," see John M. G. Barclay, *Paul and the Gift* (Grand Rapids: Eerdmans, 2015).
[78] Eyl, *Signs, Wonders, and Gifts*, 148.

revelation, Paul says, that he received the "good news that is proclaimed by me" (τὸ εὐαγγέλιον τὸ εὐαγγελισθεν, Gal 1:11). In this sense Paul's vision was understood not just as a necessary prelude to future divinatory acts, but as divinatory in and of itself. We have already seen how this is the case in 1 Cor 15:1–8. Galatians adds to, and somewhat complicates, this picture by its particular focus on Paul's mission to Gentiles, and the issues of Gentile circumcision and Torah obedience. Gentile circumcision represents a "different good news" (Gal 1:6), and when Peter withdrew from table fellowship with Gentiles in Antioch he was "not walking straight with the truth of the good news" (Gal 2:14). From Galatians alone, the message that Paul received would seem to be directly related to the terms of Gentile acceptance by God and the community.

When scholars assess this discrepancy, they generally take the commission to the Gentiles, and Paul's particular views about Gentile inclusion, to be a later interpretation which follows from an initial vision of a resurrected Christ. The dots are joined in different ways – the interpretation may follow immediately from a chain of logical inferences,[79] or develop more slowly after the practical experience of evangelising Gentiles[80] – but Paul's initial vision itself did not explicitly communicate a commission to the Gentiles.[81] Joshua Garroway has recently attempted to overcome this discrepancy by positing two separate revelations within Gal 1 itself: one in which *Christ* was revealed to Paul (Gal 1:15–16), and a second in which *"the gospel"* was revealed to him (Gal 1:11–12).[82] "The gospel" for Garroway refers specifically to the message of salvation without the law, which was unique to Paul in contrast to the more general preaching of the resurrected Christ which was common to all the apostles. This is an attractive solution but unconvincing in its details. His thesis founders on the fact that Paul introduces the events of 1 Cor 15:3–5 as τὸ εὐαγγέλιον ὃ εὐηγγελισάμην, "the gospel that I proclaimed." For Garroway, this is "one part of the gospel," but not "the aspect

---

[79] Seyoon Kim, *The Origin of Paul's Gospel*, WUNT 2/4 (Tübingen: Mohr Siebeck, 1984); Seyoon Kim, *Paul and the New Perspective: Second Thoughts on the Origin of Paul's Gospel* (Grand Rapids: Eerdmans, 2002); F. F. Bruce, *The Epistle to the Galatians*, NIGTC (Grand Rapids: Eerdmans, 1982), 89, 93.

[80] Albert Schweitzer, *The Mysticism of Paul the Apostle*, trans. William Montgomery, 2nd ed. (London: Black, 1953; repr. Baltimore: Johns Hopkins University Press, 1998), 181; Paula Fredriksen, "Paul and Augustine: Conversion Narratives, Orthodox Traditions, and the Retrospective Self," *JTS* 37 (1986): 3–34. Somewhere between these two positions are James D. G. Dunn, "'A Light to the Gentiles', or 'The End of the Law'? The Significance of the Damascus Road Christophany for Paul," in *Jesus, Paul, and the Law: Studies in Mark and Galatians* (London: SPCK, 1990), 100; Terence L. Donaldson, *Paul and the Gentiles: Remapping the Apostle's Convictional World* (Minneapolis: Fortress, 1997), 82.

[81] Hurtado ("Revelatory Experiences," 476) is agnostic about whether the call to the Gentiles was part of Paul's initial experience or not, but calls it "another major revelatory component."

[82] Garroway, *Beginning of the Gospel*, 52–58.

of the gospel that distinguished it from other preaching."[83] But if the distinguishing aspect of the gospel (the thing that makes it "the gospel") is specifically a law-free salvation, then it seems incredible that Paul could give any précis of the gospel that does not include this aspect. For Garroway's thesis Paul should have no reason to call what he narrates in 1 Cor 15:3–5 "the gospel" at all. Once this restrictive definition of the gospel breaks down, there is no convincing exegetical reason to separate out the revelation of Gal 1:11–12 from that of Gal 1:15–16.

Since we cannot recover Paul's experience itself, we must remain at the culturally conditioned level of interpretation and narration, and here I have already argued that there would be no barrier to an initial vision also including further messages and instructions, indeed it would be expected. While Garroway's thesis does not stand up to scrutiny, there is also nothing inherently implausible about the idea that Paul learnt multiple things over the course of multiple visions, or that he may have sought further visions to interpret and clarify earlier visions. This is in fact the picture that Acts paints, in which his initial vision on the Damascus road only tells him to enter the city, and the implications and interpretations of this initial vision are worked out by means of further visions both to himself and to others (Acts 9:1–19; 22:17–21).

The Interpretation of Dreams and Visions

Symbolic dreams or visions have the most obvious need for interpretation, since epiphany visions – at least in the form they are usually narrated – are more straightforward and explicit. Artemidorus in his book on dream interpretation purposefully omits any explanation of epiphanies (what he calls ὅραμα and χρηματισμός dreams) since he believes these to be self-explanatory, and focuses instead on interpreting the more symbolic aspects of dreams.[84] This can include dreams in which gods or heroes appear but do not speak. Instead they signify something by their appearance. For example, a hero or heroine seen looking small and downcast signifies that they are not receiving the worship or honour that they are due (Artemidorus 4.71–79).[85] Artemidorus also acknowledges, however, that the gods can speak enigmatically (αἰνίσσονται), so that even the plain speech of the god in a vision should not always be taken at face value, but requires some interpretation (Artemidorus 4.71).[86]

---

[83] Garroway, *Beginning of the Gospel*, 29–30.
[84] Gil H. Renberg, "The Role of Dream-Interpreters in Greek and Roman Religion," in *Artemidor von Daldis und die antike Traumdeutung: Texte – Kontexte – Lektüren*, ed. Gregor Weber, Colloquia Augustana 33 (Berlin: de Gruyter, 2015), 252.
[85] See commentary in Daniel E. Harris-McCoy, *Artemidorus' Oneirocritica: Text, Translation and Commentary* (Oxford: Oxford University Press, 2012), 486–92.
[86] Artemidorus includes one dream that would seem to fulfil this category (5.89).

Paul responds to the possibility that he may have sought an interpretation when he says he did not immediately consult (προσανεθέμην) any human authorities, including the other apostles, after his vision (Gal 1:16–17). The verb προσανεθέμην in this context implies the consultation of a specialist regarding the interpretation of divinatory phenomena.[87] The Stoic Chrysippus tells a story of a man who consults a dream interpreter with this same word (προσαναθέσθαι ὀνειροκρίτῃ [*SVF* 1202]).[88] Diodorus Siculus also relates the story of how an imprisoned native managed to escape his bonds and enter the palace of Alexander the Great. He put on Alexander's robes and diadem and sat on his throne. This was unusual enough to be understood as an omen (σημεῖον), so Alexander consulted (προσαναθέμενος) his seers in search of an interpretation (Diodorus Siculus 17.116). To this we could also possibly add Philodemus, writing in the first century BCE, who describes a self-willed man as "one who does not consult with anyone (οἷος μηδενὶ προσαναθέμενος) about going abroad, about buying or selling, about starting something or bringing other matters to completion."[89] This does not explicitly mention divination, but the topics of inquiry here are exactly the topics oracles were used to dealing with.

Dream-interpreters are well attested as a specific sub-group of divinatory specialists. It is only in Graeco-Egyptian cults, such as the cult of Sarapis in Athens or on Delos, that dream-interpreters appear to have had an official role in the cult hierarchy, but independent or freelance diviners with no official affiliation would also have been readily available to offer their own interpretations, normally for a fee.[90] Dream interpretation was also not opposed by Jewish sensibilities, as the biblical precedents of Joseph and Daniel attest. Josephus describes himself as an interpreter of dreams and one who is "skilled in divining the meaning of ambiguous utterances of the deity" (Josephus, *B.J.* 3.352). On a different social level, Juvenal also mocks Jews who, he says, "will sell you whatever dreams you like for the tiniest coin" (Juvenal, *Sat.* 6.542–47).

In claiming not to have consulted flesh and blood, Paul is saying he has not referred his vision to anyone for interpretation, specialist or otherwise. This

---

[87] James D. G. Dunn, "The Relationship Between Paul and Jerusalem According to Galatians 1 and 2," in *Jesus, Paul and the Law*, 109–110. Lightfoot (*Galatians*, 83) noted the use of this word in a divinatory context, but took it as only indirectly illustrating Paul's usage.

[88] The next line also refers to the dream interpreter as a μάντις. The lexicon the fragment is taken from locates the story in his book "On Oracles" although Cicero attributes the same story to "On Dreams" (*Div.* 2.134).

[89] Cited in Dunn, "Paul and Jerusalem," 109.

[90] Renberg, "Role of Dream-Interpreters," 240–46; Derek S. Dodson, *Reading Dreams: An Audience-Critical Approach to the Dreams in the Gospel of Matthew*, LNTS 397 (London: T&T Clark, 2009), 36–42. For the referral of dreams to divinatory specialists, see Plutarch, *Alex.* 2.3; Cicero, *Div.* 1.22.

could be because his vision was direct and explicit enough not to require any interpretation,[91] or at least that he had managed to interpret it for himself after some thought and reflection.

Dream Oracles in Arabia?

Paul's subsequent reference to Arabia in Gal 1:17 presents another option for how he interpreted his vision. Scholars have typically understood this enigmatic reference to refer to a period of either solitary reflection or of Gentile evangelism.[92] The latter view is the most popular – by going to the Gentile territory of Arabia he immediately put into action the commission he was given and began proclaiming his good news to Gentiles, before any interaction with the Jerusalem apostles. J. B. Lightfoot, and later N. T. Wright, have interpreted Arabia more specifically to imply Mount Sinai. As Wright notes, "The word 'Arabia' is very imprecise in Paul's day, covering the enormous area to the south and east of Palestine; but one thing we know for sure is that, for Paul, 'Arabia' was the location of Mount Sinai."[93] This is because, outside of Gal 1:17, Paul's only other use of the word Ἀραβία is to clarify the location of Mount Sinai in Gal 4:25: "now Hagar is Mount Sinai in Arabia."[94] In this explicit mention of Sinai, it serves as the negative side of Paul's allegory, which represents slavery. It is "according to the flesh" and corresponds to the present day Jerusalem. Such a negative characterisation led Lightfoot to interpret the Arabia reference in Gal 1:17 as part of Paul's negative re-evaluation of the law:

> Standing on the threshold of the new covenant, he was anxious to look upon the birthplace of the old: that dwelling for a while in seclusion in the presence of 'the mount that burned with fire,' he might ponder

---

[91] This is the position of Dunn ("Paul and Jerusalem," 110) and Michael Wolter (*Paul: An Outline of his Theology*, trans. Robert L. Brawley [Waco, TX: Baylor University Press, 2015], 26).

[92] Solitary reflection: Lightfoot, *Galatians*, 88–89; Ernest de Witt Burton, *A Critical and Exegetical Commentary on the Epistle to the Galatians*, ICC (Edinburgh: T&T Clark, 1921), 55; Richard N. Longenecker, *Galatians*, WBC 41 (Dallas: Word, 1990), 34. Gentile evangelism: Jerome Murphy-O'Connor, "Paul in Arabia," *CBQ* 55 (1993): 732–37; F. F. Bruce, *Paul: Apostle of the Free Spirit* (Exeter: Paternoster, 1977), 81–82; Betz, *Galatians*, 74; Martin Hengel, "Paul in Arabia," *BBR* 12 (2002): 47–66.

[93] N. T. Wright, "Paul, Arabia and Elijah (Galatians 1:17)," *JBL* 115 (1996): 686. On the territory of Arabia in Paul's time, see Betz, *Galatians*, 73–74.

[94] The readings of 𝔓46 and ℵ are even more emphatic, "for/now Sinai is a mountain in Arabia." I favour the NA28 reading as the *lectio difficilior*. Lightfoot's argument in favour of ℵ is not implausible (*Galatians*, 192–93), however superior attestation makes an original δέ more likely than γάρ (Metzger, *Textual Commentary*, 527).

over the transient glories of the 'ministration of death,' and apprehend its real purpose in relation to the more glorious covenant which was now to supplant it.⁹⁵

Wright, however, draws on the parallels between Paul's experience and that of Elijah in 1 Kings 19. Both Paul and Elijah describe themselves as zealous persecutors of those they saw as God's enemies (Gal 1:13–14; 1 Kings 19:14). Then at a time when this zeal had seemed to fail them in some way, they both travel to Sinai (or Arabia as Paul has it: Gal 1:17; 1 Kings 19:8), and then both return specifically to Damascus (Gal 1:17; 1 Kings 19:15). Elijah returns with the commission from God to anoint two new kings over Aram and Israel, as well as a prophetic successor for himself. Paul returns with the commission to proclaim a different anointed one.⁹⁶ In this context, Paul could be seen as following the model of his prophetic successor Elijah in going to Sinai to seek an audience with God. The motive for this audience, Wright suggests, would be either to resign his previous role as zealous persecutor or, as Wright thinks more likely, to complain of his new commission, according to the model of Moses, Jeremiah, and others.⁹⁷

Another option which Wright does not consider is that Paul would seek clarification and interpretation of his vision.⁹⁸ This arises most naturally from the syntax of vv. 16–17, as the action of travelling to Arabia contrasts not just the alternative possibility of travel to Jerusalem, but also the possibility of consulting (προσανεθέμην) "flesh and blood." "Flesh and blood" represent what is mortal and perishable, in contrast with "beings of a higher order, especially with God" (1 Cor 15:50; cf. Sir 14:18; 17:31; Eph 6:12; Matt 16:17).⁹⁹ We may extend the implications of Paul's language then by paraphrasing: "I did not consult with flesh and blood, nor did I go up to Jerusalem . . . but I went to Arabia (to consult with God)."¹⁰⁰

There are numerous examples in the ancient world of people going to oracles or otherwise inquiring directly of a god for clarification or interpretation of their visions. In Plutarch's *Life of Alexander*, Alexander's father Philip has a dream that he seals his wife's womb with a seal bearing the image of a lion. This dream receives interpretation from the seers, but later when he

---

⁹⁵ Lightfoot, *Galatians*, 88–89.
⁹⁶ Wright, "Paul, Arabia and Elijah," 685–87.
⁹⁷ Wright, "Paul, Arabia and Elijah," 687.
⁹⁸ This is suggested fleetingly by Tobias Nicklas, who follows Wright in seeing a journey to Sinai, Nicklas, "Paulus – der Apostel als Prophet," 83.
⁹⁹ Burton, *Galatians*, 54.
¹⁰⁰ This is essentially how Burton reads it, but he does not see the "communion with God" that Paul sought to be at Sinai, but rather in solitude in the wilderness, Burton, *Galatians*, 55.

believes he has seen an apparition (φάσμα) of Zeus, in the form of a snake, lying down next to his wife in bed, he sends an emissary to Delphi to inquire the meaning of this vision (Plutarch, *Alex.* 2.2–3.2). Aelius Aristides in his many dreams and waking visions of Asclepius that he records, on occasion asks Asclepius to clarify the meaning of a previous dream that he had been given (Aelius Aristides, *Or.* 47.55). When Aristeas, whom we discussed earlier, appeared to the Metapontines, they did not immediately obey his request for an altar to Apollo and a statue of himself. Rather, Herodotus writes, they "sent to Delphi to inquire of the god what the vision (τὸ φάσμα) of the man might be" (Herodotus 4.15). Since Aristeas appears to be demanding worship for both Apollo and himself, we may interpret the Metapontines' actions as going back to the source to check whether Apollo agrees with the vision and whether it should be obeyed.[101] Note with this example that they still sought clarification from Apollo, even though the commands in the vision were given in a straightforward manner with no obvious need for decoding. If the dead but resurrected Jesus had also appeared to Paul in such a way as to make him reconsider Jesus's role and nature in relation to God, and commanded action in keeping with this, then similar clarification from God might be sought.

We might ask whether Sinai would be a likely place for Paul to seek such clarification. As a place of revelation Sinai was most readily connected to the past, and the revelation of the law to Moses. If one were to travel anywhere to consult God, Jerusalem may seem like a more likely option for a Jew of Paul's day.[102] That being said, the historical weight of God's revelation at Sinai continued to exert pressure on contemporary apocalyptic visionaries. Bockmuehl notes: "in light of the prior authority and givenness of a written Bible (esp. the Torah), any contemporary claim of additional divine disclosures must of necessity have recourse to Mount Sinai as the unquestioned touchstone and reference point."[103]

Wright's connections with the story of Elijah provide an additional link between Sinai and visionary experiences. We know from Rom 11:2–6 that Paul was aware of the Elijah story and saw it as a previous instance of God's

---

[101] Examples of oracles interpreting visions can be multiplied: Cicero, *Div.* 1.21; Pausanias 7.5.1–3; Plutarch, *Them.* 30.2.

[102] On the (sometimes contested) significance of Sinai/Horeb as a location of God's revelations, see the essays in George John Brooke, Hindy Najman, and Loren T. Stuckenbruck, eds., *The Significance of Sinai: Traditions about Sinai and Divine Revelation in Judaism and Christianity* (Leiden: Brill, 2008). Paul's explicit mentions of Sinai and the revelation of the law to Moses, while not entirely negative, generally serve to devalue the revelation in comparison with Christ, Gal 3:19–20; 4:21–31; 2 Cor 3:7–18.

[103] Bockmuehl, *Revelation and Mystery*, 29.

revelatory activity in dreams and visions at Sinai.¹⁰⁴ Paul calls God's message to Elijah a χρηματισμός, which appears in most translations as "divine reply" (NRSV), "God's reply" (RSV, ESV), or "God's answer" (NIV). Most commentators know better and tend to translate it as "oracle," but even this may be a bit anaemic as the term also often implies a visionary component.

The verb χρηματίζω sometimes describes the functioning of the Delphic oracle (Diodorus Siculus 15.10.2; Plutarch, *Def. orac.* 435c) as well as oracular responses more generally at other sanctuaries (Diodorus Siculus 3.6.2). In the NT the verb is used in the passive voice to refer to messages received in dreams (Matt 2:12, 22) and visions (Acts 10:22), as well as further unspecified divine instructions (Luke 2:26; Heb 8:5; 11:7), the sources of which are variously described as angels, holy *pneuma*, or sometimes by implication God himself.¹⁰⁵ Artemidorus we have already seen includes the noun, χρηματισμός, as one part of his five-fold classification of dreams which, along with ὅραμα and ὄνειρος, have divinatory significance (Artemidorus 1.1–2). He does not elaborate on χρηματισμός dreams, since he deemed it unnecessary, but Macrobius, writing much later, appears to follow the same five-fold system and describes it as a dream in which instruction is received from a god or venerable figure, in the manner of an epiphany or message dream (*Commentary on the Dream of Scipio* 1.3.8).¹⁰⁶ An inscription relates the dedication of a statue of an eagle and an altar in response to the instructions of an oracle delivered in a dream (κατὰ χρηματισμὸν ὀνίρου).¹⁰⁷ This fits well with the way the verb is being used elsewhere in the NT, and makes it probable that this is also how Paul understands and characterises Elijah's encounter with God at Sinai.¹⁰⁸ If this was Elijah's experience, Paul may have reasonably expected a similar one "in the present time" (cf. Rom 11:5).

---

¹⁰⁴ In 1 Kings 19, Elijah is fleeing to Mount Horeb and Yahweh is actually the one to initiate the conversation. In Paul's presentation, however, the episode conforms to the standard oracle-report of a request or petition followed by an oracle.

¹⁰⁵ In Heb 12:25, Moses is also portrayed as the one delivering the divine instructions (τὸν χρηματίζοντα).

¹⁰⁶ Kessels believes the agreement between Artemidorus and Macrobius sufficient to make it "quite certain that they both directly or indirectly made use of the same source," A. H. M. Kessels, "Ancient Systems of Dream-Classification," *Mnemosyne* 22 (1969): 395. Harris-McCoy concedes that Macrobius is the best source of information available for clarifying Artemidorus, but advises caution against simply applying the definitions from one to the other, Harris-McCoy, *Oneirocritica*, 422.

¹⁰⁷ G. H. R. Horsley, "χρηματισμός," *NewDocs* 4 (1987): 176.

¹⁰⁸ Dunn suggests there could have been a tendency in Jewish circles to link this word specifically with revelations given at Sinai, which would strengthen the case being made here. He can only do this, however, by misreading 2 Macc 2:4. The oracle in this text commands Jeremiah to go to Mount Nebo ("where Moses ... had seen the inheritance of God"), not Mount Sinai. Of the two other instances of the noun in Jewish or Christian literature, 1 Clem. 17:5 does refer to a revelation at Sinai, but Prov 31:1 does not, James D. G. Dunn, *Romans 9–16*, WBC 38B (Dallas: Word, 1988), 637.

Summary

Paul's initial vision of Jesus fulfils a number of functions relating to his divinatory calling and abilities. As is the case with many epiphanies in the ancient world, Paul's vision provided him with the conviction that he had been favoured by his God to deliver a particular message on his behalf. It did this primarily by communicating the content of this message itself, that Jesus had been raised to life by this God, and enjoyed a special divine status alongside him. With this revelation come a host of further implications about the resurrection of the dead, the Messianic kingdom and the status of the Gentiles within it. How he drew these implications from the initial vision is not immediately clear, but a comparative study of dreams and visions suggests a range of suitable options. These include explicit commands in the vision itself, further interpretation by Paul, as well as the seeking out of additional guidance and interpretation from God himself through further visions and other divinatory media.

Further Visions and Revelations

I have considered the possibility above that a single vision of Jesus was not sufficient for all of Paul's divinatory needs, but that he continued to seek and be guided by further visions and revelations. This is consistent with the way he is portrayed by Acts, in which multiple dreams and visions guide his whole career. It is also what we see in Paul's letters. In Gal 2:2, Paul mentions in passing another revelation (ἀποκάλυψις), which caused him to go to Jerusalem with Barnabus and Titus. In Phil 3:15, he is confident that God himself will reveal (ἀποκαλύψει) the truth to the Philippians of any matters in which they are currently deficient. These passages do not require these revelations to be visionary, but especially in the case of Gal 2:2, which comes so closely after the similar language of Gal 1:12, 16, we can assume that Paul did not have a drastically different scenario in mind than the revelations he had already related.[109]

Paul explicitly mentions visions in 2 Cor 12:1, in which he says he could boast of multiple ὀπτασίας καὶ ἀποκαλύψεις κυρίου, "visions and revelations

---

[109] De Boer's rereading ("Paul," 29), in which "his visit to Jerusalem functioned as a revelation *to the apostles and the church there* (italics mine), because this visit had granted them new insight into the one and only gospel (1:7) and, thus, into the activity of God in the world," twists Paul's sense completely and imports hosts of unnecessary concepts into a simple sentence. Lührmann (*Offenbarungsverständnis*, 42) reads this passage through Acts 11:30; 15:2, in which Paul is appointed to go to Jerusalem by the Antioch *ekklēsia*, and 1 Cor 14:6, 26, in which an ἀποκάλυψις can be delivered in a congregational setting, to suggest the revelation took the form of a concrete instruction from the Antioch *ekklēsia*. This is a plausible harmonisation, but only serves to shift the experience back from Paul to others.

of the Lord." These two words are not synonymous, but neither are they to be sharply distinguished.[110] An ὀπτασία is a vision, usually of God or an angel (Mal 3:1 LXX; Sir 43:16; Ezek 1:1 [α', σ', θ']; θ' Dan 10:1, 7; Luke 1:22; 24:23; Acts 26:19 [Paul's vision of Jesus]), while ἀποκαλύψις, as we have seen, is a more general term for a divine disclosure.[111] We may think of "visions" here as the form of communication, while "revelations" expresses that these visions also had content to be disclosed.[112] Given the epiphanic nature of an ὀπτασία, the genitive κυρίου, "of the Lord," is most likely objective, as it is in Gal 1:12.[113]

Heavenly Ascent and Unspeakable Revelations (2 Cor 12:1–6)

In this context, Paul relates one particular experience of a man who was caught up (ἁρπαγέντα) to the third heaven, to paradise. There he heard unspeakable words, which were either not possible, or not permitted for humans to speak (ἄρρητα ῥήματα ἃ οὐκ ἐξὸν ἀνθρώπῳ λαλῆσαι, 2 Cor 12:4). Most scholars believe the "man" Paul talks about is himself.[114] The section begins with Paul's own ability to boast of visions and revelations, and by

---

[110] Heininger, *Paulus*, 245–46; cf. Rowland, *Open Heaven*, 380; Buchanan Wallace, *Snatched into Paradise*, 251–53; Segal, *Paul the Convert*, 35–36.

[111] See Michael Goulder, "Vision and Knowledge," *JSNT* 56 (1994): 56. But his conclusion that ὀπτασία should be understood here as "visions of the Throne in heaven" in contrast to ecstatic experiences on earth is unwarranted, and is modified to some extent in his later work, Michael Goulder, "Visions and Revelations of the Lord (2 Corinthians 12:1–10)," in *Paul and the Corinthians: Studies on a Community in Conflict, Essays in Honour of Margaret Thrall*, ed. Trevor J. Burke and J. Keith Elliott, NovTSup 109 (Leiden: Brill, 2003), 308 n. 4.

[112] Paula R. Gooder, *Only the Third Heaven? 2 Corinthians 12:1–10 and Heavenly Ascent*, LNTS 313 (London: T&T Clark, 2006), 109.

[113] Most scholars resist this conclusion as Paul does not specifically mention a vision of Christ in the following verses, but Thrall notes the objective reading would be more consistent with Paul's usage elsewhere, Margaret E. Thrall, *2 Corinthians 8–13*, ICC (London: T&T Clark, 2000), 775. Lincoln understands Christ to be "both giver and content" in Gal 1:12, 16, but this is contradicted by Gal 1:16, in which God is explicitly the revealer, and Christ the revealed, Andrew T. Lincoln, "'Paul the Visionary': The Setting and Significance of the Rapture to Paradise in 2 Corinthians 12:1–10," *NTS* 25 (1979): 205–206. Cf. 1 Cor 12:4–6, in which God is the one who ultimately produces (ἐνεργῶν) pneumatic gifts in people. Goulder maintains the *kyrios* must be God and not Jesus, but this would be highly unusual for Paul, even if it could be demonstrated that he was quoting his opponents, Goulder, "Visions and Revelations," 305–306.

[114] Dissenting views are few and unconvincing: Goulder, "Visions and Revelations," 303–12 (Paul resorts to the experience of a colleague because he himself had no such experiences); Smith, "History," 16 (Paul refers to Jesus, the only person in whom he says he will boast); Hans-Josef Klauck, "With Paul through Heaven and Hell: Two Apocryphal Apocalypses," *BR* 52 (2007): 58 (Paul refers to Apollos).

vv. 6–7 he is again talking about his own abundance of revelations. Even if Paul does refer to someone else in vv. 2–4, he makes clear in v. 6 that he could truthfully tell similar stories about himself.

The description of being caught up to heaven places this experience in the category of "heavenly ascent" which, along with its inverse, "descent to Hades," was a common topos in Jewish and Graeco-Roman sources.[115] Scholars studying this passage have produced plentiful parallels to Paul's experience of heavenly ascent. Many have looked to *merkabah* mysticism and/or Jewish apocalypses as the primary context.[116] But others have noted the broader currency of the theme in the ancient Mediterranean world.[117] The primary point of interest for our purposes is that by Paul's time such visions were increasingly seen as a prominent way of obtaining hidden knowledge from the divine realm and were becoming increasingly associated with traditional methods of divination.

John Barton has argued convincingly that the visions and heavenly journeys associated with "apocalyptic" are nothing other than the standard post-exilic perception of prophecy.[118] This can be seen most clearly by the way the authors of apocalypses describe their own works as "prophecy" (Rev 1:3; 22:7, 10, 18–19; 4 Ezra 1:1–4), and in the way that classical prophets are, in this period, provided with their own apocalypses and heavenly ascents,

---

[115] Alan F. Segal, "Heavenly Ascent in Hellenistic Judaism, Early Christianity and their Environment," *ANRW* 23.1:1333–94; Martha Himmelfarb, *Tours of Hell: An Apocalyptic Form in Jewish and Christian Literature* (Philadelphia: University of Pennsylvania Press, 1983); Martha Himmelfarb, *Ascent to Heaven in Jewish and Christian Apocalypses* (Oxford: Oxford University Press, 1993); Adela Yarbro Collins, "Ascents to Heaven in Antiquity: Toward a Typology," in *A Teacher for All Generations: Essays in Honour of James C. VanderKam*, ed. Eric F. Mason, JSJSup 153 (Leiden: Brill, 2012), 2:553–72; Jan N. Bremmer, "Descents to Hell and Ascents to Heaven in Apocalyptic Literature," in Collins, *Oxford Handbook of Apocalyptic Literature*, 340–57.

[116] Gershom G. Scholem, *Jewish Gnosticism, Merkabah Mysticism, and Talmudic Tradition* (New York: Jewish Theological Seminary of America, 1965); Segal, *Paul the Convert*, 34–58; Christopher R. A. Morray-Jones, "Paradise Revisited (2 Cor 12:1–12): The Jewish Mystical Background of Paul's Apostolate. Part 2: Paul's Heavenly Ascent and its Significance," *HTR* 86 (1993): 265–92; Gooder, *Only the Third Heaven?*; Peter Schäfer is more sceptical of the link with *merkabah*, "New Testament and Hekhalot Literature: The Journey into Heaven in Paul and Merkavah Mysticism," *JJS* 35 (1984): 19–35.

[117] Buchanan Wallace, *Snatched into Paradise*; James D. Tabor, *Things Unutterable: Paul's Ascent to Paradise in its Greco-Roman, Judaic, and Early Christian Contexts* (Lanham, MD: University Press of America, 1986); Adriana Desto and Mauro Pesce, "The Heavenly Journey in Paul: Tradition of a Jewish Apocalyptic Literary Genre or Cultural Practice in a Hellenistic-Roman Context?" in *Paul's Jewish Matrix*, ed. Thomas G. Casey and Justin Taylor (Rome: Gregorian & Biblical Press, 2011), 167–200.

[118] John Barton, *Oracles of God: Perceptions of Ancient Prophecy in Israel After the Exile*, 2nd ed. (London: Darton, Longman & Todd, 2007), 122–24. Cf. Hindy Najman, "The Inheritance of Prophecy in Apocalypse," in Collins, *Oxford Handbook of Apocalyptic Literature*, 36–48.

such as in the *Ascension of Isaiah*. On the Greek and Roman side, Struck has also pointed to a newly forged link between otherworldly journeys and divination by the first century BCE. In Cicero's *Dream of Scipio*, for example, the titular character's deceased grandfather leads him on a tour of the cosmos, where he learns all about its structure as well as the place of the earth and human beings within it. He also learns truths about the composition of the human person and the nature of the soul (Cicero, *Rep.* 6.9.10–29). Cicero's most prominent literary predecessor is Plato's myth of Er. This myth includes similar revelatory insights, but Plato portrays them as the results of a near death experience rather than divination. Cicero, on the other hand, portrays such a journey as specifically enabled by a divinatory dream.[119] The same can be said of Aeneas's journey to the underworld in book 6 of Virgil's *Aeneid*. Here Aeneas learns the fate of souls and gains insights into the broad scope of human history by means of an oracular consultation with the Cumaen Sibyl, who in many ways is modelled on the Pythia of Delphi. It is she who facilitates the journey and guides Aeneas on his tour. Plutarch's myth of Timarchus, in which his soul is transported to various parts of the cosmos where he learns the nature and fate of souls, is also occasioned by a visit to the oracle of Trophonius (Plutarch, *Gen. Socr.* 589f–592e).[120]

These are literary tropes, employed by their authors for various ends in epic poetry and at the end of philosophical works.[121] As such they attest more to cultural expectations of divination and otherworldly journeys than they do to actual practice.[122] Even if cultural expectation is all that can be securely recovered, this is still significant as it affects how Paul's audience would have received such claims from him, and indeed how Paul himself understood such claims. These visions and journeys typically impart knowledge concerning fundamental philosophical questions such as the structure of the universe, the nature of human beings and the meaning of life.

---

[119] Struck, *Divination and Human Nature*, 219–21.

[120] Adela Yarbro Collins ("Ascents to Heaven," 570) includes this story as an example of a "journey of the soul after death," even though it quite clearly takes place in the context of an oracle, and for the purpose of receiving information on a specific matter.

[121] Hans Dieter Betz, "The Problem of Apocalyptic Genre in Greek and Hellenistic Literature: The Case of the Oracle of Trophonius," in Hellholm, *Apocalypticism in the Mediterranean World*, 577–97.

[122] The oracle of Trophonius was a functioning oracle which Pausanias claims to have consulted (Pausanias 9.39). By his account inquirers sometimes received their information by sight and sometimes by hearing, so visions can be plausibly associated with this oracle. The nature of the information is only described as τὰ μέλλοντα, "the future," which does not particularly distinguish the information gained at this oracle from any other. Philostratus had Apollonius of Tyana consult the oracle in which the topic of consultation appears to have been the finer points of Pythagorean philosophy (*Life of Apollonius* 4.24; 8.19), see Iles Johnston, *Ancient Greek Divination*, 95–97.

Paul fails to relate any of this information in 2 Cor 12, but instead speaks only of "unutterable words, which it is not permitted for a person to speak" (ἄρρητα ῥήματα ἃ οὐκ ἐξὸν ἀνθρώπῳ λαλῆσαι). Many scholars take Paul to be subverting his audience's expectations here and parodying the genre of ascent in support of a broader point about the respective worth of visionary experiences.[123] The revelation he boasts of in fact reveals nothing. But this misreads the place of vv. 2–4 within the rhetorical context of 2 Cor 11–12. Here in the "fool's speech" Paul oscillates between "madly" matching the boasts of his competitors (11:21–29),[124] and then insisting that he will only truly boast in things that show his weakness (11:30–33).[125] At 12:1 he is back to outdoing the boasts of his opponents and presents a remarkable experience of visionary revelation. The corresponding weakness will come with his thorn in the flesh in v. 7, but there is nothing particularly ironic about the account of the ascent itself, which is calculated to impress.[126] Whether the "unutterable words" are inexpressible[127] or forbidden[128] is not particularly important, as the main point is their superlative value (cf. v. 7). Paul has heard things that are too great and too sacred to be communicated. This may be a source of frustration for his listeners as they would want to hear these revelations, but it would be a frustration that would only bolster their opinion of him not diminish it, as he has been privileged to receive this revelation that has been blocked to others.

---

[123] Hans Dieter Betz, *Der Apostel Paulus und die sokratische Tradition*, BHT 45 (Tübingen: Mohr Siebeck, 1972), 72–95. Most authors do not read the passage as a conscious parody, but do think Paul subverts expectations and in these subversions portrays a distinctive attitude towards visionary experiences, Lührmann, *Offenbarungsverständnis*, 58; Lincoln, "Paul the Visionary," 209–210, 216; Heininger, *Paulus*, 248–49; Gooder, *Only the Third Heaven?*, 192–95, 209–211; Joseph R. Dodson, "The Transcendence of Death and Heavenly Ascent in the Apocalyptic Paul and the Stoics," in Blackwell, Goodrich, and Maston, *Paul and the Apocalyptic Imagination*, 169–71.

[124] I take the catalogue of hardships to demonstrate his superiority as a servant of Christ rather than as a show of weakness. Cf. Murray J. Harris, *The Second Epistle to the Corinthians*, NIGTC (Grand Rapids: Eerdmans, 2005), 816 n. 2.

[125] How one judges the sincerity of Paul's rhetoric on boasting is ultimately in the eye of the beholder. Rollens ("The God Came to Me," 58) labels it "carefully subdued conceit," which "contains just enough play to allow him to feign appropriate humility." E. P. Sanders (*Paul: The Apostle's Life, Letters, and Thought* [Minneapolis: Fortress, 2015], 251–56) recognises how it both bolsters Paul's authority and also connects to an important theme in his broader theology in which God acts through human weakness and foolishness.

[126] Rollens, "The God Came to Me," 57–58.

[127] Such as angelic languages: John C. Poirier, *The Tongues of Angels: The Concept of Angelic Languages in Classical Jewish and Christian Texts*, WUNT 2/287 (Tübingen: Mohr Siebeck, 2010), 59–63.

[128] Lincoln, "Paul the Visionary," 216; Russell P. Spittler, "The Limits of Ecstasy: An Exegesis of 2 Corinthians 12:1–10," in *Current Issues in Biblical and Patristic Interpretation: Studies in Honor of Merrill C. Tenney Presented by his Former Students*, ed. Gerald F. Hawthorne (Grand Rapids: Eerdmans, 1975), 263–64.

Nothing in the passage suggests that the unutterable words were all he heard or saw. Margaret Thrall notes that he must have at least had a vision of "paradise" for him to recognise it as such, and she thinks it likely that a vision of Christ in paradise can also be assumed.[129] Given that Paul has already set the context for this account as "visions and revelations of the Lord," I would concur that Paul's audience would likely have surmised the same. In the context of Paul's boasting, he is merely being selective about the most impressive elements of his experience before passing on to speak of his weakness. The main effect of this section is to create the impression that Paul knows, and has experienced, much more of the divine realm than he can or will ever communicate. This in turn invests the divine knowledge that he does communicate with extra reliability and authority.

In a rhetorical context such as 2 Cor 11–12 there is a sense in which, "the content of Paul's secrets and mysteries is less important than the function of secrecy itself,"[130] as this secrecy helps to elevate Paul's boast. We can push further than this though, by noting the cultural expectations that were attached to the sort of knowledge gained through otherworldly journeys. If his hearers were expecting secrets of the cosmos along with the eschatological fate of human beings and human history in general, then we can see that elsewhere Paul does not hold back in offering such information, not least when he reveals mysteries and words of the Lord in Rom 11:25; 1 Cor 15:51, and 1 Thess 4:15.[131] This suggests that far from a failed ascent, which is of no public use to anyone, such visionary experiences can be seen to provide much of the more expansive and revelatory insights in Paul's divinatory repertoire, even if he does not provide them in this passage.[132]

---

[129] Thrall, *2 Corinthians 8–13*, 797.

[130] Eyl, *Signs, Wonders, and Gifts*, 154.

[131] Rowland, *Open Heaven*, 383. Origen, in a fragment from his *Commentary on Genesis*, quotes Paul's "ineffable words" in the context of astrological and cosmological knowledge concerning "solstices, the alternation of the seasons, year cycles, and the positions of the stars." In his *Homilies on Joshua* he suggests that the knowledge was unable to be spoken to "man" because they could not receive it in their sinful state. But close colleagues such as Timothy and Luke were able to hear and understand this knowledge. See texts cited in Riemer Roukema, "Paul's Rapture to Paradise in Early Christian Literature," in *The Wisdom of Egypt: Jewish, Early Christian, and Gnostic Essays in Honour of Gerard P. Luttikhuizen*, ed. Anthony Hilhorst and George H. van Kooten, AGJU 59 (Leiden: Brill, 2005), 275–77.

[132] Bousset also suggested Paul can speak of the "heavenly dwellings" in 2 Cor 5:1 because of his experience of ascent, Wilhelm Bousset, "Die Himmelsreise der Seele," *AR* 4 (1901): 149. Dodson ("Transcendence of Death," 170) contrasts 2 Cor 12:1–10 and the mysteries usually revealed through heavenly ascent with 1 Cor 2:6–16, in which "the apostle's churches already understand these mysteries because they have the Spirit of God and the mind of Christ." As we saw in Chapter 1, however, Paul presents this as an idealised state, which the Corinthians were currently not attaining because of their fleshly desires. If Paul truly thought his communities all enjoyed constant and unhindered access to the mind of Christ, then one wonders why he would ever need to reveal such eschatological mysteries at strategic points throughout his letters.

Weakness and Healing Oracles (2 Cor 12:7–10)

Frances Flannery notes three functions of divinely sent dreams and visions which remained constant throughout the ancient Near East and the Mediterranean. Two of these have already been extensively discussed: to "convey divine sanction," and to "impart extraordinary knowledge."[133] The third is to "dispense healing," and this is precisely the context of the oracle Paul receives in vv. 7–9 when he turns to boast in his weakness. Paul says he was given a "thorn in the flesh," which he also identifies as an "angel of Satan," so that he should not "exalt" himself. The need for this thorn in the flesh, given in response to Paul's excess, or superiority of revelations (τῇ ὑπερβολῇ τῶν ἀποκαλύψεων), should be proof enough that Paul did not consider anything to be deficient with the exemplary revelatory experience of vv. 2–4.[134] The precise nature of this "thorn" is impossible to discern, but Paul evidently experienced it as a physical impediment of some sort, which he thrice pleaded (παρεκάλεσα) with "the Lord" to remove.

Turning to a god for healing is of course a common practice in both the ancient and modern world, especially when faced with chronic illnesses that medical professionals have failed to cure. In the ancient Mediterranean this was particularly associated with the incubation shrines of gods such as Asclepius, Sarapis, and Isis.[135] Here, the sick would come and sleep at the sanctuary with the hope of either being healed by means of an epiphany in their sleep, or receiving instruction for their healing from the god in a dream.[136] We do not know exactly how Paul solicited his healing. The verb παρακαλεῖν could simply mean "beseech," but when the object is a god it suggests "invoke" or "call to one's aid" and was used by those attending incubation shrines. Adolf Deissmann cites a particularly close parallel from a marble stele, which records a healing at the shrine of Asclepius at Epidaurus: "And concerning this thing I besought (παρεκάλεσα) the god."[137] Given Jesus's reputation as a healer, it may be significant that Paul addresses his prayer specifically to him (τὸν κύριον), although Paul does not reference this reputation elsewhere.[138] Dream oracles in general were usually associated with chthonic gods and divinised prophets

---

[133] Flannery, "Dreams and Visions," 107.
[134] Against the NA28 punctuation, I take v. 7a to be syntactically connected to v. 7b rather than v. 6. For discussion, see Thrall, *2 Corinthians 8–13*, 805.
[135] Renberg, *Where Dreams May Come*, 22; Matthew Dillon, *Omens and Oracles: Divination in Ancient Greece* (London: Routledge, 2017), 286–89.
[136] Renberg (*Where Dreams May Come*, 21–30) sharply distinguishes "therapeutic" incubation, in which healing is sought, from "divinatory" incubation, in which advice on any range of matters is sought. These categories would appear to blur though when the dreamer receives advice on how to obtain healing as is often the case.
[137] Deissmann, *Light from the Ancient East*, 310–11. Cf. BDAG, s.v. "παρακαλέω"; LSJ, s.v. "παρακαλέω".
[138] Thrall, *2 Corinthians 8–13*, 820.

or heroes rather than the Olympian gods.[139] Paul too, never claims to see God himself in a dream or vision, but rather the resurrected divine man Jesus. The combination of Paul's request for healing followed by an oracle certainly evokes the context of therapeutic dreams and visions.[140]

Compared with the superlative and unspeakable revelations of vv. 2–4, such a divinatory encounter in the context of healing certainly better illustrates Paul's weakness and dependence on Christ. Especially as the only prescription the oracle provides is to be content with Christ's favour (χάρις), "for power is perfected in weakness" (v. 9). The refusal of a physical cure need not be read as an ironic parody of a healing story. Oracles could often refuse the premise of the questions they were asked. One is less likely to publicise the refusal of healing so there are fewer surviving examples of this, but this is exactly Paul's point. The parallel examples we do have illustrate the differences in Paul's attitude towards this oracle. Aune points to an episode in which Asclepius appears to Aelius Aristides, who "asks three times to save his friend Zosimus." Asclepius refuses the first two requests, but the third time provides the information for a cure (*Or.* 47.71).[141] The eventual granting of the request transforms the story and highlights the value of Aelius Aristides's persistence. Hans Dieter Betz points to Cassius Dio's account of Antoninus who was physically and mentally sick, but was unable to procure healing from any of the healing gods after visiting them in person.[142] No cure is granted in this example, but this only tells Dio that the gods disregarded the offerings of Antoninus and refused healing on account of his wicked deeds. The one oracle he does record is from the soul of the dead Commodus and ominously warns, "Draw nearer judgement, which gods demand of you" (78.15.5). When people tried to publicise this oracle, Dio says they were abusively threatened (ἐπηρεάσθησαν). Paul on the other hand boasts in his oracle, because it does not show God's displeasure with him but his favour, which is manifested through his weakness.

Paul's juxtaposition of a superlative heavenly ascent and a (maybe disappointing) healing oracle perfectly accomplishes the rhetorical tightrope walk he is attempting in this passage without devaluing or parodying visionary experiences as a meaningful method of divination. On the contrary, this passage demonstrates that both the highs and paradoxical lows of Paul's apostolic endeavours are attended by visions of Jesus – and the information gained from them – in ways that are consonant with Paul's ancient context.

---

[139] Renberg, *Where Dreams May Come*, 30–33.
[140] Hans Dieter Betz, "Eine Christus-Aretalogie bei Paulus (2 Kor 12:7–10)," *ZTK* 66 (1969): 288–305; Aune, *Prophecy*, 249.
[141] Aune, *Prophecy*, 423 n. 12.
[142] Betz, "Eine Christus-Aretalogie," 301.

Conclusion

In the ancient world, divinely sent dreams and visions conveyed divine sanction, dispensed healing, and imparted extraordinary knowledge.[143] Paul's letters attest to all three of these functions. His initial vision of a resurrected Jesus conveyed divine sanction for his role as an apostle and messenger on Christ's behalf, and further visions cemented his legitimacy as one, even though he would rather direct attention to Christ's power in his weakness in 2 Cor 12. This passage also shows Paul engaging in the therapeutic use of dreams and visions to obtain healing, although the information received serves to reorient his perspective (on weakness, not on visions). The impartation of extraordinary knowledge is the most pertinent function to this study and is one that can often get lost in scholarly studies that focus on dynamics of power and control. These two functions are indeed inextricably intertwined – divine sanction and authority come through the assumption of extraordinary knowledge – but one should not be made to subsume the other. Rather Paul, like most other people of his time, believed that he received genuinely new insights through visionary experiences, which directed his actions and organised his behaviour. Most pertinent for Paul is the insight that Jesus has been raised, and God's transformation of creation has begun. This forms the basis of Paul's "good news," which leads in turn to a host of other implications and interpretations. Further visions may clarify aspects of this message for Paul, but also, in some exceptional circumstances, provide him with first-hand knowledge of the cosmos and eschatology, some of which he may reveal to his congregations as mysteries, others which he may not.

The study of visionary experiences has focused on the visual apprehension of things usually hidden from the mortal realm. But as this study has shown there was no binary opposition in the ancient world between visual and auditory divination, and visual epiphanies could be expected to also include verbal instruction. This verbal aspect of divination in Paul, which forms the subject of the next chapter, sometimes overlaps with visionary experiences and sometimes stands apart as a separate phenomenon.

---

[143] Flannery, "Dreams and Visions," 107.

CHAPTER 3

Speech

In the previous chapter, I argued that visionary experiences play a key role in Paul's reception of divine knowledge. It also became clear that in the ancient world such visions were not limited to sight alone, but could also convey verbal, oracular instruction. Paul's healing oracle in 2 Cor 12:9 is one such example in which Paul can report the words of the Lord in a context which presupposes a visionary experience. This chapter is concerned with similar instances of Paul reporting divine speech.

Chapter 1 highlighted the prominence of *pneuma*, and "words taught by *pneuma*" (1 Cor 2:13) in Paul's reception of divinatory knowledge. Part one of the present chapter examines the words Paul says are *spoken* by *pneuma*, which, perhaps surprisingly, fail to provide any divinatory knowledge at all. Instead, each time Paul makes *pneuma* the subject of a verb of communication the speech is always directed from humans to God, and is always in a language unintelligible to the speaker. Part two of this chapter turns to the topic of prophecy as the sort of speech that does communicate divinatory knowledge for Paul. This is speech ἐν πνεῦμα, which involves the anthropological partnering of the mind (νοῦς). Paul's letters provide glimpses of his own prophetic speech, and of his oracular role in general, such as when he makes short-term predictions of his own suffering, when he gives commands from the Lord and his own pneumatic judgement on certain topics, and when he provides details of more expansive eschatological scenarios.

The Audible *Pneuma*

Wordless Prayers (Romans 8:26)

In Rom 8:26, Paul says that when believers do not know what to pray the *pneuma* petitions God on their behalf with wordless groans (στεναγμοῖς ἀλαλήτοις). In this way the *pneuma* aids believers in their weakness. God knows the intentions of the *pneuma* because it can petition God in the right way.¹ A στεναγμός is a groan or sigh often used in conjunction with γόος, "weeping" or "wailing," to denote audible sorrow (Sophocles, *Oed. tyr.* 30; Euripides, *Orest.* 959; Plato, *Resp.* 578a). Such sighs could also be used in ritual contexts of prayer and healing in conjunction with other inarticulate words and sounds. Amid a number of spells, a papyrus gives the following instruction:

> (Breathe out, in. Fill up); "EI AI OAI" (pushing more, bellow-howling.) "Come to me, god of gods, AĒŌĒI ĒI IAŌ AE OIŌTK" (Pull in, fill up, / shutting your eyes. Bellow as much as you can, then, sighing (στενάξας), give out [what air remains] in a hiss). (*PGM* XIII.942–946)²

Another papyrus invokes a goddess with a number of sounds that accompany her name, "the first . . . silence, the second a popping sound, the third groaning (στεναγμός), the fourth hissing, / the fifth a cry of joy, the sixth moaning," and so on (*PGM* VII.765–780). In Mark 7:32 Jesus heals a man by, among other things, looking to heaven, giving out a sigh (ἐστέναξεν) and uttering the Aramaic word εφφαθα, which Mark translates as "be opened." That Jesus should speak in Aramaic is unremarkable, but that Mark should quote it in Aramaic (as he also does in the raising of Jairus's daughter [Mark 5:41]) suggests that a Greek speaking audience detected a special divine power at work in the sigh and the unintelligible Aramaic words.³

Both contexts of audible lamentation and ecstatic prayer are relevant to Paul here.⁴ Most importantly, Paul describes the groans as the product of the *pneuma* itself. He places this groaning in the context of the groaning of all creation, which waits for its eschatological redemption. In v. 23 this includes the groaning of believers waiting for the redemption of their mortal bodies, which is also connected with their possession of *pneuma*: "we ourselves, who have the first fruits of the *pneuma*, groan in ourselves (ἐν ἑαυτοῖς στενάζομεν)." The same

---

¹ The phrase κατὰ θεόν may simply mean "before God," as is evidently true in this instance, but probably also carries the sense of "according to God," which mirrors καθὸ δεῖ in v. 26. The believer does not know the proper way or the proper things for which they should pray, but the *pneuma* petitions in a way that is appropriate to God. See James D. G. Dunn, *Romans 1–8*, WBC 38A (Dallas: Word, 1988), 477.
² Translation from Betz, *Greek Magical Papyri*, 193. Text from Karl Preisendanz, ed., *Papyri Graecae Magicae: Die griechischen Zauberpapyri*, 2 vols, 2nd ed. (Stuttgart: Teubner, 1973–1974).
³ Adela Yarbro Collins, *Mark*, Hermeneia (Minneapolis: Fortress, 2007), 371–72; cf. Campbell Bonner, "Traces of Thaumaturgic Technique in the Miracles," *HTR* 20 (1927): 171–74; Martin Dibelius, *From Tradition to Gospel*, trans. Bertram Lee Woolf (Cambridge: James Clarke & Co., 1971), 85–86.
⁴ Smith, "Pauline Worship," 247.

thought (and the same word) appears in 2 Cor 5:1–5, where believers groan (στενάζομεν) for the tents of their mortal bodies to be swallowed up by the life of their heavenly bodies. Paul, again, connects this with their possession of *pneuma*, "given as a deposit" (2 Cor 5:5). This groaning does not materialise in actual words, but it is not meaningless. The presence of the *pneuma* is the firstfruits and guarantee of what is to come, so for Paul the groans are an audible manifestation of immortal *pneuma* in mortal bodies, offering prayers to God through and for the believer.[5]

Prayers in Aramaic (Romans 8:15; Galatians 4:6)

Earlier in the same chapter of Romans this same *pneuma* of adoption (πνεῦμα υἱοθεσίας) inspires the Aramaic prayer ἀββά, to which Paul adds its Greek translation ὁ πατήρ (Rom 8:15). In this verse, it is the believer who utters the cry by means of the *pneuma* (ἐν ᾧ κράζομεν), but in the parallel passage of Gal 4:6 the *pneuma* itself cries out in Aramaic from within the hearts of the believers. Scholars domesticate these passages when they treat the *abba* cry as a liturgical (most often baptismal) formula,[6] or view the utterance as what people are now enabled to say because of the change in relationship effected by the *pneuma*.[7] These interpretations miss the force of both texts in which the *pneuma* does not just provide the conditions in which *abba* may be uttered, but directly causes the utterance itself. The verb κράζω, used in both instances, indicates a loud scream or shriek, signifying intense emotion, which is also at home in ecstatic ritual contexts alongside the groans discussed above. Paul's only other use of the verb introduces the prophetic cry of Isaiah in Rom 9:27, but other sources use it of the cry of daimons or sorcerers.[8] In Rom 8:16 Paul further describes this cry as the *pneuma* bearing witness with (συμμαρτυρεῖ) the *pneuma* of believers that they are children of God. This indicates that the cry is produced by the joining together of divine *pneuma* with human *pneuma*, which

---

[5] This is more than Keener's claim that the *pneuma* "interprets the inner groans of believers for God." Rather, the groans themselves are those of the *pneuma*, Craig S. Keener, *The Mind of the Spirit: Paul's Approach to Transformed Thinking* (Grand Rapids: Baker Academic, 2016), 180.

[6] Martyn, *Galatians*, 392.

[7] This is the impression given by Caroline Johnson Hodge (*If Sons, Then Heirs: A Study of Kinship and Ethnicity in the Letters of Paul* [Oxford: Oxford University Press, 2007], 72) and Paula Fredriksen (*Pagans' Apostle*, 151), in which the role of *pneuma* is restricted to joining Gentiles to Christ, but plays no explicit communicative role. The same is true for Engberg-Pedersen (*Cosmology and Self*, 66–67), for whom the cry "evidently reflects the state of their own pneuma."

[8] For the full range of meaning, see Robert Jewett, *Romans*, Hermeneia (Minneapolis: Fortress, 2007), 498–99. Grundmann notes the magical, ecstatic connotations of the word, but denies them for Paul, Walter Grundmann, "κράζω, κτλ.," *TDNT* 3:898–903.

both cause and verify the words spoken.⁹ James Dunn remarks of this passage, "The sense of inspiration is very strong . . . the consciousness of being moved upon by divine power, of words being given to say."¹⁰

The Aramaic cry may well indicate the language of the one who was thought to be inspiring believers. Since Paul identifies the *pneuma* of adoption that speaks in Rom 8 with the *pneuma* of God's son in the Galatians passage, it makes sense that the cry would be in Jesus's own language.¹¹ This reverses the usual explanation, that the Aramaic cry is preserved from Palestinian liturgical forms, possibly reflecting memories of Jesus's own distinctive forms of prayer (Mark 14:36; Luke 11:2).¹² Rather it is as the inspiring deity that Jesus's use of Aramaic is decisive in this context. Ancient sources often assign gods different languages, sometimes dependent on their ethnicity.¹³ Cicero, in sceptical mode, denies authenticity to a number of oracles passed down in Chrysippus's collection because "Apollo never spoke in Latin" (*Div.* 2.116). Presumably for Cicero the only authentic oracles of Apollo must be given in his own language, which is Greek. Others denied the use of any human language by the gods. Dio Chrysostom asks, "Do you think Apollo speaks Attic or Doric? Or that men and gods have the same language (διάλεκτον)?" (*Serv.* 23; cf. *Troj.* 22).¹⁴ This lack of shared language explains for Dio why people constantly misunderstood oracles, as the meaning is missed and misinterpreted in translation.¹⁵ Clement of Alexandria also cites an otherwise unknown text of Plato to the effect that the gods have their own dialect. He says Plato formed this conjecture "mainly from dreams and oracles, and especially from demoniacs, who do not

---

[9] Exactly how all the various types of *pneuma* are related in Rom 8 is complex. For a good reading that highlights the problems and ambiguities, see Dale B. Martin, *Biblical Truths: The Meaning of Scripture in the Twenty-First Century* (New Haven: Yale University Press, 2017), 233–34.

[10] Dunn, *Romans 1–8*, 453; see further Dunn, *Jesus and the Spirit*, 240–41. Steven Muir recognises the "ecstatic" nature of the cry, but his treatment of Rom 8:22–26 and Rom 8:15–16 as separate developmental stages of a single ritual that Paul tries to theologically control is entirely speculative, Steven C. Muir, "Accessing Divine Power and Status," in DeMaris, Lamoreaux, and Muir, *Early Christian Ritual Life*, 38–54.

[11] Also noted by Giovanni B. Bazzana, *Having the Spirit of Christ: Spirit Possession and Exorcism in the Early Christ Groups*, Synkrisis (New Haven: Yale University Press, 2020), 201.

[12] As argued by Dunn, *Romans 1–8*, 453–54.

[13] For the ethnicity of gods in general, and for Paul in particular, in which language is an important factor, see Paula Fredriksen, "How Jewish is God? Divine Ethnicity in Paul's Theology," *JBL* 137 (2018): 193–212, esp. 209.

[14] For the language of the gods, Dio variously uses διάλεκτος, φωνή, and γλῶττα, the Attic form of γλῶσσα.

[15] When exactly this mistranslation occurs is not entirely clear. According to Forbes (*Inspired Speech*, 115), "Dio is suggesting . . . that oracles become obscure as they pass from the divine to the human realm, and are thus translated from the divine language into the normal human language of the Pythia." Fritz Graf (*Apollo*, 67) suggests that the Pythia herself acted as the "translator of Apollo's thoughts."

speak their own language or dialect, but that of the demons who have taken possession of them" (*Strom.* 1.21 [*ANF* 2:332]). Possession by a divine being or *pneuma*, then, is likely to result in speech in the language of that *pneuma*. Paul is evidently not as reticent as Cicero to let his God speak other languages too. Paul readily quotes the words of God and Jesus in Greek, and was most probably reading the words of God in his sacred texts in Greek too. However these references to the speech of the *pneuma* in different languages suggests an immediacy of connection to divine power, which expresses itself most readily in a different language.

Prayers in the Languages of Humans and Angels (1 Corinthians 12–14)

The question of divine languages is also relevant for the final instance in Paul in which *pneuma* is made the subject of a verb of communication. According to Paul, there are a number of γένη γλωσσῶν, "types of languages,"[16] which are given to believers as manifestations of a single *pneuma* (1 Cor 12:10, 28). When someone speaks in one of these languages,[17] no one else in the assembly understands what is being said, but according to Paul, they are speaking to God.[18] Further elaborating the mechanics of this, Paul describes this speech as the speech of *pneuma*: "if I pray in a language, my *pneuma* prays, but my mind (νοῦς) is unfruitful." This is consistent with what we have already seen happen when *pneuma* is the direct subject of communication. The speech is always directed to God, and in a language other than the speaker's native Greek. That Paul speaks of "his" *pneuma* praying as a result of a gift from the one *pneuma* also mirrors Rom 8:16 in which the *pneuma* of adoption joins together with the *pneuma* of believers to create the *abba* cry.[19] In addition to *pneuma*

---

[16] Cf. 1 Cor 14:10 where Paul talks about multiple γένη φωνῶν, "types of voice," which appears to be a broader category than γένη γλωσσῶν.

[17] Paul's wording varies between a singular γλῶσσα (1 Cor 14:2, 4, 9, 13, 14, 19, 26, 27) and the plural, which sometimes refers to a single person speaking multiple languages (1 Cor 12:10; 13:1; 14:5, 6, 18), and sometimes refers to multiple people speaking multiple languages (1 Cor 12:30; 14:5, 23, 39). The best pattern I can discern is that when Paul speaks of the general ability he uses the plural, and when he is referring to a specific instance he uses singular, but this is not absolute.

[18] Paul uses various terms for the lack of understanding that accompanies glossolalia clustered around the concepts of hearing, knowing, and understanding: ἀκούειν (14:2); εἰσακούειν (14:21); γινώσκειν (14:9); εἰδέναι (14:16). He also says people become foreigners (barbarians, non-Greek speakers) to each other (14:11).

[19] Some scholars have connected the pneumatic nature of the *abba* cry with glossolalia in 1 Cor 14: Smith, "Pauline Worship," 247; Werner Bieder, "Gebetswirklichkeit und Gebetsmöglichkeit bei Paulus," *TZ* 4 (1948): 24; Harry O. Maier, *New Testament Christianity in the Roman World* (Oxford: Oxford University Press, 2018), 61. Most, however, if they mention the passage at all in this connection, have sought to keep them apart: E. A. Obeng, "Abba, Father: The Prayer of the Sons of God," *ExpTim* 99 (1988): 365; Dunn, *Jesus and the Spirit*, 241.

being the subject of prayer, Paul can also describe speaking in languages as speaking by or with *pneuma*, using the dative case: speaking mysteries with *pneuma* (πνεύματι: 14:2), praying (προσεύξομαι), singing (ψαλῶ),[20] or praising (εὐλογῇς)[21] with *pneuma* ([τῷ] πνεύματι, 14:15–16).[22] In each case it is clear that speaking πνεύματι has the same meaning of speaking to God in a language not understood by the hearer.[23]

In the history of scholarship there have been three main options for how Paul understands the nature of such speech. Much of the debate centres around how one understands Paul's poetic reference in 1 Cor 13:2 to speaking ταῖς γλώσσαις τῶν ἀνθρώπων . . . καὶ τῶν ἀγγέλων, "in the languages of humans and of angels." Dale Martin takes the two types of language to be in opposition to each other, so the languages of humans refers to normal human speech, while only the languages of angels refers to "glossolalia," or what Paul calls λαλῶν γλώσσῃ. Otherwise, he sees "no indication that Paul viewed glossolalia as human language."[24] Forbes on the other hand, takes "the languages of humans" as decisive for his interpretation of glossolalia as unlearned human languages.[25] He tentatively suggests divine angelic languages could also be included, but is more inclined to see the line "and of angels" as a rhetorical flourish. Just as in 13:2, Paul is not claiming to know *all* mysteries and *all* knowledge, so he is not actually claiming to be able to speak angelic languages, but is rhetorically taking glossolalia to its logical extreme.[26] Anthony Thiselton appears to take the whole phrase as rhetorical and hypothetical, so that "Paul begins with the notion of tongues as that which gives expression to the yearnings and praise of the depths of the human heart, and escalates to a hypothesis considered at Corinth but not

---

[20] The verb in this context and elsewhere refers to singing or making music *to* God, cf. Eph 5:19; Ps 7:18; 9:3, 12 LXX.

[21] "Praise" should be preferred to "say a blessing" as the NRSV and many commentators have it, since later in the same verse it is described as a εὐχαριστία, "thanksgiving," and for Paul all glossolalia is properly speech to God, not to people.

[22] The original text of 14:16 either contains πνεύματι without the article ($\mathfrak{P}$46 ℵ* A F G) or with the participle ἐν πνεύματι (ℵ² B Dˢ P), and there is not much to decide between them on textual grounds. Pace Fee (*First Corinthians*, 740 n. 518): Paul does not "clearly intend the Holy Spirit" in this instance, as the immediately preceding verse is talking about human *pneuma*.

[23] A possible exception is 1 Cor 12:3: "no one is able to say, 'Jesus is Lord,' except in holy *pneuma* (ἐν πνεύματι ἁγίῳ)." Here speaking ἐν πνεύματι produces an exclamation in Greek. The construction with ἐν is slightly different to the simple datives in 14:2, 15 (and possibly 14:16), but would mirror Rom 8:15 (ἐν ᾧ κράζομεν). More importantly though, there is no equivalent instance where the *pneuma* itself says Κύριος Ἰησοῦς. This is in contrast to early Christian texts, particularly Revelation and Acts, in which *pneuma* is identified as not just the means, but the source of much prophetic speech, see Aune, *Prophecy*, 329.

[24] Dale B. Martin, "Tongues of Angels and Other Status Indicators," *JAAR* 59 (1991): 559 n. 23.

[25] Forbes, *Inspired Speech*, 63.

[26] Forbes, *Inspired Speech*, 61–62.

necessarily endorsed by Paul, that tongues is the angelic language of heaven."[27] Glossolalia for Thiselton is pre-linguistic, forming no discernible words in any language, and is principally "the language of the unconscious."[28]

Each of these three options (heavenly language, human language, pre-linguistic language of the unconscious) can find some support in the various ways Paul talks about *pneuma* making itself audible through human bodies. The wordless sighs of Rom 8:26 support the language of pre-linguistic groanings; the *abba* cry of Rom 8:15 and Gal 4:6 supports the idea of human languages; and the languages of angels appears to have been at least one of the ways in which the phenomenon was understood in Corinth. For this reason I am unconvinced by any attempts to limit glossolalia to either human or divine languages. Paul's mention of γένη γλωσσῶν, "types of languages," suggests that Paul did not limit the audible manifestation of *pneuma* to any one particular type of language, be it human, divine, or even inarticulate.[29] Morton Smith explained the varieties of ecstatic speech described above as various ways Paul interpreted a single phenomenon in various situations: "When he could, he found meanings for the utterances," as with the translation of "father" for *abba*. "When he had to admit that the sounds were incomprehensible, he explained that the reward destined for Christians exceeds imagination," as with the inarticulate groanings of Rom 8:26. When their use was causing division and pride in the *ekklēsia*, then he emphasises the need to discipline such speech and subordinates it to prophecy.[30] This aligns reasonably well with what Paul himself says about the use of languages in 1 Cor 14, albeit in a more critical register: when there is an interpretation, it should be interpreted (v. 27), if there is no interpretation it should be kept to oneself as a personally edifying but unintelligible prayer (v. 28). What ties all these examples together for Paul is that they are all examples of the speech of *pneuma*. They are what happens when *pneuma* becomes audible.

---

[27] Thiselton, *First Corinthians*, 1033; Poirier (*Tongues of Angels*, 51–53) is also ambivalent about whether an angelic language is Paul's own understanding or that of the Corinthians.

[28] Drawing on Gerd Theissen (*Psychological Aspects of Pauline Theology*, trans. John P. Galvin [Edinburgh: T&T Clark, 1987], 267–320) and Krister Stendahl ("Glossolalia – The New Testament Evidence," in *Paul Among Jews and Gentiles*, 109–12).

[29] Thiselton (*First Corinthians*, 970) warns against trying to make glossolalia "one thing" on the basis of the γένη γλωσσῶν of 12:10. Martin ("Tongues of Angels," 548 n. 4), despite denying the inclusion of human language within glossolalia for Paul, earlier notes how the distinction between human and divine languages need not be as absolute as we often assume: "many of those societies [who practice glossolalia] would not differentiate between 'natural' and 'supernatural' in the same way that we modern westerners would. They might take a speech-act to represent a language of the 'gods' or 'spirits,' but the difference between it and ordinary language would be one of hierarchy or degree, not of kind."

[30] Smith, "Pauline Worship," 247.

The Audible *Pneuma* and Divination

The audible expression of *pneuma* can be viewed as one of the most direct contacts with the divine world, but even so, it has little divinatory value for Paul as the words expressed are unintelligible and understood as direct communication back to God rather than the communication of divine truths to humans: "For the one who speaks in a language does not speak to people but to God" (1 Cor 14:2). For this reason Paul is careful to limit the use of glossolalia in community settings, precisely because of its lack of divinatory value. The situation changes slightly when someone is able to interpret the words spoken in a language. Paul lists the ἑρμηνεία γλωσσῶν, "interpretation of languages," as a particular gift enabled by *pneuma* (1 Cor 12:10), and only when this gift is employed does he deem languages to be of use in group settings. This is different to the interpretation of oracles delivered by prophets, which also required some form of interpretation by those who are pneumatic (1 Cor 2:13; 14:29). Rather than the συγκρίνω/διακρίνω terminology used of interpreting the words of prophets, Paul uses the terms ἑρμηνεία and διερμηνεύω to speak of interpreting languages. In context this suggests "translation" rather than "interpretation," translating the speech into intelligible words as opposed to discerning the meaning and significance of the utterances suggested by the συγκρίνω/διακρίνω terminology.[31]

Since Paul suggests that interpreted languages edify the assembly in the same way that prophecy does (1 Cor 14:3–5), many interpreters have understood interpreted languages to take on the status of prophetic, revelatory words addressed to the community.[32] This is to mistake the *effect* of interpreted languages for their *content*. Paul nowhere suggests that the content of glossolalia changes from prayer to prophecy once interpreted. In 1 Cor 14:15–16 prayer and praise which involve the *nous* as well as the *pneuma* still function as prayer and praise; they

---

[31] For "interpretation" as a translation of συγκρίνω/διακρίνω, see Gerhard Dautzenberg, "Zum religionsgeschichtlichen Hintergrund der διάκρισις πνευμάτων (1 Kor 12:10)," *BZ* 15 (1971): 93–104; Dautzenberg, "Botschaft und Bedeutung," 154–55. I do not actually agree with Dautzenberg that this is the correct interpretation of 1 Cor 12:10, but it does fit the context of 1 Cor 2:13 and 14:29, pace Wayne A. Grudem, "A Response to Gerhard Dautzenberg on 1 Cor 12:10," *BZ* 22 (1978): 269–70.

[32] C. K. Barrett, *The First Epistle to the Corinthians*, BNTC (London: A&C Black, 1968), 316; E. Earle Ellis, "Prophecy in the New Testament Church – and Today," in Panagopoulos, *Prophetic Vocation*, 53; Gerhard Dautzenberg, "Glossolalie," *RAC* 11:227–29; Tibbs, *Religious Experience*, 213; M. Eugene Boring, *Sayings of the Risen Jesus: Christian Prophecy in the Synoptic Tradition*, SNTSMS 46 (Cambridge: Cambridge University Press, 1982), 108; Forbes recognises that it does not prove an equivalency, but does "suggest that there is some parallel between the two in Paul's thought," and counts it as a plank in his argument that interpreted languages are still "revelatory," *Inspired Speech*, 95.

do not become prophecy.³³ The only instance in which Paul might suggest some divinatory content to glossolalia is 1 Cor 14:2, in which the one speaking in languages is described as πνεύματι δὲ λαλεῖ μυστήρια, "speaking mysteries by *pneuma*." The term μυστήριον elsewhere in Paul refers to "previously hidden but now knowable" divine truths, such as the meaning of a crucified Messiah (1 Cor 2:1, 7) and eschatological forecasts (Rom 11:25–26; 1 Cor 15:51–52),³⁴ so some reason that glossolalia was seen as containing similar mysteries that were revealed to the community once interpreted.³⁵ This argument runs up against the larger sentence in which this clause is placed. It is hard to escape Thiselton's conclusion that, "Paul's usual meaning [of revealed eschatological secrets] cannot make sense here without undermining his own argument."³⁶ The mysteries are expressly spoken by *pneuma* to God, in which case it makes little sense for the glossolalist to be communicating eschatological mysteries back to God.³⁷ Paul consistently describes glossolalia as prayer and praise directed to God, and this does not change once it is interpreted. The edification that the assembly receives is from understanding what prayers are being offered, so that they are able to add their own "amen" (1 Cor 14:16), rather than from any new divinatory content from God. The flow of communication remains from humans (via *pneuma*) to God, not *vice versa*. While from an etic position we may profitably categorise glossolalia and prophecy together as types of divine or inspired speech, Paul is more drastic in his distinctions. Glossolalia is not just "an oracle whose words and sounds are left unintelligible"³⁸ but represents a different direction of communication, which serves a different function altogether.

---

³³ Fee, *First Corinthians*, 663.
³⁴ In a more generalised sense, also 1 Cor 4:1; 13:2. See especially Lang, *Mystery*, 39.
³⁵ For Dunn (*Jesus and the Spirit*, 244) "the subject matter is the eschatological secrets known only in heaven."
³⁶ Thiselton, *First Corinthians*, 1085.
³⁷ Luz translates the dative here as "for God," which "thus comes close to prayer," but in terms of content, prophecy is "not different from glossolaly," Ulrich Luz, "Stages of Early Christian Prophetism," in Verheyden, Zamfir, and Nicklas, *Prophets and Prophecy*, 65. Paul does not seem so circumspect, cf. 1 Cor 14:14–16. T. J. Lang (*Mystery*, 39–40) has sought to overcome this problem by reading the δέ of 14:2b as contrastive so that "the person speaking in indecipherable tongues speaks only to God *even though* she speaks mysteries in the Spirit … Paul is lamenting that private interaction between the believer and God in incomprehensible tongues obscures what would otherwise be profitable for the whole community." On this reading, though, one would expect Paul to urge interpretation for individual tongue-speaking just as much as for communal, as an individual would surely profit from understanding the unintelligible mysteries they were uttering as much as a community. Paul does not make this move though. One might also more naturally expect εἰ καί, εἴπερ, καίπερ or something similar to express "even though," rather than δέ.
³⁸ Eyl, *Signs, Wonders, and Gifts*, 99.

Prophecy: *Pneuma* and *Nous*

In contrast to unintelligible pneumatic languages, Paul urges the use of prophecy, which is intelligible language, not spoken to God, but to people (1 Cor 14:3). Eyl notes how Paul, like other Jewish authors such as Philo, constructs prophecy as "the most legitimate Israelite and Judean divinatory practice."[39] This is in large part because of the prominent role given to prophets in Jewish tradition and their sacred texts. Deuteronomy 18:10–15 had already singled out the prophet (נביא, προφήτης) as the one legitimate spokesperson for Yahweh in contrast to the various other divinatory roles one could fulfil in the broader culture. For Paul, in this context prophecy is superior because, unlike languages, it is able to provide edification (οἰκοδομή), exhortation (παράκλησις), and encouragement (παραμυθία) to the *ekklēsia* through intelligible messages (1 Cor 14:3). Despite this rhetorical privileging of prophecy, scholars often disagree about what sort of activity Paul is referring to when he uses the words προφητεία and προφητεύειν.[40] Some understand prophecy as mainly an interpretive activity in the Pauline assemblies, consisting of inspired interpretations of Jewish scripture, or of the "early Church kerygma."[41] This sort of function easily shades into prophecy as a form of "exhortatory pastoral preaching."[42] As a functional definition – and with a host of necessary caveats – this may not be wrong, but as a historical description it serves to make Pauline prophecy look more like a modern sermon than a first-century divinatory practice.[43]

---

[39] Eyl, *Signs, Wonders, and Gifts*, 99.

[40] Cf. Shantz, *Paul in Ecstasy*, 184: "precisely what prophecy is remains a point of contention." Prophecy in Paul has often been subsumed within (and also made determinative for) the broader category of "early Christian prophecy" which presents further complications. On this, see Nasrallah, *Ecstasy of Folly*, 66–69.

[41] For "charismatic exegesis" of scripture, see Édouard Cothenet, "Les prophètes chrétiens comme exégètes charismatiques de l'écriture," in Panagopoulos, *Prophetic Vocation*, 77–107; Ellis, *Prophecy and Hermeneutic*, part two of which is entitled "Prophecy as Exegesis"; Boring, *Sayings*, 100–101. For interpretation of the kerygma, see Thomas W. Gillespie, *The First Theologians: A Study in Early Christian Prophecy* (Grand Rapids: Eerdmans, 1994); Helmut Merklein does not limit prophecy to interpreting the kerygma, but makes prophecy dependant on it: filling in gaps between kerygma and the needs of the present, "Der Theologe als Prophet: Zur Funktion prophetischen Redens im theologischen Diskurs des Paulus," in *Studien zu Jesus und Paulus II*, WUNT 105 (Tübingen: Mohr Siebeck, 1998), 377–404.

[42] So Gillespie, *First Theologians*, 164: "Specifically, prophecy is the theological and ethical exposition of the gospel." This conclusion becomes particularly easy when the effects of prophecy in 1 Cor 14:4 are taken to be a generic marker of its contents, so Ulrich B. Müller, *Prophetie und Predigt im Neuen Testament: Formgeschichtliche Untersuchungen zur urchristlichen Prophetie*, SNT 10 (Mohn: Gütersloh, 1975); David Hill, "Christian Prophets as Teachers or Instructors in the Church," in Panagopoulos, *Prophetic Vocation*, 108–30. Hill is slightly more circumspect in his later *New Testament Prophecy* (London: Marshall, Morgan & Scott, 1979), 137–38.

[43] It would not be unfair to point out that many of the works on Paul and early Christian prophecy in the last 50 years are explicitly and self-consciously concerned with what place prophecy should have in the contemporary church and so are perhaps prone to eliminate historical difference.

Focusing on such a definition also elides the primary feature of prophecy, which is the divine source of the message.[44] Aune's definition is more appropriate to the ancient evidence: "Prophecy is a specific form of divination that consists of intelligible verbal messages believed to originate with God and communicated through inspired human intermediaries."[45] This, rather than finding its comparison in the twenty-first-century pulpit can be (and has been) more fruitfully compared with the practice of inspired speech in the broader Graeco-Roman world.

This sort of inspired speech is most famously associated with the official oracle sanctuaries, especially at Delphi, as well as inspired figures of the legendary past such as the Sibyl and Cassandra.[46] Outside of these contexts a number of texts make oblique references to figures called ἐγγαστρίμυθοι, literally "belly-talkers."[47] Plutarch reports that they used to be called "Eurycleis," named after a particularly famous Athenian example, but in his day were called "Pythones," presumably exploiting the connection between this prophetic gift and the official version at Delphi (Plutarch, *Def. or.* 414e).[48] These figures, according to Plutarch, claimed to have the god, or perhaps a daimon, inside them, who spoke from within them using their mouths as instruments.[49] According to Acts 16:16, Paul encountered a slave girl with a πνεῦμα πύθωνα, "Python spirit," by which she could perform divination (μαντευομένη), and which Paul promptly exorcised.[50] We do not know much about such figures. The sources mention them only in passing and often only as a means of comparison for

---

[44] Regarding the inspired interpretation of Jewish scripture, I will argue in the next chapter that the interpretation of written oracles was indeed a large part of Paul's divinatory repertoire, but there is no real evidence to suggest that this happened as the result of particular revelations, or that the interpretation itself was what Paul called προφητεία. Cf. David E. Aune, "Charismatic Exegesis in Early Judaism and Early Christianity," in *The Pseudepigrapha and Early Biblical Interpretation*, ed. James H. Charlesworth and Craig A. Evans, JSPSup 14 (Sheffield: Sheffield Academic, 1993), 146–48; Forbes, *Inspired Speech*, 233–36.

[45] Aune, *Prophecy*, 339.

[46] Delphi is most prominently associated with divine speech; the case is harder to judge with some of the other oracle sanctuaries. Plato lists the priestesses of Dodona with the Pythia and Sibyl as examples of divine *mania* (*Phaedr.* 244b), but other sources suggest a variety of methods of divination used at Dodona not involving inspired speech, such as lots or the rustling of leaves. See the discussion in Esther Eidinow, *Oracles, Curses, and Risk Among the Ancient Greeks* (Oxford: Oxford University Press, 2007), 67–70. On the oracle sanctuaries, see Iles Johnston, *Ancient Greek Divination*.

[47] See Dodds, *Greeks and the Irrational*, 71–72; Aune, *Prophecy*, 40–41; Forbes, *Inspired Speech*, 295–98.

[48] For Eurycles, see Plato, *Soph.* 252c; Aristophanes, *Vesp.* 1019–20. On Pythones, see Iles Johnston, *Ancient Greek Divination*, 140–41, who also notes an alternative interpretation of the name.

[49] Cf. Hippocrates, *Epid.* 5.63, in which a patient made a noise from her chest, "like the so-called belly-talkers," and Lucian, *Lex.* 20, where the daimon itself appears to be called an ἐγγαστρίμυθος.

[50] Belly-talkers mostly appear to be female, see Forbes, *Inspired Speech*, 295–96. For the gendered dynamics of prophecy see Wire, *Corinthian Women Prophets*; Marshall, *Women Praying and Prophesying*.

something else, but this in itself suggests they were common enough to be readily understood by ancient readers without further explanation.

Prophecy and Inspiration

In Chapter 1, I surveyed the mechanics of how people were thought to be able to receive divine knowledge. When dealing with divinatory speech we may ask some further questions about mechanics: how is the speech itself produced, and how much control is the prophet thought to have over what is said? In 1 Cor 2:13, Paul claims that he and his fellow apostles speak "words taught by *pneuma*." The reception and interpretation of the words are pneumatic, but the speech itself merely reports what has been taught (διδακτοῖς). It is the content rather than the manner of speech that is remarkable. Is this also how Paul understands the speech of prophets? Or does he understand them to be "channelling the speech of divine beings" in the manner of belly-talkers?[51] Ancient writers countenanced both explanations of prophetic speech. The belly-talker view, which Plutarch dismisses, is supported in an oft-quoted text of Philo.

> For indeed the prophet, even when he seems to be speaking, really holds his peace, and his organs of speech, mouth and tongue, are wholly in the employ of Another, to shew forth what He wills. Unseen by us that Other beats on the cords with the skill of a master-hand and makes them instruments of sweet music, laden with every harmony (Philo, *Her.* 266).[52]

For Philo this is the corollary of the absence of *nous*, "which is evicted at the arrival of the divine *pneuma*," and results in ἔκστασιν καὶ θεοφόρητον μανίαν, "ecstasy and inspired mania" (*Her.* 265).[53] As I argued in Chapter 1, Paul certainly understands himself and the rest of his assemblies to possess, and even to be possessed by, God's *pneuma*. In this sense, the difference between Pauline prophecy and the slave girl in Acts 16 could be more to do with which spirit is possessing the host, rather than the nature of the possession itself.[54] Paul also talks of this *pneuma* speaking through human bodies in unintelligible languages in a way that bypasses the mind (1 Cor 14:14).[55] The mechanics of

---

[51] As argued by Eyl, *Signs, Wonders, and Gifts*, 98; who follows Tibbs, *Religious Experience*, passim.
[52] Cf. Plutarch, *Def. orac.* 404e; Lucan 5.166–169.
[53] This clearly owes a lot to Plato's discussions of divine mania, and the absence of reason in divination, *Tim.* 71e–72a; *Ion* 534c–d; *Phaedr.* 244b–d.
[54] Bazzana (*Having the Spirit*, 30–31) notes the ambiguity of the language of possession, which ultimately leaves open who is in possession of whom. This guards against simplistic notions of control and agency (see the discussion below on "ecstasy").
[55] Forbes (*Inspired Speech*, 64; followed by Tibbs, *Religious Experience*, 246) is correct to note that Paul's description of the *nous* as ἄκαρπός does not necessarily mean it is bypassed or inactive,

glossolalia then seem to follow the belly-talker model. Prophecy, however, Paul categorises with other forms of intelligible, inspired speech in which both *pneuma* and *nous* work together.⁵⁶ He therefore portrays prophecy and glossolalia as divine, pneumatic speech channelled through different anthropological routes.⁵⁷ The cooperation of the mind brings Paul's understanding of prophecy closer to that of Theon in Plutarch's *De Pythia oraculis*. For Theon, when the Pythia utters her oracles,

> The voice (ἡ γῆρυς) is not that of a god, nor the sound (ὁ φθόγγος), nor the diction (ἡ λέξις), nor the metre (τὸ μέτρον), but all these are the woman's; he puts into her mind only the visions (τὰς φαντασίας), and creates a light in her soul in regard to the future; for inspiration (ἐνθουσιασμός) is precisely this (*Pyth. orac.* 397c).

Such a view of prophetic speech can also work in conjunction with a possession model. Hippolytus, writing at the beginning of the third century CE, describes prophetic inspiration thus:

> For these [the prophets] were all furnished with the prophetic spirit, and worthily honoured by the *logos* himself; being united with them after the manner of instruments, having the *logos* in them always, like a plectrum, by which they were moved and announced the things God willed . . . first of all they were correctly given wisdom by the *logos*, and

---

just that it is unfruitful in the sense that it cannot understand or benefit from the speech. Verses 15–19, however, indicate a more active role for *nous* in producing intelligible speech, which was absent for glossolalia (e.g., τῷ νοΐ μου λαλῆσαι).

⁵⁶ To be slightly pedantic, it is not simply the case that "speaking τῷ νοΐ μου corresponds to prophecy" (Sandnes, *Paul – One of the Prophets?*, 99). In 14:13–19, speaking with the *nous* refers to the interpretation of languages, and the result is not prophecy, but praying and singing intelligibly with *nous*. But to the extent that *nous* seems to be involved in all intelligible speech for Paul, it is implied that prophecy must also involve both *nous* and *pneuma*.

⁵⁷ Tibbs (*Religious Experience*, 243–51) understands all inspired speech in Paul as spirit possession, in which "a holy spirit had gained temporary control of the medium's vocal chords [sic]" (176). He can only do this by denying any anthropological nuance to Paul's statements so that *pneuma* refers not to Paul's own transformed *pneuma*, but the temporary possession of a foreign spirit, and *nous* refers not to the involvement of Paul's own mind in producing speech, but merely to the fact that the words can be understood. He translates τὸ πνεῦμά μου προσεύχεται in 14:14 as "the spirit, indeed, prays [through] me." The grammar of προσεύξομαι τῷ πνεύματι, "I pray by the *pneuma*," in 14:15 is reversed to mean "the spirits should indeed utter prayers through the agency of a human medium." Then in the clearly parallel phrasing προσεύξομαι δὲ καὶ τῷ νοΐ, "I also pray with the *nous*," the *nous* is translated as an adverb which means "intelligibly" (247). This is even so when Paul later refers to τῷ νοΐ μου in v. 19, which Tibbs translates as "speak five words that I understand" (250). This is surely a case in which what Paul says gets in the way of what Tibbs wants Paul to mean.

then were rightly instructed in the future by visions. And then, being thus sent, they spoke those things which had been revealed by God to them alone.

οὗτοι γὰρ πνεύματι προφητικῷ οἱ πάντες κατηρτισμένοι καὶ ὑπ' αὐτοῦ τοῦ λόγου ἀξίως τετιμημένοι, ὀργάνων δίκην ἑαυτοῖς ἡνωμένοι ἔχοντες ἐν ἑαυτοῖς ἀεὶ τὸν λόγον ὡς πλῆκτρον, δι' οὗ κινούμενοι ἀπήγγελλον ταῦτα ἅπερ ἤθελεν ὁ θεός . . . πρῶτον μὲν διὰ τοῦ λόγου ἐσοφίζοντο ὀρθῶς, ἔπειτα δὲ δι' ὁραμάτων προεδιδάσκοντο τὰ μέλλοντα καλῶς· καὶ εἶθ' οὕτως πεμπόμενοι ἔλεγον ταῦτα, ἅπερ αὐτοῖς μόνοις ἦν ὑπὸ θεοῦ ἀποκεκαλυμμένα. (*Antichr.* 2)[58]

Here is the familiar imagery of the body as an instrument (ὄργανον) played by the deity, which for Hippolytus is the *logos* in conjunction with the prophetic *pneuma*. There is also a form of possession as the *logos* is "in" and "united with" the prophet, but it is not the prophet's vocal cords that are being played by the god. The deity does not appear to provide any words at all. Rather, prophetic inspiration comes from being endowed with wisdom, and through visions, the content of which the prophet is then commissioned to speak.[59] This comes quite close to Paul's perspective in 1 Cor 2:13.

Inspiration and Ecstasy

It would be a mistake to call this form of inspiration "non-ecstatic."[60] Much modern scholarship has been too preoccupied with the binary terms of Plato and Philo's definitions, so that rationality and ecstasy are defined as mutually exclusive categories, and any involvement of the mind signals the loss of ecstatic frenzy and its replacement with rationality and lucidity.[61] Both ancient witnesses and modern anthropological studies of altered states of consciousness call this position into question.[62] In the case of Plutarch's own

---

[58] Text from Hans Achelis, ed., *Hippolyt's kleinere exegetische und homiletische Schriften* (Leipzig: J. C. Hinrichs'sche, 1897).

[59] In place of πεμπόμενοι, "sent," some manuscripts read πεπεισμένοι, "becoming convinced," which would further heighten the engagement of the prophet's cognitive faculties in the process.

[60] As done by Terence Callan, "Prophecy and Ecstasy in Greco-Roman Religion and in 1 Corinthians," *NovT* 27 (1985): 129–30, 139.

[61] See Allen R. Hunt, *The Inspired Body: Paul, the Corinthians, and Divine Inspiration* (Macon, GA: Mercer University Press, 1996), 125–27; Callan, "Prophecy and Ecstasy," 126; Wayne A. Grudem, *The Gift of Prophecy in 1 Corinthians* (Lanham, MD: University Press of America, 1982; repr. Eugene, OR: Wipf & Stock, 1999), 150. For a similar approach to Delphic inspiration, Joseph Fontenrose, *The Delphic Oracle: Its Responses and Operations* (Berkeley: University of California Press, 1978), 206–12.

[62] See Lisa Maurizio, "Anthropology and Spirit Possession: A Reconsideration of the Pythia's Role at Delphi," *JHS* 115 (1995): 69–86; Graf, "Apollo, Possession, and Prophecy," 592. On

discussion, while the god makes use of the Pythia's mental faculties she is evidently not in complete control.

> For [Apollo] makes known and reveals his own thoughts, but he makes them known through the associated medium of a mortal body and a soul that is unable to keep quiet, or, as it yields itself to the One that moves it, to remain of itself unmoved and tranquil, but, as though tossed amid billows and enmeshed in the stirrings and emotions within itself, it makes itself more and more restless . . . what is called inspiration (ἐνθουσιασμός) seems to be a combination of two impulses, the soul being simultaneously impelled through one of these by some external influence, and through the other by its own nature. (*Pyth. orac.* 404e–f [Babbitt, LCL])

Elsa Giovanna Simonetti concludes from this account of the Pythia's soul that, "according to Plutarch, the psychic state reached by the priestess during the mantic session is neither an uncontrolled, raving frenzy . . . nor a completely calm, reasonable state of lucidity."[63] While she retains enough mental control to translate the images and thoughts she receives into her own intelligible words, reason is not entirely opposed to ecstasy.[64] A similarly variable mix of control and compulsion is present in accounts of the Sibyl's inspiration.[65] She evidently was thought to retain enough control to be able to speak in her own first person, in contrast to the Pythia who almost always spoke in the person of Apollo himself. She is at the same time under compulsion to speak when stirred by God, and depicted with the usual signs of divine mania.

> When God had quieted my all-wise song
> At my imploring, once more in my breast
> He stirred the joyful voice of inspired words.
> My whole form shivering, I tell these words:
> I know not what I say, God bids me speak.
>
> (Sib. Or. 2.1–5)[66]

---

varying levels of control within altered states of consciousness, see Shantz, *Paul in Ecstasy*, 193–97.

[63] Simonetti, *Perfect Medium*, 46; Graf calls it "a sophisticated Platonic transformation of the Body Snatcher [by which he means possession] template," Graf, "Apollo, Possession, and Prophecy," 595.

[64] Cf. Aune, *Prophecy*, 33: "Ecstasy and rationality, however, should not be regarded as two mutually exclusive states of consciousness."

[65] Literary depictions of the Pythia and Sibyl tended to influence each other so cannot be sharply differentiated. Poetic depictions tended towards a picture of uncontrolled frenzy. See Jane L. Lightfoot, *The Sibylline Oracles: With Introduction, Translation, and Commentary on the First and Second Books* (Oxford: Oxford University Press, 2007), 9–11.

[66] Translation from Lightfoot, *Sibylline Oracles*.

Paul seems to assume something similar to Plutarch when he instructs prophets to prophesy one by one, and if something is revealed (ἀποκαλυφθῇ) to another, then the one speaking should be silent so that the new prophecy can be heard (1 Cor 14:29–31). Prophecy here is positioned as the result of a revelation, which is then spoken to the assembly. A position which could be further strengthened by Paul's list of beneficial speech in 14:6, which he lists as revelation (ἐν ἀποκαλύψει), knowledge (ἐν γνώσει), prophecy (ἐν προφητείᾳ), and teaching ([ἐν] διδαχῇ). Some have taken this to represent two pairs: prophecy deriving from revelation, and teaching deriving from knowledge.[67] This is an attractive solution, but has to be read into Paul's syntax, as he merely lists them one after the other. Nevertheless, despite myriad other differences over the details, the idea that prophecy functions for Paul as the public report of a revelation is agreed on by most.[68]

This revelation could possibly take the form of a vision, as in Hippolytus, and in the visions and revelations we have already discussed in Paul. According to Martti Nissinen this was "one of the basic methods of obtaining a prophetic message" for the Hebrew prophets.[69] The involvement of the *nous*, which results in intelligible speech, would suggest that Paul understands the words to be the prophet's own.[70] There is an element of compulsion as the floor must be ceded to make room for the new revelation as it is delivered, although Paul also presumes enough control on the part of the previous prophet to stop what he is saying when this happens.[71] In general Paul urges more control over the moments of inspiration than is apparent with either Plutarch or the Sibyl, which is in keeping with his desire for order and clarity in this passage: "the *pneumata* of the prophets are subject to the prophets, for God is not of disorder but of peace" (1 Cor 14:32–33). This does not make him emerge as a champion of rationality over frenzy.[72] He rather distinguishes between

---

[67] Forbes, *Inspired Speech*, 226; Tibbs, *Religious Experience*, 224.

[68] E.g., Callan, "Prophecy and Ecstasy," 138; Smith, "Pauline Worship," 247; Forbes, *Inspired Speech*, 220; Hill, *New Testament Prophecy*, 130; Gerhard Dautzenberg, *Urchristliche Prophetie: Ihre Erforschung, ihre Voraussetzungen im Judentum und ihre Struktur im ersten Korintherbrief*, BWA(N)T 10 (Stuttgart: Kohlhammer, 1975); Ulrich Luz, "Stages of Early Christian Prophetism," in Verheyden, Zamfir, and Nicklas, *Prophets and Prophecy*, 65 n. 36; Sandnes, *Paul – One of the Prophets?*, 92, 99.

[69] Nissinen, *Ancient Prophecy*, 184–85. He cites Ezek 1; 10; Amos 7:1–9; 8:1–3; 9:1–4; Zech 1–6.

[70] Pace Eyl, *Signs, Wonders, and Gifts*, 98; Tibbs, *Religious Experience*, passim.

[71] Forbes (*Inspired Speech*, 225 n. 21) suggests it is the one giving interpretative comment that must cede the floor to new revelation, but ὁ πρῶτος in v. 30 makes most sense in the context of the δύο ἢ τρεῖς prophets speaking in v. 29.

[72] For Schweitzer (*Mysticism*, 171–72): "Hardly anywhere does Paul appear so markedly as possessing the greatness which not only belongs to its own time, but also stands above it," as when he champions the rational over the ecstatic in this passage, for "How sure an instinct guided

two types of ecstatic speech, one which involves only the *pneuma* and one which involves both *nous* and *pneuma*, and encourages the Corinthians towards greater control of their pneumatic gifts for the sake of the community.[73] Neither, I must add, does Paul replace a Hellenistic view of ecstasy with a Jewish or Christian view of prophecy, as has often been supposed.[74] Debates about the nature of inspiration and the psychological state of the prophet occurred across purported Jewish and Hellenistic boundaries, and ecstasy was not foreign to Israelite prophecy.[75]

Inspiration and Interpretation

This paradigm of inspiration, as Fritz Graf notes, has its drawbacks as a mode of divination, which its ancient proponents recognised.[76] For Dio Chrysostom, the translation of the dialect of the gods into human dialect causes confusion and obscurity. For Plutarch also, the use of a human body to express divine thoughts inevitably results in some contamination of the message. The god makes use of the Pythia's soul, and the soul in turn makes use of the body as an instrument (ὄργανον). According to Plutarch, the virtue of an instrument is to,

> Conform as exactly as possible to the purpose of the agent that employs it ... but to make this known, not in the form in which it was existent in its creator, uncontaminated, unaffected, and faultless, but combined with much that is alien to this. For pure design cannot be seen by us, and when it is made manifest (φαινόμενον) in another guise and through another medium, it becomes contaminated with the nature of this medium. (*Pyth. orac.* 404b–c [Babbitt, LCL])

Plutarch compares this to malleable materials such as wax, which take on the form they are given when moulded, but always contribute something of their own nature to the finished product. He also cites the myriad distortions

---

him could first be appreciated by men of the present day, who have learned to recognise ecstatic speech as a merely psycho-physical phenomenon." But as Laura Nasrallah points out, throughout 1 Corinthians Paul "claims to stand on the side of folly, and challenges human pretensions to wisdom," Nasrallah, *Ecstasy of Folly*, 93; cf. Bazzana, *Having the Spirit*, 179, 192.

[73] Shantz, *Paul in Ecstasy*, 196–97.

[74] Adolf Schlatter, *Paulus: der Bote Jesu: eine Deutung seiner Briefe an die Korinther* (Stuttgart: Calwer, 1934), 372–73; Hill, *New Testament Prophecy*, 121; Hunt, *Inspired Body*, 131; Sandnes, *Paul – One of the Prophets?*, 92.

[75] "If Ezekiel does not have ecstatic experiences, then we have no criteria to judge that *anyone* of antiquity had such experiences," Grabbe, *Priests, Prophets, Diviners, Sages*, 110. On various views of ecstasy in Jewish literature, see Nissinen, *Ancient Prophecy*, 183–91.

[76] Graf, "Apollo, Possession, and Prophecy," 593.

of a single shape when seen in mirrors, whether flat, concave or convex (ἐν κατόπτροις ἐπιπέδοις τε καὶ κοίλοις καὶ περιηγέσι [*Pyth orac.* 404d]). The listing of the different types of mirror suggests that the particular type of distortion depends on the nature of the particular type of mirror used, which contributes something of its own nature to the image it is reflecting.

Paul, of course, also describes the state of present divinatory knowledge, including prophecy and languages, as seeing δι' ἐσόπτρου ἐν αἰνίγματι, "by means of a mirror in an enigma" (1 Cor 13:12).[77] Paul does not elaborate in the same way as Plutarch does about the nature of this correspondence between mirrors and divination, but he does not seem to be talking about catoptromancy.[78] The imagery of mirrors could imply either clarity or distortion depending on the context in which it is used[79] so it is unnecessary to debate the relative merits of Corinthian bronzeware as is sometimes done.[80] However good Corinthian mirrors were, the context of the metaphor is the decisive factor, and Paul describes the result as an enigma or riddle (ἐν αἰνίγματι). The enigmatic nature of many oracles is well documented, and suggests that the mirror analogy likewise indicates the obscurity and need to correctly interpret much prophetic speech.[81]

For Paul the primary context is eschatological: "For we know in part, and we prophesy in part, but when the perfect comes the partial will be rendered unnecessary" (13:9). "Now I know in part, but then I will fully know, just as

---

[77] Many commentators see this phrase as a form of Midrash on Num 12:6–8: "When there are prophets among you, I the Lord make myself known to them in visions; I speak to them in dreams. Not so with my servant Moses.... With him I speak face to face – clearly, not in riddles (MT: ומראה ולא בחידת; LXX: ἐν εἴδει καὶ οὐ δι' αἰνιγμάτων); and he beholds the form of the Lord." See Michael Fishbane, "Through the Looking Glass: Reflections on Ezek 43:3, Num 12:8 and 1 Cor 13:8," *HAR* 10 (1986): 63–75. The LXX makes an interesting comparison with Plutarch as here αἰνίγματα are contrasted with an εἶδος. In Plutarch, a single εἶδος when reflected through a mirror results in multiple distortions.

[78] On which see Iles Johnston, *Ancient Greek Divination*, 98–99; Dillon, *Omens and Oracles*, 268–71.

[79] Wilfred L. Knox, *St Paul and the Church of the Gentiles* (Cambridge: Cambridge University Press, 1939), 121 n. 4.

[80] Thiselton, *First Corinthians*, 1068; Fee, *First Corinthians*, 718; Christophe Senft, *La première Épître de Saint Paul aux Corinthiens*, rev. ed., CNT 7 (Geneva: Labor et Fides, 1990), 171.

[81] For the link between αἴνιγμα and oracles, see Peter T. Struck, *Birth of the Symbol: Ancient Readers at the Limits of their Texts* (Princeton: Princeton University Press, 2004), 171–77. Plutarch elsewhere describes the presence of the divine in inanimate (ἀψύχοις) and disembodied (ἀσωμάτοις) objects as an αἴνιγμα, whereas animate beings are a clearer mirror (ὡς ἐναργεστέρων ἐσόπτρων) of the divine (*Is. Os.* 76 [382b]). In this sense a mirror is an accurate representation of what it reflects, but is nonetheless still a reflection, which introduces distortions of its own nature. This tension is expressed well by Samuel E. Bassett, "1 Cor 13:12: βλέπομεν γὰρ ἄρτι δι' ἐσόπτρου ἐν αἰνίγματι," *JBL* 47 (1928): 236. Paul, however, calls the mirrored image itself an αἴνιγμα. Robertson and Plummer (*First Corinthians*, 298–99), who stress the distortion inherent in mirrors, still appear closer to Paul's meaning and his ancient context than their detractors.

I have been fully known" (13:12). As I argued in Chapter 1, eschatology, cosmology, and anthropology are all closely intertwined in Paul's understanding of divination, so some of Plutarch's concerns are relevant to Paul's discussion here. In Paul's present, the pure speech of *pneuma* is unintelligible and only useful as a language of prayer to God. Divine speech must cooperate with the human *nous* in order to be intelligible, and therefore useful as a means of knowledge, but is still in need of interpretation. In Paul's future all knowledge is pneumatic, and even the human bodies through which knowledge is communicated are pneumatic (1 Cor 15:44), so the translation required between different levels of being is no longer needed.[82] This does not cause Paul to denigrate or dispose of prophecy in the present, neither does he marginalise the role of *nous* as an element that introduces distortion. Rather he stresses the necessity of *nous* for understanding prophecy in the present, and accounts for its deficiencies by stressing the need for interpretation in 1 Cor 14:29.[83] Paul thus sits closer to Plutarch, who stresses the cooperative nature of inspiration in order to explain its variable features, than Dio Chrysostom, who uses it to diminish the utility of oracular pronouncements.[84]

Paul's Prophetic Speech

In his discussion of inspired speech in 1 Cor 12–14, Paul claims to speak in languages more than any of the Corinthians (1 Cor 14:18). Given his comparative privileging of prophecy in this context, it is perhaps ironic that, aside from a single hypothetical situation in 1 Cor 14:6, Paul never claims to be a prophet or to prophesy. This is no doubt largely due to his further privileging of the role of "apostle" (1 Cor 12:28), a type of super-prophet who, rather than prophesying, proclaims (κηρύσσω) and announces good news (εὐαγγελίζομαι). His occasional claims to speak "in Christ" or "in the Lord" parallel his description

---

[82] David H. Gill ("Through a Glass Darkly: A Note on 1 Corinthians 13:12," *CBQ* 25 [1963]: 427–29) follows J. Behm ("Das Bildwort vom Spiegel 1 Korinther 13:12," in *Reinhold-Seeberg-Festschrift*, ed. Wilhelm Koepp [Leipzig: Deichert, 1929], 1:315–42) in understanding δι' ἐσόπτρου as "through the medium of creatures." Plutarch's *Is. Os.* 382b, quoted above, is often cited as a parallel text, but I am yet to find anyone who references *Pyth. orac.* 404d. The language does not match as precisely, but it is arguably a closer conceptual parallel as it concerns prophetic knowledge. I also find this parallel more convincing than Richard Seaford's confident suggestion that "Paul is here imagining eschatological transitions in terms taken from the transition ... from ignorance to knowledge in mystery-cult," which could be effected by riddling language and mirrors, Richard Seaford, *Dionysos* (London: Routledge, 2006), 123.
[83] The two-stage process of prophecy as revelation followed by interpretation is emphasised by Dautzenberg, *Urchristliche Prophetie*, 43–121.
[84] Cf. the even more pessimistic comments of Pindar (*Ol.* 12.7–12): "Never yet has anyone who walks upon the earth found a reliable symbol from the gods concerning a future matter."

of prophetic speech as "in *pneuma*" (2 Cor 2:17; 12:19; Rom 9:1; 1 Thess 4:1). While various spirits may inspire the speech of the Corinthians, Paul's speech is always specifically inspired by the *pneuma* of Christ. This is made most explicit in 2 Cor 13:3, in which Paul responds to the desire for proof that τοῦ ἐν ἐμοὶ λαλοῦντος Χριστοῦ, "the one who speaks in me is Christ." On a very rare occasion Paul can even say it is God who is communicating through him and other apostles (2 Cor 5:20), although Christ and the Lord are more usual. In these instances it is hard to pinpoint any particular content to what he is saying, rather this seems to be a way of characterising his speech in general, particularly in argumentative contexts in which he needs to defend his position and authority.[85] On other occasions, Paul provides glimpses of what may have been the form of his prophetic speech to his communities.

Predictions

On three occasions Paul reminds his audiences of predictions he made to them, using the word προλέγειν: "I foretell (προλέγω) to you, just as I foretold (προεῖπον), that those who practise such things shall not inherit the kingdom of God" (Gal 5:21). "For when we were with you, foretelling (προελέγομεν) to you, 'we are about to be afflicted' (μέλλομεν θλίβεσθαι), just as also came to pass and you know" (1 Thess 3:4). "The Lord is an avenger in these things, just as we foretold (προείπαμεν) to you and testified (διεμαρτυράμεθα)" (1 Thess 4:6). On each occasion Paul refers to a time in the past in which these predictions were being made, leading many to translate the verbs in question as "said beforehand," which is a legitimate translation of the προ- prefix (cf. 2 Cor 7:3). The word is also frequently used in oracular contexts to introduce prophetic speech, and further examination of these passages suggests that this is a more appropriate way to understand Paul's use of the word in these instances.[86] In 1 Thess 3:4, Paul's words clearly refer to what was about to happen (μέλλομεν) in the near future, the fulfilment of which he can now point to to verify his prediction.[87] The fulfilment of his prediction was proof that affliction was part

---

[85] This would fit with Aune's general conclusion (*Prophecy*, 338) that "Christian prophetic speech ... is Christian discourse presented with divine legitimation, either in the absence of more rational structures of institutional authority, or in conflict with them." As a generalisation though, this is somewhat lacking (see Chapter 2).

[86] Herodotus 1.53 and 8.136 and other references in LSJ, s.v. "προλέγω," "προεῖπον." In Rom 9:29 Isaiah foretells (προείρηκεν) the (conditional) fate of Israel; cf. Acts 1:16: "the holy *pneuma* foretold (προεῖπεν) through the mouth of David concerning Judas."

[87] Cf. Plato, *Euthyphr.* 3c: In a discussion of Socrates's δαιμόνιον, "whenever I address the Assembly on religious matters (περὶ τῶν θείων) and predict to them what's going to happen (προλέγων αὐτοῖς τὰ μέλλοντα), they laugh at me as if I'm mad ... although nothing of what I've told them by way of prediction (εἴρηκα ὧν προεῖπον) has been untrue."

of their appointed lot in God's purposes and so they should not be troubled by it (εἰς τοῦτο κείμεθα [v 3]). The predictions of Gal 5:21 and 1 Thess 4:6 are of eschatological judgement for those who continue in particular vices (the works of the flesh and *porneia*), occuring in 1 Thess 4:6 just after Paul has declared "the will of God" for them. "Warn" could also capture the force of προεῖπον in these cases, but even this requires divinely sanctioned knowledge of what the eschatological fate of such people will be.[88] A warning in this context is no different than a conditional prediction.[89] In these instances, then, Paul refers to predictive oracles he has orally delivered to his assemblies that both exhort (παράκλησις) and encourage (παραμυθία).[90]

Oracular Responses to Specific Questions

One may also glimpse Paul's prophetic or oracular role in his responses to specific questions about daily life in 1 Corinthians. In 1 Cor 7:1, Paul moves from discussing things he has heard (ἀκούεται, 1 Cor 5:1) about the Corinthian congregation to things that they have specifically asked him about in writing: Περὶ δὲ ὧν ἐγράψατε, "Now about the things you wrote." The immediately following responses concern issues of marriage, abstinence, and divorce. Sex and marriage were common topics among the questions individuals brought to oracles (cf. Plutarch, *E Delph.* 386c; *Pyth. orac.* 408c). The specifics of many questions put to the oracle at Dodona have been preserved on lead tablets, giving us a first-hand witness to what sort of questions were asked and how they were phrased. One Gerioton, for example "asks Zeus about a woman, whether (he would do) better if he married."[91] Onasimos asks, "Will it be better for Onasimos to marry the woman?"[92] And another asks, "About a woman, whether I will be fortunate taking Klelais as a wife?"[93] Others asked whether

---

[88] For a similar sense, see the words of Hermes in Aeschylus, *Prom.* 1071–1075: "Well, remember what I warn/predict (προλέγω), and when disaster hunts you down do not complain about your fate, nor ever say that Zeus cast you into a calamity that you had not foreseen (ἀπρόοπτον)." Paul also warns (προείρηκα καὶ προλέγω) in 2 Cor 13:2, but the warning is of his own future actions so not oracular.

[89] In the case of Gal 5:21, the fact that προλέγω appears in both the present and aorist form further suggests that previous instruction is not what the προ- prefix is meant to denote, as that is adequately expressed by the juxtaposition of the aorist and present. Contrast Gal 1:9: ὡς προειρήκαμεν καὶ ἄρτι πάλιν λέγω.

[90] Aune calls them paraenetic oracles, and attempts reconstructions of what the original oracles may have looked like, *Prophecy*, 258–60; cf. Nicklas, "Paulus – der Apostel als Prophet," 98–100.

[91] Γηριότον Δία ἐπερωτῆι περὶ γυναικὸς ἢ βέλτιον λαβόντι, Eidinow, *Oracles*, 85.

[92] Ὀνασίμοι ἄμεινον τὰν γυναῖκα κομίδεσται, Eidinow, *Oracles*, 84.

[93] περὶ γυναικὸς πότερον κα τ[υγ]χάνοιμι λαμβάνων Κλέολαϊν, Eidinow, *Oracles*, 84.

they should seek another (or a different) wife, and some of the questioners may have asked whether they should abstain from sexual intercourse.[94]

A number of the questions begin with περί followed by the subject of the question, in these cases mostly γυναικός, "about a woman/wife," but also περὶ γενεᾶς, "about offspring," περὶ τᾶς οἰκήσις, "about a place to dwell," or περὶ τᾶς ὁρμᾶς, "about a voyage."[95] This seems to be echoed in one of the few preserved responses. In response to a question περὶ παμπ[ασίας], "concerning all my property," the back of the tablet preserves the words, "to Zeus the father, concerning (περί) . . . to Fortune a libation, to Herakles."[96] The response is fragmentary, but would seem to prescribe various sacrifices or libations to specific gods, with περί marking out the various aspects of the question, or property to which the prescription corresponds. A similar formula begins an oracular response preserved on papyrus, ὑπὲρ ὧν ἠξίωσας, "concerning the things about which you asked," which G. H. R. Horsley remarks "may remind us of 1 Cor 7:1."[97] The phrase περὶ δέ in 1 Corinthians has been much discussed, and fits into a number of contexts in ancient literature. Margaret Mitchell's caution is salutary, that the "formula is nothing more or less than a way of introducing a topic the only requirement of which is that it be readily known to both writer and reader."[98] The word περί itself does not prove any particular connection to oracular questions, but oracular consultations do appear as another overlooked context in which such a phrase was used in a formulaic way.

Another common feature of many of the questions put to oracles is to ask whether it will be "better" to take a particular course of action. The most common form of this is λῷον καὶ ἄμεινόν ἐστι ἐμοί . . . "is it better and more good for me . . . ?" although there is some variation.[99] This phrasing is then typically repeated in the response λῷον καὶ ἄμεινόν ἐστι, "it is better and more good."[100]

---

[94] Seeking another wife: ἒ ἀτέραν ἄγομει, "Whether I should marry another woman?"; ἦ ἄλλαν μαστεύων, "Whether I should seek another woman?" Although in this case, Eidinow acknowledges the feminine form could apply to another feminine noun such as land. Questions about intercourse rely on reading θίγō as a partial corrupt form of θιγγάνω: Ἐ μὲ θίγō[---], "Should I not have intercourse?"; θίγō Ἀγēσαρέτα, "(If) I have intercourse with Agesareta." Eidinow, Oracles, 86, 93.

[95] This is also a common feature of oracular questions in the literary tradition concerning Delphi and Didyma, Eidinow, Oracles, 47–29, 125–26.

[96] Διὶ πατρῴωι περί . . . ιο /Τύχαι λοιβὰν/ Ἡρακλεῖ . . .

[97] G. H. R. Horsley, "Answer from an Oracle," NewDocs 2 (1982): 37–38. On περί and ὑπέρ as synonymous in this period, see Margaret M. Mitchell, "Concerning περὶ δέ in 1 Corinthians," NovT 31 (1989): 234.

[98] Mitchell, "περὶ δέ," 236.

[99] Eidinow, Oracles, 135–36; Fontenrose, Delphic Oracle, 37–38, H5; H21; H25; H33; H36; H54.

[100] Fontenrose, Delphic Oracle, 14; variations include Δίκαιον ποιεῖν, "it is right to do," Joseph Fontenrose, Didyma: Apollo's Oracle, Cult, and Companions (Berkeley: University of California Press, 1988), 180.

Paul does not use these words, but follows a similar formula with the words καλὸν ἀνθρώπῳ γυναικὸς μὴ ἅπτεσθαι. Most scholars see Paul's words here as a quotation of the Corinthian position on the issue, which is phrased as a statement: "it is good for a man not to touch [i.e., have intercourse with] a woman."[101] But it is equally likely that Paul is quoting a question posed by the Corinthians: "is it good for a man not to touch a woman?" to which Paul then offers his response.[102] Indeed, this is the scenario presupposed by scholars when they speak of Paul responding to queries from the Corinthians. To the unmarried and widowed, he also gives a response in this form, καλὸν αὐτοῖς ἐὰν μείνωσιν, "it is good for them if they remain [as they are]" (v. 8), followed by an alternative scenario using the comparative form, "it is better (κρεῖττον) to marry than burn."

Commentators often take the word καλός in a purely moral sense, which would sharply distinguish it from ἀγαθός in the oracular tablets. Gordon Fee, however, notes in his commentary that the Pauline use in this context "means something closer to 'it is desirable, or to one's advantage.'"[103] This much is clear from his advice to the unmarried in vv. 25–38. In v. 28 he states that whether they marry or not "there is no sin" rather the advice is "for their own benefit." "Those who marry will experience distress in this life" but his advice will lead to a life "free from anxieties" (v. 32). "So then, the one who marries his virgin does well (καλῶς) and the one who does not marry does better (κρεῖσσον)" (v. 38). This focus on a more advantageous or desirable outcome makes Paul's use of καλός functionally equivalent to λῷον καὶ ἄμεινόν in the oracular context.

Paul's subsequent uses of περὶ δέ in 1 Corinthians are not necessarily related to 7:1 so need not all mark responses to previous questions asked by the Corinthians. He may be simply changing topic. At least the next three occurrences, however, concern topics that would also not be out of place among questions asked at an oracle sanctuary. Περὶ δὲ τῶν παρθένων, "concerning virgins" in v. 25 continues the questions about marriage and relationships. If παρθένος here refers to virgin daughters being given in marriage by their fathers as Lightfoot read it, then there are similar questions among the Dodona catalogue.[104] Περὶ δὲ

---

[101] John C. Hurd, *The Origin of 1 Corinthians* (London: SPCK, 1965), 120–23; Wolfgang Schrage, "Zur Frontstellung der paulinischen Ehebewertung 1 Kor 7:1–7," *ZNW* 67 (1976): 214–34; Wire, *Corinthian Women Prophets*, 80; Martin, *Corinthian Body*, 205; Deming, *Marriage and Celibacy*, 107–9; Thiselton, *First Corinthians*, 498–500; Fee, *First Corinthians*, 306–7.

[102] Conzelmann (*1 Corinthians*, 115 n. 10) recognises that Paul is responding to questions rather than slogans, but takes 7:1 as Paul's answer since the later uses of καλόν in 7:8 and 7:26 show it to be "Pauline style." This is easily countered by pointing to the repetition of the same formula in both the oracular questions and answers.

[103] Fee, *First Corinthians*, 306.

[104] "Reveal, O Zeus, whether it is more serviceable to give my daughter to Theodoros or to Tessias as a wife," Eidinow, *Oracles*, 85; J. B. Lightfoot, *Notes on the Epistles of St Paul from Unpublished Commentaries* (London: Macmillan, 1895), 231.

τῶν εἰδωλοθύτων, "concerning food sacrificed to idols" in 8:1, 4 concerns issues of correct cult, and which sacrifices one should or should not be involved in, which is a very well attested topic for oracles.[105]

Περὶ δὲ τῶν πνευματικῶν in 12:1, if read as a neuter adjective "pneumatic things," would reflect questions about the inner workings of the divine world, and how one relates to it. These sorts of questions are much rarer among the lead tablets collected at Dodona, but start to become more popular in later periods. By the second century CE someone had asked the oracle of Apollo at Claros "Who or what is God?" A question that fits into a context of the increasing use of oracles for theological and philosophical questions.[106] We have already seen in chapter two that information about the gods and the cosmos could be associated with dreams and chthonic oracles (e.g., Plutarch, *Gen. Socr.* 589f–592e). The second-century *Chaldean Oracles* also combines oracular and philosophical form to present short, pithy statements on cosmology and metaphysics.[107] If, on the other hand, τῶν πνευματικῶν is read as a masculine ending, "pneumatic people," then the topic may find a parallel in a question asked at Dodona: "To Zeus Naios and Dione, whether or not they should hire Dorios the soul-raiser (ψυχαγωγῶι)?"[108] If the underlying question is about the usefulness of particular "religious experts," this could make sense in the immediate context, as Paul then reminds them how they were previously led astray to mute idols, and immediately gives them criteria for distinguishing when a person is speaking with God's *pneuma* or not – in other words, which religious experts should be listened to.

Given the similarities I have noted in both form and content to an oracular consultation, it is also important to notice the differences. Rather than addressing the details of individual circumstances he gives more generalised advice to different groups of people. This is not unusual in itself for an oracle, which would often respond to community inquiries. In the Dodona catalogue, however, questions about marriage and divorce are normally asked by individuals. Paul's responses are also remarkably measured and negotiated. Although he does offer some binary responses of what is "good" and "better," these do not appear as pronouncements from on high but as carefully crafted philosophical and rhetorical arguments.[109] Other responses are given as

---

[105] Eidinow, *Oracles*, 112–13; Fontenrose, *Delphic Oracle*, 24–25.
[106] Robert Parker, "Seeking Advice from Zeus at Dodona," *Greece & Rome* 63 (2016): 73; Robin Lane Fox, *Pagans and Christians* (New York: Knopf, 1986), 168–171.
[107] Ruth Majercik, *The Chaldean Oracles: Text, Translation, and Commentary* (Leiden, Brill, 1989).
[108] [- - -Διὶ] τῶι Νάωι καὶ τᾶι Διώναι· ἢ μὴ χρηῦται Δωρίωι τῶ[ι] ψυχαγωγῶι; Eidinow, *Oracles*, 112.
[109] See Margaret M. Mitchell, *Paul and the Rhetoric of Reconciliation: An Exegetical Investigation of the Language and Composition of 1 Corinthians* (Louisville: Westminster John Knox, 1992); Wire, *Corinthian Women Prophets*, 81.

Paul's judgement (γνώμην 7:25, 40). The ensuing discussions about idol-meat (1 Cor 8–10) and pneumatic matters (1 Cor 12–14) are also intricate pieces of logical and philosophical argumentation, and do not appear as straightforward oracular responses to questions. This may lead one to place Paul in the context of philosopher rather than seer in this instance. Philosophers could also be approached with questions about marriage (Plutarch, *Amat.* 750a; Diogenes Laertius, *Lives* 6.3; Epictetus, *Diatr.* 3.22.67, 77), and saw it as their job to pronounce on what courses of action were good (ἀγαθόν) and fitting (προσηκόντων) for people.[110] But in many ways this is a false choice given the way divinatory and philosophical expertise could be combined by the freelance religious experts of Paul's era.[111] Paul's responses come across as a peculiar blend of philosophical and oracular advice.

Two factors foreground the divinatory aspect of Paul's advice in these chapters. First, interspersed with the argumentation and negotiation are more straightforward "commands of the Lord." In 1 Cor 7:10, the Lord commands (παραγγέλλω, οὐκ ἐγὼ ἀλλ' ὁ κύριος), "a wife not to be separated from her husband ... and a husband not to divorce his wife." In 1 Cor 9:14, Paul recalls that the Lord commanded (διέταξεν) those who proclaim the gospel, that they should also get their living from the gospel. In 1 Cor 14:37, Paul challenges those who see themselves as prophets or "pneumatic" to recognise what he has just written as κυρίου ... ἐντολή, "the Lord's command."[112] The first two of these are commonly viewed as pieces of "Jesus tradition," given their similarity to tradition that would later appear in the Synoptic Gospels.[113] Paul himself, however, does not designate them as such. By citing "the Lord" he invokes the same source and authority as the healing oracle of 2 Cor 12:8–9 (cf. 1 Cor 14:37; 1 Thess 4:15 discussed below). It is impossible to know the exact source of the commands and the exact manner in which Paul received them, particularly given the uncertainty over the transmission

---

[110] See the careful work by Deming, *Paul on Marriage and Celibacy*, 110–12.
[111] Wendt, *At the Temple Gates*, 188–89.
[112] The textual tradition testifies to difficulty with relating the singular ἐντολή to the plural relative pronoun ἅ. Some MSS (D* F G b) omit the word ἐντολή thus creating a more general sense that what has been written is "of the Lord." D¹ K L Ψ change the singular to plural ἐντολαι, which again moves the focus off of a specific command. See Fee, *First Corinthians*, 774 n. 697.
[113] The most cautious of scholars will still refer to 1 Cor 7:10 and 9:14 as "the only explicit references to an actual saying of Jesus," Frans Neirynck, "Paul and the Sayings of Jesus," in *L'apôtre Paul: personalité, style et conception du ministère*, ed. A. Vanhoye (Leuven: Leuven University Press, 1986), 277; cf. Nikolaus Walter, "Paul and the Early Christian Jesus-Tradition," in *Paul and Jesus: Collected Essays*, ed. A. J. M. Wedderburn, JSNTSup 37 (Sheffield: Sheffield Academic, 1989), 54; Traugott Holtz, "Paul and the Oral Gospel Tradition," in *Jesus and the Oral Gospel Tradition*, ed. Henry Wansbrough, JSNTSup 64 (Sheffield: Sheffield Academic, 1991), 383–85; David L. Dungan, *The Sayings of Jesus in the Churches of Paul* (Philadelphia: Fortress, 1971).

of gospel traditions before they received their written form.[114] What matters more is that Paul presents these as commands issued in the present from the same divine source that he evokes elsewhere in his letters.[115] There is nothing to distinguish Paul's citation of these commands from the other command of the Lord in 1 Cor 14:37. The precise content of the command in 1 Cor 14:37 is hard to determine, but it seems to refer to the general command for order and unity that informs 1 Cor 14 as a whole.[116] Paul presents this as a prophetic command, since he challenges others who see themselves as prophets or pneumatic people to recognise it as such. These prophetic oracles punctuate Paul's reasoned responses to the questions put to him.[117]

Second, when Paul does not produce a specific command, he still qualifies his own judgement (γνώμη) as one that is deemed trustworthy by the Lord (7:25) and enabled by God's *pneuma* (7:40). The distinction between pneumatic judgement and a command of the Lord makes it likely that 1 Cor 14:37 refers to a specific oracle rather than Paul's general apostolic authority. In the absence of such commands, though, the appeal to the *pneuma* invests Paul's more negotiated and pragmatic advice with its own oracular character. Paul is being consulted on these matters not because of his philosophical expertise but because of his access to the mind of Christ (1 Cor 2:16). The Corinthians themselves

---

[114] Since Paul is the only real evidence for the pre-synoptic transmission of tradition the data set is meagre, and arguments about the Pauline handling of such tradition are inevitably circular. See Eric Eve, *Behind the Gospels: Understanding the Oral Tradition* (Minneapolis: Fortress, 2014), 159–63; Christine Jacobi, *Jesusüberlieferung bei Paulus? Analogien zwischen den echten Paulusbriefen und den synoptischen Evangelien*, BZNW 213 (Berlin: de Gruyter, 2015).

[115] This is certainly true of 1 Cor 7:10, cf. Raymond F. Collins, *First Corinthians*, SP 7 (Collegeville, MN: Liturgical Press, 1999), 264–65; Conzelmann, *1 Corinthians*, 120. The command of the Lord in 1 Cor 9:14 is given more of a historical context. It is the aorist tense, and is not addressed specifically to Paul or the Corinthians but to "those who proclaim the good news." Nevertheless, it is not this historical context that is important for Paul, but the fact that the Lord said it. It comes just after Paul has also quoted an oracle from "the Law of Moses" to show that what he is saying rests not on merely human authority, but is derived from God's own words and intentions. The appeal to the "Lord" has a similar function.

[116] Aune, *Prophecy*, 257–58. Some have seen 1 Cor 14:37 as an appeal to "Jesus tradition." Gerhardsson suggests an *agraphon*, a piece of tradition which circulated as a saying of Jesus, but was not preserved in any extant Gospel, Birger Gerhardsson, *Memory and Manuscript: Oral Tradition and Written Transmission in Rabbinic Judaism and Early Christianity*, trans. Eric J. Sharpe, ASNU 22 (Lund: Gleerup, 1961), 306. Stettler suggests Jesus's command to love one's neighbour provides the basis for 1 Cor 13 and the ensuing discussion, Christian Stettler, "The 'Command of the Lord' in 1 Cor 14:37 – A Saying of Jesus?" *Biblica* 87 (2006): 42–51.

[117] The liturgical tradition of 1 Cor 11:23–26 is also "received from the Lord," and some scholars argue for a visionary or revelatory source: Francis Watson, "'I Received from the Lord ...': Paul, Jesus, and the Last Supper," in *Jesus and Paul Reconnected: Fresh Pathways into an Old Debate*, ed. Todd D. Still (Grand Rapids: Eerdmans, 2007), 103–24; Garroway, *Beginning of the Gospel*, 26.

should also theoretically have this access, but Paul deems it sadly lacking in 1 Cor 3:1.[118] Paul's responses also, while philosophical in much of their character and content, are not ultimately justified with appeals to reason but to the Lord and the *pneuma*. In the words of Wendt, "Though he makes ample use of intellectual skills, the immediate and ongoing involvement of God, Christ, and *pneuma* in his practices is vital to his form of expertise."[119] In this way Paul performs the function of an oracle with regard to the Corinthian community. The Corinthians refer the usual topics of oracle consultations (which concern matters of proximate concern such as marriage and cult) to Christ rather than to Zeus or Apollo, and seek the answers through Paul rather than the Pythia.

Freelance diviners had various ways of relating themselves to the more official oracular institutions, which were often cooperative rather than competitive.[120] I have already mentioned how the designation of the slave girl in Acts 16 as one with a πνεῦμα πύθωνα, "Python spirit," serves to link her divination with the inspiring power of Delphi. In this way she and other bellytalkers who bore the name "Pythones" could offer the same service as one would receive from an official visit to Delphi but through a more local proxy. Some magical papyri also exhibit this link to institutional oracles, such as one in which Apollo is called on to answer questions about divinatory matters (χρημάτισόν μοι, περὶ ὧν ἀξιῶ). The invoker wears white prophetic (προφητικῷ) robes and holds a branch of laurel to mimic the Pythia, then calls on Apollo to "leave Mount Parnassus and the Delphic Pytho" to come and answer his own questions (*PGM* I.262–300; cf. III.236–240). Another papyrus addresses Apollo as "Renowned Paian, who lives in Kolophon," evoking Apollo's oracle at Claros (*PGM* II.82–85).[121] Along with Apollo the invocation also calls on Iao, Michael, Gabriel, and Adonai to join him in his prophecies showing the possibility of cooperation across different ethnic religious and oracular traditions in this context (*PGM* I.300–305).

Alexander of Abonoteichus is said to have set up his own oracle in Paphlagonia, which delivered oracles from the snake god Glycon, himself a manifestation of Asclepius (Lucian, *Alex.* 14).[122] This new oracle, like its more

---

[118] The use of κἀγώ, "I also," suggests Paul's claim to pneumatic judgement is in part reactionary against others who are also utilising their pneumatic judgement, but wrongly in Paul's view. It at least assumes that he is not alone in being able to make this claim, Fee, *First Corinthians*, 393.

[119] Wendt, *At the Temple Gates*, 168.

[120] See Esther Eidinow, "Oracles and Oracle-Sellers: An Ancient Market in Futures," in *Religion and Competition in Antiquity*, ed. David Engels and Peter van Nuffelen, Collection Latomus 343 (Brussels: Latomus, 2014), 55–95.

[121] Iles Johnston, *Ancient Greek Divination*, 153–54.

[122] Lucian's portrayal of Alexander's oracle is highly satirical and derogatory, but there is enough evidence that the oracle was in fact highly popular and enduring. See Lane Fox, *Pagans and Christians*, 241–50; Iles Johnston, 101–5.

established counterparts, was tied to a specific location in a way the above examples were not. It also did not derive legitimacy from the institutions of Apollo, but from his son Asclepius whose incubation sanctuaries were already popular in Asia Minor. But even this oracle did not operate in open competition with the Apolline sanctuaries, rather Lucian says Alexander ingratiated himself to the priests of Claros, Didyma, and Mallos by sending some of his visitors to them for further consultation (*Alex.* 29).[123]

Paul's relationship to the institutional options available to the Corinthians was undoubtedly more antagonistic. All of Paul's claims should be filtered through his basic expectation of his converts to "turn from idols to serve the true and living God" (1 Thess 1:9). "When you were Gentiles," he reminds the Corinthians, "you were led astray to mute idols" but now believers are only to heed God's *pneuma* (1 Cor 12:2–3). This *pneuma* is not totally independent either as it carries its own set of connections. As the ethnic designation "when you were Gentiles" suggests, this *pneuma* connects believers to the God who is in Jerusalem via his "image," the Lord Jesus.[124] The primary "institutional" means of divination for this God is no longer the Urim and Thummim but the oracles recorded in the Jewish scriptures (on which see Chapter 4). But Paul also provides a more direct connection to this God through the *pneuma* of his son Jesus. The presence of this particular *pneuma* is vital for providing answers to the questions Paul receives, the actual means for which appears to be a mixture of pneumatic judgement and prophetic oracles given either to Paul himself or another prophet. Written oracles also come to play a part in informing the answers Paul gives and possibly remembered traditions about Jesus's earthly words, which are treated in a similar way.

Eschatological Mysteries

On three further occasions Paul reveals particular information about the eschaton, which he frames as new knowledge of hidden mysteries. They share a number of similar features, and are the passages scholars will most readily identify as oracular in some sense.[125]

Words of the Lord (1 Thessalonians 4:13–18)

In 1 Thess 4, Paul has already reminded the Thessalonians of a number of divine instructions given διὰ τοῦ κυρίου Ἰησοῦ, "through the Lord Jesus,"

---

[123] Wendt, *At the Temple Gates*, 16.
[124] See Matthew V. Novenson, "Messiahs and their Messengers," *STK* 95 (2019): 13–14; Wendt, *At the Temple Gates*, 148–50.
[125] They are the "only three 'safe' traces of Christian prophecies," in Paul for Luz, "Early Christian Prophetism," 65. Cf. Nicklas, "Paulus – der Apostel als Prophet," 92; Hill, *New Testament Prophecy*, 130–31 (though he demurs on 1 Thess 4:15). For synoptic comparisons, see Bockmuehl, *Revelation and Mystery*, 171; Merklein, "Theologe als Prophet," 389–90.

which include the eschatological warnings in 4:6 discussed above. In v. 13, he turns to a message of eschatological comfort with the wish that his audience not be ignorant (ἀγνοεῖν). In contrast to the surrounding reminders of prior knowledge (οἴδατε 4:2; 5:2), this suggests that he is about to disclose new information that they have not previously heard. This information concerns the eschatological fate of those who have died before Christ's parousia, so we can safely say that it concerns information not normally available by ordinary human means. His first general point is that God will raise the dead, which he justifies by the shared belief that God has already raised Jesus (v. 14). His next, more specific, point is spoken ἐν λόγῳ κυρίου, "by a word of the Lord."

The mention of the κύριος leads many to look for a source in the sayings of Jesus, some noting parallels in content with Jesus's eschatological discourse in Mark 13:26–27/Matt 24:30–31.[126] Whatever sources Paul may have had at his disposal, this word, more than any other in Paul, is presented with the biblical vocabulary of a prophetic oracle to the Thessalonians.[127] The phrase λόγος κυρίου, "word of the Lord," is a frequent idiom in the Greek Bible to denote prophetic revelation, rendering דבר יהוה. Nearly all of the prophetic books begin with a variant of the phrase "The word of the Lord came to [prophet's name]," which is then frequently repeated throughout the book to introduce new oracles.[128] The exact phrase that Paul uses, ἐν λόγῳ κυρίου, is less frequent, but occurs a number of times in a particular story in 3 Kgdms 13. Commentators often give this passage a perfunctory citation, but the frequency of the phrase here, and its relative scarcity elsewhere, warrants further attention.[129]

In 3 Kgdms 13 a "man of God" comes from Judah to Bethel and predicts the birth of Josiah, foretelling that he will desecrate the altar at Bethel by sacrificing priests on it. The narrator describes the initial journey from Judah to Bethel as happening ἐν λόγῳ κυρίου, "by a word of the Lord," (3 Kgdms 13:1) presumably meaning that he was instructed to go there in a revelation. This would be parallel to Paul's claim in Gal 2:2 that he went to Jerusalem κατὰ ἀποκάλυψιν, "according to a revelation." The man of God addresses his prediction to the

---

[126] Seyoon Kim, "The Jesus Tradition in 1 Thess 4:13–5:11," *NTS* 48 (2002): 225–42; David Wenham, *Paul: Follower of Jesus or Founder of Christianity?* (Grand Rapids: Eerdmans, 1995), 305–7.

[127] J. G. Davies, "The Genesis of Belief in an Imminent Parousia," *JTS* 14 (1963): 105–6.

[128] ἐγένετο λόγος κυρίου πρός ... Mic 1:1; Jonah 1:1; Zech 1:1; Jer 1:4; Ezek 1:3; λόγος κυρίου, ὃς ἐγενήθη πρός ... Hos 1:1; Joel 1:1; Zeph 1:1; ἐγένετο λόγος κυρίου ἐν χειρὶ Αγγαιου τοῦ προφήτου: Hag 1:1; λῆμμα λόγου κυρίου ἐπὶ τὸν Ισραηλ ἐν χειρὶ ἀγγέλου αὐτοῦ: Mal 1:1. Amos, Obadiah, Nahum and Isaiah, on the other hand, all feature introductions that foreground visionary experiences with the words Ὅρασις, "vision," and εἶδεν, "he saw" (though cf. Isa 1:10 Ἀκούσατε λόγον κυρίου).

[129] Cf. Aune, *Prophecy*, 255. Amidst the detailed linguistic analysis of the various elements of the phrase by Michael Pahl, he devotes no space to specifically examining the phrase as a whole in the Greek versions, Michael W. Pahl, *Discerning the 'Word of the Lord': The Word of the Lord in 1 Thessalonians 4:15*, LNTS 389 (London: T&T Clark, 2009), 106–115.

altar, "and he addressed the altar by a word of the Lord (ἐν λόγῳ κυρίου) and said 'Altar, altar, thus says the Lord: behold a son will be born to the house of David, Josiah his name'" (13:2). He then gives a sign (ἔδωκεν ... τέρας), by which his message and prophetic status will be validated, "this is the word (τὸ ῥῆμα), which the Lord spoke, saying, behold, the altar shall be torn down, and the fatness that is on it shall be poured out" (13:3). A few verses later, when the fulfilment of this sign is reported, it is described as having been given ἐν λόγῳ κυρίου, "by a word of the Lord" (13:5).

The king invites the man of God to come home with him to receive a gift, but the man refuses saying that he had been commanded by another word of the Lord (οὕτως ἐνετείλατό μοι ἐν λόγῳ κύριος λέγων) not to return the way he had come (13:9). As a sequel to this story a Bethelite prophet also attempts to bring the man of God back to his house for a meal. The man of God again refuses, citing the word of the Lord he had received (ἐντέταλταί μοι ἐν λόγῳ κύριος [13:17]), but the Bethelite prophet responds that he too is a prophet, and (falsely) that an angel had spoken to him by a word of the Lord (ἐν ῥήματι κυρίου) telling him to take the man into his house (13:18). When seated together at his house, the prophet receives another word of the Lord, this time using the more traditional prophetic formula, "And a word of the Lord came to the prophet (καὶ ἐγένετο λόγος κυρίου πρὸς τὸν προφήτην) ... and he said to the man of God who came from Judah, saying, 'thus says the Lord: because you embittered the word of the Lord (τὸ ῥῆμα κυρίου) and have not kept the commandment (τὴν ἐντολήν), which the Lord your God commanded you ... your body shall not enter the tomb of your fathers'" (13:20–22).

The translator of this passage appears to take λόγος κυρίου and ἐν λόγῳ κυρίου as set phrases that translate דבר יהוה and בדבר יהוה respectively and refer to the process or event of divine revelation itself. The content of that revelation he describes consistently as τὸ ῥῆμα (κυρίου), variously rendering המופת, "the sign" (13:3); פי יהוה, "mouth of Yahweh" (13:21, 26), and הדבר, "the word," when it occurs on its own (13:32, 33, 34).[130] The MT describes the false message that the Bethelite prophet claims to have received "by a word of the Lord" the same way as the true revelations (בדבר יהוה), but the LXX uses the slightly different phrase ἐν ῥήματι κυρίου. This would seem to reflect a desire to reserve ἐν λόγῳ κυρίου for a moment of true revelation. This phrase can function as the complement to a number of different verbs. By a word of the Lord, one can arrive somewhere (παρεγένετο [13:1]), address someone or something (ἐπεκάλεσεν [13:2]), give a sign (τὸ τέρας, ὃ ἔδωκεν [13:5]), receive a command (ἐνετείλατό μοι [13:9, 17]), or speak a word (τὸ ῥῆμα, ὃ ἐλάλησεν

---

[130] Verses 33 and 34 do not refer to the content of the prophecy, and are usually translated "event," or "matter," but הדבר is still rendered as τὸ ῥῆμα.

[13:32, cf. 13:18]). All of these constructions make the best sense if ἐν λόγῳ κυρίου means something akin to "in accordance with, or by the authority of a prior revelation."[131] The phrase is usually used to refer back to a revelation given in the past, and on the one occasion a present moment of revelation is explicitly narrated, the narrator uses the more common prophetic formula καὶ ἐγένετο λόγος κυρίου πρὸς τὸν προφήτην, "the word of the Lord came to the prophet" (13:20).[132]

The remaining three uses of this phrase in the Greek Bible confirm this general sense of "in accordance with, and by the authority of a prior revelation," with various emphases depending on context. In 3 Kgdms 21:35, a prophet "said to his neighbour by a word of the Lord (εἶπεν . . . ἐν λόγῳ κυρίου), 'Strike me!'" The words themselves are not exactly an oracle, although they are described in the next verse as τῆς φωνῆς κυρίου, "the voice of the Lord." The phrase indicates that the prophet utters them with the authority of the Lord, and presumably in accordance with what he has been told to do by the Lord, as being struck enables the prophet to then stage a scenario in which he can deliver an oracle to the king. In Sir 48:3, Elijah is said to have "shut up the sky by a word of the Lord (ἐν λόγῳ κυρίου ἀνέσχεν οὐρανόν)," which again emphasises the divine authority of his words, but also implies he was acting at the Lord's behest. In 2 Chr 30, Hezekiah invites all of Israel and Judah to a Passover in Jerusalem. Most of the Israelite tribes ignore the summons, but the text says, "the hand of the Lord was on Judah (ἐν Ιουδα ἐγένετο χεὶρ κυρίου) to go and do according to the ordinance of the king and the rulers by a word of the Lord (ἐν λόγῳ κυρίου)" (30:12).

The phrase ἐν λόγῳ κυρίου here may modify τὸ πρόσταγμα, implying that the ordinance of the king was issued with divine authority, perhaps in accordance with previous revelations they had received or were in possession of. Summing up Hezekiah's reform efforts in 2 Chr 31:21 the narrator states that all of Hezekiah's work for the house of the Lord was ἐν τῷ νόμῳ καὶ ἐν τοῖς προστάγμασιν "according to the law and the ordinances," which suggests that the work of the king was in accordance with the prior commands of the Lord.[133] Every other

---

[131] This correlates with Pahl's locative and instrumental uses of ἐν, *Word of the Lord*, 109–110.
[132] Verse 2 is the most ambiguous as the message addressed ἐν λόγῳ κυρίου is introduced as the present speech of the Lord: τάδε λέγει κύριος in the same way as v. 20. The sign that is given in v. 3, however, reports the words the Lord spoke (ἐλάλησεν), and each further occurrence of the phrase explicitly refers back to past revelations.
[133] His installation of the priestly musicians was also according to what had previously been revealed to King David, "according to the command of King David and Gad the king's seer and Nathan the prophet, because the ordinance was through a command of the Lord by the hand of the prophets (δι' ἐντολῆς κυρίου τὸ πρόσταγμα ἐν χειρὶ τῶν προφητῶν [29:25])." And his general cleansing of the temple was κατὰ τὴν ἐντολὴν τοῦ βασιλέως διὰ προστάγματος κυρίου, "according to the command of the king through the ordinance of the Lord" (29:15).

instance of ἐν λόγῳ κυρίου, however, has directly modified a verb, so the text as it stands may instead modify the construction ἐλθεῖν τοῦ ποιῆσαι. This would imply that the Judahites obeyed the command of the king in accordance with a separate revelation. The phrase ἐν Ιουδα ἐγένετο χεὶρ κυρίου, "the hand of the Lord was on Judah," parallels statements of divine inspiration, especially in Ezekiel, καὶ ἐγένετο ἐπ' ἐμὲ χεὶρ κυρίου, "and the hand of the Lord was upon me" (Ezek 1:3; 3:14, 22; 8:1), which led to visions and oracles, so it is possible the translator understood a collective revelation prompting Judah's obedience in this matter.

When Paul says, τοῦτο γὰρ ὑμῖν λέγομεν ἐν λόγῳ κυρίου, "for this we say to you by a word of the Lord," it is likely, then, that he intends his words to be received with the authority of the Lord's words, and understood as resting on a previously received revelation.[134] The κύριος for Paul is fairly consistently Jesus, but this does not mean that the basic sense of the phrase is radically altered. In the same way Paul can use a biblical prophetic concept such as ἡμέρα κυρίου, "the day of the Lord" (Isa 13:6, 9; Joel 1:15; 2:1; 4:14; Zeph 1:14; Obad 1:15; Ezek 7:10; 13:5; Jer 32:33; Mal 3:19) and use it in a way that is substantially unaltered, but with a subtly different referent (1 Thess 5:2).

The content of the revelation consists of a short statement that expresses Paul's main point in this context, "we who live, who are left until the parousia of the Lord will certainly not precede those who sleep" (v. 15). Next comes an eschatological scenario that either contextualises, or provides the basis for, the original terser statement. This includes the voice of an archangel, the blast of a trumpet, the Lord descending from heaven, the dead being raised, and the living meeting the Lord in the air. While elements of the eschatological scenario may be common to more generally held eschatological beliefs, it is going too far to call it "familiar eschatological tradition."[135] It may be familiar to scholars acquainted with the broad sweep of Jewish literature, but Paul's audience would still assume such knowledge to have a basis in revelation, whether that revelation has been passed on in tradition from previous visionaries or given directly to Paul himself.

Knowledge of the eschatological and cosmological fate of the dead is not of the same order as the more "proximate concerns about specific courses of action" discussed in the previous sections.[136] Eschatological forecasts are, however, what one might expect to hear from someone who has experienced

---

[134] Pahl's argument (*Word of the Lord*) that the "word of the Lord" refers to "the gospel" in some way rests mainly on the later evidence of Acts. Paul's solitary use of the phrase ὁ λόγος τοῦ κυρίου in 1 Thess 1:8 is not enough evidence to suggest a new "Christianised" use of the term for Paul himself.

[135] As done by Bockmuehl, *Revelation and Mystery*, 172. It seems what he mainly means here is "Jesus-tradition" as these are the examples he explicitly cites, although he notes them "in addition to commonplace apocalyptic expectations."

[136] Struck, *Divination and Human Nature*, 217.

ascents to heaven (2 Cor 12:1–10), and has received revelation of "what God has prepared for those who love him" (1 Cor 2:9).[137] Cicero relates the same sort of information in his *Dream of Scipio*, when Scipio asks Africanus "whether he and my father Paulus and the others whom we think of as dead, were really still alive" (*Rep.* 6.9.14). The response reveals to him that true life is only found in escape from the body, "For man was given life that he might inhabit that sphere called Earth . . . and he has been given a soul out of those eternal fires which you call stars and planets" (*Rep.* 6.9.15). Living with justice and duty towards family and fatherland is "the road to the skies, to that gathering of those who have completed their earthly lives and been relieved of the body, and who live in yonder place which you now see" (*Rep.* 6.9.16).[138] The specific content is of course not the same as Paul's, but the eschatological and cosmological nature of the information is similar. An eschatological prediction for Paul also serves the prophetic function of παράκλησις, perhaps best rendered "comfort" in this case, as Paul exhorts his audience to παρακαλεῖτε ἀλλήλους ἐν τοῖς λόγοις τούτοις, "comfort one another by these words" (1 Thess 4:18; cf. 1 Cor 14:3).

Mysteries (1 Corinthians 15:51–52; Romans 11:25–27)

The mystery revealed in 1 Cor 15:51 also concerns the fate of the dead at the resurrection, and shares the concern for the equality of those who are living and who have died at Jesus's return. While in 1 Thess 4 the focus was on the presence of both the dead and living together with Jesus, answering the question: how will the dead be able to meet Jesus at his return?, in 1 Cor 15:51, the focus is the nature of the resurrected bodies, answering the implicit question: how will the living receive immortal bodies without dying first? This is a fair question given Paul's earlier statement that "What you sow [the animate body] does not come to life [as a pneumatic body] unless it dies" (1 Cor 15:36). Similar information was revealed to Scipio: souls, made from the stuff of the stars, can only enjoy life in the immortal spheres once the soul has been relieved of the body. Paul, again, gives a pithy statement, "We will not all sleep, but we will all be changed," followed by an eschatological scenario which explains the statement and follows the same outline as the scenario in 1 Thess 4:16–17. This includes the sound of a trumpet, the resurrection of the dead first, and then "we" who are still alive being transformed. Rather than a "word of the Lord," Paul introduces this information as a "mystery": ἰδοὺ μυστήριον ὑμῖν λέγω, "Behold I tell you a mystery" (15:51).[139]

---

[137] Cf. Himmelfarb (*Ascent to Heaven*) and the discussion in Chapter 2.
[138] The Milky Way, crucially above the moon, where everything is eternal (*Rep.* 6.9.17).
[139] On the term μυστήριον, see Günther Bornkamm, "μυστήριον, μυέω," *TDNT* 4:802–28; Raymond E. Brown, *The Semitic Background of the Term "Mystery" in the New Testament* (Philadelphia: Fortress, 1968); A. E. Harvey, "The Use of Mystery Language in the Bible," *JTS* 31 (1980): 320–36; Lang, *Mystery*, 9–20.

This term is less precise than a "word of the Lord" for discerning the source and means of revelation. The visionary, Enoch, claims to know mysteries because he has seen the heavenly tablets and understood their contents (1 Enoch 103:1), mysteries are revealed to Daniel in a vision, which enable him to interpret Nebuchadnezzar's dreams (Dan 2:19, 27–28). The Teacher of Righteousness knew the mysteries contained in prophetic texts because God had put "understanding in his heart" to interpret the eschatological secrets written down by previous prophets (1QpHab 2:8–10; 7:4–5).[140] Paul can appeal to a similar array of divinatory methods, including: wisdom revealed by God's *pneuma* (1 Cor 2:10–16), visionary experiences (2 Cor 12:1–10), and the interpretation of written prophecies (Rom 1:2), so that exactly how he arrived at the mystery he now speaks is undetermined, but consonant with Paul's general claims to divine revelation and of a piece with the previous "word of the Lord."[141]

Written prophecies do appear to play some role in this case, as part of the eschatological scenario described is explained in terms of a composite citation from Isa 25:8 and Hos 13:14, "Death has been swallowed up in victory, where, death, is your victory? Where death is your sting?" Paul then stops to interpret elements of this oracle in v. 56. T. J. Lang points out that this is not a "prooftext" from which Paul derives his mystery of the pneumatic transformation of bodies at the parousia. Rather the text receives a new interpretation and specificity in the light of that mystery.[142] The composite oracle is one component among many that help to form the revealed eschatological scenario. It both receives its interpretation from the revealed mystery, and adds further specificity and a level of interpretation to the mystery itself.

Written prophecies are even more closely intertwined with eschatological revelation in Rom 11:25–27. So much so, that some see Paul's interpretation of scripture as the sole source of the revealed mystery in this instance.[143] Like 1 Thess 4:15, this passage starts with a desire to correct his audience's ignorance (οὐ γὰρ θέλω ὑμᾶς ἀγνοεῖν [v. 25]), and like 1 Cor 15:51, reveals a "mystery." Instead of being concerned with the respective fates of the living

---

[140] The words ב[לבו בינ]ה are admittedly conjectural, but reconstructed from similar phrasing in 1QHab 6.19. See Timothy H. Lim, *The Earliest Commentary on the Prophecy of Habakkuk* (Oxford: Oxford University Press, 2020), 51.

[141] Bockmuehl (*Revelation and Mystery*, 174–75) suggests "a dynamic inter-reaction of Scripture, [exegetical] tradition, and religious experience (which may or may not *include* a vision). The catalyst ... is a Biblical meditation sparked by a problem of current concern." This would see the biblical text functioning very much like an oracle to which questions are posed and an inspired answer sought.

[142] Lang, *Mystery*, 47–48.

[143] E.g., N. T. Wright, *Paul and the Faithfulness of God* (London: SPCK, 2013), 2:1232.

and the dead at the parousia, this passage is concerned with the respective fates of Jews and Gentiles.

> A hardening has come upon part of Israel, until the full number of the Gentiles has come in. And so all Israel will be saved; as it is written, "Out of Zion will come the Deliverer; he will banish ungodliness from Jacob." "And this is my covenant with them, when I take away their sins." (Rom 11:25–27)

Again, this citation is not a proof text from which Paul reasons to the mystery. In comparison with 1 Cor 15:51 and 1 Thess 4:15, the citation serves the same function as the narration of an eschatological scenario, against which the main statement makes sense, and would also have been assumed to stem from revelation. Aune includes the citation as part of the oracle itself on form-critical grounds.[144] If this is accepted, it would be comparable to other contexts in which new oracles use the words of older texts. Cassius Dio reports consultations taking place at the oracle of Zeus Belus in Apamea. The responses received here consisted of lines from well-known literary texts from Homer and Euripides. Scholars have speculated that the oracle may have functioned as a sort of lot oracle, in which dice rolls may have pointed one to the right text to read out as a response.[145] As far as Dio's account is concerned, however, the god simply spoke (εἰρήκει, ἔφη) the words of Homer and Euripides to his consultees (79.8.6–8; 79.40). For Paul, in this instance, the words of two ancient oracles are appended to his own to form a new oracle, which collectively reveals a mystery about the eschatological salvation of Jews and Gentiles.

Conclusion

This chapter has surveyed the various forms of speech through which divine information can be received and conveyed for Paul. This ranges from the direct and unrestrained groanings and babblings produced by *pneuma*, to prophecies in which pneumatic knowledge and visionary experiences are filtered and interpreted through the *nous*. Our clearest glimpse of this direct sort

---

[144] Aune, *Prophecy*, 252.
[145] The dice hypothesis is based on *PGM* VII. 1–148, which lists 216 discrete quotations from the *Odyssey* and *Iliad*. These are listed next to possible permutations of three dice rolls, so that each permutation leads one to a particular quote as a divinatory answer. See Betz, *Greek Magical Papyri*, 112–19; Pieter W. van der Horst, "Sortes: Sacred Books as Instant Oracles in Late Antiquity," in *Japheth in the Tents of Shem: Studies on Jewish Hellenism in Antiquity*, CBET 32 (Leuven: Peeters, 2002), 179–80.

of prophetic speech is when Paul refers back to oral prophecies he delivered to his assemblies, which predicted future suffering and warned of eschatological judgement. On other occasions he references words and commands of the Lord, which may refer back to earlier moments of inspiration and revelation, but can now be deployed in the context of more involved argumentation and interpretation of written texts. These are brought forward in response to smaller scale queries of proximate concern, such as whether to marry or remarry, how one should or should not be involved in sacrificial cult, and how to understand and engage with things of the *pneuma*. To larger and more expansive questions about the fate of different people-groups at Christ's parousia (dead, living, Jew, Gentile) Paul deploys his most traditionally Jewish and apocalyptic prophetic terminology to provide details about the events of the eschaton. This process begins to move away from the spontaneous utterance of a prophecy, towards knowledge derived from visions of heaven, as well as the preservation and subsequent use of prophecies and oracles for various purposes.[146] The next chapter will consider in greater detail how Paul uses his largest repository of previously revealed divine wisdom – the texts of his Jewish scriptures.

---

[146] Although see Bent Noack ("Current and Backwater in the Epistle to the Romans," *ST* 19 [1965]: 165–66), who attempted to overcome the apparent inconsistency between Rom 9 and 11 by suggesting that the oracle of 11:25–26 was spontaneously received while in the process of dictating this part of the letter!

CHAPTER 4

Texts

The last chapter examined the phenomenon of prophetic speech in Paul's letters. Prophetic speech was not always spontaneous but sometimes drew on oracles that had been delivered previously and stored up in tradition or in writing. When Paul explicitly quotes speech from a divine being, his largest source by far is the various texts that make up the Jewish sacred writings, which he says preserve the "oracles of God" (Rom 3:2; cf. 11:4). Written oracle collections were a common feature of the ancient world, where they were generally understood to be the written records of oracles previously uttered under inspiration, either by the priest at an official oracle sanctuary, such as Delphi or Dodona, or by independent inspired figures of the legendary past, such as Bacis, Musaeus, or the Sibyl.[1] This chapter further examines Paul's use of sacred texts both as a part of his own divinatory repertoire, and as part of the divinatory use of texts in the ancient world.

Scholars have generally resisted seeing any analogy between Paul's use of scripture and such oracle collections of the ancient world, more often viewing "scripture" as a uniquely Jewish category, with Paul as a uniquely Christian interpreter of it.[2] Recently, however, those who have applied the term

---

[1] Bacis and Sibyl appear to have been the most popular seers to have had their oracles quoted, to the extent that it is unclear whether these designations sometimes function just as generic names for male and female seers. See Fontenrose, *Delphic Oracle*, 159–61; Stoneman, *Ancient Oracles*, 171.
[2] Literature on "Paul's use of scripture" is voluminous. Works that pay particular attention to the wider Jewish and Christian contexts include Otto Michel, *Paulus und seine Bibel* (Gütersloh: Bertelsmann, 1929); C. H. Dodd, *According to the Scriptures: The Sub-Structure of New Testament Theology* (London: Collins, 1952); E. Earle Ellis, *Paul's Use of the Old Testament* (Edinburgh: Oliver & Boyd, 1957); Richard N. Longenecker, *Biblical Exegesis in the Apostolic Period* (Grand Rapids: Eerdmans, 1975), 104–32; Dietrich-Alex Koch, *Die Schrift als Zeuge des Evangeliums: Untersuchungen zur Verwendung und zum Verständnis der Schrift bei Paulus*, BHT 69 (Tübingen: Mohr Siebeck, 1986); Richard B. Hays, *Echoes of Scripture in the Letters of Paul* (New Haven: Yale University Press, 1989); Timothy H. Lim, *Holy Scripture in the Qumran Commentaries and Pauline*

"divination" to Paul have made "textual divination" a matter of first importance in comparing Paul with his environment. Wendt and Eyl have both recontextualised Paul's textual practices within the divinatory use of texts such as Homer, Orphic literature, or the Chaldean Oracles.[3] Eyl notes that divinatory interpretations of texts exist on a sliding scale, with bibliomancy on one end: "the practice of opening (or unrolling) a text, pointing to a random passage, and imagining that it delivers a prophetic message to or about an inquirer."[4] On the other end of the scale are interpretations that employ "a greater cognitive investment through intellectual concepts such as metaphor, allegory, theories about the cosmos and gods, complex textual interpretations, and even more complex reinterpretations."[5] Both Eyl and Wendt draw on the work of Struck to posit allegory, understood in a broad sense, as the basic hermeneutical stance underwriting all such divinatory practice in Paul and his wider context.[6] The basic presupposition is that such texts are repositories of hidden truth, possessing deeper meaning than

---

Letters (Oxford: Oxford University Press, 1997); Watson, *Paul and the Hermeneutics of Faith*; Stanley E. Porter and Christopher D. Stanley, eds., *As It Is Written: Studying Paul's Use of Scripture*, SymS 50 (Atlanta: SBL Press, 2008); Christopher D. Stanley, ed., *Paul and Scripture: Extending the Conversation*, ECL 9 (Atlanta: SBL Press, 2012).

[3] Wendt, *At the Temple Gates*, 129–33, 151–56; Eyl, *Signs, Wonders, and Gifts*, 102–112. Christopher Stanley's work also stands out for its readiness to compare Paul's use of scripture with the broader Graeco-Roman world. His first works compared Paul's citations with citations of Homer by Greek writers as an example of "archetypal texts of their culture": Christopher D. Stanley, "Paul and Homer: Greco-Roman Citation Practice in the First Century CE," *NovT* 32 (1990): 48–78; Christopher D. Stanley, *Paul and the Language of Scripture: Citation Technique in the Pauline Epistles and Contemporary Literature*, SNTSMS 74 (Cambridge: Cambridge University Press, 1992). In a later work, taking an audience-centred approach, he tentatively asks "might Paul have been regarded as a sort of 'diviner' in his use of quotations from the Jewish Scriptures?": Christopher D. Stanley, *Arguing with Scripture: The Rhetoric of Quotations in the Letters of Paul* (New York: T&T Clark, 2004), 59.

[4] Eyl, *Signs, Wonders, and Gifts*, 102–3. On bibliomancy, see Harry Gamble, *Books and Readers in the Early Church: A History of Early Christian Texts* (New Haven: Yale University Press, 1995), 239–41; van der Horst, "Sortes," 159–90; Robert Wiśniewski, "Pagans, Jews, Christians, and a Type of Book Divination in Late Antiquity," *JECS* 24 (2016): 553–68. It is hard to believe such a practice did not exist in Paul's time, but it should be noted that most of the clear evidence for it is considerably later than Paul, and the practice appears much more clearly as a feature of late antiquity. First Maccabees 3:48, which is sometimes cited to show the early Jewish adoption of bibliomancy, certainly shows Jewish scripture being used in a divinatory way, but nowhere says the consultation was random. For a detailed examination of the divinatory elements in this passage, see Tervanotko, "Searching the Book of Law," 121–37.

[5] Eyl, *Signs, Wonders, and Gifts*, 104.

[6] Struck, *Birth of the Symbol*, 165–92. This is not to say that all allegory is therefore divination, as this very much depended on the individual interpreter and the view they held of the text they were interpreting. One of the strongest and most famous statements of the divine inspiration of poets is in Plato (*Ion* 534d), but Struck notes how this view was "nuanced, modified, denatured into a literary trope, and even rejected by some" (*Birth of the Symbol*, 168), and so the extent to which allegorists saw their work as accessing divine knowledge will vary depending on the extent to which they subscribed to such a theory of poetic inspiration.

what is apparent on the surface. Bringing Paul into conversation with such textual practices reframes our existing categories, and invites fresh exegesis which more closely considers the similarities and differences between these various textual forms of divination.

In doing this it will be impossible to exhaustively analyse every Pauline citation across all of his letters. Rather, after some general comments on Paul's understanding of the nature of his sacred texts, I will opt for detail over comprehensiveness and focus on some select examples that illustrate all the most pertinent aspects of his textual divination. I also deliberately restrict my analysis in this chapter to explicit citations. Paul undoubtedly alludes to his sacred texts at a number of points, but pinpointing such allusions with certainty is a much harder task about which there is little agreement in method or practice.[7] To slightly preempt the discussion below, in my view, most of Paul's allusions reflect the way Paul's language and modes of thought have been influenced by his ancestral scriptures (for example, the language of prophetic calling in Gal 1:15–16), which is different to the explicit citation and interpretation of a divine, oracular source of authority.

Types of Authority

One of the biggest obstacles to seeing an analogy between Paul's use of scriptural texts and oracle collections is the unconscious (or sometimes conscious) assumption that Jewish scripture in Paul's day was a single, unified body of literature, with a fixed canon, that held normative authority for all of Jewish society.[8] Such a canon appears "radically different" from the various different oracle collections conceptualised by modern scholars as a "rag-bag of sayings and cryptic wisdom."[9] Paul himself can sometimes seem to reinforce this view when he cites from an undifferentiated ἡ γραφή, and the texts he directly quotes can all be found within the standard canons of a modern OT.[10]

---

[7] See Paul Foster, "Echoes without Resonance: Critiquing Certain Aspects of Recent Scholarly Trends in the Study of the Jewish Scriptures in the New Testament," *JSNT* 38 (2015): 96–111.
[8] These features are explicitly brought forward (to various degrees) to reject any comparison by W. D. Davies, "Reflections about the Use of the Old Testament in the New in its Historical Context," *JQR* 74 (1983): 105–36; Koch, *Die Schrift*, 190; Wright, *Paul and the Faithfulness of God*, 1351–52.
[9] Wright, *Paul and the Faithfulness of God*, 1351.
[10] His most cited books are Isaiah (21x), Psalms (16x), Deuteronomy (12x) and Genesis (11x). Most other books of the traditional Hebrew canon receive at least one citation or allusion from Paul, but not Esther, Song of Songs, Ruth, or Ezra-Nehemiah. It is sometimes said that Paul's Bible was exclusively the Septuagint, although the boundaries for this are no easier to define in the first century CE. Timothy Lim also sounds some words of caution on identifying Paul's scriptures too easily with the LXX, Timothy H. Lim, *The Formation of the Jewish Canon* (New Haven: Yale University Press, 2013), 165–66. First Corinthians 2:9 contains a quotation introduced with Paul's usual καθὼς γέγραπται, which cannot be convincingly traced to a source in the Hebrew Bible or Greek Septuagint, and there is no agreement on what the source may be (see Chapter 1, n. 85).

As David Lincicum has recently cautioned, however, "there was no single book that contained all the authoritative scriptural traditions of Israel in Paul's day."[11] Rather there were collections of individual scrolls with variously secure authoritative status.[12] Most recent scholars now question the existence of a closed Jewish canon in the first century CE, and prefer to speak of a "diversity of collections of authoritative scriptures"[13] or a "more amorphous sense of revealed and authoritative literature"[14] whose text was not rigidly controlled.[15] Closer examination of Paul's own citations also reveals a more varied texture to his understanding of the material, which distinguishes different levels and sources of authority that speak within these different texts.

Ancestral, Oracular, and Prophetic

Rather than seeing Jewish sacred texts as a single, homogeneous collection, which is divinely revealed in its entirety, George van Kooten has identified three levels of authority which Paul ascribes to the Jewish sacred texts. These are ancestral, oracular, and prophetic.[16] Ancestral authority for van Kooten is operative when Paul attributes citations to human authors such as David, Isaiah, and Moses, and in his references to "the law," which he cites as revered ancestors and ancestral tradition respectively. He contrasts this with oracular authority in which God (or the κύριος) speaks directly in the first person, which Paul often acknowledges with phrases such as εἶπεν ὁ θεός (2 Cor 6:16;

---

[11] David Lincicum, "How Did Paul Read Scripture?" in Longenecker, *The New Cambridge Companion to St Paul*, 226.

[12] Stanley E. Porter, "Paul and His Use of Scripture: Further Considerations," in Porter and Land, *Paul and Scripture*, 10–11.

[13] Lim, *Jewish Canon*, 185–86.

[14] Eva Mroczek, *The Literary Imagination in Jewish Antiquity* (Oxford: Oxford University Press, 2016), 13.

[15] The following works all differ from each other in significant aspects, but all, in their own way, argue against the existence of a single closed canon of texts normative for all Jewish people at the time of Paul: Barton, *Oracles of God*, 35–95; John J. Collins, "Before the Canon: Scriptures in Second Temple Judaism," in *Old Testament. Past, Present, and Future: Essays in Honor of Gene M. Tucker*, ed. J. L. Mays, D. L. Petersen, and K. H. Richards (Nashville: Abingdon, 1995), 225–41; Lim, *Jewish Canon*; Mroczek, *Literary Imagination*; Michael L. Satlow, *How the Bible Became Holy* (New Haven: Yale University Press, 2014).

[16] George H. van Kooten, "Ancestral, Oracular and Prophetic Authority: 'Scriptural Authority' According to Paul and Philo," in *Authoritative Scriptures in Ancient Judaism*, ed. Mladen Popović, JSJSup 141 (Leiden: Brill, 2010), 267–308. Satlow (*How the Bible Became Holy*, 4–5) also proposes three different kinds of authority which he applies to texts in general: literary (earlier texts that are used as models and inspiration for new texts), oracular (texts that contain messages from the divine realm), and normative (texts that dictate behaviour). He places Paul's use of scripture in the oracular category.

cf. 2 Cor 4:6), λέγει κύριος (Rom 12:19; 14:11; 1 Cor 14:21; 2 Cor 6:17, 18), or simply λέγει where God or the Lord is clearly the speaker (Rom 9:12, 15, 25; 2 Cor 6:2; Gal 3:16). Crucially, in each of these cases God is also the speaker in Paul's source text, so Paul does not view "the writings" as a whole as the direct speech of God, but is aware of the specific oracles that they contain.[17] Oracular terminology such as λόγια in Rom 3:2 and χρηματισμός in Rom 11:3 further contribute to the impression that Paul sees his sacred texts as receptacles of divine oracles, uttered in the past to and through certain prophetic figures.[18] They are records of previous divinatory encounters.

Van Kooten's third category of "prophetic authority" derives from a distinction Philo theorises, but Paul appears to presuppose, in which some oracles are spoken directly by God in his own person, while others are spoken under divine influence, but in the prophet's own voice, using the prophet's own words (Philo, *Mos.* 2.187–91). This is somewhat akin to the distinction between the Pythia and the Sibyl in their modes of inspiration; the former spoke the words of Apollo directly, whereas the latter spoke her own words under Apollo's influence. For Philo, Moses can operate in both modes at different times. In the last chapter, I surveyed the variety of ways Paul understood divine speech to function, and argued that Paul distinguished within his own speech between direct prophetic oracles and his own pneumatic judgement (1 Cor 7:10–40).[19] Paul also acknowledged similar distinctions in the speech of Moses, Isaiah, and David.

An important example of this may be found in Paul's treatment of the story of Abraham in Rom 4. In contrast to Gal 3:7–9 and 3:16–18 where the words of God's promise are the focus of attention, Rom 4:1–25 focuses on the phrase "Abraham believed God, and it was reckoned to him as righteousness" (Rom 4:3, 9, 22, 23). In this case, unusually, Paul does not report the speech of God, but the prophetic comment of the narrator, presumably Moses, whom

---

[17] Van Kooten, "Ancestral, Oracular and Prophetic," 279. 1 Cor 14:21 is the only ambiguous case. Paul evidently quotes it as God's words with the first-person singular form λαλήσω, but the LXX has the third-person plural λαλήσουσι referring to the priest and prophet of Isa 28:7. The MT, with Paul, understands God as the one who will speak, but expresses it in the third person ידבר. Christopher Stanley (*Paul and the Language of Scripture*, 197–205) describes Paul's relationship to the LXX in this passage as "one of the greatest challenges in the entire corpus of Pauline citations." Overall he opts for a Hebraising revision of the LXX as Paul's *Vorlage* to which Paul has added a number of his own alterations.

[18] "Jeremiah, who is known as the author of the book of Jeremiah, is a prophet not because he wrote a book but because he received oracles," van Kooten, "Ancestral, Oracular and Prophetic," 281.

[19] Cf. van Kooten, "Ancestral, Oracular and Prophetic," 298–99. He rightly notes that Paul's classification of contemporary prophetic speech generally fits in the more "prophetic" as opposed to "directly oracular" category.

he credits with privileged insight and understanding into God's response to Abraham's faithfulness. This insight is still authoritative and prophetic as it could not be known by ordinary means, and was written not just as a statement about Abraham's righteousness, but also for the sake of Paul's generation, "who trust in the one who raised Jesus our Lord from the dead" (Rom 4:24).[20]

Some nuance of van Kooten's categories is needed though. While on some occasions Paul does appear to quote Isaiah or David for examples of their human experience (Rom 4:6–8; 10:16), on other occasions he cites these human authors as reporting the first-person speech of God. In Rom 10:19–21, for example, Moses is credited with saying, "I will make you jealous by those who are not a nation; with a foolish nation I will make you angry," and Isaiah says, "I have been found by those who did not seek me; I have shown myself to those who did not ask for me." This suggests Paul cites Moses and Isaiah not merely as revered ancestors but as ancient prophets, which would place these instances into van Kooten's oracular category. This is not an unusual way to cite oracles, as Delphic oracles are also interchangeably attributed to the god Apollo and the Pythia. Diodorus Siculus, for example, is representative of a common formula when he says, "Myscellus . . . went from Rhypê to Delphi and inquired of *the god* concerning the begetting of children. And *the Pythia* answered in this way" (Diodorus Siculus 8.17.1).[21] Apollodorus equally implies no discontinuity between speakers when he gives the reverse: "[Aegeus] went to *the Pythia* and consulted the oracle concerning the begetting of children. And *the god* gave an oracle to him." (Apollodorus 3.15.6). In the same way a citation attributed to David or Isaiah does not rule out the citation of an oracle.

Paul's citation of "the law" as an ancestral authority is also complicated. On the one occasion Paul discusses the origin of the Jewish law he describes it as διαταγεὶς δι' ἀγγέλων, "constituted through angels" (Gal 3:19). Paul uses the mediating nature of angels to rhetorically devalue the law in relation to Christ and the promise given to Abraham, but by doing this it is clear that Paul ascribes to the law more than a purely human authority. When he cites from "the law of Moses" in 1 Cor 9:9, the law is explicitly adduced in contrast to "human authority" and treated as an oracle. The following question, "Is it for oxen that God is concerned?" shows that the words of this law at least reflect God's concerns when interpreted properly.[22] These factors suggest that Paul's

---

[20] "Recounting details about the past which had not been recorded elsewhere is an equally suitable task for a prophet, since it too requires supernatural illumination," Barton, *Oracles of God*, 224. Cf. Homer's description of the augur Calchas as one who had knowledge of "things that were, and that were to be, and that had been before" (*Il.* 1.70).

[21] Cf. Diodorus Siculus 9.3.2; 12.10.5; Aelian, *Var. hist.* 2.32; Plutarch, *Quaest. rom.* 265a.

[22] On different approaches to "divine law," see Christine Hayes, *What's Divine About Divine Law? Early Perspectives* (Princeton: Princeton University Press, 2015), esp. 140–64.

varied citation practice indicates different sources of authority, but not necessarily different levels, as they can all be classed as divine in some sense. The majority of Paul's citations, though, tend to fall into the oracular or prophetic categories.

Paying attention to Paul's citations, and the sources to which he attributes his various references, shows him to be more discriminating than his generic references to ἡ γραφή can lead one to believe. Rather than a single, transparently divine text, Paul cites various ancient "prophets in the holy writings" such as David, Moses, and Isaiah, through whom the Jewish god has previously spoken. Viewing the scriptures as an oracle collection in this way more readily invites comparison with the various ways the oracles of other inspired figures of the legendary past, such as Bacis, the Sibyl, or the Pythia, were used and interpreted in the ancient world. This is arguably a closer and more straightforward point of comparison than the more sophisticated and intentional allegorical exegeses of Homeric texts, although the basic interpretative principle remains the same.[23] In the following section I will examine Paul's predictive use of oracles, which includes both oracles that predict events in recent history and oracles that predict events that are still future for Paul. Following this, I will examine a further use for oracles that is more neglected in scholarly studies, which sees in them more general divine wisdom, and truths about the character and nature of gods.

Predictive Oracles: Present and Future

One of the most obvious and well-known uses of a written oracle is as a prediction of future events, most often events that are seen to be fulfilled in the interpreter's own day. One need only think of the many oracles (λόγιά) "uttered long ago" that Thucydides reports were circulated in the Peloponnesian War, which predicted the outcome of various battles (Thucydides 2.8.3; 2.21.3; 2.54.2; 5.26.3–4). Closer to Paul's own time the Sibylline books at Rome were thought to contain predictions of the whole of Rome's history.[24] A college of priests, the *(quin)decimviri sacris faciundis*, consulted these oracles throughout the Roman Republic and early Empire in response to prodigies

---

[23] Paul engages in conscious allegory of a narrative text once in Gal 4:21–31. Material from the Pentateuch offers more opportunity for such reading, but most of the time he simply claims to interpret God's speech in oracles. Eyl (*Signs, Wonders, and Gifts*, 108–9) is correct that this still requires "decontextualization, transportation, translation, and recontextualized reinterpretation," but it is less clear that Paul engages this "prophetic-allegorical" strategy consciously, or that he would have himself seen the similarities between these reading strategies.

[24] Wendt, *At the Temple Gates*, 41.

and portents, which were interpreted as signs that the Romans needed to seek peace with the gods.²⁵ The oracles, it seems (at least before 83 BCE), consisted in a prediction of the particular prodigy and a series of ritual expiations that were needed to placate the gods.²⁶ While it is the ritual prescriptions that are often foregrounded by Roman historians, the popular conception and use of the oracles focused on their predictive value, with the populace at times of crisis matching the predicted prodigies and portents to present realities (e.g., Cassius Dio 57.18.4–5; 62.18.3–5).

Paul regularly claims that recent events have been foretold by his sacred texts, often describing them with verbs prefixed with προ-. So in Rom 1:2 Paul's good news is pre-promised (προεπηγγείλατο) by God through his prophets in holy writings. In Gal 3:8 the writing foresees (προϊδοῦσα) that God would justify the Gentiles by faith, so pre-proclaims the good news (προευηγγελίσατο) to Abraham. In Gal 3:1 Jesus's death, and specifically his crucifixion, is forewritten (προεγράφη).²⁷ The main tenets of his good news in 1 Cor 15:3–4, including the Messiah's death for sins and resurrection on the third day, all happened "in accordance with the writings." In Rom 15:4 everything that has been forewritten (προεγράφη) is said to be instructive for Paul's readers so that they may have hope. This last statement occurs in a chapter of Romans that is dense with scriptural citations that Paul uses in diverse and interesting ways. Rather than attempt a comprehensive overview of Paul's predictive citations, an exegesis of Paul's citations in Rom 15 will form a useful case study of how

---

[25] The standard scholarly view of prodigies as signs that the *pax deum* has been breached and needs to be restored has recently been questioned by Susan Satterfield ("Prodigies, the Pax Deum and the Ira Deum," *CJ* 110 [2015]: 431–45), who draws on Federico Santangelo, "Pax Deorum and Pontiffs," in *Priests and State in the Roman World*, ed. James H. Richardson and Federico Santangelo (Stuttgart: Steiner, 2011), 161–86. In this revised view, the *pax deum* was "neither stable nor long-lasting" but constantly had to be sought (rather than restored) in times of crisis. Prodigies, thus, can signal divine displeasure, but can equally warn of coming disasters that have no link to wrongful Roman action.

[26] For the predictive and prescriptive nature of these oracles, see John North, "Diviners and Divination at Rome," in *Pagan Priests: Religion and Power in the Ancient World*, ed. Mary Beard and John North (Ithaca, NY: Cornell University Press, 1990), 54–55; Tadeusz Mazurek, "The decemviri sacris faciundis: supplication and prediction," in *Augusto augurio: Rerum humanarum et divinarum commentationes in honorem Jerzy Linderski*, ed. C. F. Konrad (Stuttgart: Steiner, 2004), 151–68. The nature of the oracles probably also changed in the first century BCE when the collection was reconstituted after being destroyed by fire, John J. Collins, "The Jewish Adaptation of Sibylline Oracles," in *Seers, Sibyls and Sages in Hellenistic-Roman Judaism*, JSJSup 54 (Leiden: Brill, 1997), 182–84.

[27] This example is normally translated as "proclaimed" or "publicly portrayed," which is a legitimate translation. Given the context though, a predictive sense should not be ruled out. On this verse and the predictive force of προγράφω in other texts, see Wendt, "Textual Prophecy," 369–89.

scriptural oracles function predictively for Paul, and will also illustrate a number of wider features of his divinatory use of texts.

Predictions of Past Events

Commentators mostly weaken the force of προεγράφη in Rom 15:4 to refer to things that were simply written in the past, which then have abiding value.[28] But Paul has just quoted a psalm that predicted the suffering of the Messiah, which invests it with a level of divine, or theological, interpretation. "The reproaches of those who reproach you have fallen on me" (Rom 15:3; Ps 69:9 [68:10 LXX]). The predictive nature of the psalm in this instance is bound up with the question of who the "me" of the citation refers to. Paul introduces the quotation by urging his readers to not look out for their own interests, but those of their neighbour because even the Messiah did not please himself. He then adduces the first-person words of the psalm in support of this statement with his favourite formula καθὼς γέγραπται, "as it is written." On the simplest reading the words must be those of the Messiah himself, so that Jesus the Messiah speaks through the mouth of David the psalmist and prophet.[29] This view has become generally accepted in recent scholarship, but explanations for why and how Paul treats these words as Jesus's own are various.

The Speaker of Psalm 68:10 LXX

The most common position sees the psalm functioning "typologically" so that the sufferings of David (or more generally a "righteous sufferer") are understood as a type, which in some way prefigures Jesus's own suffering. This reading has stronger and weaker iterations. Scott Hafemann understands the typological link as little more than a comparison, in which "Christ did not please himself *just as* the suffering righteous of the psalm experienced the rebellion of the unrighteous that was aimed at God himself."[30] The words of the psalm only function as the words of Jesus in the sense that some correspondence

---

[28] Dunn, *Romans 9–16*, 843; Jewett, *Romans*, 880–81; Joseph A. Fitzmyer, *Romans: A New Translation with Introduction and Commentary*, AB 33 (New York: Doubleday, 1993), 703.

[29] Eva Mroczek (*Literary Imagination*, 67–69) sees a range of possibilities for how people understood the connection between David and the Psalms in the first century, not all of which imply Davidic authorship. Paul, however, explicitly cites David as author and speaker of at least two psalms (Rom 4:6; 11:9) and it would be reasonable to suppose this is how he viewed the collection as a whole.

[30] Scott Hafemann, "Eschatology and Ethics: The Future of Israel and the Nations in Romans 15:1–13," *TynB* 51 (2000): 164–65 (italics original). Cf. Dunn, *Romans 9–16*, 838–39; Fitzmyer, *Romans*, 702–3.

can be seen in the situations of the two people. Richard Hays on the other hand sees a much stronger typological link, identifying the Davidic ascription of the psalm and Paul's reference to the title ὁ Χριστός as the specific rationale for Paul's identification. He offers a complex double typology in which "The Messiah embodies Israel's destiny in such a way that David's songs can be read retrospectively as a prefiguration of the Messiah's sufferings and glorification."[31]

A. T. Hanson, reacting against the typological readings of a previous generation, understood Paul's logic to be much simpler and more concrete. Starting from the position that Jesus was, for Paul, evidently pre-existent and active in the history of Israel (1 Cor 10:1–11 is his foundation text) he takes this text as an utterance of the pre-existent Christ, in which Jesus speaks directly to David about his own future suffering in the first person.[32] Matthew Bates continues much of Hanson's conclusions but shifts the focus onto a method of exegesis rather than beliefs about Christ's actual presence to David. This verse is for Bates an example of "prosopological exegesis," in which, because the text is seen as divinely inspired in a general sense, sections of text can read from the point of view of different dramatis personae. On this reading, Christ is not directly inspiring the oracle, but because David's words are divinely inspired, Paul can understand them to be spoken in the dramatic persona, or *prosopon*, of Christ. This view shares some features with first-century interpretations of Homer, and thus provides a link with the wider divinatory uses of texts in the Graeco-Roman world, albeit in a highly specialised sense.[33]

---

[31] Richard B. Hays, "Christ Prays the Psalms: Israel's Psalter as Matrix of Early Christology," in *The Conversion of the Imagination: Paul as Interpreter of Israel's Scripture* (Grand Rapids: Eerdmans, 2005), 115. Matthew Novenson puts similar emphasis on the Davidic and Messianic links, but is more circumspect about its specific nature preferring to opt for "a general perceived correspondence between David the χριστός and Jesus the χριστός [which] will have allowed for the psalms of David to be read as words of Christ," Matthew V. Novenson, *Christ Among the Messiahs: Christ Language in Paul and Messiah Language in Ancient Judaism* (Oxford: Oxford University Press, 2012), 156.

[32] A. T. Hanson, *Jesus Christ in the Old Testament* (London: SPCK, 1965), 153–160; A. T. Hanson, *Studies in Paul's Technique and Theology* (London: SPCK, 1974). He is followed by Leander E. Keck, "Christology, Soteriology, and the Praise of God (Romans 15:7–13)," in *The Conversation Continues: Studies in Paul and John in Honor of J. Louis Martyn*, ed. Robert T. Fortna and Beverly Roberts Gaventa (Nashville: Abingdon, 1990), 85–96. Bates misreads and complicates Hanson's thesis by labelling it a "sacramental" reading, and then critiques him for not explaining adequately "the mechanism by which the real presence of Jesus could be available to Paul via the text," Matthew W. Bates, *The Hermeneutics of the Apostolic Proclamation: The Center of Paul's Method of Scriptural Interpretation* (Waco, TX: Baylor University Press, 2012), 248 n. 65. Hanson is clear, though, that when he talks of "real presence" he means "the pre-existent Jesus actually present in OT events," that is, the real presence of Jesus to David in inspiring prophecy, not the real presence of Jesus to Paul in the text, Hanson, *Jesus Christ*, 176.

[33] The primary comparative evidence for prosopological exegesis as a reading strategy comes from the Church Fathers. The evidence from the wider Hellenistic world is much sparser and

Most oracle collections of the ancient world, however, were not attributed to a general sense of divine inspiration but connected to particular legendary seers who spoke for specific gods or divine beings. Bacis was supposed to have been inspired by nymphs (Pausanias 4.27.4; 10.12.11) and it is to them that the information he provides can be attributed (Aristophanes, *Pax* 1070), although other passages in Aristophanes seem to assume that Bacis's guidance ultimately comes from Apollo (*Eq.* 1002–96, 1229–40). Epimenides was also associated with nymphs although it is not as clear that they were the source of his divinatory capabilities.[34] Musaeus, as his name suggests, probably had a connection to the Muses. Elsewhere Pausanias says he had read the verses (ἔπη) of a nymph herself, Erato, who functioned as the prophetess of Pan's oracles. These oracles, presumably, although described as the nymph's, could ultimately be attributed to Pan (Pausanias 8.37.11–12).[35]

The multiple Sibyls generally spoke for Apollo, and this seems to be the case even in the Roman context of the Sibylline books, where the *(quin)decemviri*, who interpreted the Sibylline books, also functioned as priests with a particularly close association with Apollo.[36] The extant *Sibylline Oracles* explicitly repurpose the Sibyl to make her speak for the great God of the Hebrews (*Sib. Or.* 4.4–7). In the case of oracular shrines, the link to a particular god was even more explicit, and the form of inspiration most direct, as the Pythia at Delphi spoke the words of Apollo in the first person. Written collections of these oracles are more likely to be attributed directly to the god (Aristophanes, *Av.* 959–91). In this context then, oracle collections, while primarily ascribed to a particular seer, were also connected to a particular divinity who inspired them.

Paul's treatment of David as the psalmist could also make sense in this context as a prophet with a particular connection to Jesus as both his fleshly descendent and Messiah. David utters the oracles of the Messiah and at times can speak first-person prophecies in his voice. This is not to say that Paul would have taken every passage of the Psalms to be an oracle of the Christ, for neither did the legendary seers attributed to oracle collections only write oracles. Epimenides's oracles probably formed a "single composition of rather

---

more varied, see Bates, *Hermeneutics*, 209–12. In my view, the best example of prosopological exegesis in Paul is when he assigns speech to abstract principles such as "the righteousness from faith" in Rom 10:6–9. This is closer to Bates's example from Heraclitus in which the speech of a goddess, Athena, is abstracted to represent the speech of "reason" (Heraclitus, *All.* 62.1–2). In Paul's use of the Psalms he usually adds gods (or Messiahs) rather than removes or abstracts them.

[34] On the nymphs as a source of oracles, see H. W. Parke, *Sibyls and Sibylline Prophecy in Classical Antiquity* (London: Routledge, 1988), 180–81. Plutarch knew of an ancient nymph-oracle on Cithaeron (*Arist.* 11.4).

[35] Dillon, *Omens and Oracles*, 21.

[36] Jerzy Linderski, "Quindecimviri sacris faciundis," *BNP* 11:346.

miscellaneous content" including a theogony and instructions on purification.³⁷ Pausanias quotes both oracles and poems of Musaeus, and the only writing of his he actually thinks genuine is a hymn (Pausanias 1.22.7; 10.5.6; 10.9.11). Herophile the Sibyl is also said to have composed a hymn to Apollo as well as speaking on his behalf in her oracles (Pausanias 10.12.2–3). Many Jews of the Second Temple period saw the figure of David in a similar way. Josephus variously describes David as someone who both composes hymns to God and prophesies in his name. The text "David's Compositions" in 11QPsa presents David as a composer of psalms and songs for liturgical and exorcistic purposes, "all of which he composed through prophecy (בנבואה)."³⁸ Paul quotes psalms for a number of reasons and in a number of ways. Elsewhere in Romans psalms are quoted as prayers directed to God (Rom 3:4; 8:36). On other occasions, the psalmist seems to provide general wisdom (Rom 4:7–8; 1 Cor 3:20; 2 Cor 9:9). In 1 Cor 15:27 a psalm is understood as a prophecy about Jesus's role in the eschaton, and, in a further few instances, psalms can be plausibly read as words of Jesus himself (2 Cor 4:13; Rom 11:9–10; 15:3, 9).³⁹

Psalm 68:10 LXX as prediction

Using a predictive oracle to illustrate an aspect of Jesus's life shows the sort of information Paul believed to be contained in his sacred texts. His deployment of the oracle in this context also shows how this information could be used. In this case it serves to invest the predicted aspect of Jesus's life with a level of divine and theological interpretation. As C. H. Dodd commented on this verse, "if you can cite Scripture for a fact, you show, not only that it was so, but that it must have been so, in the eternal purpose of God."⁴⁰ For Hanson,

---

³⁷ Parke, *Sibyls and Sibylline Prophecy*, 175.

³⁸ On the varied roles and abilities attributed to David in Jewish tradition, see Mroczek, *Literary Imagination*, 71–84. Mroczek has cautioned against applying references which talk about David's literary output directly to the book of Psalms as it is now available (35–38). We do not know in what form Paul would have encountered the psalms he quotes (a single scroll of 150 psalms? various scrolls containing various collections of psalms?), but it is reasonable to assume that traditions about the nature of David's literary output would colour how Paul read the various Davidic compositions he does quote.

³⁹ Hays (*Echoes of Scripture*, 224 n. 28) gives cautious assent to such a reading of 2 Cor 4:13, cf. Hanson, *Studies*, 17–18; Bates, *Hermeneutics*, 275–85, 304–25. On the phenomenon of placing psalms in the mouth of Jesus in the New Testament more broadly, see Harold W. Attridge, "Giving Voice to Jesus: Use of the Psalms in the New Testament," in *Psalms in Community: Jewish and Christian Textual, Liturgical, and Artistic Traditions*, ed. Harold W. Attridge and Margot E. Fassler, SymS 25 (Atlanta: SBL, 2003), 101–12.

⁴⁰ C. H. Dodd, *The Epistle of Paul to the Romans*, MNTC 6 (London: Hodder & Stoughton, 1932), 221.

the psalm is "an interpretation of his sufferings, given us by the Messiah himself."⁴¹ Paul can then use this interpretation to elicit the appropriate response from his audience.

At Qumran psalms of David were also read, along with other more obviously "prophetic" books, to provide information about events in the past life of the community. Interpretations that refer the text to past events generally use the perfect *qatal* form, while knowledge of future events is communicated with the imperfect *yiqtol* form.⁴² So, for example, the pesherist renders Ps 37:7 as "[Be si]lent before [Yahweh and] wait for him, do not be annoyed with one who has success, with someone [who hatch]es plots" (4QpPsa 1.25–2.1).⁴³ This person who has success and hatches plots is interpreted as referring to "the Man of Lies who misdirected (התעה) many with deceptive words, for they have chosen (בחרו) worthless things and did not lis[ten] ([ולוא שמ[עו) to the Interpreter of Knowledge."

Thus the psalm is used to interpret a situation in which many have not followed the community leader, but instead followed another, dubbed "the Man of Lies."⁴⁴ The divine oracle confirms that although he has success at the moment, he is actually opposed to Yahweh, and those who are on the side of Yahweh need not worry about his seeming success, but only wait for Yahweh's intervention. This interpretation of past events leads to a conclusion about the future of those who have been led astray by the "Man of Lies"

---

⁴¹ Hanson, *Jesus Christ*, 155. In order for the oracle to make Paul's broader practical point about pleasing others and not oneself in 15:3, almost all commentators have needed to look to other verses in the broader context of the Psalm. Thompson moves back in the context of Psalm 68 to v. 8 to show that the reproaches Christ bore were for God's sake, not his own, Michael B. Thompson, *Clothed with Christ: The Example and Teaching of Jesus in Romans 12:1–15:13*, JSNTSup 59 (Sheffield: Sheffield Academic, 1991), 223. Hafemann moves forward in the psalm to argue that the primary point of Paul's quotation is to show that those who give of themselves for others can have hope that God will vindicate them, Hafemann, "Eschatology and Ethics," 168.

⁴² Maurya P. Horgan, *Pesharim: Qumran Interpretations of Biblical Books* (Washington DC: Catholic Biblical Association of America, 1979), 248.

⁴³ Text and translation from Florentino García Martínez and Eibert J. C. Tigchelaar, *The Dead Sea Scrolls Study Edition*, 2 vols (Leiden: Brill, 1997). This particular psalm is an acrostic, which was also a feature of many Sibylline oracles (Cicero, *Div.* 2.54.112). After the Capitoline fire of 83 BCE, when a new collection of Sibylline oracles was being assembled, the acrostic framework of a text was supposedly the main test to verify whether the oracle was genuine or not (Dionysius of Halicarnassus 4.62.6).

⁴⁴ The pesharim, while referring the text to contemporary events, still cloak those events in a certain amount of obscurity so that sobriquets such as "Man of Lies" and "Teacher of Righteousness," which would presumably have been meaningful to the community interpreting the text, do not help us to identify these figures with any more clarity. See e.g., William H. Brownlee, "The Wicked Priest, the Man of Lies, and the Righteous Teacher: The Problem of Identity," *JQR* 73 (1982): 1–37.

expressed in the *yiqtol* form: "they will die (יובדו) by the sword, by hunger and by plague." The pesherist does not identify the "man of Lies" as the first-person speaker of any of these psalms, like Christ in Romans, rather he is merely predicted by the psalmist. Paul and the pesherist interpret the psalms in similar ways, though, which add a divine context and layer of interpretation to recent events.

At one stage further removed, this is something like the role of prediction in the Sibylline books. First is an event requiring interpretation, such as a famine, a plague, or the birth of a hermaphrodite. This event occasions the consultation of the text, which shows that the event was both foretold, and that it signifies impending disaster. The remaining ritual prescriptions instruct the people how to prevent the coming disaster that the prodigy foretold. As in the previous examples, the consultation of a sacred, oracular text serves to interpret a recent event by placing it into a divine context, and provides guidance on how to act accordingly.

Predictions of Still-Future Events

While Paul cites many predictions that he claims have already been fulfilled in recent events, other predictions for Paul are still to be fulfilled or are in the process of being realised. In the last chapter, I showed how scriptural oracles could be brought in to enhance eschatological mysteries in 1 Cor 15:54–55 and Rom 11:26–27. In some cases, Paul sees it as his job to help bring these predictions to fulfilment, particularly those oracles that speak of the allegiance of the Gentiles to the Messiah.

The Allegiance of the Gentiles (Romans 15:7–13)

Immediately after Paul's statement in Rom 15:4–6 about the value of written predictions, Paul offers another imperative to his audience that is again grounded in both the deeds of the Messiah and in written prophecies about him.[45] "Welcome one another, just as the Messiah welcomed you" (15:7). The Messiah's welcome is first backed up by Paul's own statement that he "became a servant to circumcision [Jews] for the sake of God's truthfulness in order to confirm the promises given to the patriarchs and, for the sake of mercy, in order that the Gentiles might glorify God."[46] The Messiah confirms promises

---

[45] For the structural parallel between vv. 1–6 and 7–13, see Keck, "Christology, Soteriology, and the Praise of God," 86; J. Ross Wagner, "The Christ, Servant of Jew and Gentile: A Fresh Approach to Romans 15:8–9," *JBL* 116 (1997): 474 n. 10.

[46] For the difficult syntax of this sentence, see Wagner, "Servant"; Engberg-Pedersen, *Paul and the Stoics*, 356–57 n. 29. Garroway's alternative translation sees the Messiah as "agent of circumcision,"

or prophecies that were written to the Jewish forefathers, and this results in the merciful inclusion of Gentiles in the worship of the one God; a sentiment that echoes Paul's programmatic statement about his good news in Rom 1:1–6. Paul then cites four oracles from LXX Ps 17:50; Deut 32:43; Ps 117:1; and Isa 11:10 that are linked by the word ἔθνη and talk of the Gentiles praising God together with Jews.

The first of these, like Rom 15:3 discussed above, is a psalm of David spoken from the person of Jesus the Messiah. As in v. 3 it occurs immediately after a description of the Messiah's deeds and illuminates them with first-person speech. The only difference is that whereas 15:3 was in the aorist tense and illuminated the sufferings the Messiah had already gone through, 15:9 is in the future tense and speaks of the Messiah's future intention and goal: "I will confess (ἐξομολογήσομαι) you among the Gentiles and sing (ψαλῶ) to your name." While Paul believes this has already begun in the Gentile communities that are already dedicated to the Messiah, it is a vision that is not yet complete and which he strives to help bring to completion himself.[47] The next two quotations consist in imperatives to the nations (Gentiles) to praise God with the Jews (μετὰ τοῦ λαοῦ αὐτοῦ). The speaker of these passages is ambiguous, and possibly not that important for Paul's purposes. Unlike the previous two quotations, neither are designated "Psalms of David" and the first is not a psalm at all, which loosens the link with Christ as the speaker. The Ps 117:1 quotation also contains a third person reference to τὸν κύριον, "the Lord," which Paul had erased from his previous quotation of Ps 17:50.[48] On the other hand, the introductory formula πάλιν λέγει if understood as "again he says" would signify a continuity of speaker, and Paul does not explicitly indicate a change of speaker until v. 12. In v. 12, Paul does feel the need to specify a

---

that is, the one who "facilitates the admission of Gentiles into the patriarchal covenant that has genital circumcision as its entrance requirement." This translation arguably fits better with Paul's other uses of διάκονος (Gal 2:17; 2 Cor 3:6) and the flow of the present argument, which maintains focus on Gentile inclusion throughout. Garroway's concept of a "real, but imperceptible, circumcision" is more questionable though, Joshua D. Garroway, "The Circumcision of Christ: Romans 15:7–13," *JSNT* 34 (2012): 303–13; Joshua D. Garroway, *Paul's Gentile-Jews: Neither Jew nor Gentile, but Both* (New York: Palgrave Macmillan, 2012), 118–22.

[47] Richard Hays (*Echoes of Scripture*, 71) stresses the fulfilment of this oracle for Paul's situation: "Paul rests his case on the claim that his churches, in which Gentiles do in fact join Jews in praising God, must be the eschatological fulfilment of the scriptural vision." Looking forward to 15:14–21 however, Paul is not content to merely rest his case, but sees much more to be done to bring this vision to fulfilment.

[48] Both Bates (*Hermeneutics*, 299–300) and J. Ross Wagner (*Heralds of the Good News: Isaiah and Paul "in Concert" in the Letter to the Romans*, NovTSup 101 [Leiden: Brill, 2002], 312–13 n. 23) make much of the fact that Paul erases reference to the κύριος in the earlier quotation in order to avoid confusion between Jesus as both the κύριος and as the speaker of the psalm. Cf. Stanley, *Paul and the Language of Scripture*, 180.

new speaker, perhaps because the figure of Isaiah is particularly important to him, but perhaps also because he is sensitive to the change from the first- and second-person discourse of the previous four quotations to third person in the Isaiah quotation.[49] Whether or not the Messiah was speaking the last two passages, he is obviously not speaking the Isaiah passage and so a new speaker must be specified. The passage predicts that "the root of Jesse shall come, the one who rises to rule the Gentiles, in him the Gentiles shall hope." Paul brings out this reference to hope in his benediction in v. 13, which explicitly connects the hope of his Gentile audience in Rome with the Gentiles of the Isaiah passage who hope in the Messiah.

In the specific context of the letter, these citations all serve to support and amplify the initial imperative to "welcome one another, just as the Messiah welcomed you" (Rom 15:7). They demonstrate that the acceptance of Paul's Gentile audience was foreseen and part of God's plan for the world and for his Messiah. In addition to the specific function in this chapter, Matthew Novenson has highlighted the role these texts play in Paul's general understanding of his mission to the Gentiles. The "obedience of the Gentiles" to the Messiah that Paul sees as the purpose of his apostleship in Rom 1:5 is a concept only explicitly attested elsewhere in Greek in Ps 17 and Isa 11 LXX, both of which Paul quotes together in this catena. Once Jesus is identified as the Messiah, it follows for Paul that Gentile obedience and allegiance to him is the next step in God's purpose.[50] In this sense, the oracles function more like the Sibylline oracles that the Roman populace quoted against Nero. One oracle read "When thrice three hundred revolving years have run their course, Civil strife upon Rome destruction shall bring, and the folly, too, Of Sybaris . . ." Cassius Dio, who records the oracle, refutes its use by the populace as it did not fit the period of the city's history. But if one can calculate the present time to be 900 years since the city's founding, as some evidently did, then the resulting strife would be sure to come (Cassius Dio 57.18.4–5). Similarly, "Last of the sons of Aeneas, a mother-slayer shall govern" depends on the verification of Nero committing matricide. Once that identification is made, the Roman people can declare that

---

[49] *Pace* van Kooten ("Ancestral, Oracular and Prophetic," 268–69), it does not seem to imply any downgrading of the authority of the quotation to a merely human ancestral or prophetic level in distinction to first-person oracular speech.

[50] Matthew V. Novenson, "The Jewish Messiahs, the Pauline Christ, and the Gentile Question," *JBL* 128 (2009): 357–73; Novenson, *Christ Among the Messiahs*, 156–160. Fredriksen argues for a similar logic based in the biblical oracles but moving in the opposite direction: "Paul seems to name the Gentiles' turning through Christ to worship the God of Israel as the eschatological event confirming Jesus' status as (Davidic) Messiah," Paula Fredriksen, *Jesus of Nazareth, King of the Jews: A Jewish Life and the Emergence of Christianity* (New York: Knopf, 1999), 153, more fully 125–37. The logic, to me, seems to run the other way, especially in the context of Romans. For a critique of the particular texts to which Fredriksen appeals, see Donaldson, *Paul and the Gentiles*, 187–97.

he will be the last to reign. This oracle Dio deems to have come true, since Nero was the last of the Julio-Claudian line (Cassius Dio 62.18.3–5). Paul's oracles are not structured quite so neatly, but the logic underlying their interpretation is the same.[51] If Jesus can be identified as the Messiah, and his oracles speak of Gentile nations paying obeisance to that Messiah, then it is time for the Gentiles to give their allegiance to Jesus.

Promise and Fulfilment

After quoting these oracles, Paul goes on to tell his addressees of his success in producing obedience among the Gentiles and his further ambitions to go where the Messiah has not yet been proclaimed. This ambition is itself guided by a further oracle from Isa 52:15: "Those who have never been told of him shall see, and those who have never heard of him shall understand." The fact that Paul works to help bring these oracles to fulfilment is noteworthy, and highlights an important point in Paul's engagement with scriptural prophecies.[52]

In the Roman context, and in the examples from Cassius Dio cited above, the prodigies that prompted the consultation of the Sibylline books almost always received a negative interpretation as they warned of disasters to come. The role of the texts was to interpret what the prodigy foretold and how to avoid it. Rather than disasters to be averted, Paul's main category for thinking about predictions in sacred texts is that of promise (ἐπαγγελία). Paul's language of "promise" clusters around the passages that also feature the highest density of explicit scriptural citations.[53] The singular noun always refers to God's promise to Abraham and appears when this is the focus of discussion in chapters 4 and 9 of Romans, and chapters 3 and 4 of Galatians. The plural can refer to promises made to Abraham (Gal 3:16, 21) but can also refer more generally to promises made to the Israelites (Rom 9:4), the patriarchs (Rom 15:8) and other prophecies in the Jewish writings (2 Cor 7:1).[54] The word "promise"

---

[51] For this protasis/apodosis form in omen lists and the pesharim, see Armin Lange, "Interpretation als Offenbarung: zum Verhältnis von Schriftauslegung und Offenbarung," in *Wisdom and Apocalypticism in the Dead Sea Scrolls and in the Biblical Tradition*, ed. Florentino García Martínez, BETL 168 (Leuven: Peeters, 2003), 17–33.

[52] Paul's own role in fulfilment is highlighted in differing ways by Munck, *Paul*, 42–49; Hays, *Echoes of Scripture*, 171–73; Wagner, *Heralds of the Good News*, 356; Fredriksen, *Pagans' Apostle*, 164–66.

[53] The noun ἐπαγγελία or the verb ἐπαγγέλω appear five times in Rom 4 (vv. 13, 14, 16, 20, 21), which also features five scriptural citations, three times in Rom 9:1–18 (vv. 4, 8, 9) amid six citations (and many more in the rest of 9–11), once in Rom 15:8, with six citations in the chapter as a whole, once in 2 Cor 7:1 immediately after a catena of three citations, and 11 times in Gal 3–4 (3:14, 16, 17, 18 (twice), 19, 21, 22, 29; 4:23, 28) amid 10 citations. The only time the word appears in a context that does not have a sustained focus on scriptural texts is 2 Cor 1:20, which refers more generally to all God's promises that are fulfilled in Christ. The only other passage that contains a similar density of scriptural citation without the word ἐπαγγελία appearing is 1 Cor 15.

[54] On the promises to the patriarchs for Paul, see Garroway, *Paul's Gentile-Jews*, 120–21.

in Paul is also particularly linked to God's speech. Of the five times in Paul's letters that God is explicitly the subject of a verb of speech (Rom 9:12; 2 Cor 4:6; 6:2, 16; Gal 3:16) Paul characterises three of them as a promise (four if 2 Cor 6:2 is included in the purview of 7:1, which I think it should be). The only direct speech of God that he does not explicitly describe as a promise is God's act of creation in 2 Cor 4:6. This default understanding of divine speech as promise explains Paul's eagerness to work for the realisation of these promises, rather than to avert them, and is a common response to prophecies that predict a favourable outcome for certain parties.

A number of Roman sources, for example, relate rumour of an oracle from the Sibylline books which circulated near the end of Caesar's life, which predicted that "the Parthians would never submit to the Romans until the latter should be commanded by a king" (Appian, *Bell. Civ.* 2.110; cf. Suetonius, *Jul.* 79; Cicero, *Div.* 2.110; Plutarch, *Caes.* 60, 64). In response, some sought to grant Caesar the title of king (of those nations subject to Rome but not of Rome itself). Roman authors usually include this oracle in the context of other attempts to grant Caesar the title of king towards the end of his life, so one might suspect that the granting of the title was the real end goal, rather than the predicted victory over the Parthians. This is certainly how Plutarch understood the scenario. Taken at face value, though, this oracle also follows an "if A then B" pattern which people work to help along to fulfilment. It predicts rule over a foreign nation by a certain individual matching a certain description: a king. Once Caesar is aligned with that description victory over the Parthians can be assured, and the oracle brought to fulfilment.[55]

This is also similar in nature to Josephus's "ambiguous oracle" from the Jewish sacred texts (ἐν τοῖς ἱεροῖς . . . γράμμασιν) that "at that time one from their country would become ruler of the world" (*B.J.* 6.312).[56] Josephus refutes

---

[55] Satterfield ("Prodigies," 432 n. 7, 442) provides another anomalous example in which a prodigy was interpreted positively as a prophecy of Roman victory (Livy 42.20.1–6). It is not certain that the Sibylline books played a role, though, as this interpretation was given by the haruspices and not the decemviri who simply responded with a list of rituals to be performed. In this case, the expiatory rituals could have functioned to ensure that the victory portended would indeed come to pass.

[56] The identification of this oracle has itself remained ambiguous. Most interpreters assume it refers to "Old Testament prophecy," with either Numbers 24:15–19 or various portions of Daniel being the most popular suggestions, see Martin Hengel, *The Zealots*, trans. David Smith (Edinburgh: T&T Clark, 1989), 237; N. T. Wright, *The New Testament and the People of God* (London: SPCK, 1992), 312–14; Anthony J. Tomasino, "Oracles of Insurrection: The Prophetic Catalyst of the Great Revolt," *JJS* 59 (2008): 86–111. It should be noted that other oracles that Josephus cites from "the records of the ancient prophets" bear no resemblance to any known biblical texts (*B.J.* 4.386–88; 6.109–10, 309–11). The closest parallel to one oracle is actually found in a Sibylline Oracle (4.115–29), which suggests Josephus is working from a broader pool of ancient prophecies than a modern OT.

the interpretation of this oracle by the wise men, like Cassius Dio would later do of the Roman populace, by questioning its application to present circumstances.[57] The oracle did not refer to a Judean, as everyone supposed, but to the emperor Vespasian who was proclaimed Emperor on Judean soil. But, for some, the fit of the oracle with present circumstances was evidently enough to incite war in the hope that this ruler would emerge and the oracle be brought to fulfilment.[58] Paul is already sure in his identification of Jesus with the Messiah, the root of Jesse, so it now follows for him that the obedience and allegiance of the Gentiles is the next step in God's purpose, and that God has called him to help bring it to fulfilment. In this way, his actions are guided by the predictive power of oracles.

Summary

The oracles of Romans 15 show how Paul understood certain passages in the Jewish sacred writings to contain both predictions of recent events as well as further promises for the future. Some of these are first-person oracles from the Messiah himself that both explain and interpret his own recent suffering, and express his future intentions. Others are spoken in the voice of Isaiah the ancient prophet, conveying the words of God about the future obedience of the Gentiles to the Messiah. All of these oracles for Paul speak directly to his present situation and this is the primary context for which they are intended.

Timeless Oracles: Examples and Proverbs

Beyond this predictive function, various literary traditions recorded and preserved oracles in writing. Plutarch lists a number of figures who for various reasons had compiled collections of oracles, such as Herodotus, in his histories; Philochorus, who we know wrote a book *On Divination*; Ister, who wrote books on the epiphanies of Apollo and Heracles; as well as Theopompus.[59] These collections could form the basis for philosophical and theological reflection, as often happens in Plutarch's own dialogues, in which the content and nature of oracles provide information on the nature of divine communication (e.g., *Def. or.* 399c). Porphyry's third-century CE work *Philosophy from Oracles* may be seen as the peak of this particular practice. For Porphyry and other

---

[57] Cf. T.W. Manson, "The Argument from Prophecy," *JTS* 46 (1945): 130.
[58] This argument supplements Novenson's comparison of the ambiguous oracle in Josephus with Paul's use of Messiah texts, "Jewish Messiahs," 363–64.
[59] Stoneman, *Ancient Oracles*, 171–73.

Neoplatonists, "all knowledge which humans have concerning the gods comes from the gods themselves," so oracles become an important source for understanding the nature of different gods and the inner workings of the divine realm.[60] The collectors of these oracles did not generally claim that they had been fulfilled in the present day of the writer, nor were they stored up in the hope of a future fulfilment; their fulfilment, if one was required, was already seen to lie in the past. In such contexts, the oracle had now become part of the shared cultural story of the interaction of the gods with their people, and the content of the oracle still had much to reveal about the more general will and character of the gods in its function as a record of divine speech.

Exemplary Oracles and the Character of God (Romans 9:6–18)

Paul uses oracles in this way in Rom 9:6–18 where he draws conclusions about the nature of God's election by producing three examples of God favouring one party over another from the Pentateuch: Isaac and Ishmael (vv. 7–9), Jacob and Esau (vv. 10–13), and Moses and Pharaoh (vv. 14–18). The first two directly illustrate Paul's ambiguous statement that "not all those descended from Israel are Israel."[61] The third example directly answers the question of whether God's election is unjust. Commentators habitually refer to this section of Rom 9 as Paul's retelling of the story of Israel or as Paul looking back on God's past dealings with his people, as if these things can be read directly off of the events of Israel's past.[62] Paul is more subtle and specific though, as he does not technically interpret events here but oracles. In the first 18 verses

---

[60] Crystal Addey, *Divination and Theurgy in Neoplatonism: Oracles of the Gods*, Ashgate Studies in Philosophy & Theology in Late Antiquity (Farnham: Ashgate, 2014), 13, 96–98.

[61] On the difficulties in translating this verse, see Mark D. Nanos, "'The Gifts and the Calling of God Are Irrevocable' (Romans 11:29): If So, How Can Paul Declare That 'Not All Israelites Truly Belong to Israel' (9:6)?" *SCJR* 11 (2016): 14–17 (although, his solution is no more convincing than the standard translations). Gaventa's reading of the syntax is the most convincing, in which οὐ negates the entire statement, thus "For it is not the case that all those who are from Israel ... these people are ... Israel," Beverly Roberts Gaventa, "On the Calling-Into-Being of Israel: Romans 9:6–29," in *Between Gospel and Election: Explorations in the Interpretation of Romans 9–11*, ed. Florian Wilk and J. Ross Wagner, WUNT 257 (Tübingen: Mohr Siebeck, 2010), 259.

[62] Wright (*Paul and the Faithfulness of God*, 1181) sees the whole of 9:6–29 as a retelling of the story of Israel. Fredriksen (*Pagans' Apostle*, 160) calls this section "the formative history of Israel." Stanley K. Stowers (*A Rereading of Romans: Justice, Jews, and Gentiles* [New Haven: Yale University Press, 1994], 299–300) refers to "the patterns of God's activity whereby he directs history and uses historical forces and actors." For Wagner (*Heralds of the Good News*, 47 n. 12), Paul's understanding "is driven by the very particular story of God's relationship with Israel ..." Gaventa ("Calling-Into-Being," 268) combines both themes for "a brief and radical recasting of Israel's history in terms of God's creative actions" and "The history of God's creation and redemption."

of chapter 9 Paul quotes from his sacred texts six times, and each time he directly quotes the words of God in the first person.[63] He is not simply quoting his Bible, but searching for examples in the past where God has made himself known through his oracles. It is from these past oracles that Paul then draws more general conclusions about God's character. These are not entirely abstract generalisations; they are still connected to the very particular story of God's dealings with Israel.[64] In this context, though, they are still generalisable statements about God's character. Each example contains an introduction to the example in question followed by a direct quote from an oracle spoken by God. Each oracle is then interpreted with an antithesis about God's election in the form οὐ . . . ἀλλά, "not . . . but," formulated in general terms, and followed by another supporting oracle that illuminates a point either in the previous oracle or in Paul's interpretation of it.[65]

In the case of Isaac and Ishmael, Paul's introductory point is that the seed is counted not through all children of Abraham but only through Isaac. The main oracle he quotes is from Gen 21:12, "in Isaac your seed shall be called," which he interprets with the antithesis that it is "not the children of the flesh who are children of God, but the children of the promise are reckoned as seed" (Rom 9:8). This interpretation is then supported by another oracle delivered to Abraham, "at this time I will come and Sarah will have a son" (Rom 9:9). Paul explicitly designates this a word of promise, which aligns Isaac's birth with the category of promise from the previous antithesis rather than flesh.

Paul's next example takes his argument a stage further by showing that even within Isaac's line, God chooses to use some for his purposes while rejecting others. Paul's introductory comment stresses the situation in which the oracle was given, in which both parties were of the same mother and the same father, and that election occurred prior to any deeds performed by either child, good or bad. The main oracle of this example is in the words spoken to Rebekah "the greater shall serve the lesser" (Rom 9:12). Paul's interpretative antithesis precedes the oracle itself in this case, but is structurally the same as in the Isaac and Ishmael example. It is Paul's logical conclusion from the words of the oracle, coupled with the context in which it was given: "not from works, but from the one who calls" (Rom 9:11). If God's words show that he has chosen

---

[63] Francis Watson (*Paul and the Hermeneutics of Faith*, 18) notes the preponderance of first-person singular divine speech in Rom 9. John Barclay (*Paul and the Gift*, 532) links this pattern in 9:6–29 with Paul's focus throughout Rom 9–11 on God's agency and sovereign will that is "unknown and in principle unknowable."

[64] Wagner, *Heralds of the Good News*, 53.

[65] On the formulation οὐ . . . ἀλλά in Paul, see Folker Siegert, *Argumentation bei Paulus, gezeigt an Röm 9–11*, WUNT 34 (Tübingen: Mohr Siebeck, 1985), 182–85. On the antitheses themselves, see Jonathan A. Linebaugh, "Not the End: The History and Hope of the Unfailing Word in Romans 9–11," in *God and Israel: Providence and Purpose in Romans 9–11*, ed. Todd D. Still (Waco, TX: Baylor University Press, 2017), 151–55; Barclay, *Paul and the Gift*, 529.

one to serve the other before any indication of worth, either through family or deeds, then this is Paul's logical conclusion. The point is supported and strengthened again by a second oracle, this time from the prophet Malachi, again speaking the words of God in the first person: "Jacob I loved, but Esau I hated" (Rom 9:13). Paul may have taken this prophetic oracle as an authoritative commentary on the Torah and thus as providing a deeper level of insight into God's actions. Alternatively, if Paul is understanding the oracle in the context of Malachi's own oracle collection, then he may have used it as a testimony to the ongoing effects of God's election which resulted in the preferential treatment for Israel against Edom as the surrounding context of Mal 1:2–5 explicitly spells out.

The third pairing, Moses and Pharaoh, Paul introduces with a question left lingering from the last example, as to whether God is just to love one over the other on the basis of divine choice alone. Paul's first answer is to quote his next oracle, given to Moses in Exod 33:19, from which he draws his next antithesis: "it is not of the one who wills, nor the one who runs, but of the God who has mercy" (Rom 9:16). This antithesis specifically draws out an aspect of God's character as "the one who has mercy."[66] This is then supported by more of God's words, to Pharaoh this time, which receive their own interpretation.[67] This interpretation serves as a summary to the section as a whole, that God has mercy on whom he wills and hardens whom he wills (Rom 9:18).

Thus, Paul presents three generalised antitheses about the nature of God and his election, each one pointing to God's will as the only criterion of election.[68] Not children of flesh, but children of promise, not from works, but from the one who calls, not from will or effort, but from God who has mercy. Paul is not claiming these as prophecies that are fulfilled in Jesus or the Gentile mission, rather they are all generalised conclusions about God's nature, deduced from God's past words in specific situations.[69]

---

[66] Linebaugh, "Not the End," 154;

[67] The introductory formula designates "scripture" itself as the present tense speaker λέγει γὰρ ἡ γραφὴ τῷ Φαραώ. Given Paul's focus on past events as past events throughout this section, I am inclined to view this formula merely as designating the source for the oracle that Paul is quoting, rather than ascribing any particular agency to scripture itself as a "living voice," *pace* Wagner, *Heralds of the Good News*, 53 n. 34.

[68] Cf. Barclay, *Paul and the Gift*, 528–33; Michael Wolter, "'It Is Not as Though the Word of God Has Failed': God's Faithfulness and God's Free Sovereignty in Romans 9:6–29," in Still, *God and Israel*, 34–42.

[69] Cf. L. Ann Jervis, "Promise and Purpose in Romans 9:1–13: Toward Understanding Paul's View of Time," in Still, *God and Israel*, 5 n. 17: "Paul uses Scripture in order to state who God is; to give a glimpse into the realm of God's life, of God's mind. Scripture is a window into God's purpose. It helps Paul to communicate the significance of what he thinks God is demonstrating about Godself. It is not a collection of promises awaiting fulfillment." Jervis is wrong, in my view, to claim this as a general rule that shows Paul's distinctive understanding of time. She is correct, however, in this characterisation of the oracles cited in Rom 9:6–18 and 11:1–6.

This use of oracles fits with a demonstrable pattern in the ancient world, particularly amongst philosophers and orators, in which a god's oracles illustrate his character. Plutarch, in his *Life of Numa*, also asks whether it is possible and indeed proper that a god should harbour affection and love for particular people, in this case based on their character and virtues. Among other examples, he cites the story that whenever Hippolytus would set sail towards Delphi, the Pythia would chant: "Lo, once more doth beloved Hippolytus hither make voyage" (*Numa* 4.5). Plutarch takes these words as an oracle, which illustrates the joy with which Apollo awaited his arrival, and thus demonstrates the more general character of the god who harbours affection for certain people.

Dio Chrysostom, in his seventeenth oration, *On Covetousness*, seeks to show the evil effects of this vice, which are illustrated by a list of historical and legendary examples (*Avar.* 9–15). After listing such general, historical examples he shifts to focus on divine attitudes towards covetousness, as illustrated from Apollo's oracles.

> These [previous] instances, in order that they be warning examples to you, I have taken not only from exceedingly ancient, but also from subsequent times, and as related both in poetry and in narrative prose. It is also [this is where he shifts] worth pondering the god, how he also by his very nature punishes the covetous. (*Avar.* 16; adapted from Cohoon, LCL)

This is illustrated by the account of how the Spartans, when flourishing and prospering, were not satisfied to remain at peace, but consulted the Delphic oracle as a prelude to invading Arcadia. The god, Dio says, not only refused them Arcadia, but rebuked their insatiable greed with the words "Arcadia you ask of me? You ask much, I will not give it to you" (17.16). The episode, with the accompanying oracle, of which Dio quotes only the first line, is recorded in Herodotus, and functions for Dio as a record of previous divine communication, from which one can discern the nature and character of the god, as well as the behaviours he approves or condemns.

Dio also adduces a supporting oracle to help explain an ambiguous feature of the oracle he has just quoted. While the first line of the oracle in Herodotus denies the Spartans Arcadia, the rest of it appears to grant them Tegea. The Spartans, acting on this assumption, attempted to invade Tegea, but had no success. This failure Dio also attributes to the Spartans' greed, which prevented them from understanding the oracle correctly. This he illustrates with another oracle in which the Athenians also suffered dire consequences as a result of greedily over-interpreting the god's words. In this case they invaded the island of Sicily, when the god had actually granted them only a hill called Sicily.

Pausanias draws on both the oracles of Zeus and past natural disasters that had divinatory value to support conclusions about the attitude of the gods towards their suppliants. He first attributes the destruction of the city of Helike by earthquake and flood to the wrath of Poseidon after suppliants were removed from his sanctuary there and killed (7.24.5–13). The destruction of the city, he says, was "one of the many proofs that the wrath of the God of Suppliants is inexorable." Pausanias finds another proof in an oracle given to the Athenians at Dodona, which "manifestly advises us to respect suppliants" (7.25.1). Here the words of the oracle are combined with other divinatory signs such as floods and earthquakes, to draw a general conclusion about the attitude and workings of the gods, as well as the appropriate human response to this, that we, his readers, should also respect suppliants.

Dio Chrysostom found his oracles in Herodotus, but we do not know in what text, if any, Pausanias or Plutarch found their oracles. Plutarch introduces his oracle with φασιν "they say," which suggests an oral source in popular tradition, rather than a written text. This hardly matters, though, as if the words can be attributed to the god, then they can also provide information about the character of the god, and divinity in general.[70] All the examples surveyed, Paul included, derive this information both from particular keywords in the oracles themselves and from the contexts in which they were given. In Dio Chrysostom and Pausanias, the knowledge of the god's character serves to direct present behaviour by warning of certain vices to avoid. Paul's usage is closer to Plutarch at this point as they both turn to oracles to resolve potential problems concerning the nature of gods and their relationship to humans. Is it consistent with a god's nature to harbour particular affection for certain people, and what form does this take? This question stands in different ways behind both Paul and Plutarch's examples. Plutarch's answer is maybe, but it is equally likely that these figures invented their special relationships with the gods in order to hold power over the masses. Paul's answer is more complicated and involved. It requires a higher concentration of examples which then serve as a springboard for the discussion of further oracles in the rest of Rom 9 and 10, which do seem to more directly predict the Gentile situation into which Paul is writing.[71]

Paul returns to this exemplary function of oracles again in Rom 11:1–6. We have already had occasion (in Chapter 2) to examine the nature of the oracle Paul narrates here, which he calls a χρηματισμός, an epiphanic dream-vision. The whole encounter, as Paul narrates it, is reminiscent of an oracular inquiry in which Elijah petitions God (ἐντυγχάνει τῷ θεῷ), and receives an oracular

---

[70] Cf. Iles Johnston (*Ancient Greek Divination*, 137): "By 'text' I mean not only written documents, but also compositions that were transmitted orally, as was a lot of important material in ancient Greece."

[71] See Lincicum, "How Did Paul Read Scripture?" 233–34.

vision in response.[72] Paul takes the content of this oracle, which relates God's retention of a faithful remnant in the face of mass unfaithfulness, as evidence of God's habitual way of operating. Like the oracles in Rom 9:6–18, Paul gives prominence to the context of the oracle, and the way he commences his application (woodenly: "therefore in this way also, in the present time") makes it explicit that Paul does not see the oracle as a veiled prediction of future events that needs to be allegorised and reapplied. Rather he understands it as a precedent in former times that now gives insight into God's present and future action, in this case his choice of a faithful remnant.[73] Like his previous use of oracles in chapter 9 Paul uses a sharp antithesis to expresses the main point about God's character that he wants to extract from the oracle, "and if by grace, no longer from works."[74]

Proverbial Oracles

One final use of oracles to consider is as a source of general wisdom in the form of proverbs or maxims. The most famous piece of Delphic wisdom is the maxim γνῶθι σαυτόν, "know yourself," which was inscribed in the pronaos of Apollo's temple at Delphi. According to Pausanias, the inscriptions were made by sages (σοφούς) who dedicated this and other maxims to Apollo (10.24). (Pseudo) Plutarch cites it as one of two inscriptions (γραμμάτων) on which all the others depend (*Cons. Apoll.* 116c). He thus regards it as the pinnacle of Delphic wisdom, but not explicitly as an oracle. Seneca, however, attributes it to the Pythian oracle herself (*Dial.* 6.11.2), and Cicero calls it "Apollo's maxim" (*Tusc.* 1.22.52), later introducing the proverb as the straightforward speech of Apollo (*Tusc.* 5.25.70; cf. *Leg.* 1.22.58; Dio Chrysostom, 4 *Regn.* 57).[75]

Plutarch cites a number of other oracles as universally applicable wisdom, although they were originally given in specific circumstances. Thus, "soon shall your swarms of honey-bees turn out to be hornets" illustrates the general truth

---

[72] Cf. Plutarch, *Quaest. rom.* 265a: "Aristinus ... sent to Delphi and urged the god (δεῖσθαι τοῦ θεοῦ) to release him from the difficulties in which he was involved because of the custom; and the Pythia said ..."

[73] Linebaugh, "Not the End," 145.

[74] This interpretation that focuses on grace is not an obvious one, given the oracle explicitly mentioned not bowing the knee to Baal as the criterion of God's choice. It is helped along, however, by Paul's addition of ἐμαυτῷ to his *Vorlage*, which emphasises that the choice rests with God alone. See Barclay, *Paul and the Gift*, 545. For the generally free translation style of this quotation, see Stanley, *Paul and the Language of Scripture*, 152–58.

[75] These authors are most likely following Clearchus who gave the saying a context as a response of the Pythia to Chilon the Spartan. Most others attribute the saying to a sage as in Pausanias's story. See H. W. Parke and D. E. W. Wormell, *The Delphic Oracle* (Oxford: Blackwell, 1956), 1:387.

that friends can turn out to be enemies (*Amic. mult.* 96b), and "A deaf man's hearing, a blind man's sight" illustrates the nature of memory as it hears and sees things that no longer are (*Def. orac.* 432b). Second-century collections of proverbs compiled by figures such as Zenobius and Diogenianus also include a number of oracles. These compilers always give their oracles a historical setting in an oracular consultation of the past, but include them for their timeless wisdom. Whether or not any of these proverbs can be traced to genuine oracular responses is beside the point.[76] Once it is written down as an oracle it becomes an oracle, and takes on the status of divine wisdom. So proverbs such as "accept the gift that you are given" (Zenobius, *Prov.* 3.42), "take the top and you will have the middle" (Zenobius, *Prov.* 1.57), and "love of money and nothing else will destroy Sparta" (Diogenianus 2.36) are all cited as oracles that have become proverbial.

Paul will occasionally cite texts that have a proverbial character and offer general wisdom for the current situation, although it is also possible to read many of these examples with a more predictive force. So, in 1 Cor 9:9, he quotes from "the law of Moses, 'You shall not muzzle an ox while it treads out the grain.'" Paul explicitly introduces this citation of the law as an example of divine authority, in contrast to human authority (v. 8), and treats the words as God's own (vv. 9–10). But he explains that God was not really talking about oxen, but about "us," his audience.[77] The oracle is to be interpreted more generally to the effect that the one who works should also have a share in the fruits of that work.[78] When Paul says that God spoke it "entirely for our sake" does he mean simply that it is a point of general wisdom for people, rather than for animals?[79] Or is he thinking more specifically that this oracle was spoken with his present community's situation in mind "upon whom the end of the ages has come" (1 Cor 10:11)?[80] The generic nature of the saying inclines me to the

---

[76] Fontenrose doubts the authenticity of any oracle that has proverbial character, although his reasons for doing so are somewhat circular, *Delphic Oracle*, 86–87.

[77] Or perhaps, even more specifically, Paul and Barnabas, Hays, *Echoes of Scripture*, 166; Fee, *First Corinthians*, 449 n. 234.

[78] This text has proven a popular battle-ground for whether Paul's scriptural interpretation is to be understood as "literal" or "allegorical," see Hanson, *Studies*, 161–66; David Instone Brewer, "1 Corinthians 9:9–11: A Literal Interpretation of 'Do Not Muzzle the Ox'," *NTS* 38 (1992): 554–65; Raymond F. Collins, "'It Was Indeed Written for Our Sake' (1 Cor 9:10): Paul's Use of Scripture in the First Letter to the Corinthians," *SNTSU* 20 (1995): 160–62; Fee, *First Corinthians*, 449–51; Jan L. Verbruggen, "Of Muzzles and Oxen: Deuteronomy 25:4 and 1 Corinthians 9:9," *JETS* 49 (2006): 699–711.

[79] This is the position of Conzelmann (*First Corinthians*, 154–55) and Senft, (*Première Épître*, 119 n. 17) who both adduce a quote from Philo that "the law does not prescribe for unreasoning creatures, but for those who have mind and reason" (*Spec. leg.* 1.260). Cf. Eduard Lohse, "'Kümmert sich Gott etwa um die Ochsen?' Zu 1 Kor 9:9," *ZNW* 88 (1997): 314–15.

[80] Hays, *Echoes of Scripture*, 165–66; Joop F. M. Smit, "'You Shall not Muzzle a Threshing Ox': Paul's Use of the Law of Moses in 1 Cor 9:8–12," *Estudios Bíblicos* 58 (2000): 239–63.

former in this instance, but both readings are possible, and both readings are consistent with the way oracles were interpreted in Paul's culture.

The case is the same in Rom 1:17 and Gal 3:11 where Paul cites the maxim "the righteous one will live from faith." Much has been written about this citation, how it should be translated, and its relation to the various textual forms of Hab 2:4.[81] For now, we need only ask whether Paul understands these words, spoken by God to the prophet Habbakuk, to contain general proverbial wisdom and a rule for life? Or does he see in it a more specific prediction of the Messiah (the righteous one) and his faithfulness?[82] Paul's understanding of δικαιοσύνη, and indeed Paul's thought in general, always has an eschatological bent, so he probably sees a predictive element to the oracle that speaks of the condition of eschatological righteousness and life.[83] On the other hand, both citations occur in contexts that stress this condition is generally true for all people. In Rom 1:16–17, "the good news is the power of God for salvation to all who are faithful, the Jew first and the Greek," and in Gal 3:11, "by the law no one is justified with God, because the righteous one will live from faith." In these contexts the oracle functions as a general maxim about the state of eschatological righteousness. Whether one chooses to foreground the predictive or proverbial aspect of Paul's interpretation, both are accepted ways to understand oracles given in the past. The pithy, proverbial character of the oracle presents the opportunity for both of these interpretations.

Another example that dispenses general wisdom but with a prophetic edge is the oracle Paul quotes from Isa 29:14 in 1 Cor 1:19: "I will destroy the wisdom of the wise, and the discernment of the discerning I will thwart." The future oriented oracle predicts a specific time in which this will happen, which

---

[81] Much of the traditional debate concerned whether ἐκ πίστεως modifies δίκαιος ("the one-who-is-righteous-from-faith shall live") or ζήσεται ("the righteous shall live from faith"). Other questions include whether ὁ δίκαιος refers "to the righteous person" in general or more specifically the Messiah, understood as "the righteous one," and consequently whose faith or faithfulness is then in view, Manson, "Argument from Prophecy," 133–36; D. Moody Smith, "Ο ΔΕ ΔΙΚΑΙΟΣ ΕΚ ΠΙΣΤΕΩΣ ΖΗΣΕΤΑΙ," in *Studies in the History and Text of the New Testament in Honor of Kenneth Willis Clark*, ed. B. L. Daniels and M. J. Suggs, SD 29 (Salt Lake City: University of Utah Press, 1967), 13–25; H. C. C. Cavallin, "The Righteous Shall Live by Faith: A Decisive Argument for the Traditional Interpretation," *ST* 32 (1978): 33–43; R. M. Moody, "The Habakkuk Quotation in Romans 1:17," *ExpTim* 92 (1981): 204–8; Watson, *Paul and the Hermeneutics of Faith*, 38–47, 144–50.

[82] Hanson, *Studies*, 42–45; Dodd, *According to the Scriptures*, 51; Richard B. Hays, *The Faith of Jesus Christ: The Narrative Substructure of Galatians* 3:1–4:11, 2nd ed. (Grand Rapids: Eerdmans, 2002), 132–41; Hays, *Echoes of Scripture*, 39–41; Douglas A. Campbell, "Romans 1:17 – A Crux Interpretum for the πίστις χριστοῦ Debate," *JBL* 113 (1994): 265–85; Stephen L. Young, "Romans 1:1–5 and Paul's Christological Use of Hab 2:4 in Rom 1:17: An Underutilized Consideration in the Debate," *JSNT* 34 (2012): 277–85.

[83] "To be righteous means to acquire ... a claim to be pronounced righteous at the coming Judgement," Schweitzer, *Mysticism*, 205, see further 205–26.

Paul interprets as Jesus's crucifixion. Like the oracle of Rom 15:3 it predicts Jesus's crucifixion and interprets it within the plan of God as an inversion of human wisdom. At the same time, it can also function as a general statement about the nature of divine wisdom in relation to humans, which allows Paul to draw broader conclusions on this topic in the chapters that follow, so that by 1 Cor 3:19–20 he can cite further oracles from Job 5:13 and Ps 94:11 that express the same point about the futility of human wisdom, but in the form of more general proverbial truths.

Summary

Paul's "use of scripture" overlaps with the ancient use of oracles in more ways than just prediction. In addition to providing foreknowledge of present and future events, oracles could also be a source of general wisdom, and knowledge of the nature and character of the gods. We may want to question the extent to which we should apply the label "divination" to these latter two usages. The social contexts in which they arise are not especially divinatory contexts, and it is unlikely Plutarch, Pausanias, or Paul for that matter, thought they were engaging in *mantikē* when they interpreted their oracles in these ways. These examples do, however, reflect the interrelationship of divinatory media with other enterprises such as philosophy or theology; a point which has recurred in each chapter of this study. They are also examples of continued attempts to retrieve information about the gods and the world, which can only be accessed from the gods themselves. As such, these examples highlight various overlooked facets of the afterlives of oracles, and their continued use, which forms an important plank in Paul's various methods of hearing and interpreting messages from the divine realm.

Conclusion

When Paul quotes his sacred texts he is rarely simply quoting an inspired text with a general normative authority. Rather, he pays attention to the specific oracles and records of past divinatory phenomena that the text preserves. These past oracles preserve the words of God himself, and occasionally also the Messiah Jesus, and serve a variety of functions, all of which can be paralleled with the ways divine oracles were transmitted and interpreted in the wider Greek and Roman worlds. These include predicting current and future events, providing examples of God's character and habitual means of operating, as well as providing general proverbial wisdom.

Prophetic books such as Isaiah are the easiest to see as straightforward oracle collections, while David as the psalmist also appears as an ancient prophet who spoke Messianic oracles amidst his other poetic and liturgical work. Narrative material such as that found in the Pentateuch has the most varied use, sometimes acting like an omen list (1 Cor 10:1–13), and sometimes as divine commentary on the past (Rom 4:3–25). Sometimes it functions more like Herodotus, as a record of past oracles (Rom 9:6–18), and sometimes more like Homer, as an allegory waiting to be explained (Gal 4:21–31). All such uses presuppose the various sacred texts to be repositories of useful divine knowledge encompassing past, present, and future.

I have assumed throughout this chapter that Paul does actually use these texts to learn new information that is relevant to his situation. It must be noted, however, that this position runs against the grain of much scholarship on "Paul and scripture" in which it is argued that scripture is more of an argumentative tool for Paul than a genuine source of information.[84] This is no different to the problem that runs through all study of divination as to whether it serves as a genuine means of decision-making, or a legitimation for decisions already arrived at by other means. It should be repeated here that such a question is not a zero-sum game, and that interpretation and rhetoric need not cancel each other out.[85] Further, the "divine legitimation" explanation is often foregrounded in order to explain why Paul did not interpret Jewish scriptures like modern historical-critical scholars, who pay attention to the original context of the passages they cite. This chapter has hopefully shown that Paul had different expectations of his texts, which cohere with the expectations and interpretations people brought to oracles in the ancient world.[86]

On the other extreme of this question, but from a different angle, Wendt has recently argued that viewing Paul's use of scripture through the lens of ancient textual divination may suggest a much more formative role to sacred texts than

---

[84] A forceful statement of this is Adolf von Harnack, "The Old Testament in the Pauline Letters and in the Pauline Churches," in *Understanding Paul's Ethics: Twentieth Century Approaches*, ed. Brian S. Rosner, trans. George S. Rosner and Brian S. Rosner (Grand Rapids: Eerdmans, 1995), 27–49. More recently, see Stanley, *Arguing with Scripture*, 181–82; Donaldson, *Paul and the Gentiles*, 100–104; Satlow, *How the Bible Became Holy*, 218–23. Stanley does acknowledge that Paul sought to interpret his faith in Jesus as Messiah in the light of the Jewish scriptures, so he does not intend his audience-centred approach to be able to say everything about Paul's use of scriptural texts. However, by the end of the book his conclusions leave little room for any active role for these texts in shaping Paul's convictions.

[85] "To construe apostolic authority as pure abstract will-to-power is to overlook the particular theological and social vision that Paul strives to promote and realize ... Pauline theology and Pauline rhetoric are not to be detached from each other, as though they were distinct objects of study promoted by rival scholarly parties. Pauline theology is rhetorical theology; Pauline rhetoric is theological rhetoric," Watson, *Paul and the Hermeneutics of Faith*, 493–95; cf. Lincicum, "How Did Paul Read Scripture?" 236.

[86] "The answers to such questions often reveal more about the cultural assumptions of modern historians than about those of the Greeks," Flower, *Seer in Ancient Greece*, 4.

is usually acknowledged. Rather than using scriptural oracles to elaborate and interpret a core tradition inherited from other Jesus-followers, she suggests that Paul could have "pieced together the figure and eschatological significance of Christ largely from his own textual sleuthing."[87] "It was by divining prophecies from Judean writings and not from received traditions, that Paul crafted many of his teachings about Christ."[88] In terms of "eschatological significance" this certainly appears to be true. Jewish prophecies about the Messiah and Gentile allegiance to him, as argued above, help not only interpret but generate Paul's own particular form of Judaising mission towards Gentiles.

The generative role of texts should not be pushed too far though, and this is a point with which I believe Wendt would agree. The argument of this chapter has demonstrated that precisely by viewing Paul's textual practice through the lens of textual divination, one can see that texts are generally not consulted in isolation, but most often in reaction to an external stimulus. This could be other divinatory media the texts interact with, such as the visionary experiences and contemporary prophetic oracles studied in the previous two chapters. These also provide Paul with the contents of his "good news" and in different ways incorporate sacred texts into the process. There are also external "facts" in the world that prompt the consultation of a text. Wendt's *comparanda* confirm this as she discusses Josephus's and Philo's references "to recent events predicted in Judean writings."[89] The interpretive process requires both predictive writings as well as recent events in order to make sense, and the writings mean nothing without the event they are said to have predicted. The Sibylline books, for example, were consulted in response to prodigies: omens or portents, which signal a change in the relations between gods and people that requires attention. Writers do not seem to generate past events in order to explain the texts, rather the texts explain and interpret the past events. This requires certain aspects of Paul's teaching about Christ to precede his interpretation of sacred texts, otherwise there would be nothing to interpret.

Jesus's Messiahship is one thing that appears as an assumption, rather than a result in Paul's textual sleuthing, as does his crucifixion.[90] Taken together these prove a problem, or indeed an omen, that it is necessary to turn to prophetic texts to solve. Without some of these givens, and particularly unusual givens, such as a crucified Messiah, there is no reason to turn to a text to divine anything at all, so it is to the topic of signs and omens in Paul's letters that we finally turn.

---

[87] Wendt, "Textual Prophecy," 389.
[88] Wendt, "Textual Prophecy," 389.
[89] Wendt, "Textual Prophecy," 386.
[90] Cf. Allison, *Constructing Jesus*, 392.

CHAPTER 5

Signs

The basic unit of divination is the sign, "something that represents something else," which is then "taken as the basis for a process of inference."[1] This is most obvious for so-called artificial means of divination, in which the flight of a bird or the shape of a liver represents success in battle or something similar, but it also applies to inspired visions and prophecy. Anne Marie Kitz breaks down the process of divination in general into three defining characteristics: first, the divine manipulation of earthly material (ranging from stones used for lot-casting to animals to human mediums), second, the sign (the way the lots fall, the particular flight of the birds, the vision seen or the words uttered in prophecy), and third, the interpretation of the sign.[2] This is a useful model with which to see the structural similarities across different methods of divination and highlights how, in all methods, there remains a sign that needs to be interpreted. This is no less true for visions or prophecy than it is for the interpretation of texts.[3]

In each of the preceding chapters, I have shown how these various forms of divination either interact with signs in the external world, or can themselves function as signs that need interpreting. In this chapter, I turn more focused attention to signs and omens in Paul's letters, those things in the world from which he draws inferences about divine activity and disposition. The first half of the chapter will survey the various ways signs could be interpreted in the ancient world and how Paul's appeals to signs and omens fit within this context. The second half will be devoted to analysing the role of divine signs in

---

[1] Giovanni Manetti, *Theories of the Sign in Classical Antiquity*, trans. Christine Richardson (Bloomington: Indiana University Press, 1993), 14.
[2] Anne Marie Kitz, "Prophecy as Divination," *CBQ* 65 (2003): 27–33.
[3] Prophecies can themselves be included in lists of divine signs, e.g., Plutarch, *Dem.* 19.1.

Rom 1–3. These opening chapters of Romans show a sustained engagement with the question of *how* certain things have been revealed, and also contain what many scholars have taken to be Paul's central and defining comments on the topic of "revelation."

Interpreting Signs and Omens

Varieties of Signs and Interpretations

A great variety of things could be read as signs, and different signs could be interpreted with various levels of sophistication. On the one hand, certain objects acquired, through convention, specific semiotic value, such as the flight of birds, or the liver or entrails of an animal. On the other hand, one could bestow divinatory value on any remarkable, or otherwise inexplicable, occurrence as it makes known the will of a deity.[4] As in the case of dreams and visions, these signs could carry their own symbolic interpretive logic, which any onlooker could readily interpret, or they could also be referred to professional seers or oracles to explain their significance.

In Herodotus, for example, an omen (τέρας) in which a mare gives birth to a hare is said to be easy to interpret: "Xerxes was to march his army to Hellas with great pomp and pride [like a mare], but to come back to the same place fleeing for his life [like a hare]" (Herodotus 7.57). Xerxes ignored this and other signs, but he was a fool to do so. Dionysius of Halicarnassus records another sign (σημεῖον, φάσμα) with a figurative interpretation, but this time given by the omen interpreters (οἱ τερατοσκόποι). Roman javelin tips spontaneously burst into flame, and since "everything yields to fire and there is nothing not consumed by it," this was interpreted as signalling divine favour and victory for the Romans (*Ant. rom.* 5.46).[5]

Not all interpretations were coded or symbolic. Fire in other contexts could simply signal divine displeasure. A temple that burned down on the eve of an expedition was taken as a bad omen, and the expedition called off (Pausanias 3.9.2). The timing of the omen was significant for its interpretation in this case. The Romans also understood the Great Fire of Rome simply as a sign of divine anger, which provided occasion for the consultation of the Sibylline books in an attempt to "appease heaven" (Tacitus, *Ann.* 15.44).

---

[4] Bouché-Leclercq, *Histoire de la divination*, 1:113–14.
[5] Cited by Eyl, *Signs, Wonders, and Gifts*, 90. For the role of the seer on the battlefield, see Iles Johnston, *Ancient Greek Divination*, 116–18; Flower, *Seer in Ancient Greece*, 153–87.

Natural and Given Signs

Not all signs are divine signs, and there are some subtle distinctions that will be helpful when organising the evidence and evaluating exactly how a sign is interpreted. One important distinction is between natural and given signs, which relates to communicative intentionality.

> Very roughly speaking, natural meaning, which belongs to natural signs as such, is the evidential support that a sign furnishes for a conclusion, while given signs are used by humans, or beings relevantly like them, in order to convey their thoughts to other such beings.[6]

Thus when Paul says in 1 Thess 2:18, "we wanted to come to you ... but the Satan hindered us (ἐνέκοψεν ἡμᾶς ὁ σατανᾶς)," we see the end point of what was presumably a chain of inferences from "natural" events. That Paul suffered setbacks in trying to visit is given a level of non-human intentionality and taken as a sign that a low-rank divine being was trying to thwart him. As such, the setbacks Paul experienced function as a natural sign, or evidence, of activity in the divine world. This is not the same as supposing that the Satan was using these events to try and communicate his displeasure to Paul, or that Paul reached this conclusion as a result of trying to seek the Satan's will for his enterprise. The focus is on the act of hindrance itself rather than any message that was being conveyed through it. In this sense the setbacks are evidential support for a conclusion rather than the product of divine communication, and I would hesitate to call it an example of divination.

This distinction is useful, but difficult to maintain absolutely. James Allen notes in the case of Stoic attitudes towards divination that signs are both "natural," in that they are part of the order of the cosmos and interpreted through repeated observation and experience, but also "given," in the sense that they are part of "the providential order of nature, intended by God to serve humankind as signs."[7] In the case of the Great Fire of Rome, was the fire understood as a sign sent to alert the Romans of divine anger, or was the devastation it caused evidence of such anger? Miguel Requena Jiménez has recently argued that prodigies in Republican Rome should be understood generally as evidence of the absence of the gods' protective power rather than a deliberate signalling of their intentions. The divination comes in trying to

---

[6] James Allen, "Greek Philosophy and Signs," in *Divination and Interpretation of Signs in the Ancient World*, ed. Amar Annus, OIS 6 (Chicago: Oriental Institute of the University of Chicago, 2010), 30; cf. James Allen, *Inference from Signs: Ancient Debates about the Nature of Evidence* (Oxford: Clarendon, 2001), 4–5.

[7] Allen, *Inference from Signs*, 4–5.

analyse and interpret the reasons for the absence.[8] Similar difficulties exist with Paul whose sign-reading has much in common with Roman prodigies. Many of the things he designates signs, and other instances from which he draws inferences of divine activity, do not seem to primarily have a communicative function, and serve more of an evidentiary role. The thing they provide evidence for, however, is divine action or intention, which he then uses as a basis for further action. So, God's activity and attitude can still be discerned through certain signs, even though the signs themselves often primarily serve other functions.

Signs, Omens, and Divine Politics

Paul's closest verbal link to divinatory signs is when he speaks of σημεῖα καὶ τέρατα, "signs and omens," which accompanied and validated his preaching to the Gentiles (Rom 15:19; 2 Cor 12:12). The pairing of σημεῖα καὶ τέρατα is common in both Jewish and Greek sources to denote omens, portents, and prodigies from the gods.[9] In Greek sources, these include springs and rainwater turning to blood, sweating statues, temples being struck by lightning, mules giving birth, dogs howling like wolves, wolves running through the city, and newborn babies speaking. All such signs portended a significant political or military upheaval (Polybius 3.112.8; Appian, *Bell. civ.* 2.144; 4.4; Aelian, *Var. hist.* 12.57).

In the Greek Bible the phrase is most commonly used of the Exodus plagues and the signs performed by Moses and Aaron.[10] These signs, which include the rivers turning to blood, hailstorms, thunder, and plagues of frogs, gnats, flies, and locusts all parallel the sort of signs reported by the Greek writers, and in similar style portended defeat for the Egyptians. In the world of divine politics they also served the further function of displaying the power and superiority of

---

[8] Miguel Requena Jiménez, "Prodigies in Republican Rome: The Absence of God," *Klio* 100 (2018): 480–500.

[9] See Molly Whittaker, "'Signs and Wonders': The Pagan Background," *SE* 5 (1968): 155–58; K. H. Rengstorf, "σημεῖον κτλ," *TDNT* 7:200–26; Rengstorf, "τέρας," *TDNT* 8:113–26; S. Vernon McCasland, "Signs and Wonders," *JBL* 76 (1957): 149–52.

[10] The secondary literature can sometimes give the impression that the phrase becomes restricted in its use to only refer to the events of the Exodus. So, Graham H. Twelftree ("Signs, Wonders, Miracles," *DPL* 875) says, "In the LXX the phrase is *generally confined* to" the Exodus, or Rengstorf ("σημεῖον κτλ," 221) concludes that "in Greek-speaking Judaism … the formula … seems *to be reserved* for God's wonders in the days of Moses" (italics mine). It would be more accurate to think of the Exodus as representing an instance of God's signs and wonders *par excellence*, which does not exhaust the continuing revelation of divine signs. Jeremiah 32:20 (39:20 LXX) states "you who performed signs and wonders in Egypt *until this day* both among Israel and among the earthborn and made a name for yourself *as this day*." For examples of the phrase outside of an Exodus context: Deut 13:2; 28:46; Isa 8:18; 20:3; OG Dan 4:37; θ' Dan 4:2; 6:28; Sir 36:5; Wis 8:8; cf. 3 Kgdms 13:3, 5; 2 Chr 32:31; Joel 3:3.

the Jewish God. Yahweh regularly prefaces the sending of plagues in Exodus with statements such as, "By this you shall know that I am Yahweh" (Exod 7:17), "that you may know that I, Yahweh, am in this land" (Exod 8:22), "that you may know that there is no one like me in all the earth" (Exod 9:14). More than just wearing down the Egyptians, the plagues signified to the Egyptians and the Israelites alike where power and favour resided in the divine realm.

This function of signs and omens is characteristic of most Jewish sources, in which a sign primarily indicates God's power and favour. For this reason, signs are not generally given elaborate or symbolic decoding. Dreams and visions receive such interpretations in Jewish literature but signs in the natural world generally only signal divine pleasure or displeasure. There are of course exceptions to this. Josephus records omens and portents in much the same manner as any Roman historian, although not without some modifications.[11] Some astrological and physiognomic texts from Qumran also involve more advanced systems of interpretation (4Q186, 4Q534, 4Q561). A zodiacal calendar (4Q318) predicts various forms of famine or invasion by foreign armies depending on whether it thunders in Gemini or Taurus. Even the physiognomies, though, only purport to reveal what proportion of a person's soul belongs to light or darkness.[12] Yahweh sometimes commands the prophets Isaiah and Ezekiel to enact signs and omens, which symbolically enact Yahweh's message (Isa 8:18; 20:3; Ezek 12:6, 11; 24:24, 27). As such, these are an interesting example of the divine manipulation of human beings into symbolic signs but are not quite in the same category as interpretations of natural or social phenomena. The pattern of Exodus remains the most common, in which the Nile turning to blood portends defeat for the Egyptians not because it is given a symbolic interpretation, but because it demonstrates the superior power of Yahweh and legitimates Moses as his true spokesperson.[13]

---

[11] S. Vernon McCasland, "Portents in Josephus and in the Gospels," *JBL* 51 (1932): 323–35; Francis Schmidt, "Signes et prodiges chez Flavius Josèphe et Tacite (*Guerre des juifs* 6.288–315; *Histoires* 5.13)," in *La Raison des signes: présages, rites, destin dans les sociétés de la Méditerranée ancienne*, ed. Stella Georgoudi, Renée Koch Piettre, and Francis Schmidt, RGRW 174 (Leiden: Brill, 2012), 253–89.

[12] See Mladen Popović, "Reading the Human Body and Writing in Code: Physiognomic Divination and Astrology in the Dead Sea Scrolls," in *Flores Florentino: Dead Sea Scrolls and Other Early Jewish Studies in Honour of Florentino García Martínez*, ed., Anthony Hilhorst, Émile Puech, and Eibert Tigchelaar, JSJSup 122 (Leiden: Brill, 2007), 271–84.

[13] The plagues were sent "non comme des avertissements mais comme l'annonce d'événements qui ne peuvent être évités." As such, they function as "les actions à travers lesquelles Dieu manifeste sa force," Ileana Chirassi Colombo, "Teras ou les modalités du prodige dans le discours divinatoire grec: une perspective comparatiste," in Georgoudi, Piettre, and Schmidt, *La Raison des signes*, 226. Chirassi Colombo attributes this difference to the divide between monotheism and polytheism. If so, it is a specifically competitive monotheism, which seeks to show the superiority of the true God over the other (very real) contenders.

One could also predict a sign, as with the "man of God" in 3 Kgdms 13:3–5 who "gave a sign (τέρας)" predicting that the altar would be torn down. The fulfilment of this sign leads to the vindication of the "man of God" as a prophet. The prophet Joel predicts omens (τέρατα: blood, fire, smoke, the sun going dark, the moon turning to blood) which, when they appear, will be signs of the proximity of the day of the Lord, and the fulfilment of the rest of Joel's prophecy (Joel 2:30–31 [3:3–4 LXX]; cf. Matt 24:30; Luke 21:25).[14] This is also the role of the predictions in 2 Thess 2:1–12, which appear to have been derived from sacred texts, and function as signs to be observed before Christ's parousia. Stowers has opined that the "most important motivation [among scholars] for denying the Pauline authorship of 2 Thessalonians" is the desire to make Paul "apocalyptic, but not too apocalyptic."[15] Such eschatological timetables that rely on the observation of signs are seen as a step too far for a refined and restrained apocalypticist such as Paul. Whether or not this is a genuine motivation, we have already seen in the last chapter that Paul is indeed working to an eschatological timetable, which he has divined from sacred texts. This involves the recognition of the Messiah and the necessary allegiance of the Gentiles. The broader use of signs in 2 Thessalonians is consistent with the use of signs in the undisputed letters, and so will be included in the discussions below.

Divine Signs in Paul: Approval and Judgement

Signs and Omens (σημεῖα καὶ τέρατα) in Paul

The signs and omens Paul points to appear generally positive in nature, and serve the function of demonstrating the power of his God. The signs prove that his message is true, and that his camp is the one in which divine favour resides. Gentiles became obedient to Christ, he says in Rom 15:19, by the power of signs and omens and by the power of God's *pneuma* (ἐν δυνάμει σημείων καὶ τεράτων, ἐν δυνάμει πνεύματος [θεοῦ]). In 2 Cor 12:12, signs, omens, and works of power (σημείοις τε καὶ τέρασιν καὶ δυνάμεσιν) are among the signs of an apostle which ought to have proved his legitimacy as one sent by God before the Corinthians.

---

[14] See further Klaus Berger, "Hellenistisch-heidnische Prodigien und die Vorzeichen in der jüdischen und christlichen Apokalyptik," *ANRW* 23.2:1436–47; Edward Adams, *The Stars Will Fall From Heaven: 'Cosmic Catastrophe' in the New Testament and its World*, LNTS 347 (London: T&T Clark, 2007), 46–47, 176–177.

[15] Stanley K. Stowers, "Paul's Four Discourses About Sin," in *Celebrating Paul: Festschrift in Honor of Jerome Murphy-O'Connor, O.P. and Joseph A. Fitzmyer, S.J.*, ed. Peter Spitaler (Washington, DC: Catholic Biblical Association of America, 2011), 117.

Without the language of signs, but surely referring to similar occurrences, virtually every undisputed letter of Paul contains reference to visible displays of *pneuma* and power (δύναμις) that accompanied his initial preaching.[16] In each case, as also in the examples above, Paul exhibits these as divine confirmation of his message, and his status as a message bearer for the divine. To the Thessalonians he writes that "our good news did not come to you in word alone, but also in power and in holy *pneuma* and full assurance (πληροφορίᾳ πολλῇ)." The word πληροφορία could be translated as "fullness," and refer to a preponderance of miraculous signs.[17] But it is usually rendered as "conviction" or "assurance," referring to either the conviction of Paul's preaching or the assurance that the Thessalonians received about his message.[18] In this case, the displays of divine power appear to serve as divine confirmation for everyone involved. Paul first mentions them as the reason why he and his associates know the Thessalonians are chosen by God (εἰδότες . . . τὴν ἐκλογὴν ὑμῶν, ὅτι . . .),[19] and then notes that in the same way (καθώς) the Thessalonians also knew what sort of people Paul and his associates were.[20] Divine signs that accompanied his message served both as confirmation for Paul of the efficacy of his message and that his audience were loved and chosen by God, as well as confirmation to his audience of what sort of people Paul and the apostles were, that is, people with divine approval.

To the Corinthians he recalls that the persuasiveness of his initial preaching was not in the wisdom of his words, but in demonstrations of *pneuma* and of power (ἐν ἀποδείξει πνεύματος καὶ δυνάμεως). It is these that rightly won their trust, rather than his manner of speaking "so that your trust might not be in human wisdom but in the power of God." In Galatians 3:1–5 he contrasts his own message with that of his opponents. Before turning to sacred writings to support his claim, Paul first points to the fact that the Galatians

---

[16] Jacob Jervell, "The Signs of an Apostle: Paul's Miracles," in *The Unknown Paul: Essays on Luke-Acts and Early Christian History* (Minneapolis: Augsburg, 1984), 91–93.

[17] Gene L. Green, *The Letters to the Thessalonians*, PNTC (Grand Rapids, Eerdmans, 2002), 96.

[18] Charles A. Wanamaker, *The Epistles to the Thessalonians*, NIGTC (Grand Rapids: Eerdmans, 1990), 79; F. F. Bruce, *1 & 2 Thessalonians*, WBC 45 (Dallas: Word, 1982), 15. Bruce opts for the latter, but attempts to distance the assurance received from the miracles, referring to it as "a token of the Holy Spirit's work in their hearts, more impressive and more lasting than the persuasion produced by spectacular or miraculous signs."

[19] The ὅτι may be causal, "because," or epexegetic, "knowing the manner of your election" (see Gordon D. Fee, *God's Empowering Presence: The Holy Spirit in the Letters of Paul* [Peabody, MA: Hendrickson, 1994], 40 n. 4; Lightfoot, *Notes*, 12). Either way, Paul is offering up the nature of his initial preaching as evidence for the genuineness of their calling.

[20] F. F. Bruce (*1 & 2 Thessalonians*, 15) notes the correspondence implied by καθώς, "we know what kind of people you turned out to be when you received the gospel *as* you know what kind of people we were when we brought it to you," (italics original).

themselves received *pneuma* from God and witnessed miracles (δυνάμεις). This proves which message – works of the law or the message of faith – had divine approval. The assumption throughout is that these divinely wrought signs attest to Paul's legitimacy and played a large part in convincing his audience that his message came with divine approval.

Divine signs for Paul, then, mainly serve the role of confirmation and indicate divine approval. They do not need complex decoding, but act more like the signs in the *Iliad*, such as a flash of lightning on the right, which indicates a nod of approval from Zeus for the Achaean expedition, and a promise of their success (2.347–353). Thunder and lightning later serve a similar function for the Trojans in battle (8.170–171; 9.232–239). When Ajax challenges Hector and predicts the sack of Troy, the Achaeans are encouraged by a bird flying by on the right. This is taken as divine confirmation and validation of the truth of Ajax's words (13.815–823). Closer to Paul's own time, Suetonius records various signs, which accompanied the rise to power of certain Roman emperors: trees with enormous and unnatural growth, a rainbow-like circle around the sun, lightning strikes, as well as extraordinary auspices (Suetonius, *Aug.* 94–95; *Vesp.* 5.2–3). These signal both divine favour for the emperor and a "great and happy future" for Rome under his rule.

The fact that divine signs can accompany people with different religious allegiances is recognised in 2 Thess 2:8–12. Here it is not Paul but the "lawless one" who produces power, signs, and omens, all of which are branded false (ψεύδους [v. 9]).[21] That is not to say that these signs do not reveal divine power. Rather in this case God has deliberately sent a force of deception so that people will believe what is false (v. 11). Whether performed by Paul or the lawless one, the desired function of divine legitimation remains the same. The difference is that whereas Paul's signs are interpreted as genuine signs of divine favour, the signs of the lawless one, Paul warns, are divine deceptions, and are signs that fulfil a particular eschatological timetable.

Paul does not specify what his signs or wonders were. Thunderbolts, miraculous healings, or glossolalia are all plausible speculations that fit Paul's language and context.[22] The latter two suggestions can also be supported from Paul's own letters. Paul gives a prominent role to God's *pneuma* in four of the five passages cited above, so his list of manifestations of God's *pneuma* in 1 Cor 12 provide the firmest idea as to what he may be referring to.[23] These manifestations include healings, prophecy, and the ability to speak other languages, as well as the interpretation

---

[21] Van Kooten takes 2 Thess as post-Pauline and links these signs and omens with Nero, whose life and career were also said to have been accompanied by various signs and portents. George van Kooten, "'Wrath Will Drip in the Plains of Macedonia': Expectations of Nero's Return in the Egyptian Sibylline Oracles (Book 5), 2 Thessalonians, and Ancient Historical Writings," in Hilhorst and van Kooten, *The Wisdom of Egypt*, 201–3.

[22] Eyl, *Signs, Wonders, and Gifts*, 89.

[23] Wanamaker, *Thessalonians*, 79.

of languages.²⁴ It is also worth noting that this list includes the more general ἐνεργήματα δυνάμεων, "works of power," (12:10) so it is probably unwise to narrow the options too much as Paul himself remains staunchly vague and generic.²⁵

Prophecy and Languages as Signs

Of these manifestations of *pneuma* Paul does explicitly call prophecy and languages "signs," although the more specific he becomes about this, the harder it is to discern with confidence what he means by it.²⁶ The key statement is in 1 Cor 14:22, αἱ γλῶσσαι εἰς σημεῖόν εἰσιν οὐ τοῖς πιστεύουσιν ἀλλὰ τοῖς ἀπίστοις, ἡ δὲ προφητεία οὐ τοῖς ἀπίστοις ἀλλὰ τοῖς πιστεύουσιν, "languages serve as a sign²⁷ not to believers but to unbelievers, but prophecy [serves as a sign]²⁸ not to unbelievers but to believers." The main issue with this passage is how the key statement of v. 22 relates both to the quotation from Isa 28:11 that precedes it,²⁹ and to the two illustrations that follow, which seem to directly contradict v. 22 in some aspects. The flow of thought from the citation to the illustrations

---

[24] Esler draws attention to the role glossolalia played in the book of Acts, which convinced others of that person's possession by *pneuma*, Philip F. Esler, "Glossolalia and the Admission of Gentiles into the Early Christian Community," *BTB* 22 (1992): 136–42. In this instance, it is also possible that such signs could have been taken as signs of the "last days" as in Acts 2:14–36. The language of signs and wonders is used in this passage to speak both of portents of the end (in the Joel quote), and the signs which attested Jesus as a man of God.

[25] Engberg-Pedersen's suggestion that Paul's preaching was accompanied by visions of Christ for his hearers (*Paul and the Stoics*, 144) is possible, but less likely, as his textual basis for this is Gal 3:1 which I take to refer to written oracles rather than a visionary experience (cf. Wendt, "Textual Prophecy"). Visions of Christ himself are generally reserved for Paul and other apostles (see Chapter 2), but 2 Cor 3:18–4:6 may suggest a more general inner illumination available to all.

[26] Eyl (*Signs, Wonders, and Gifts*, 88) dismisses this use of σημεῖον as evidential in contrast to Paul's different usage in Rom 15 and 2 Cor 12, but this is unwarranted given the obviously divine nature of the sign.

[27] Wayne A. Grudem ("1 Corinthians 14:20–25: Prophecy and Tongues as Signs of God's Attitude," *WTJ* 41 [1979]: 388 n. 23) takes εἰς σημεῖόν εἰσιν as a Semitism which functions as a regular predicate nominative but all the supporting examples he cites (with the exception of 1 John 5:8) are either with γίνομαι or the future tense of εἰμί in which the preposition appropriately conveys the movement into a state of affairs (BDF §145.1; BDAG, s.v. "εἰς"). In the present tense the addition of "serve as a sign" would convey the force of the preposition better (BDF §145.2; BDAG, s.vv. "εἰμί," "εἰς"). This wording reflects the fact that the primary function of glossolalia for Paul is not as a sign but as prayer. It can however serve a secondary function as a sign. The same would also apply to prophecy.

[28] It is important for some that only glossolalia is explicitly labelled a (mere) sign here, while prophecy is taken to be something different and better, see Stendahl, "Glossolalia," 116 n. 9; Joop F. M. Smit, "Tongues and Prophecy: Deciphering 1 Cor 14:22," *Biblica* 75 (1994): 185, 189. The clear parallelism, however, makes it most likely that εἰς σημεῖόν εἰσιν should be assumed for the second half of the clause.

[29] "In the law it is written, 'by people of other languages and by the lips of foreigners will I speak to this people, and even then they will not obey me, says the Lord'" (1 Cor 14:21).

appears simple enough. The citation demonstrates that divine speech in foreign languages will not lead to obedience, and the illustrations confirm this point: unbelievers encountering glossolalia remain unaffected, whereas an unbeliever hearing prophecy "will bow down before God and worship him." In what way then do languages function as a sign for unbelievers, but not for believers?

The most popular current interpretation understands σημεῖον here to indicate a sign of judgement on unbelievers. The exclamation μαίνεσθε uttered by the outsider in response to hearing glossolalia is understood as a rejection of God's message ("you are mad") confirming the unbeliever in their unbelief and leaving them in a state of judgement. Support for this comes from the citation of Isa 28:11, in which the foreign tongues of the Assyrian conquerors are a sign of judgement on God's people for not listening to his message.[30] In the same way, for Paul, glossolalia is taken to be a sign of God's judgement on unbelievers because it confirms, and even hardens them, in their unbelieving status.[31] This is not a satisfactory reading, as it transforms a sign *to* unbelievers into a sign *about* unbelievers. It is hard to see how unbelievers themselves would recognise glossolalia as a sign of their own judgement, so some commentators get around this by making it instead a sign to believers of God's judgement on unbelievers.[32] But at this point we are far removed from the plain syntax of v. 22.

---

[30] The NRSV of Isa 28:11–13 reads: "Truly, with stammering lip and with alien tongue he will speak to this people, to whom he has said, 'This is rest; give rest to the weary; and this is repose'; yet they would not hear. Therefore the word of the Lord will be to them, 'Precept upon precept, precept upon precept, line upon line, line upon line, here a little, there a little [the Hebrew is essentially gibberish]'; in order that they may go, and fall backwards, and be broken, and snared, and taken."

[31] There are variations within this common perspective. For F. F. Bruce (*1 & 2 Corinthians* [London: Marshall, Morgan & Scott, 1971], 133), "strange tongues addressed to the deliberately disobedient will confirm them in their disobedience." For C. K. Barrett (*First Corinthians*, 323), "tongues serve to harden and thus condemn the unbeliever ... they are a sign by which believers are distinguished from unbelievers, since the latter reveal themselves by the reaction described in verse 23." For Fee (*First Corinthians*, 756), "Because what is spoken in tongues is unintelligible, unbelievers receive no revelation from God; they cannot thereby be brought to faith. Thus by their response ... they are destined for divine judgement." For Fee, however, this is an effect of tongues rather than God's intent for tongues. All of these explanations stretch the definition of "sign" beyond recognition.

[32] E.g., Barrett, *First Corinthians*, 323. Stephen Chester ("Divine Madness? Speaking in Tongues in 1 Corinthians 14:23," *JSNT* 27 [2005]: 431–32) notes the problems with an unbeliever being unable to understand a sign that is ostensibly for them. T. J. Lang ("Trouble with Insiders: The Social Profile of the ἄπιστοι in Paul's Corinthian Correspondence," *JBL* 137 [2018]: 993–94) argues the most compelling recent case for this line of interpretation I have seen. For Lang, the ἄπιστοι are not generic unbelievers but members of the *ekklēsia* who do not remain exclusively faithful to the one God. Glossolalia is a sign of judgement for them as it publicly demonstrates to people who thought that they were insiders, that they are in fact unfaithful and under divine judgement. I remain unconvinced it is a sign of judgement at all, for the reasons argued below.

A further problem with this reading is that the concept of "a sign of judgement" is nowhere present in Paul's text, or his wider discussion of glossolalia. Rather, it is imported from the wider context of Isa 28 in the MT. In this text, it is true, the foreign languages through which God speaks are those of the Assyrians, which are the result of God's judgement on his people for not listening to his intelligible message in v. 12: "This is rest; give rest to the weary; and this is repose." The LXX of this passage, however, conveys quite a different meaning.[33] The intelligible message in v. 12 is one of doom, "This is the rest for the hungry, and this is the destruction," and is spoken not by Yahweh, but by the Assyrians.[34] The people's refusal to listen to this message from the Assyrians, rather than unfaithfulness, could be interpreted as their refusal to capitulate to foreign invaders.[35]

Paul's citation is selective, and does not fully represent either text, so it is best to pay attention to the specific wording he employs in the context of his argument, rather than the unstated context of a text he may not have known.[36] Most significantly, Paul replaces the third person singular of the MT (ידבר referring to Yahweh) and the third person plural of the LXX (λαλήσουσι, referring to either the Assyrians or the priests and prophets) with the first-person singular λαλήσω, and concludes the citation with λέγει κύριος. This causes the whole passage to become a first-person oracle of the Lord. Paul also omits the intelligible message of Isa 28:12a, which has a profound effect on the meaning of the text. With the intelligible message intact, the foreign tongues appear as a punishment for not heeding this message. Without the intelligible message of v. 12, the tongues themselves become the message that is not heeded. As Paul has rendered the citation then, it becomes an "oracle about how to give an oracle."[37] It is about what happens when God communicates in foreign languages, and the result is that the people do not respond.[38] There is not a hint in Paul's use of this oracle that "unknown tongues are not God's

---

[33] "Because of contempt from lips, through a different tongue, because they will speak to this people, saying to them, 'This is the rest for the hungry, and this is the destruction'; yet they would not hear. And the oracle of the Lord God will be to them affliction upon affliction, hope upon hope, yet a little, yet a little, in order that they may go and fall backward, and they will be in danger and crushed and taken" (NETS).

[34] The third-person plural is ambiguous and could also refer to the drunken priests and prophets in v. 7.

[35] This is how the text is understood by David E. Lanier, "With Stammering Lips and Another Tongue: 1 Cor 14:20–22 and Isa 28:11–12," *CTR* 5 (1991): 263–64, who is followed by Chester, "Divine Madness?" 440.

[36] For a full discussion of the complex issues, see Stanley, *Paul and the Language of Scripture*, 197–205.

[37] Peter Nagel, "1 Corinthians 14:21: Paul's Reflection on ΓΛΩΣΣΑ," *JECH* 3 (2013): 46.

[38] B. C. Johanson, "Tongues, A Sign for Unbelievers? A Structural and Exegetical Study of 1 Corinthians 14:20–25," *NTS* 25 (1979): 182.

greeting to a believing congregation but His rebuke to an unbelieving one."[39] Such an estimation runs counter to his general estimation of glossolalia in this passage as a personally beneficial means of prayer, which he claims to practice more than anyone.

If languages are not a sign of judgement, then what do they signal? The best indication should be found in the responses uttered by the unbelievers in each example. Both the response to glossolalia (μαίνεσθε) and to prophecy (ὄντως ὁ θεὸς ἐν ὑμῖν ἐστιν) can be read as recognitions of divine presence and activity. Clearly for Paul the second response is the more satisfactory, as it leads to the obedience that is lacking from the Isaiah quote. But as many have previously noted, μαίνεσθε may also imply a recognition of divinely bestowed madness, and is best translated as "you are inspired," or "you are possessed."[40] This would not necessarily have the effect of driving the unbeliever away in contempt as most interpret it, but would lead to a general recognition that a divine presence is at work. As with glossolalia in the rest of 1 Cor 14, this does not seem to be a problem in itself for Paul, it simply is not as effective a sign as prophecy, as it does not communicate clearly or precisely enough. Jane Lightfoot notes the "double-edged" nature of the madness motif, which could be used both to verify true prophecy and to ridicule false alternatives.[41] It therefore serves as an ambiguous sign.

Prophecy on the other hand is the sort of sign the faithful should seek as it points more clearly to the correct god, and the correct interpretation. Note the specificity of the information conveyed through the prophets in v. 25, who reveal the secrets of the unbeliever's heart. This leads to a similarly specific conclusion that recognises not just the general presence of divine activity, but that *the* God (ὁ θεός) is present in the assembly.[42] Paul's language is reminiscent of

---

[39] Derek Kidner, "Isaiah," in *The New Bible Commentary, Revised*, ed. Donald Guthrie and J. A. Motyer (London: InterVarsity, 1970), 606. Kidner is quoted approvingly by Grudem ("Prophecy and Tongues," 387) and Lanier ("Stammering Lips," 272 n. 40).

[40] Stephen Chester ("Divine Madness?") has provided the fullest case in support of this, but Roberts had already argued a similar case: P. Roberts, "A Sign – Christian or Pagan?" *ExpTim* 90 (1979): 199–203. Cf. Gillespie, *First Theologians*, 156–57. Paul Trebilco (*Outsider Designations and Boundary Construction in the New Testament: Early Christian Communities and the Formation of Group Identity* [Cambridge: Cambridge University Press, 2017], 57 n. 62) believes Chester's proposal unlikely because it "requires considerable reading between the lines." But as shown above, the view of divine judgement requires just as much, if not more, reading between the lines of what Paul has actually written.

[41] Lightfoot, *Sibylline Oracles*, 18–19. Both uses are already present in Plato, cf. *Phaedr.* 244a–b; *Euthyphr.* 3c.

[42] The term ὁ θεός, without further qualification, for Paul always means the God of Israel, see Fredriksen, *Pagans' Apostle*, 126. The verb ἀπαγγέλλειν is used in Gen 41:8 and Judg 14:12 LXX to refer to the interpretation of a dream or riddle, so one could read a further nuance to the term that treats the unbeliever's conclusion as his interpretation of the divine sign, see LSJ, s.v. "ἀπαγγέλλω."

Isa 45:14: ἐν σοὶ ὁ θεός ἐστι, καὶ ἐροῦσιν οὐκ ἔστι θεὸς πλὴν σοῦ, "God is among you, and they will say there is no God beside you." If Paul is evoking this and similar passages, this further reinforces the sense of identifying the one true God from amongst the range of possible divinities (cf. 3 Kgdms 18:39; Dan 2:47; Zech 8:23).[43]

Romans 8:16 may furnish another example in which languages, when they are interpreted, serve as a divinatory sign. Paul says, "the *pneuma* itself bears witness with our *pneuma* that we are children of God." Here the cry of *abba* uttered by the *pneuma* when given its interpretation into Greek still functions primarily as prayer, but also serves as a sign that tells believers about their status with God. The configuration of divine and human *pneuma* that produces the ecstatic *abba* cry directed towards God serves as confirmation and supporting evidence that believers are in fact God's children. Paul uses the same phenomenon to draw the same conclusion in Gal 4:6, where the cry of *abba* is followed by Paul's conclusion: "therefore you are no longer a slave but a son."

Signs of Judgement

Languages do not function as a sign of judgement in Paul's letters, but there are many other things in the ancient world that could display a god's displeasure. Discerning and interpreting these became particularly institutionalised in Roman divination and its recording of prodigies. A prodigy was, according to Susan Satterfield, "an aberration in what the Romans considered the natural order of things: a talking chicken, a hermaphrodite birth, a plague, etc."[44] The presence of a prodigy was either read as a warning of coming disaster or an expression of divine anger. Underlying both possibilities could be the assumption that a prodigy provided evidence that a god had removed his or her protection from the people.[45] Once prodigies were identified, they were then subjected to interpretation, often by means of the Sibylline books. The interpretations would determine how to seek the *pax deum*, restoring the right relationship with the gods and averting disaster. Livy lists wars, famine, and disease as things people attributed to the wrath of the gods (*ira deum*: Livy 4.9.3), and notes a number of occasions in which the Romans consulted the Sibylline books and offered expiations in response to such events (Livy 4.25.3; 5.14.4; 22.9.10; 40.37.2). The cause of divine wrath was not always clear, or indeed important. The main concern was how to now seek peace with the gods. When an explanation was offered, it usually related to some form of

---

[43] "What these passages underscore is the identity of Israel's God as *exclusively* God and *exclusively* present with God's people" (italics original), Lang, "Trouble with Insiders," 994.

[44] Satterfield, "Prodigies," 432.

[45] Requena Jiménez, "Prodigies in Republican Rome."

impiety in the form of ritual error, or transgression of divine norms which threatened social or political cohesion.[46]

Paul often assumes the role of discerner and interpreter of divine wrath in response to certain circumstances. He traces sickness and death amongst some of the Corinthians to improper conduct at the ritual meal, eating the bread and drinking the cup in an unworthy manner (1 Cor 11:27–30).[47] It could be argued that this is not a sign of judgement, but judgement itself. The way Paul interprets these judgements, however, shows that there is more to it than that. Paul interprets the events as acts of divine discipline, sent so that the Corinthians can rectify their ways and avert a fuller, final judgement (1 Cor 11:32). The immediate, smaller-scale judgements thus serve a communicative intent as they show up problems in the way the Corinthians are currently acting and alert them to the need to change their actions to avert further judgement.[48]

In 1 Thess 2:14–16, Paul also discerns the presence of divine wrath against certain Judeans who opposed his message to the Gentiles. Paul adds to this opposition the charges of killing the Lord Jesus and the prophets, so that "they are continually filling up the measure of their sins. But the wrath has come upon them [leading] toward its completion."[49] Here again is the notion that immediate historical signs of wrath form part of a trajectory leading towards a full and final judgement. While the Corinthians are told to heed these signs of judgement and recognise them as acts of divine discipline, the Judeans who continue to oppose Paul's message continue to "fill up the measure of their sins" so that the proximate signs of judgement continue to point towards their final completion.[50]

Reading this text with post-70 CE eyes has led many to believe the text must be a post-Pauline interpolation that refers to the destruction of the Jerusalem temple as a final act of God's wrath on the Jews.[51] Burning temples

---

[46] David S. Levene, *Religion in Livy*, Mnemosyne 127 (Leiden: Brill, 1993), 6–8; Satterfield, "Prodigies," 431 n. 3; Jerzy Linderski, "Pax deorum (deum)," *BNP* 10:659.

[47] Shantz (*Paul in Ecstasy*, 182) sees this passage as evidence of Paul assuming a priestly role as a "magico-religious practitioner," which she distinguishes from the role of divine "messenger." In the context of divination, they both fit easily side by side. Cf. Wendt, *At the Temple Gates*, 167–68.

[48] Oracles were often consulted in response to sickness: Herodotus 1.19.2; Plutarch, *Mulier. virt.* 245c; Diodorus Siculus 4.31.5, 38.3; Pausanias 5.13.6.

[49] For this translation of εἰς τέλος, see Stowers, "Sin," 119.

[50] Stowers, "Sin," 117–21; Abraham J. Malherbe, *The Letters to the Thessalonians*, AB 32B (New York: Doubleday, 2000), 170–71.

[51] Birger Pearson ("1 Thessalonians 2:13–16: A Deutero-Pauline Interpolation," *HTR* 64 [1971]: 79–94) is usually credited with the strongest case toward this conclusion, although the identification with the fall of Jerusalem was made by F. C. Baur, *Paul the Apostle of Jesus Christ*, trans. Allan Menzies (London: Williams & Norgate, 1875), 2.87–88, who judged 1 Thessalonians in its entirety to be inauthentic. Pearson's arguments have been critiqued, however, by John Hurd ("Paul Ahead of His Time: 1 Thess 2:13–16," in *Paul and the Gospels*, ed. Peter Richardson, vol. 1 of *Anti-Judaism in Early Christianity*, SCJ 2 [Waterloo, ON: Wilfred Laurier University Press, 1986], 21–36) and Markus N. A. Bockmuehl ("1 Thessalonians 2:14–16 and the Church in Jerusalem," *TynB* 52 [2001]: 5–17).

were certainly bad omens, signalling the lack of divine presence in precisely the place where it should normally be,[52] but to assume that this was the only event of the first century that could elicit such language from Paul underestimates the range of events that could be attributed to divine anger. It also, as many have pointed out, assumes the hindsight that would have been unavailable if the text is authentically from Paul.[53]

With this in mind, Paul could have interpreted a number of miseries that befell Judea in the years preceding the writing of 1 Thessalonians in this way.[54] Political miseries and other instances of mass bloodshed connected with the temple could have been read as signs of divine anger, such as the tens of thousands of lives lost when a large deployment of Roman soldiers was sent into the temple porticoes during Passover in 49 CE (Josephus, *A.J.* 20.112; *B.J.* 2.227). Paul elsewhere suggests God's wrath could be made known through government officials (Rom 13:4–5), suggesting civil punishments could be interpreted as expressions of God's displeasure. Famines, in particular, were also frequently signs of divine anger and are well documented in Judea between 44 and 49 CE.[55]

Records of past judgements recorded in the sacred books also serve as warnings of similar disasters in response to impiety (1 Cor 10:6–11). Paul even suggests that the primary purpose of such judgements was to be a warning to the present generation. Disasters which befell the Israelites in the wilderness, such as the death by snakes recorded in Numbers 21, happened as τύποι – examples that set the pattern of divine response to idolatry and sexual immorality (10:6, 11). They were written down, Paul says, as warnings of how to avert disaster in the present (v. 11). In this instance, Paul reads the text of the Pentateuch as a sort of omen list, which records the signs of judgement that accompanied various acts of impiety for future use.[56]

Not all suffering is a sign of judgement. I have already discussed Paul's thorn in the flesh in 2 Cor 12:7–10, which Christ himself interprets for Paul as a sign

---

[52] Dillon, *Omens and Oracles,* 188; Requena Jiménez, "Prodigies in Republican Rome," 495.

[53] Robert Jewett, *The Thessalonian Correspondence: Pauline Rhetoric and Millenarian Piety* (Philadelphia: Fortress, 1986), 61; Todd D. Still, *Conflict at Thessalonica: A Pauline Church and its Neighbours,* JSNTSup 183 (Sheffield: Sheffield Academic, 1999), 35–36; Bockmuehl, "1 Thessalonians," 8.

[54] Various options are listed by B. W. Bacon, "Wrath 'Unto the Uttermost,'" *The Expositor* 8.24 (1922): 370–71; Sherman E. Johnson, "Notes and Comments (1 Thess 2:16)," *AThR* 23 (1941): 173–76.

[55] Bockmuehl, "1 Thessalonians," 25–27. This is assuming a date of c. 50 CE for 1 Thessalonians. Campbell dates the letter about a decade earlier, but can similarly point to famines or political miseries of the time to explain 1 Thess 2:16, such as the events surrounding the revolt of Theudas, Douglas A. Campbell, *Framing Paul: An Epistolary Biography* (Grand Rapids: Eerdmans, 2014), 252–53.

[56] Such examples, of course, do not approach anything like the systematic observation of signs that went into the compilation of omen lists in general. See Iles Johnston, *Ancient Greek Divination,* 133–34.

of strength and favour so that Paul can withstand all manner of hardships.[57] Paul provides similar interpretations to the Philippians and Thessalonians when they are faced with human opposition (Phil 1:27–30; 2 Thess 1:4–10). These afflictions, Paul says, are not to be averted through changed behaviour, but endured. The ability to endure these afflictions is itself a form of evidence (ἔνδειξις [Phil 1:28]; ἔνδειγμα [2 Thess 1:5]) that they will eventually be vindicated, and their opponents judged. Like the signs of judgement already discussed in this chapter, Paul places these hardships in a context of future and final judgement. Correct interpretation is needed, however, to know whether they signal judgement for you or your enemies.

Romans 1–3: Signs of Judgement and Justice

In Rom 1–3, the presence and absence of visible signs of judgement becomes the subject for a more complex chain of reasoning and reflection, but one that still conforms to the general structure of "prodigy and expiation" (to borrow from the title of a classic work on Roman divination).[58] The remainder of this chapter will be devoted to a selective reading of Rom 1–3 that highlights the divinatory elements in Paul's argument, and their applicability to a particularly Roman form of religion. Romans 1–3 is an important text deserving of sustained attention, firstly because it consists of a number of complex (and contested) arguments that are chiefly concerned with the question of how God has made certain things known.[59] Secondly, and as a consequence, this section houses what many previous interpreters have taken to be Paul's central statements about revelation.[60]

Signs of Wrath

When Paul writes to Rome that "the wrath of God is revealed from heaven upon all impiety and unrighteousness" he touches the nerve of Roman divination, which was preoccupied with discerning the *ira deum* in response to

---

[57] See Chapter 2.
[58] Bruce MacBain, *Prodigy and Expiation: A Study in Religion and Politics in Republican Rome*, Collection Latomus 177 (Brussels: Latomus, 1982). This basic structure in Rom 1–3 is tentatively noted by Berger, "Hellenistisch-heidnische Prodigien," 1436 n. 25.
[59] On this see Marcus A. Mininger, *Uncovering the Theme of Revelation in Romans 1:16–3:26*, WUNT 2/445 (Tübingen: Mohr Siebeck, 2017). My reading differs from Mininger's in a number of places and is necessarily much briefer and more selective. On the identification of "revelation" as a major theme of Romans 1–3, though, I think he is exactly right.
[60] Lührmann, *Offenbarungsverständnis*, 145–53, 158; Bockmuehl, *Revelation and Mystery*, 133–35, 138–41.

impiety. Impiety (ἀσέβεια), as opposed to more general notions of sin, deals specifically with the relations between humans and gods, and is the most common source of divine anger in the Roman world. Impiety was most evident in the negligence of proper religious observance, but could also extend to dishonouring contracts over which the gods were seen to preside.[61] Kathy Ehrensperger writes of Roman religion, "It was essential to know how to give to the gods what they were due: *scientia colendorum deorum* was considered key in all Roman activities."[62]

Romans 1:16–18 contain two programmatic statements of divine revelation as Paul claims that both God's justice (δικαιοσύνη) and wrath (ὀργή) can be discerned from events and actions in the observable world. God's justice is revealed in the "good news" that Paul announces (1:16–17), and many scholars have sought to link the revelation of wrath (v. 18) to this same event.[63] This, however, is unlikely and unnecessary in the flow of Paul's argument, as he explains what reveals God's wrath in the immediately following verses. This is not the good news of Jesus's death and resurrection, but the depraved state of (mainly Gentile) sexual and social relations.[64]

Romans 1:24–31 describes three instances of God handing people over (παρέδωκεν) to impurity (ἀκαθαρσίαν), dishonourable passion (πάθη ἀτιμίας), and a debased mind (ἀδόκιμον νοῦν) in response to the worship of images. Various compound forms of the verb δίδωμι (ἀποδίδωμι, παραδίδωμι) are used in the LXX to describe God handing the Israelites into the power of foreign enemies as expressions of his anger towards them (Judg 2:14; 3:8; 10:7; 2 Chr 29:8–9; Ps 105:40; Isa 42:24–25).[65] This already provides a hint at the way Paul

---

[61] Levene, *Religion in Livy*, 7–8.
[62] Kathy Ehrensperger, "Between Polis, Oikos, and Ekklesia: The Challenge of Negotiating the Spirit World (1 Cor 12:1–11)," in *Searching Paul: Conversations with the Jewish Apostle to the Nations*, WUNT 429 (Tübingen: Mohr Siebeck, 2019), 162–63; cf. Kathy Ehrensperger, "The Absence of εὐσέβεια in Paul: Peculiarities of Cultural Translation," in *Searching Paul*, 203–6: "Εὐσέβια/*pietas* was the visible performance of giving the gods the honour owed, for which in turn they provided for the needs of mortal humans."
[63] Günther Bornkamm, "The Revelation of God's Wrath (Romans 1–3)," in *Early Christian Experience*, trans. Paul L. Hammer (London: SCM, 1969), 47–64; Jonathan A. Linebaugh, "Announcing the Human: Rethinking the Relationship Between Wisdom of Solomon 13–15 and Romans 1:18–2:11," *NTS* 57 (2011): 227; Wright, *Paul and the Faithfulness of God*, 767; Bockmuehl, *Revelation and Mystery*, 138–40.
[64] "How is God's wrath revealed from heaven? There has been no earthly catastrophe, such as a devastating earthquake or the destruction of a city or enslavement of a people that might be called a sign of God's wrath ... God's wrath is revealed through the human behavior described in vv. 24–32. This would mean that God's handing idolaters over to wretched deeds *is* the revelation of God's wrath." Bernadette J. Brooten, *Love Between Women: Early Christian Responses to Female Homoeroticism* (Chicago: University of Chicago Press, 1996), 221; cf. Mininger, *Uncovering*, 146–53.
[65] Mininger, *Uncovering*, 144–45; Beverly Roberts Gaventa, *Our Mother Saint Paul* (Louisville: Westminster John Knox, 2007), 115.

is reading the signs of divine displeasure. Just as military defeat could be a sign of God's anger and his relinquishing of his people to another power, impurity, passion, and debasement serve as similar signs for Paul that they have been "handed over" by God in his anger.

Each instance of handing over in Rom 1:24–31 is accompanied by an observable effect, or consequence, which reveals God's anger at idolatry and suppression of the truth. Being handed over to impurity is evidenced by people with dishonoured bodies (v. 24). Being handed over to dishonourable passions is evidenced by sexual acts Paul deems against or beyond nature (vv. 26–27).[66] Being handed over to a debased mind is evidenced by a long string of antisocial behaviours and dispositions (vv. 28–31). Paul presents these as aetiologies moving from God's actions to the human consequences, but in the context of v. 18 the observable consequences take on the role of signs through which God's wrath is revealed. It is not just that "Paul turns to an account of events in the past to explain the current situation of those who have refused to recognize God."[67] He also turns, on the vertical plane, to God's actions to explain the current state of human behaviour. Put differently, he interprets certain human behaviours as signs of God's displeasure.

Some of these signs Paul singles out as being unnatural (παρὰ φύσιν: 1:26). Matthew Dillon writes of the dysfunctional, abnormal nature of prodigies, especially in the Roman world.

> *Terata* . . . reflected the inversion of the norms of the natural and human world. Prodigies were dysfunctional manifestations of the gods' displeasure, such as babies that spoke intelligible words, torched trees that miraculously resprouted, and malformed beasts like Lampon's one-horned ram.[68]

Aristotle classifies a τέρας as decidedly παρὰ φύσιν, "contrary to nature" (*Gen. an.* 4.770b; cf. Plato, *Crat.* 393c–394d), and lists a number of examples, including animals with human-looking heads (or *vice versa*), people with additional body parts, and ambiguously sexed individuals born with both male and female genitalia (*Gen. an.* 4.772a–b). Aristotle is concerned to explain how such irregular formations are biologically generated, but the more common approach is to take them as ominous portents, reflecting a cosmic imbalance.[69]

---

[66] Mininger (*Uncovering*, 147) notes how the conjunction γάρ in v. 26 explicitly serves the function of explaining how one can know God's action: "In other words, the fact that these people practice sexual relations that go against nature (παρὰ φύσιν) provides evidence that they were handed over to dishonorable passions."

[67] Stowers, *Rereading of Romans*, 90. In fairness to Stowers, he also acknowledges the vertical aspect on page 177.

[68] Dillon, *Omens and Oracles*, 206.

[69] Luc Brisson, *Sexual Ambivalence: Androgyny and Hermaphroditism in Graeco-Roman Antiquity*, trans. Janet Lloyd (Berkeley: University of California Press, 2002), 8–30; Chirassi Colombo, "Teras," 222–23.

A τέρας usually implies a physical abnormality, but in the case of people who are ambiguously sexed the reasoning could sometimes be extended to sexual behaviour. This is especially true for female homoeroticism, which Roman writers of the Imperial era often described with the language of prodigies and omens. Martial (*Ep.* 1.90) lambastes a certain Bassa, whom he had never seen coupling with men but was always surrounded by women. At first he thought her a model of chastity (a Lucretia), but then realised she was a *fututor* – a masculine word that denotes an active, penetrative sexual relation.[70]

Sexual relations in the Roman world, as is well known, were hierarchical and centred around the act of penetration, in which the dominant partner penetrated the subordinate, regardless of gender.[71] Women (along with boys and slaves) occupied the subordinate, penetrated category, so when Martial describes Bassa with the masculine form he implies that her actions reveal an ambiguous gender. By engaging in sexual relations with other women, Martial says she feigns masculinity with her *prodigiosa venus*. Some take *venus* here to refer generally to passion or "lust."[72] This is how the same phrase appears to be used in Ovid's *Metamorphoses* when Iphis calls her love for a woman *prodigiosa* (*Metam.* 9.727). She likens this to other *monstra* such as the love between Pasiphaë and a bull, which produced the minotaur (*Metam.* 9.736). Diana Swancutt is correct however that in Ovid's context, "'love' does not refer here to an orientational desire but to a particular act, penetration, that requires a 'male' – a penetrator."[73] Martial maintains the same focus on the act of penetration, whom Swancutt reads as making an anatomical reference: "Martial's use of the phrase 'monstrous *venus*' implies that Bassa has a highly unfeminine phallus." Bassa feigns masculinity by assuming the role of the penetrator, and thus "s/he is represented as hermaphroditic."[74] Pseudo-Lucian also describes

---

[70] Martial can use the feminine form *fututrix* elsewhere (*Ep.* 11.22.4; 11.61.10). See Judith P. Hallett, "Female Homoeroticism and the Denial of Roman Reality in Latin Literature," in *Roman Sexualities*, ed. Judith P. Hallett and Marilyn B. Skinner (Princeton: Princeton University Press, 1997), 262; Brooten, *Love Between Women*, 47; Diana M. Swancutt, "Still Before Sexuality: 'Greek' Androgyny, the Roman Imperial Politics of Masculinity and the Roman Invention of the *Tribas*," in *Mapping Gender in Ancient Religious Discourses*, ed. Todd Penner and Caroline Vander Stichele, BibInt 84 (Leiden: Brill, 2007), 11–62.

[71] See Craig A. Williams, *Roman Homosexuality*, 2nd ed. (Oxford: Oxford University Press, 2010), 7–8, 178–79, 258–62.

[72] This is how it is translated by Hallett ("Female Homoeroticism," 262) and Brooten (*Love Between Women*, 47). Brisson's translator renders the phrase "prodigious coupling," Brisson, *Sexual Ambivalence*, 69.

[73] Swancutt, "*Still* Before Sexuality," 46.

[74] Swancutt, "*Still* Before Sexuality," 38. She notes how *venus* can sometimes be used as a synonym for *mentula* (Martial 1.46.2; 3.75.6; Juvenal 11.167; Lucretius 4.1270). Kamen and Levin-Richardson view the phrase as a double entendre, meaning both "monstrous love" and "monstrous organ," Deborah Kamen and Sarah Levin-Richardson, "Lusty Ladies in the Roman Imaginary," in *Ancient Sex: New Essays*, ed. Ruby Blondell and Kirk Ormand (Columbus: Ohio State University Press, 2015), 244.

a contrived phallus, used for sex between women, as a τεράστιον αἴνιγμα, "ominous enigma" (*Am.* 28).

All these sources use terms derived from omens and prodigies (*prodigiosa/ monstrum/* τεράστιον) to describe the abnormality of penetrative sex between women.[75] The gender ambiguity assigned to female homoeroticism resembles the hermaphrodite that manifests disordered nature. Martial goes on to tell Bassa that she has created for herself a portent (*monstrum*) "worthy of the Theban riddle" (*Ep.* 1.90). Her resultant state is an enigma or riddle that needs decoding.

Paul does not use the language of omens, as τέρας is reserved in his vocabulary for the wondrous signs that validate his preaching. But given the ubiquitous Roman view of female homoeroticism, it is no coincidence that he singles out "their women"[76] committing sexual acts contrary to nature (παρὰ φύσιν) as his prime example of how God has signalled his wrath against idolatry (Rom 1:26).[77] Like a hermaphrodite birth, they are dysfunctional manifestations of God's displeasure. This is the first tangible proof Paul cites of the revelation of God's wrath, which specifies his earlier more general claim that "God handed them over in the desires of their hearts to the impurity of dishonouring their bodies among themselves" (Rom 1:24).[78]

Hallet ("Female Homoeroticism," 268) draws attention to the "widely held Roman notion that female homoeroticism could not be expressed without masculine sexual parts," cf. Phaedrus, *Fab.* 4.16; Seneca, *Ep.* 95.20–21; Martial 7.67, 70.

[75] See Sandra Boehringer, "'Ces monstres de femmes': topique des thaumata dans les discours sur l'homosexualité féminine aux premiers siècles de notre ère," in *Conceptions et représentations de l'extraordinaire dans le monde antique: Actes du Colloque international, Lausanne, 20–22 mars 2003*, ed. Olivier Bianchi and Olivier Thévenaz (Bern: Lang, 2004), 90.

[76] Paul's reference to "their women" reflects the "language of otherness" that Paul uses to talk of idolatrous Gentiles (Thiessen, *Gentile Problem*, 47–48), but would also resonate at this point with a Roman audience for whom female homoeroticism was consistently portrayed as a foreign Greek practice (Hallet, "Female Homoeroticism"; Swancutt, "*Still Before Sexuality*"). Paul himself was probably less sensitive to this distinction as everyone in Romans is either a Jew or a Greek (Rom 1:16; 2:9–10; 3:9).

[77] It is sometimes argued that παρὰ φύσιν could refer to a number of sexual acts deemed unnatural, and not specifically female homoeroticism, e.g., James Miller, "The Practices of Romans 1:26: Homosexual or Heterosexual?" *NovT* 37 (1995): 1–11; Klaus Haacker, "Exegetische Gesichtspunkte zum Thema Homosexualität," *TBei* 25 (1994): 173–80; David Wheeler-Reed, Jennifer W. Knust and Dale B. Martin, "Can a Man Commit πορνεία with His Wife?" *JBL* 137 (2018): 391–93 (argued in relation to Philo rather than Paul). Paul may have a wider range of sexual acts in mind, but as Brooten (*Love Between Women*, 248 n. 99, 251–52) argues, "The type of sexual relations engaged in by women most often called 'contrary to nature' (*para physin*) in the Roman world is sexual relations between women." The framing of these acts as indicators of God's wrath in the Roman context further reinforces this conclusion by connecting Paul to the broader Roman discourse on female homoeroticisim.

[78] Commentators generally agree that the "dishonouring of their bodies" refers to the sexual behaviours he will go on to describe (cf. 1 Cor 6:18), thus making Rom 1:26 the first concrete example of this: Jewett, *Romans*, 169; Dunn, *Romans 1–8*, 62; C. K. Barrett, *The Epistle to the Romans*, BNTC (London: Black, 1957), 38.

Paul's next claim that men's shameful acts with each other also forsake the "natural use" of women, and by extension could also be seen as contrary to nature, will have appeared more controversial to a Gentile Roman audience, but is in keeping with other Jewish estimations of Gentile behaviour. Philo calls the passive partner in a pederastic relationship an androgyne – a man-woman hybrid (τὸν ἀνδρόγυνον: *Spec.* 3.38, 40). The active partner is equally culpable for (among other reasons) pursuing a pleasure that is contrary to nature (τὴν παρὰ φύσιν ἡδονήν), and encouraging effeminacy in others (*Spec.* 3.39).[79] Roman writers of the Republican era generally saw male homoeroticism as an example of Greek licentiousness, but by the Imperial period it seems to be a generally accepted practice, as long as the penetrator and penetrated conformed to the usual social hierarchies.[80] Violations of this natural order, such as freeborn adult males being willingly penetrated, were open to ridicule, and the questioning of their manliness.[81] But they were never described with the same teratological language as women who took male roles.[82] This is partly due to the idea that female penetration required some sort of physical abnormality in order to be possible in a way that male penetration did not. It is also true that women were generally associated with "body over mind" in a way that made them closer to the animal world of nature through which divine signs could be revealed.[83]

The third "handing over," is evidenced by a string of antisocial behaviours – things that generally "ought not to be done" (Rom 1:28) which portray a society in turmoil and point unequivocally to divine judgement (Rom 1:32).[84] There is a certain irony to Paul's diagnosis, since he labels the very things that most Romans would have seen as piety, the worship of their gods, as impiety and the key reason for God's wrath against them.[85]

---

[79] For other Jewish estimations, see Thiessen, *Gentile Problem*, 48.
[80] Hallett, "Female Homoeroticism," 269–70. Musonius Rufus describes sex between males in general as παρὰ φύσιν, which, according to Williams (*Roman Homosexuality*, 272), "is at odds not only with widespread Roman beliefs and practices but also with those of other Stoics."
[81] Williams, *Roman Homosexuality*, 183–84, 197–200.
[82] Boehringer, "Ces monstres de femmes," 96.
[83] Struck, *Divination and Human Nature*, 4.
[84] Wright (*Paul and the Faithfulness of God*, 766–67) argues that God's wrath could not be simply read off of the world around because "God's wrath" for Paul points to God's future and final judgement on sinners. In 1 Cor 11:27–32 though (discussed above) Paul can point to discrete acts of judgement that point towards, and discipline one for, future judgement. Seeing the behaviours listed in these verses as *signs* of wrath, which warn of a future wrath, makes the most sense of Paul's language and thought here.
[85] See Ehrensperger ("Absence of εὐσέβεια," 200–3) for the ways other Jews negotiated Graeco-Roman understandings of piety: "In different ways, both Philo's and Josephus's agenda was to demonstrate, that contrary to the perception of their Greek and Roman neighbors, Jews were actually εὐσεβής not ἀσεβής." This differing Roman idea of piety is what Ehrensperger believes led Paul to abandon the terminology altogether for himself. Romans 1:18 however is one instance where Paul does use the language of piety, albeit in its negative form.

God's Wrath for the Jew?

In Rom 1:18–32, Paul announces and interprets the signs of God's wrath on the idolatrous Gentile world. It is not enough, however, for a diviner to diagnose a problem, they must also be able to divine a solution.[86] Paul provides this solution in Rom 3:21–26, but before doing this he makes the further claim that not only Gentiles, but "all, both Jews and Greeks are under sin" (Rom 3:9). This is something Paul says that "we have already charged" (προῃτιασάμεθα). Most take this claim to refer to a charge previously made in the letter, but exactly when is controversial. It is impossible, and unnecessary, to give a full account of all the interpretive problems in Rom 1–3, but a general account of the intervening material between 2:1 and 3:21 is necessary to properly understand Paul's divinatory reasoning between "prodigy and expiation."

Some consider the whole of Rom 1:18–3:8 to be an indictment of universal sinfulness, so that Rom 3:9 is a natural conclusion to everything that precedes it. As many commentators have pointed out, however, Rom 1:18–32 is presented as the revelation of God's wrath against idolatry, rather than sinful humanity in general. The impiety and injustice against which God's wrath is revealed belongs to "people who suppress the truth in injustice," not "people, who suppress the truth in injustice." It is true that Paul is aware of times when Israel has fallen into idolatry (Rom 11:1–4; 1 Cor 10:7–10), and, importantly, whenever they have, the resulting enslavement to passions and sexual immorality would also appear to take place (1 Cor 10:7–8). Paul does not think Jews have a genetic immunity to idolatry, and therefore I am wary of claims that Rom 1:18–32 speaks explicitly and exclusively of Gentiles. That being said, the charge of idolatry pertains to the Gentile world *en masse*, and matches contemporary Jewish portraits of Gentile behaviour, in a way that does not pertain in the same way to Jews.[87] Paul does not appear to think that his contemporary compatriots were as a whole guilty of idolatry and the resulting malformations that it produces. This is how he characterises idolatrous Gentiles as a whole (1 Thess 4:3–5; 1 Cor 5:1, 9–10; 6:9–11), who do not pursue righteousness (Rom 9:30). Jews, on the other hand do, overall, pursue a law of righteousness

---

[86] The logic of plight and solution has been strongly resisted by some Pauline scholars. I do not go so far as to say whether Paul's own divinatory reasoning moves in a linear state from wrath to propitiation, but this is unquestionably how he presents the logic of his position in Rom 1–3. Those who deny this logic to Paul's own thought also work the hardest to undermine the place of Rom 1–3 as representative of Paul's own thought, e.g., E. P. Sanders, *Paul, the Law, and the Jewish People* (Philadelphia: Fortress, 1983), 123–32; Campbell, *Deliverance of God*, 469–761.

[87] See Thiessen, *Gentile Problem*, 47–51. George van Kooten (*Paul's Anthropology*, 343–56) makes a compelling case that Paul's tale of decline from a monotheistic past would particularly resonate with a Roman audience, and can be read as his indictment of Roman religion in particular.

(Rom 9:31), and have zeal for God (Rom 10:2). Their performance of both is flawed in Paul's opinion, but not in the manner of Rom 1:18–32.[88]

If Rom 1:18–32 refers most readily to Gentiles, the diatribe that commences at Rom 2:1 is typically read as the point at which Paul targets Jewish exceptionalism and hypocrisy.[89] Here Paul addresses a fictive interlocutor (ὦ ἄνθρωπε [2:1]) who joins in the condemnation of idolatry, while still engaging in the same thing himself. Against the specifically Jewish identity of this interlocutor, a number of scholars have pointed out that Paul explicitly addresses his letter as a whole to Gentiles alone. In Rom 1:5–6, Paul defines the purpose of his apostleship: "to bring about the obedience of faith for the sake of his name among all the Gentiles, including you" (his audience). In Rom 1:13–14, he also includes "you," his audience among "the rest of the Gentiles," among whom he hopes to reap a harvest when he visits. Towards the end of the letter in Rom 11:13, after speaking about the current plight of his fellow Jews in the third person, he addresses his audience directly again as Gentiles: "But I speak to you Gentiles." In Rom 15:15–16, he justifies his boldness in speaking to his Roman audience by appeal to his role as "minister of Christ Jesus to the Gentiles." These explicit addresses all suggest that, whoever was actually present in Rome to listen to the letter being read, Paul directs the contents of the letter to Gentiles.[90] This in turn suggests that the interlocutors he addresses at points throughout the letter are also best understood as Gentiles, who represent possible positions among the letter's intended recipients.[91]

This is even the case when, in Rom 2:17, Paul addresses σὺ Ἰουδαῖος ἐπονομάζῃ "you who call yourself a Jew." Interpreters who follow this line of

---

[88] See Matthew V. Novenson, "The Self-Styled Jew of Romans 2 and the Actual Jew of Romans 9–11," in *The So-Called Jew in Paul's Letter to the Romans*, ed. Rafael Rodríguez and Matthew Thiessen (Minneapolis: Fortress, 2016), 153–60.

[89] Dunn, *Romans 1–8*, 79; Simon J. Gathercole, *Where is Boasting? Early Jewish Soteriology and Paul's Response in Romans 1–5* (Grand Rapids: Eerdmans, 2002), 203–5; Jonathan A. Linebaugh, *God, Grace, and Righteousness in Wisdom of Solomon and Paul's Letter to the Romans: Texts in Conversation*, NovTSup 152 (Leiden: Brill, 2013), 101–2.

[90] Stowers, *Rereading of Romans*, 21–22. Barclay (*Paul and the Gift*, 458 n. 20) agrees that the implied audience is consistently Gentile, but thinks Paul also writes for the "actual audience of the letter" which he knows will include Jews. This is based on the presence of Jewish names in the greetings of Rom 16:3–16, but as many have pointed out these figures are not directly greeted by Paul in the letter, rather the Gentile audience is instructed to greet them on Paul's behalf.

[91] This is argued with regard to ancient epistolary conventions by Runar M. Thorsteinsson, *Paul's Interlocutor in Romans 2: Function and Identity in the Context of Ancient Epistolography*, ConBNT 40 (Stockholm: Almqvist & Wiksell, 2003; repr., Eugene, OR: Wipf & Stock, 2015), 144: "unless otherwise stated or implied, the epistolary interlocutor represents or speaks for the letter's recipient(s)." The general point is repeated by Thiessen, *Gentile Problem*, 43–44; Fredriksen, *Pagans' Apostle*, 156.

reasoning point out that Paul does not straightforwardly address a Jew here, but one who "is called a Jew" or who "calls himself a Jew."[92] This address arguably implies a Gentile Judaiser, such as those whom Paul argues against in Galatians and Philippians, rather than an ethnic Jew. The profile of such a character in Rom 2 who boasts in God and relies on the Jewish law (2:17–18), most especially represented by circumcision (2:25–29), but still falls back into Gentile sins (stealing, adultery, sacrilege [2:21–23]) also supports this conclusion.[93]

What all this means for our purposes is that in Rom 2 Paul is not seeking to show that Jews, as a whole, also exhibit the same signs of divine wrath as idolatrous Gentiles. Rather he is arguing against one possible solution for averting that wrath: Gentile Judaising, and more specifically Gentile circumcision. In the Roman context, as discussed earlier, the sighting of a prodigy would be met with a means of ritual expiation, most often detailed by the Sibylline books. The correct performance of ritual was vital to maintaining the *pax deum* and as such forms the topic of many oracle questions and responses. It is possible that those Gentiles seeking to become circumcised and take on the Jewish law likewise saw circumcision as a ritual prescription from the Jewish sacred books, which grants them Jewish identity and thus guards them against God's wrath.[94] Paul presents circumcision in this context, however, as a failed ritual. Karin Neutel and Peter-Ben Smit have both analysed circumcision in Paul's letters through the lens of ritual studies and argue that Paul presents circumcision as a ritual "failure" or "disruption" when performed by Gentile Judaisers.[95]

[92] Thorsteinsson, *Paul's Interlocutor*, 204; Thiessen, *Gentile Problem*, 54–59; Rafael Rodríguez, *If You Call Yourself a Jew: Reappraising Paul's Letter to the Romans* (Eugene, OR: Wipf & Stock, 2014), and the essays collected in Rafael Rodríguez and Matthew Thiessen (eds.), *The So-Called Jew in Paul's Letter to the Romans*, (Minneapolis: Fortress, 2016). Lionel J. Windsor (*Paul and the Vocation of Israel: How Paul's Jewish Identity Informs His Apostolic Ministry, with Special Reference to Romans*, BZNW 205 [Berlin: de Gruyter, 2014], 148) argues that ἐπονομάζῃ must be translated as passive: "if you are publicly acknowledged as entitled to the name Jew." For a convincing argument for a middle translation ("if you call yourself") see Ryan D. Collman, "The Apostle to the Foreskin: Circumcision in the Letters of Paul" (PhD diss., University of Edinburgh, 2021).

[93] Novenson, "Self-Styled Jew," 145–47; Thiessen, *Gentile Problem*, 59–63; Fredriksen, *Pagans' Apostle*, 157.

[94] Wendt argues that the Romans, at a slightly later date, viewed the Jewish sacred texts very much as another oracle collection comparable with the Sibylline books, Heidi Wendt, "'Entrusted with the Oracles of God': The Fate of the Judean Writings in Flavian Rome," in *A Most Reliable Witness: Essays in Honor of Ross Shepard Kraemer*, ed. Susan Ashbrook Harvey et al., BJS 358 (Providence, RI: Brown University, 2015), 101–9.

[95] Karin B. Neutel, "Circumcision Gone Wrong: Paul's Message as a Case of Ritual Disruption," *Neot* 50 (2016): 373–96; Peter-Ben Smit, "In Search of Real Circumcision: Ritual Failure and Circumcision in Paul," *JSNT* 40 (2017): 73–100.

Rituals could fail for a number of reasons.⁹⁶ They could be performed by the wrong people or in the wrong circumstances. The wrong words could be said to the wrong god, or the right god could be addressed by the wrong name. Precision was an important part of Roman ritual observance.⁹⁷ Paul's main reason for seeing a ritual failure in Rom 2 is that it is the wrong ritual to achieve the desired outcome. Attempting to become Jewish through circumcision will not be effective because even circumcised Jews will still be punished if they sin.

> There will be affliction and distress for every human soul who does evil, the Jew first and also the Greek, but glory and honour and peace to all who do good, the Jew first and also the Greek, for there is no partiality with God. For all who have sinned without the law will also perish without the law, and all who have sinned in the law will be judged by the law. (Rom 2:9–12)

Circumcision by itself does nothing to change that. If we adopt Thiessen's reading, there is an additional problem for circumcised Gentiles: the wrong ritual is performed in the wrong way. For Thiessen, Paul is committed to eighth day circumcision as the only ritually correct version of circumcision, so that adult proselyte circumcision is itself a transgression of the law.⁹⁸ This would help make sense of Rom 2:27, which on a plain reading refers to those who "through (διά) the letter and circumcision transgress the law." This is normally read as if the interlocutor transgresses the law *despite* their circumcision,⁹⁹ but the preposition διά much more naturally suggests the act of circumcision itself is the transgression. In this case the ritual fails because of misapplication (performed by inappropriate persons or in inappropriate circumstances) and is thus ineffectual (fails to precipitate anticipated empirical change).¹⁰⁰ Not only

---

⁹⁶ Smit ("Real Circumcision," 76) reproduces a helpful taxonomy of ritual failures from Ronald L. Grimes, "Ritual Criticism and Infelicitous Performances," in *Ritual Criticism: Case Studies in its Practice, Essays on its Theory* (Columbia: University of South Carolina Press, 1990), 191–209. In the case of Rom 2:25–29, Smit identifies "misapplication: a ritual fails because it is performed by an inappropriate person" (one who transgresses the law) or "defeat: one ritual is defeated by another," (in which transgression of the law itself is an alternative ritual).

⁹⁷ "One had to know which god to invoke for what purpose and in what ways. The rites had to be performed with upmost [sic] precision," Ehrensperger, "Absence of εὐσέβεια," 204.

⁹⁸ Matthew Thiessen, "Paul's Argument Against Gentile Circumcision in Romans 2:17–29," *NovT* 56 (2014): 373–91; Thiessen, *Gentile Problem*, 64–68.

⁹⁹ See Windsor, *Paul and the Vocation of Israel*, 180; Barclay, *Paul and the Gift*, 470 ("the circumcised, but law-breaking Jew").

¹⁰⁰ Smit, "Real Circumcision," 76.

does proselyte circumcision fail to avert God's wrath, but potentially incurs it all the more for being a transgression of the law.

If Paul does not make the charge that Jews are under sin in Rom 2, then where does he do it, and how does he claim to know? Identifying the audience of Romans, and the interlocutor of Rom 2, as Gentile does not mean that Paul has nothing of relevance to say about Jews. On the contrary, the opening statement about his good news claims that it is the power of God for salvation to the faithful Jew, just as much as to the Gentile (before the Gentile in fact, 1:16). This in itself could possibly amount to a claim that both Jews and Gentiles are under sin, since they are both recipients of the same power for salvation. We have also already seen that Jews will also receive impartial judgement from God (2:9–10). In Rom 3:1 Paul affirms that the circumcised Jew receives many advantages, the foremost of which is being entrusted with God's oracles. Some have not been faithful with this trust, but their unfaithfulness does not nullify God's faithfulness (3:3–4). Paul's word choices here are important. He does not say that Jews have been unrighteous (ἄδικος) with regard to the law (νόμος).[101] Rather they have not believed (ἠπίστησάν) the oracles (λόγια). These are the same oracles spoken by the "prophets in the holy writings" that pre-promised Paul's good news about Jesus. This coheres with Paul's main concern with his fellow Jews later in Romans, that their zeal and pursuit of righteousness have continued without regard to Jesus as their Messiah (Rom 9–11).[102]

Jews as a whole, then, are not portrayed by Paul as malformed omens of idolatry. Despite this, Paul still claims that "all, both Jews and Greek are under sin" (Rom 3:9). Wherever Paul thinks Jewish sin may be discerned, his clearest evidence for it comes not before Rom 3:9, but directly after it in the catena of scriptural citations in vv. 10–18. These citations, taken from the Psalms and Isaiah, portray a host of evil deeds and disregard for God, which all support the claim that "There is no one righteous, not one." And this time Paul does clearly apply this judgement to Jews: "we know that as much as the law says, it says to those who are in the law." As with his use of oracles and omens that we have previously discussed, Paul explains the communicative intent of these words: "*in order that* every mouth be shut and the whole cosmos be held accountable to God." Whether or not it is obvious from their behaviour, scripture itself declares Jews to also be under sin. In the words of Novenson: "That the gentiles are under sin is empirically demonstrable . . . That the Jews

---

[101] The words ἀδικία, ὀργή, and ἁμαρτωλός are all included in 3:5–8, but Garroway convincingly argues that these verses refer to the Gentile interlocutor who queries his own position in relation to what Paul has said about Jews, Joshua D. Garroway, "Paul's Gentile Interlocutor in Romans 3:1–20," in Rodríguez and Thiessen, *The So-Called Jew*, 91–94.

[102] Novenson, "Self-Styled Jew," 153–60.

are under sin is known from the testimony of the law – that is to say, from scripture rather than experience."¹⁰³ Or, with more divinatory terminology, we might also say: from oracles rather than omens.

The Revelation of God's Justice

Now Paul has divined sin for both Jew and Gentile, he is in a position to offer his solution to the wrath of God and the impurity which results. For Paul this is the blood of Jesus, which God has provided as a propitiation or expiation.

> But now the justice of God has been manifested apart from the law, although it was attested by the law and the prophets, the justice of God through the faithfulness of Jesus Christ to all who are faithful. For there is no distinction, for all have sinned and lack the glory of God, being justified as a gift by his favour through the redemption that is in Christ Jesus, whom God put forward as a propitiation through faithfulness in his blood.
>
> Νυνὶ δὲ χωρὶς νόμου δικαιοσύνη θεοῦ πεφανέρωται μαρτυρουμένη ὑπὸ τοῦ νόμου καὶ τῶν προφητῶν, δικαιοσύνη δὲ θεοῦ διὰ πίστεως Ἰησοῦ Χριστοῦ εἰς πάντας τοὺς πιστεύοντας. οὐ γάρ ἐστιν διαστολή, πάντες γὰρ ἥμαρτον καὶ ὑστεροῦνται τῆς δόξης τοῦ θεοῦ δικαιούμενοι δωρεὰν τῇ αὐτοῦ χάριτι διὰ τῆς ἀπολυτρώσεως τῆς ἐν Χριστῷ Ἰησοῦ· ὃν προέθετο ὁ θεὸς ἱλαστήριον διὰ [τῆς] πίστεως ἐν τῷ αὐτοῦ αἵματι. (Rom 3:21–25)

Much ink has been spilled over interpreting these verses as well as the verses in the surrounding context.¹⁰⁴ The crucial word for our purposes is ἱλαστήριον, which Paul only uses in this verse, making interpretation particularly fraught.

The basic meaning of the word group represented by ἱλάσκεσθαι is generally agreed to be "to appease" or "placate."¹⁰⁵ Dirk Büchner's phrase "restoring relations by soothing" nicely encapsulates the main elements involved.¹⁰⁶ Within

---

¹⁰³ Novenson, "Self-Styled Jew," 152. So, too, Garroway ("Paul's Gentile Interlocutor," 89), "The purpose of the catena is to prove the Jewish component of the blanket indictment, that Jews in particular are sinful and unrighteous."

¹⁰⁴ For a particularly lucid account of the interpretative issues, see Douglas A. Campbell, *The Rhetoric of Righteousness in Romans 3:21–26*, JSNTSup 65 (Sheffield: Sheffield Academic, 1992), 22–37.

¹⁰⁵ LSJ, s.v. "ἱλάσκομαι"; C. H. Dodd, "ΙΛΑΣΚΕΣΘΑΙ, Its Cognates, Derivatives and Synonyms in the Septuagint," *JTS* 32 (1931): 352–60; Leon Morris, "The Use of ἱλάσκεσθαι etc. in Biblical Greek," *ExpTim* 62 (1951): 227–33.

¹⁰⁶ Dirk Büchner, "ἐξιλάσασθαι: Appeasing God in the Septuagint Pentateuch," *JBL* 129 (2010): 241. It has often been argued that the use of the word-group in the Septuagint marks a different semantic range, centring around "cleansing" and "purging," Dodd, "ΙΛΑΣΚΕΣΘΑΙ," 352–60. This has been refuted effectively by Morris ("Use of ἱλάσκεσθαι," 227–33) and more recently, on different grounds, by Büchner.

this word-group a ἱλαστήριον denotes a votive offering for the purpose of reconciliation or propitiation.[107] The use of the word to translate כפרת in the Septuagint has led many scholars to suppose that Paul in this verse intends a direct reference to the "mercy seat," or at least the festival of Yom Kippur. As many others have pointed out, however, there is nothing in Paul's text to signal such a reference other than the word itself. And as Leon Morris pointed out over half a century ago,

> The word itself means "propitiatory," and if the mercy-seat could be so designated, so also could one of the ledges on Ezekiel's altar (or even Noah's ark, according to Symmachus). ἱλαστήριον might denote the כפרת, but that was because it referred to its function, and not because it formed an exact translation of the Hebrew term. If the כפרת was "propitiatory," so too, were other things.[108]

Surviving inscriptions and literary references suggest items such as bowls and monuments were the standard type of objects offered.[109] Dio Chrysostom could also refer to the Trojan horse as a ἱλαστήριον to Athena (*Troj.* 122).

Prescribing the correct propitiations to offer was, generally speaking, the job of a diviner, and would be discerned through divination. In response to a proliferation of signs and omens (σημείων . . . καὶ τεράτων), Polybius writes that "vows, sacrifices, supplicatory processions and litanies pervaded the town. For in seasons of danger the Romans are much given to propitiating (ἐξιλάσασθαι) both gods and men" (Polybius 3.112.8). The temple chronicle from Lindos

---

[107] Adolf Deissmann, "ἱλαστήριος und ἱλαστήριον: Eine lexikalische Studie," *ZNW* 4 (1903): 193–212; Daniel P. Bailey, "Jesus as the Mercy Seat: The Semantics and Theology of Paul's Use of Hilasterion in Romans 3:25," *TynBul* 51 (2000): 156–57; Adela Yarbro Collins, "The Metaphorical Use of ἱλαστήριον in Romans 3:25," in *Sōtēria: Salvation in Early Christianity and Antiquity: Festschrift in Honour of Cilliers Breytenbach on the Occasion of his 65th Birthday*, ed. David S. du Toit, Christine Gerber, and Christiane Zimmermann, NovTSup 175 (Leiden: Brill, 2019), 273–86; Stefan Schreiber, "Das Weihegeschenk Gottes: eine Deutung des Todes Jesu in Röm 3:25," *ZNW* 97 (2006): 88–110; Stefan Schreiber, "Weitergedacht: Das versöhnende Weihegeschenk Gottes in Röm 3:25," *ZNW* 106 (2015): 207–8. In Schreiber's first article he saw ἱλαστήριον as essentially synonymous with ἀνάθημα, the word for a votive offering. He nuances this in his second article so that ἱλαστήριον is a particular type of ἀνάθημα focused on reconciliation alongside other such offerings such as χαριστήριον, εὐχαριστήριον, and δῶρον.

[108] Leon Morris, "The Meaning of ἱλαστήριον in Romans 3:25," *NTS* 2 (1955): 36. See also Stowers (*Rereading of Romans*, 210): "The translators of the LXX got the word *hilastērion* from ordinary Greek usage.... Even though *hilastērion* does not seem to have been a common word, there is nothing mysterious about its meaning in everyday speech.... Its relation to the more common cognate forms would be clear even for a Greek speaker who had never heard the word before; either an adjective meaning propitiatory/conciliatory or, when used as a substantive, a conciliatory/propitiatory thing, place, or act."

[109] The relevant texts are helpfully presented in Yarbro Collins, "ἱλαστήριον," 278–82.

records that the ἱλαστήριον presented there was in accordance with the words of Lycian Apollo, indicating that it was prescribed by an oracle.[110] Plutarch narrates the process through which seers would carry out divinatory sacrifices which reveal both the wrath of the gods and the propitiatory prescription. In the case of Camillus, who held back a promised tithe to Apollo and consulted the Senate about the matter, "the seers reported on the basis of the sacrifices the wrath of the gods was manifest, requiring propitiation and thank-offerings (ἱλασμοῦ καὶ χαριστηρίων)" (Plutarch, *Cam.* 7). Elsewhere Plutarch speaks of the seers (οἱ μάντεις) who advocated the averting of omens and the propitiating of the gods (*Fab.* 18),[111] and the Delphic oracle, which demanded propitiations and honours for the dead (*Sera* 560c).[112]

During the Cylonian pollution, according to Plutarch, the need for action was first signalled by military defeats, "superstitious fears, and apparitions (φόβοι τινὲς ἐκ δεισιδαιμονίας ἅμα καὶ φάσματα)." These led the seers to perform sacrifices, which "revealed (προφαίνεσθαι) pollutions and defilements which demanded expiation (καθαρμῶν)." In this case the seers themselves did not say what expiation was needed, but sent for Epimenides, "a man beloved of the gods, and endowed with a mystical and heaven-sent wisdom in religious matters." It was he who through "certain rites of propitiation, expiation, and sacred foundations (ἱλασμοῖς τισι καὶ καθαρμοῖς καὶ ἱδρύσεσι) . . . hallowed and consecrated the city" (*Sol.* 12).[113] Occasionally people appear to offer ἱλασμούς without prompting from divinatory experts or oracles; in these cases they are offered in response to visits from a god or a dead person in a dream, which serves as a more immediate and readily available form of divination (Plutarch, *Sera* 555c; *Soll. an.* 972c). Josephus records a ἱλαστήριον μνῆμα which Herod the Great erected in response to a blaze of fire which killed two of his bodyguards (*A.J.* 16.182). In this context it is the fire that functions as an omen signalling God's displeasure. In the same way, Paul identifies the wrath of God in response to impiety in Rom 1:18 and the lack of divine δόξα due to sin in 3:23. He wards off a potential means of propitiation in the form of proselyte circumcision before prescribing the correct ἱλαστήριον in the blood and faithfulness of Jesus.[114]

---

[110] Τήλεφος Ἀθάναι ἱλατή[ρι]ον, ὡς ὁ Λύκιος Ἀπόλλων εἶπε (the lack of the sigma reflects the Doric dialect).

[111] ὅσα μέντοι πρὸς ἱλασμοὺς θεῶν ἢ τεράτων ἀποτροπὰς συνηγόρευον οἱ μάντεις ἐπράττετο.

[112] ἱλασμούς τε πολλοὺς προσφέρειν τῶν κατοιχομένων . . . ἀπαιτεῖν.

[113] Cf. the Sibylline oracle recorded in Phlegon of Tralles, *Macr.* 5.4, which commands a gift of first fruits to be brought as ἱλάσματα, and Livy 5.14.4; 22.9.10; 40.37.2. The piling up of terms for propitiation, expiation, supplication, and averting omens suggests some of the debates over whether ἱλαστήριον should mean "propitiation" or "expiation" are creating unnecessary distinctions.

[114] Berger ("Hellenistisch-heidnische Prodigien," 1433–34) notes how prescriptions from the Sibylline books often involved the introduction of new oriental deities and parallels this with the announcements of wrath and repentance in the Judeo-Christian *Sibylline Oracles*.

How exactly Jesus's death is meant to function as a ἱλαστήριον is another, larger question to consider. The closest parallel to Paul's language here has long been recognised to be 4 Macc 17:22 in which the death of the Maccabean martyrs is labelled ἱλαστηρίου. There is clearly some metaphorical level present as the death of Jesus, or the Maccabean martyrs for that matter, cannot be wholly equated with a bowl or monument. There could be some parallels to the use of humans in apotropaic rituals, which are widely attested in different forms across the ancient Mediterranean. Such a parallel is recognised by Origen: "Jesus, who had been recently crucified, voluntarily died for humanity, like those who died for their fatherland to avert plague, epidemics, famines, and shipwreck" (*Cels.* 1.31 [*ANF* 4:409]).[115] Although for Origen Jesus's death parallels these practices by averting evil spirits rather than divine wrath. Paul's readers make this propitiation effective by undergoing the ritual of baptism, which Paul presents as a ritual identification with Jesus's death and resurrection (Rom 6:3–11). Paul claims to have discerned this propitiation in part from his knowledge of Jewish oracles as it was "testified by the law and the prophets" (v. 21). But importantly for Paul, the propitiation does not lie in the performance of the law itself but in the faithfulness of the Messiah, which the law and prophets predict, and which believers make their own through baptism.

The verb προτίθημι in 3:25, may mean "purposed" or "intended," in which case Paul would be saying nothing much different from Plutarch: that the god has made known the required propitiation intended for this purpose. Some factors in the immediate context, however, suggest the verb should be translated with the more active force of "set forth" so that God is the one offering his own propitiation.[116] Paul describes the resulting justification as a gift by his favour (δωρεὰν τῇ αὐτοῦ χάριτι v. 24) and makes much of how this demonstrates God's own justice (v. 26).[117] Livy recounts an episode in which a Roman soldier undergoes an apotropaic ritual in order to turn the tide of battle in favour of the Roman army. After devoting himself along with the enemy legions to the chthonic gods he charged into the enemy ranks to his death, throwing them into disarray in the process. Livy describes the soldier as "of an aspect more august than a man's, as though sent from heaven to expiate

---

[115] Paul's language of Christ becoming a curse (Gal 3:13), being made to be sin (2 Cor 5:21), and sin being condemned in his flesh (Rom 8:3) further heighten the parallels with apotropaic rituals. See further B. Hudson McLean, *The Cursed Christ: Mediterranean Expulsion Rituals and Pauline Soteriology*, JSNTSup 126 (Sheffield: Sheffield Academic, 1996).

[116] The discrepancy of God providing a propitiation himself is noted in BDAG (s.v. "ἱλαστήριον") and is enough for Bailey ("Jesus as the Mercy Seat," 157) to look for a different meaning of ἱλαστήριον. Elsewhere Paul also ascribes the act of sending Jesus to God's agency, Rom 8:3, 32; Gal 4:4, so that he can be seen as his own offering.

[117] Barclay (*Paul and the Gift*, 474–75) notes the "doubling of gift terms" which express God's righteousness.

all anger of the gods, and to turn aside destruction from his people and bring it on their adversaries" (Livy, 8.9.9–10 [Foster, LCL]).

In like manner, Paul describes Jesus's death as a gift from God that turns aside his anger. That God has done this seems more important for Paul in the present passage than the nature of the propitiation itself as it reveals and demonstrates something further about God, namely his justice.[118] In the space of five verses Paul mentions three times that God's act of putting forth Jesus as a propitiatory offering manifests (πεφανέρωται) or is a demonstration of (τὴν ἔνδειξιν) his justice. Twice this is identified as the purpose of God's action (vv. 25, 26), and twice Paul stresses that it is something God has done now (νυνί, v. 21) in the present time (ἐν τῷ νῦν καιρῷ, v. 26) of Paul and his readers.[119] This makes the death of Jesus itself into a "sign" for Paul that indicates God's activity and disposition through events in the world. This is how the "good news" of Jesus's death and resurrection reveal God's justice (Rom 1:16–17).[120] While the depraved actions of idolatrous Gentiles are a dysfunctional sign of God's wrath, and the sacred books condemn the Jews to sinfulness, the faithful death of Jesus the Messiah is not just the revealed means of propitiating that wrath, but also a further sign of God's justice in doing so.

The Cross as a Sign in 1 Corinthians

Paul similarly presents the cross as a sign in 1 Cor 1:21–25. He writes:

> For since in the wisdom of God, the cosmos did not know God through wisdom, God was pleased to save those who are faithful through the

---

[118] Bockmuehl (*Revelation and Mystery*, 134) notes the "striking constellation of evidential and demonstrative terminology in this passage."

[119] This must be read historically as a reference to God's new act in Jesus, not as a timeless "now" of revelation to the individual, *pace* Lührmann, *Offenbarungsverständnis*, 149, 153, 158; cf. Bultmann, *Theology*, 1:302; Bultmann, "Revelation," 78–79.

[120] Bockmuehl ("Das Verb φανερόω im Neuen Testament," *BZ* 32 [1988]: 95–96) drives a wedge between Rom 3:21 and Rom 1:17 by pointing to the perfect tense-form of πεφανέρωται in 3:25 and the present tense-form ἀποκαλύπτεται in 1:17. The former refers to "a historically perceptible manifestation of God's righteousness," while the latter is being continuously revealed in Pauline preaching (in *Revelation and Mystery*, the two passages fall under the separate headings of "past" and "present" revelation). This distinction is important for his debate with Bultmann and Lührmann, as he rightly insists that Paul appeals to historical and visible events for his gospel. I am less convinced, though, that 1:17 attaches special revelatory significance to Paul's preaching. It is revelatory in the sense that it communicates the contents of the "good news," but ἐν αὐτῷ refers to the events that the good news announce, rather than the act of announcement itself. Contrast Mininger (*Uncovering*, 349–50): "In 1:17a, Paul said that God's righteousness is revealed 'in the gospel.' Now in 3:25, the particular aspect of the gospel that Paul had most in mind there becomes explicit ... he particularly focuses on Christ's condition on the cross."

foolishness of what is proclaimed. Since Jews look for signs and Greeks seek wisdom, but we proclaim Christ crucified, a stumbling block for Jews, and foolishness for Gentiles.

ἐπειδὴ γὰρ ἐν τῇ σοφίᾳ τοῦ θεοῦ οὐκ ἔγνω ὁ κόσμος διὰ τῆς σοφίας τὸν θεόν, εὐδόκησεν ὁ θεὸς διὰ τῆς μωρίας τοῦ κηρύγματος σῶσαι τοὺς πιστεύοντας· ἐπειδὴ καὶ Ἰουδαῖοι σημεῖα αἰτοῦσιν καὶ Ἕλληνες σοφίαν ζητοῦσιν, ἡμεῖς δὲ κηρύσσομεν Χριστὸν ἐσταυρωμένον, Ἰουδαίοις μὲν σκάνδαλον, ἔθνεσιν δὲ μωρίαν.

Paul foregrounds the message about the Messiah's death on a cross as the primary content of his proclamation to both Jews and Greeks, the foolishness of which is not acceptable to either. It is interesting, given the usual scholarly separation of Jewish prophecy and Greek divination, that, of the two ethnicities, Paul singles out Jews as those most likely to look for divinatory signs, although he is obviously speaking in broad generalisations.[121] A crucified Messiah, however, is not an acceptable sign for most Jews of his acquaintance. That being said, we must resist the notion that Paul is disparaging the notion of signs altogether here. We have already seen his positive use of this language in Rom 15:19 and 2 Cor 12:12, and the same concept will appear a few verses later in 1 Cor 2:4–5. Rather, he seems to be saying that the sign of a crucified Messiah is not an easy one to accept or interpret correctly.

In the parallel case of wisdom, Paul says the Greeks are not liable to accept it, but his message *is* still wisdom nonetheless (1 Cor 2:6). As discussed in Chapter 1, it is a wisdom that is not of this age and only accessible through the receipt of divine *pneuma*. If the logic of 1 Cor 2 follows on from 1 Cor 1, then the wisdom that *pneuma* provides in this context explicitly deals with how to interpret the message of the cross.[122] In this way, a crucified Messiah is also a genuine divine sign, but one that can only be interpreted with the aid of divine *pneuma* that is not from the cosmos. That is why Paul says in 1 Cor 1:24 "but to those who are called, both Jew and Greek, Christ [is] the power of God and the wisdom of God (θεοῦ δύναμιν καὶ θεοῦ σοφίαν)."

---

[121] "I suspect Paul would be ... perfectly happy to allow that just as many Greeks sought after a sign, and just as many Jews after wisdom." Edwin Judge, "St Paul and Classical Society," in *Social Distinctives of the Christians in the First Century: Pivotal Essays by E. A. Judge,* ed. David M. Scholer (Peabody, MA: Hendrickson, 2008), 89.

[122] Ehrensperger ("Between Polis, Oikos, and Ekklesia," 173) also sees the correct interpretation of the cross as the context for 1 Cor 12:3, in which one speaking through *pneuma* recognises the crucified Jesus as κύριος, while without God's *pneuma* he is ἀνάθεμα: "An understanding of Jesus crucified is impossible through the channels of divine communication with which the Corinthians had been familiar in their lives thus far."

We have already seen earlier in this chapter how Paul's language of signs is closely related to power and is part of a cluster of words (σημεῖα, τέρατα, δύναμις, πνεῦμα), which he uses interchangeably and in different combinations to denote the same basic experience.[123] This seems to reflect Paul's overall view of signs and omens: that through the enabling of *pneuma* they demonstrate God's power. The death of the Messiah on a cross appears as one of the most foundational signs for Paul and his message, which when interpreted properly through the enabling of *pneuma* and the help of ancient oracles, signify and demonstrate God's justice and God's power.

Conclusion

All types of divination involve a divine sign in some sense, whether that sign is a vision, a prophetic oracle, or a divinatory text. This chapter has focused on the signs of divine activity that can be read off of events in the natural world of weather, plants, and animals, or the social world of human beings and their behaviours. Paul, in keeping with most of his Jewish co-religionists, does not leave any evidence of organised systems of sign-reading, as were applied by others to the entrails of animals or the flight of birds. He also does not generally read signs as symbolically encoded indications of the future. Rather the signs he interprets are more limited in scope and point either to divine presence and approval, or divine anger and judgement.

Signs for Paul are unusual or abnormal occurrences that show the hand of a deity at work, whether the wondrous signs and manifestations of divine *pneuma* that accompanied his activity among Gentiles, or the sickness and dysfunction that point to cultic error and a society gone wrong. In this he shares a number of similarities with the role of prodigies in Roman religion that signalled divine displeasure at a general level, which then required further elucidation and interpretation by other divinatory means to clarify the correct response. Paul himself can function as the discerner and interpreter of prodigies: noting their presence, tracing them to their cause, and providing the means of expiation to avoid further judgement.

This is where his full repertoire of divinatory methods and reasoning come into play as visionary revelations and textual oracles, all interpreted by means

---

[123] Rom 15:19 talks of the power *of* signs and wonders, and the power *of pneuma* (ἐν δυνάμει σημείων καὶ τεράτων, ἐν δυνάμει πνεύματος). 2 Cor 12:12 speaks of signs and wonders and [acts of (pl.)] power (σημείοις τε καὶ τέρασιν καὶ δυνάμεσιν). 1 Thess 1:5 speaks only of power and holy *pneuma* (ἐν δυνάμει καὶ ἐν πνεύματι ἁγίῳ). 1 Cor 2:4 demonstrations of *pneuma* and of power (ἐν ἀποδείξει πνεύματος καὶ δυνάμεως) and Gal 3:5 being supplied with *pneuma* and effecting acts of power (ἐπιχορηγῶν ὑμῖν τὸ πνεῦμα καὶ ἐνεργῶν δυνάμεις).

of pneumatic wisdom, help him navigate the divine will for himself and his communities. As mentioned at the end of the last chapter, the paradox of a crucified Messiah presents one of the most foundational and ambiguous signs for Paul, which, with the aid of visions, oracles, and *pneuma*, he interprets as a sign of God's power and wisdom.

CONCLUSION

Divination and Philosophy in Paul: Cosmology, Eschatology, Theology

I began this study by showing how previous scholarly categories have not been able to present a full picture of Paul's access to divine knowledge which situates him convincingly in his historical context. While Paul's letters evince diverse means of access to divine communication, categories such as "prophecy" or "revelation" account for only portions of the evidence, and neither of those categories has been able to situate Paul's full range of divinatory methods in the first-century culture of a Jew living in the Hellenistic Roman Empire. Under the rubric of "divination" I have analysed Paul's various means of divine communication under the subheadings of "visions," "speech," "texts," and "signs," elucidating their role in Paul's letters with reference to the contemporary divinatory practices of the Graeco-Roman world. I have also considered how Paul presents the mechanics of divination in conversation with contemporary philosophical reflections on the same topic.

Rather than summarise each chapter in turn, I organise my conclusions below thematically and synthetically, drawing together various strands that have emerged from the cumulative analysis of this study. Part one functions as something of a summary of Chapters 2 to 5 and focuses on the different types of knowledge each divinatory method provides. Part two considers the implications of this for how to situate the question of "revelation" in Paul's historical context. Parts three and four take up again the question of the mechanics of divination from Chapter 1, presenting some more nuanced conclusions about divination in relation to Paul's anthropology, cosmology, and theology that the ensuing chapters have made possible.

Methods of Divination in Paul

As ancient people turned to the gods for advice and information on a broad range of matters, so, too, Paul's methods of divination uncover a large range of information: from smaller scale signs and revelations that direct various aspects of everyday life, to expansive insights about cosmology and eschatology. Within this range certain methods and certain types of signs lend themselves most readily to certain types of information.

Non-verbal signs are perhaps the most limited in scope as they generally only convey divine approval or disapproval. This observation does not make them any less important an element of Paul's repertoire but merely recognises the areas in which they are most useful: flagging up ritual error, ascertaining actions to avoid, but also identifying individuals and messages that carry divine approval. Signs that require more unpacking and interpreting will typically need the assistance of other divinatory methods such as oracles or written prophecies to interpret them. If a sign is seen as the fulfilment of a previous prophecy or written oracle, then it may serve as a confirmation of that prophecy and bolster expectation of its complete fulfilment. The interpretation of signs has been the aspect of divine communication most neglected by Pauline scholarship, falling as it does on the technical, uninspired side of the traditional divide. If scholars discuss them at all they do not connect them with categories such as prophecy or revelation.[1] Restoring signs to their proper divinatory role enables one to see the important place they play within Paul's methods of divine communication.

On the opposite end of the spectrum are visions. Many scholars effectively deny the divinatory importance of visions for Paul either by relegating them to private experiences of personal edification,[2] or by studying them solely on the level of rhetoric.[3] In contrast to these tendencies, this study has shown visions to be a legitimate means of divination for Paul providing him with a wide range of information. Visions may well be involved in the more general experience of prophetic revelation and thus provide incremental pieces of information that direct Paul's travel plans or respond to prayers for healing. When Paul makes the visionary component explicit, however, it is to focus on expansive knowledge of the cosmos and foundational epiphanies of Christ. These are the most impressive means of divine communication, which themselves function as a sign of the legitimacy of the one who receives them. At times Paul downplays this aspect of visions but at other times it is important. Visions impart the most important and foundational aspects of Paul's message, including the good news that Christ has been raised. In addition to Paul's

---

[1] They play no role, for example, in the studies of Aune, *Prophecy*; Forbes, *Inspired Speech*; Lührmann, *Offenbarungsverständnis*; Bockmuehl, *Revelation and Mystery*.
[2] E.g., Baird, "Visions, Revelations, and Ministry," 651–62; Heininger, *Paulus*; Bockmuehl, *Revelation and Mystery*, 137, 144–45.
[3] E.g., Eyl, *Signs, Wonders, and Gifts*; Rollens, "The God Came to Me."

initial vision of Christ, visions are also the most likely context for the revelation of mysteries and words of the Lord that concern eschatology.

Prophecy and divine speech are harder to pin down as methods of divine communication. For Paul they more properly refer to the communication rather than the reception of divine knowledge. The direct channelling of divine speech is in fact too direct to be of any divinatory value and is therefore not properly a method of divination for Paul. In his role as a mediator of divine knowledge, however, Paul's speech can be predictive of future suffering or judgement, and he can pronounce with divine authority on aspects of everyday life (cult, marriage, and so on). Even these pronouncements often seem to rely on more than simply channelling speech from God but involve previously uttered oracles, written texts, and the sort of divine wisdom a seer might receive as a prerequisite for their craft. This finding demonstrates the utility of the category of divination, which can account for the various methods that underlie a divine pronouncement rather than "prophecy," which, if defined narrowly as inspired speech, is very hard to find an example of in Paul's letters.[4]

Written texts can also encompass the whole range of divinatory information. Some texts present general wisdom that directs aspects of everyday life or provide insight into the consistent character of God. Others predict pivotal eschatological events such as the Messiah's suffering and death, and the ingathering of the Gentiles, the transformation of mortal bodies, and the vanquishing of death. The fulfilment of these prophecies (often in unexpected ways) can function as signs that validate and bolster expectation for the fulfilment of other written prophecies, although, of course, only if interpreted in the correct way. In all these functions, Paul's "use of scripture" is not materially different from the ways sacred texts and written oracles were used in the broader Graeco-Roman world. My analysis confirms van Kooten's observation of the varied texture of divine speech in the text of scripture for Paul, as long as one recognises that Paul still sees nearly all these layers of authority as divine in some sense.

Revelation and Divination: Two Sides of the Same Coin?

The above survey shows that while much of the information divined by Paul relates to events of eschatological and salvific significance, they are still

---

[4] This is perhaps why Aune's form-critical study of prophecy in early Christianity could only offer such meagre conclusions ("the distinctive feature of prophetic speech was not so much its *content* or *form*, but its *supernatural origin*" [italics original]) as it stayed at the level of prophetic speech without investigating the divinatory methods that produce the speech, Aune, *Prophecy*, 338.

revealed and explicated in terms of familiar divinatory technology: visions, prophecies, textual interpretation, and the interpretation of signs. This highlights the major flaw of studies on Paul and revelation by Oepke, Lührmann, Bockmuehl, or the more recent apocalyptic school: that they take the identification of eschatological events as themselves a new means or idea of revelation. Revelation is seen to lie in the "Christ-event" or the continued preaching of the gospel. The eschatological and cosmological scope of the information Paul relates does indeed give a particular content to his divinations, but this is not altogether a different concept of divination or revelation than in his surrounding world. Eschatological "events" like the gospel or the Christ-event do not escape this. The statement that the gospel reveals God's righteousness relies on a number of related interpretive processes: the sign of a crucified Messiah is interpreted with respect to ancient written prophecies, his resurrection is confirmed by epiphanic visionary experiences, possibly interpreted through subsequent visionary experiences, and all are offered as the solution to other signs of divine wrath.

Struck has documented the shift in knowledge provided through divinatory means from "incremental insight to revelatory vision."[5] Recognising this shift in the broader Graeco-Roman milieu enables one to plot Paul along this line, and shows how Paul's "revelatory visions" were comprehensible and conformed in many ways to the divinatory expectations of his time. Engaging the breadth of Paul's divinatory means also shows that Paul does not entirely leave "incremental insights" behind. Rather, commands of the Lord, sacred texts, and discrete revelations can all provide Paul with incremental knowledge about how to navigate daily life. This suggests the "shift" in divinatory knowledge does not necessarily represent a replacement of one type of knowledge for another, but a widening scope that can include both. Paul calls neither type of knowledge "divination," but he does provide evidence that both types of knowledge were equally accessible through divinatory means, and are equally important for how he understands and engages in the process of divine communication.

The integration of divinatory and philosophical expertise, which is often impossible to disentangle in Paul, also fits with this widening scope of divinatory knowledge, in which philosophy is presented in divinatory forms and traditional institutions of divination are increasingly concerned with philosophical and theological questions. The integration of divination and philosophy also fits with the "eclecticism" of the freelance religious expert as described by Wendt and Iles Johnston. These experts draw freely from various areas of expertise which often defy traditional categories.

---

[5] Struck, *Divination and Human Nature*, 219–25.

Anthropology, Cosmology, and Eschatology

With these conclusions in place, we can return to some of the questions of the first chapter and draw a more nuanced picture of the role of divination within Paul's anthropology and cosmology. Here again, as is always the case with Paul, eschatology plays a prominent and distinctive role. The *pneuma* of the resurrected Christ has been poured into the hearts of believers, inwardly transforming them into the image of Christ degree by degree (2 Cor 3:17–18). This same *pneuma* is also at work in the natural world of creation and will ultimately transform the cosmos itself (Rom 8:18–25). This is the decisive eschatological event that shapes Paul's broader thinking.

While many of his philosophical contemporaries assumed a divine element to all human beings in their natural state, which was capable of correctly receiving and interpreting divine communications in the right conditions, Paul asserts that this aspect of the human person is only activated by the transformation of creation that begins with the reception of Christ's divine *pneuma*. The natural *pneuma* of human souls can only know natural human things, but God's divine *pneuma* connects believers to knowledge of the will of God (1 Cor 2:10–16). Thus divination can be located within the physical mechanisms of the cosmos (as Struck has identified for Plato, Aristotle, and the Stoics), but only as that cosmos is being renewed and recreated by the *pneuma* of the resurrected Christ. It is part of the physics of "new creation." Recognising this is a function of placing Paul in his context, rather than causing him to stand above or against it, as his language makes sense when we understand the philosophical conversations about divination and the human soul.

Placing Paul in a philosophical conversation about divination also highlights the realism with which he speaks of the anthropological elements of σάρξ, ψυχή, πνεῦμα, and νοῦς. Bultmann understood these to represent not distinguishable parts of human bodies, but the human person viewed from a particular vantage point.[6] This study has found more consonance with the Greek philosophical categories, at least at the points when Paul is speaking of the operation of divine communication.[7] Flesh, for example, stands in the way of a full appreciation of divine knowledge (1 Cor 3:1; 2 Cor 12:7). But when all people are resurrected then the flesh that clouds human access to divine thoughts will be removed, and all knowledge will occur at

---

[6] Bultmann, *Theology*, 1:209. This view is still influential: Kyle B. Wells, *Grace and Agency in Paul and Second Temple Judaism: Interpreting the Transformation of the Heart*, NovTSup 157 (Leiden: Brill, 2015), 231.

[7] This coheres with the studies of van Kooten, *Paul's Anthropology*; Wasserman, *Death of the Soul*.

the level of divine *pneuma* (1 Cor 15:49–50). Divination (the type of divine communication currently available to Paul) will be superfluous at that point because the mortal flesh will no longer exist. At that point it will cease to become divination and will simply become knowledge (1 Cor 13:8). Flesh, understood as the substance of mortal bodies, is not only an ethical but also a cognitive hindrance to the person. In the intervening time before this flesh is overcome, the *pneuma* reconstitutes the human soul and provides the channel and means of knowing and interpreting the signs God sends. These signs need interpretation from the νοῦς as they are reflected and refracted through the mortal bodies that they inhabit (1 Cor 13:12; 14:13–19). There is no natural/technical divide for Paul when it comes to methods of divine communication. While much scholarship has separated the inspired prophecy of Christianity from the technical divination of the Graeco-Roman world, this distinction does not hold for Paul. Rather the important contrast is divine knowledge with *pneuma* (whether directly revealed or interpreted) versus mundane knowledge without it.

Divination and Theology: God, Lord, *Pneuma*

Pneuma forms the crucial link between God, the cosmos, and the human person in producing meaningful communication, but what of the other beings that populate Paul's cosmos? And what can Paul's reasoning about divination tell us about his view of God? Paul's letters bear witness to a multi-layered cosmos populated by various classes of divine or semi-divine beings. Angels and daimons are present and involved in prayers, prophecy, and sacrifices (1 Cor 8–11). Multiple mediating spirits or *pneumata* are capable of communicating divinations between human and divine realms. Paul himself interacts with an angel of Satan and discerns the Satan's opposition to him in natural events that surround his mission (2 Cor 12:7; 1 Thess 2:18). The air is indeed "full of immortal souls," as Cicero put it, able to communicate information from the divine (*Div.* 1.64). The most reliable and authoritative sources of information for Paul however, and the only sources he will directly quote, are God, the Lord Jesus, and the *pneuma*.

While the *pneuma* of Christ is imperative for any meaningful communication to take place, the *pneuma* emerges in Paul principally as the means rather than the source of communication. The wisdom Paul and the apostles teach is "taught by *pneuma*" (1 Cor 2:13), but if *pneuma* itself is allowed to speak then it is unintelligible and only understood by God (1 Cor 14). Rather it is the Lord Jesus who provides intelligible words by means of *pneuma*. It is words and commands of the Lord that Paul most often conveys, and it is *in* the Lord, or *in* Christ that he speaks. It is the Lord he sees in visions and revelations. Even scriptural texts often convey the words of the Lord. We saw this in the Psalms attributed to the χρίστος. Other citations are attributed to the Lord (κύριος) which make it notoriously hard to specify exactly who Paul is talking about (Rom 12:19; 14:11; 1 Cor 14:21; 2 Cor 6:17, 18). In the context of the LXX these refer to Yahweh, but to a Gentile audience mainly familiar with Paul's letters the Lord would most readily be understood as the Lord Jesus. The context of a number of Paul's citations support this identification.[8] Just as Paul splits the *Shema* in 1 Cor 8:6 so as to distinguish one God and one Lord Jesus, so also in Rom 14:11 Paul alters Isa 45:23 so that every knee shall bow to the Lord, and every tongue confess to God (cf. Phil 2:10–11). Paul quotes these words as words of the Lord himself.

God on the other hand emerges as the somewhat hidden ultimate source who arranges everything. Paul never claims to see or hear God directly. The only speech attributed directly to God (θεός) comes in some scriptural quotations that Paul mostly characterises as "promises" (Rom 9:12; 2 Cor 4:6; 6:2, 16; Gal 3:16), and are outnumbered by the citations attributed to the Lord (κύριος). Communication from God comes in indirect and mediated form. The law of Moses reflects the will of God, even as it was delivered by angels (Gal 3:19–21; 1 Cor 9:8–10). His wrath can be discerned through the dysfunctional signs of human activity, and his justice can be discerned through the sending of Christ (Rom 1–3). Though Christ is the content of Paul's revelation in Gal 1:15–16, God is the one who reveals him to Paul. Jesus is elsewhere described as the form of God and the image of God, in whose face God's physical form can be seen (Phil 2:6; 2 Cor 4:4–6).

This all suggests some organising logic to the way Paul presents the role of these three figures in relation to the pneumatic gifts in 1 Cor 12:4–6. Here the one *pneuma* presides over the variety of gifts, which are acts of service to (or mediation of: διακονιῶν) the one Lord, which the one God activates (ἐνεργῶν) among the *ekklēsia*. This considerably nuances previous studies of revelation, prophecy, or divination in Paul, which all tend to conflate the roles of these actors as divinatory sources of information. Paul is, in fact, remarkably consistent in the roles he attributes to various inhabitants of the divine realm in the process of divine communication, and he is not alone in making such distinctions. For Apuleius, divinatory signs occur "through the will, power, and authority of the heavenly gods, but also by the compliance, service, and agency of the demons" (*De deo Socr.* 6.4–5 [Jones, LCL]). These distinctions could also be made between the heavenly gods themselves. For the authors of the Homeric hymns, Apollo at Delphi does not speak for himself but makes

---

[8] See David B. Capes, *Old Testament Yahweh Texts in Paul's Christology*, WUNT 2/47 (Tübingen: Mohr Siebeck, 1992).

known the intentions of the gods in general (*Hymn to Apollo* 483–486) or of Zeus in particular, which he has learned from Zeus's own pronouncements and subsequently passes on to mortals (*Hymn to Hermes* 532–540). For Paul, too, God is the orchestrator and organiser who makes known his intentions through Christ with the aid of *pneuma*.

Bibliography

Primary Sources

Achelis, Hans ed. *Hippolyt's kleinere exegetische und homiletische Schriften*. Leipzig: J. C. Hinrichs'sche, 1897.
Aelian. Translated by Nigel G. Wilson et al. 5 vols. LCL. Cambridge, MA: Harvard University Press, 1949–1997.
Aeschylus. Edited and translated by Alan H. Sommerstein. 3 vols. LCL. Cambridge, MA: Harvard University Press, 2009.
Aland, Barbara, Kurt Aland, Johannes Karavidopoulos, Carlo M. Martini, and Bruce M. Metzger, eds. *Novum Testamentum Graece*. 28th ed. Stuttgart: Deutsche Bibelgesellschaft, 2012.
Apostolic Fathers. Edited and translated by Bart Ehrman. 2 vols. LCL. Cambridge, MA: Harvard University Press, 2003.
Appian. Edited and translated by Brian McGing. 6 vols. LCL. Cambridge, MA: Harvard University Press, 2019–2020.
Apuleius. Edited and translated by J. Arthur Hanson and Christopher P. Jones. 3 vols. LCL. Cambridge, MA: Harvard University Press, 1989–2017.
Aristophanes. Edited and translated by Jeffrey Henderson. 5 vols. LCL. Cambridge, MA: Harvard University Press, 1998–2008.
Aristotle. Translated by H. Rackham et al. 23 vols. LCL. Cambridge, MA: Harvard University Press, 1926–2020.
Armin, Hans Friedrich August von, ed. *Stoicorum Veterum Fragmenta*. 4 vols. Stuttgart: Teubner, 1903–1924.
Babrius and Phaedrus. *Fables*. Translated by Ben Edwin Perry. LCL 436. Cambridge, MA: Harvard University Press, 1965.
Borret, Marcel, ed. *Origène: Contre Celse*. 5 vols. SC. Paris: Cerf, 1967–1976.
Callimachus. Translated by A. W. Mair et al. 2 vols. LCL. Cambridge, MA: Harvard University Press, 1921–1973.
Cassius Dio. *Roman History*. Translated by Earnest Carey and Herbert B. Foster. LCL. Cambridge, MA: Harvard University Press, 1914–1927.
Charlesworth, James H., ed. *The Old Testament Pseudepigrapha*. 2 vols. New York: Doubleday, 1983–1985.
Cicero. Translated by L. H. G. Greenwood et al. 28 vols. LCL. Cambridge, MA: Harvard University Press, 1914–2017.

Dio Chrysostom. Translated by J. W. Cohoon et al. 5 vols. LCL. Cambridge, MA: Harvard University Press, 1932–1951.

Diodorus Siculus. *Library of History*. Translated by C. H. Oldfather et al. 12 vols. LCL. Cambridge, MA: Harvard University Press, 1933–1967.

Diogenes Laertius. Translated by R. D. Hicks. 2 vols. LCL. Cambridge, MA: Harvard University Press, 1925.

Dionysius of Halicarnassus. *Roman Antiquities*. Translated by Earnest Cary. 7 vols. LCL. Cambridge, MA: Harvard University Press, 1937–1950.

Edelstein, L., and I. G. Kidd, eds. *Posidonius*. 3 vols. 2nd ed. Cambridge: Cambridge University Press, 1989–1999.

Elliger, Karl, and Wilhelm Rudolph, eds. *Biblia Hebraica Stuttgartensia*. 5th ed. Stuttgart: Deutsche Bibelgesellschaft, 1997.

Epictetus. Translated by W. A. Oldfather. 2 vols. LCL. Cambridge, MA: Harvard University Press, 1925–1928.

Euripides. Edited and translated by David Kovacs et al. 8 vols. LCL. Cambridge, MA: Harvard University Press, 1994–2008.

García Martínez, Florentino, and Eibert J. C. Tigchelaar. *The Dead Sea Scrolls Study Edition*. 2 vols. Leiden: Brill, 1997.

Harris-McCoy, Daniel E. *Artemidorus' Oneirocritica: Text, Translation and Commentary*. Oxford: Oxford University Press, 2012.

Heraclitus. *Homeric Problems*. Edited and translated by Donald A. Russell and David Konstan. WGRW 14. Atlanta: SBL Press, 2005.

Hercher, Rudolf. *Arriani Nicomediensis Scripta Minora*. Leipzig: Teubner, 1885.

Herodotus. *The Persian Wars*. Translated by A. D. Godley. 4 vols. LCL. Cambridge, MA: Harvard University Press, 1920–1925.

Hesiod. Edited and translated by Glenn W. Most. 2 vols. LCL. Cambridge, MA: Harvard University Press, 2018.

Hippocrates. Translated by W. H. S. Jones et al. 11 vols. LCL. Cambridge, MA: Harvard University Press, 1923–2018.

Homer. Translated by A. T. Murray. 4 vols. LCL. Cambridge, MA: Harvard University Press, 1919–1925.

Homeric Hymns, Homeric Apocrypha, Lives of Homer. Edited and translated by Martin L. West. LCL 496. Cambridge, MA: Harvard University Press, 2003.

Jacoby, Felix, ed. *Die Fragmente der griechischen Historiker*. Leiden: Brill, 1954–1964.

Josephus. Translated by H. St J. Thackeray et al. 10 vols. LCL. Cambridge, MA: Harvard University Press, 1926–1965.

Juvenal and Persius. Edited and translated by Susanna Morton Braund. LCL 91. Cambridge, MA: Harvard University Press, 2004.

Keil, Bruno, ed. *Aelii Aristidis Smyrnaei Quae Supersunt Omnia*. Vol. 2. Berlin: Weidmann, 1898.

Leutsch, E. L. von, and F. G. Schneidewin, eds. *Corpus Paroemiographorum Graecorum*. 2 vols. Cambridge Library Collection. Cambridge: Cambridge University Press, 2010 (1839–1851).

Livy. *History of Rome*. Translated by B. O. Foster et al. 14 vols. LCL. Cambridge, MA: Harvard University Press, 1919–2020.

Long, A. A., and D. N. Sedley, eds. *The Hellenistic Philosophers*. 2 vols. Cambridge: Cambridge University Press, 1987.

Lucan. *The Civil War (Pharsalia)*. Translated by J. D. Duff. LCL 220. Cambridge, MA: Harvard University Press, 1928.

Lucian. Translated by A. M. Harmon et al. 8 vols. LCL. Cambridge, MA: Harvard University Press, 1913–1967.

Marcus Aurelius. Edited and translated by C. R. Haines. LCL 58. Cambridge, MA: Harvard University Press, 1916.
Martial. *Epigrams*. Edited and translated by D. R. Shackleton Bailey. 3 vols. LCL. Cambridge, MA: Harvard University Press, 1993.
Maximus of Tyre. *Dissertationes*. Edited by Michael B. Trapp. Stuttgart: Teubner, 1994.
Müller, Karl, ed. *Geographi graeci minores*. 2 vols. Cambridge Library Collection. Cambridge: Cambridge University Press, 2010 (1855–1861).
Ovid. Translated by Grant Showerman et al. Revised by G. P Goold. 6 vols. LCL. Cambridge, MA: Harvard University Press, 1977–1989.
Patrologia Graeca. Edited by J.-P. Migne. 162 vols. Paris, 1857–1886.
Pausanias. *Description of Greece*. Translated by W. H. S. Jones. 5 vols. LCL. Cambridge, MA: Harvard University Press, 1918–1935.
Pease, Arthur Stanley, ed. *De divinatione*. 2 vols. Urbana: University of Illinois Press, 1920–1923.
Philo. Translated by F. H. Colson et al. 12 vols. LCL. Cambridge, MA: Harvard University Press, 1929–1962.
Philostratus. Edited and translated by Christopher P. Jones et al. 6 vols. LCL. Cambridge, MA: Harvard University Press, 1921–2006.
Phlegon of Tralles. *Book of Marvels*. Translated by William Hansen. Exeter Studies in History. Exeter: University of Exeter Press, 1996.
Pindar. Edited and translated by William H. Race. 2 vols. LCL. Cambridge, MA: Harvard University Press, 1997.
Plato. Translated by Harold North Fowler et al. 12 vols. LCL. Cambridge, MA: Harvard University Press, 1914–2017.
Pliny. *Natural History*. Translated by H. Rackham et al. 10 vols. LCL. Cambridge, MA: Harvard University Press, 1938–1962.
Plutarch. *Lives*. Translated by Bernadotte Perrin. 11 vols. LCL. Cambridge, MA: Harvard University Press, 1914–1926.
———. *Moralia*. Translated by Frank Cole Babbitt et al. 16 vols. LCL. Cambridge, MA: Harvard University Press, 1927–1976.
Polybius. *The Histories*. Translated by W. R. Paton. Revised by F. W. Walbank and Christian Habicht. 6 vols. LCL. Cambridge, MA: Harvard University Press, 2010–2012.
Preisendanz, Karl, ed. *Papyri Graecae Magicae: Die griechischen Zauberpapyri*. 2 vols. 2nd ed. Stuttgart: Teubner, 1973–1974.
Rahlfs, Alfred, ed. *Psalmi cum Odis*. Septuaginta 10. 3rd ed. Göttingen: Vandenhoeck & Ruprecht, 1979.
———. *Septuaginta*. Rev. ed. Stuttgart: Deutsche Bibelgesellschaft, 2006.
Roberts, Alexander, and James Donaldson, eds. *The Ante-Nicene Fathers*. 1885–1887. 10 vols. Repr., Peabody, MA: Hendrickson, 1994.
Schaff, Philip, ed. *The Nicene and Post-Nicene Fathers*. Series 1. 1886–1889. 14 vols. Repr., Peabody, MA: Hendrickson, 1994.
Seneca. Translated by John W. Basore et al. 13 vols. LCL. Cambridge, MA: Harvard University Press, 1913–2018.
Sophocles. Edited and translated by Hugh Lloyd-Jones. 3 vols. LCL. Cambridge, MA: Harvard University Press, 1994–1996.
Statius. Edited and translated by D. R. Shackleton Bailey. 3 vols. LCL. Cambridge, MA: Harvard University Press, 2004–2015.
Strabo. *Geography*. Translated by Horace Leonard Jones. 8 vols. LCL. Cambridge, MA: Harvard University Press, 1917–1932.
Suetonius. Translated by J. C. Rolfe. 2 vols. LCL. Cambridge, MA: Harvard University Press, 1997.

Tacitus. Translated by M. Hutton et al. 5 vols. LCL. Cambridge, MA: Harvard University Press, 1914–1937.
Thucydides. *History of the Peloponnesian War.* Translated by C. F. Smith. 4 vols. LCL. Cambridge, MA: Harvard University Press, 1919–1923.
Virgil. Translated by H. Rushton Fairclough. Revised by G. P. Goold. 2 vols. LCL. Cambridge, MA: Harvard University Press, 1999–2000.
Wevers, John William, ed. *Deuteronomium.* Septuaginta 3. 2nd ed. Göttingen: Vandenhoeck & Ruprecht, 2006.
———. *Genesis.* Septuaginta 1. Göttingen: Vandenhoeck & Ruprecht, 1974.
Willis, James, ed. *Ambrosius Theodosius Macrobius Opera.* 2 vols. 3rd ed. BSGRT. Berlin: de Gruyter, 1994.
Xenophon. Translated by Walter Miller et al. 7 vols. LCL. Cambridge, MA: Harvard University Press, 1914–2013.
Ziegler, Joseph. *Susanna, Daniel, Bel et Draco.* Septuaginta 16.2. 2nd ed. Göttingen: Vandenhoeck & Ruprecht, 1999.

Secondary Sources

Adams, Edward. *Constructing the World: A Study in Paul's Cosmological Language.* SNTW. Edinburgh: T&T Clark, 2000.
———. *The Stars Will Fall From Heaven: 'Cosmic Catastrophe' in the New Testament and its World.* LNTS 347. London: T&T Clark, 2007.
Addey, Crystal. *Divination and Theurgy in Neoplatonism: Oracles of the Gods.* Ashgate Studies in Philosophy & Theology in Late Antiquity. Farnham: Ashgate, 2014.
Aernie, Jeffrey W. *Is Paul Also Among the Prophets? An Examination of the Relationship Between Paul and the Old Testament Prophetic Tradition in 2 Corinthians.* LNTS 467. London: T&T Clark, 2012.
Algra, Keimpe. "Stoics on Souls and Demons." Pages 359–87 in *Body and Soul in Ancient Philosophy.* Edited by Dorothea Frede and Burkhard Reis. Berlin: de Gruyter, 2009.
Allen, James. "Greek Philosophy and Signs." Pages 29–42 in *Divination and Interpretation of Signs in the Ancient World.* Edited by Amar Annus. OIS 6. Chicago: Oriental Institute of the University of Chicago, 2010.
———. *Inference from Signs: Ancient Debates about the Nature of Evidence.* Oxford: Clarendon, 2001.
Allison, Dale C. *Constructing Jesus: Memory, Imagination, and History.* Grand Rapids: Baker Academic, 2010.
Amandry, Pierre. *La mantique Apollinienne à Delphes: essai sur le fonctionnement de l'oracle.* Paris: de Boccard, 1950.
Ashton, John. *The Religion of Paul the Apostle.* New Haven: Yale University Press, 2000.
Attridge, Harold W. "Giving Voice to Jesus: Use of the Psalms in the New Testament." Pages 101–12 in *Psalms in Community: Jewish and Christian Textual, Liturgical, and Artistic Traditions.* Edited by Harold W. Attridge and Margot E. Fassler. SymS 25. Atlanta: SBL Press, 2003.
Aune, David E. "Charismatic Exegesis in Early Judaism and Early Christianity." Pages 126–50 in *The Pseudepigrapha and Early Biblical Interpretation.* Edited by James H. Charlesworth and Craig A. Evans. JSPSup 14. Sheffield: Sheffield Academic, 1993.
———. "'Magic' in Early Christianity and its Ancient Mediterranean Context: A Survey of Some Recent Scholarship." *ASE* 24 (2007): 229–94.
———. *Prophecy in Early Christianity and the Ancient Mediterranean World.* Grand Rapids: Eerdmans, 1983.

Babut, Daniel. "La doctrine démonologique dans le *De genio Socratis* de Plutarque: cohérence et fonction." *L'information littéraire* 35 (1983): 201–205.
Bacon, B. W. "Wrath 'Unto the Uttermost.'" *The Expositor* 8.24 (1922): 356–76.
Bailey, Daniel P. "Jesus as the Mercy Seat: The Semantics and Theology of Paul's Use of Hilasterion in Romans 3:25." *TynBul* 51 (2000): 155–58.
Baird, William. "Visions, Revelations, and Ministry: Reflections on 2 Cor 12:1–5 and Gal 1:11–17." *JBL* 104 (1985): 651–62.
Bakhos, Carol, ed. *Ancient Judaism in its Hellenistic Context*. JSJSup 95. Leiden: Brill, 2004.
Barclay, John M. G. "Πνευματικός in the Social Dialect of Pauline Christianity." Pages 157–67 in *The Holy Spirit and Christian Origins: Essays in Honor of James D. G. Dunn*. Edited by Graham N. Stanton, Bruce W. Longenecker, and Stephen C. Barton. Grand Rapids: Eerdmans, 2004.
———. *Jews in the Mediterranean Diaspora: From Alexander to Trajan (323 BCE–117 CE)*. Berkeley: University of California Press, 1999.
———. "'O wad some Pow'r the giftie gie us, To see oursels as others see us!': Method and Purpose in Comparing the New Testament," Pages 9–22 in *The New Testament in Comparison: Validity, Method, and Purpose in Comparing Traditions*. Edited by John M. G. Barclay and Benjamin G. White. LNTS 600. London: T&T Clark, 2020.
———. *Paul and the Gift*. Grand Rapids: Eerdmans, 2015.
———. "Stoic Physics and the Christ-Event: A Review of Troels Engberg-Pedersen, *Cosmology and Self in the Apostle Paul: The Material Spirit* (Oxford: Oxford University Press, 2010)." *JSNT* 33 (2011): 406–14.
Barrett, C. K. *The Epistle to the Romans*. BNTC. London: Black, 1957.
———. *The First Epistle to the Corinthians*. BNTC. London: Black, 1968.
Barton, John. *Oracles of God: Perceptions of Ancient Prophecy in Israel After the Exile*. 2nd ed. London: Darton, Longman & Todd, 2007.
Bassett, Samuel E. "1 Cor 13:12: βλέπομεν γὰρ ἄρτι δι' ἐσόπτρου ἐν αἰνίγματι." *JBL* 47 (1928): 232–36.
Bates, Matthew W. *The Hermeneutics of the Apostolic Proclamation: The Center of Paul's Method of Scriptural Interpretation*. Waco, TX: Baylor University Press, 2012.
Baur, F. C. *Paul the Apostle of Jesus Christ*. Translated by Allan Menzies. London: Williams & Norgate, 1875.
Bazzana, Giovanni B. *Having the Spirit of Christ: Spirit Possession and Exorcism in the Early Christ Groups*. Synkrisis. New Haven: Yale University Press, 2020.
Behm, J. "Das Bildwort vom Spiegel 1 Korinther 13:12." Pages 315–42 in *Reinhold-Seeberg-Festschrift*. Edited by Wilhelm Koepp. 2 vols. Leipzig: Deichert, 1929.
Belayche, Nicole, and Jörg Rüpke. "Divination et révélation dans les mondes grec et romain." *Revue de l'histoire des religions* 2 (2007): 139–47.
Belleville, Linda L. "The Sinai-Μεσίτης Tradition in Galatians 3:19–20." Pages 325–34 in *Paul and Scripture*. Edited by Stanley E. Porter and Christopher D. Land. Pauline Studies 10. Leiden: Brill, 2019.
Benz, Ernst. *Paulus als Visionär: eine vergleichende Untersuchung der Visionsberichte des Paulus in der Apostelgeschichte und in den paulinischen Briefen*. Verlagde Akademie der Wissenschaften und der Literatur. Mainz: F. Steiner Wiesbaden, 1952.
Berger, Klaus. "Hellenistisch-heidnische Prodigien und die Vorzeichen in der jüdischen und christlichen Apokalyptik." *ANRW* 23.2:1428–69. Part 2, *Principat*, 23.2. Edited by Wolfgang Haase. Berlin: de Gruyter, 1980.
———. "Zur Diskussion über die Herkunft von 1 Kor 2:9." *NTS* 24 (1978): 271–83.
Betz, Hans Dieter. *Der Apostel Paulus und die sokratische Tradition*. BHT 45. Tübingen: Mohr Siebeck, 1972.

———. "Eine Christus-Aretalogie bei Paulus (2 Kor 12:7–10)." *ZTK* 66 (1969): 288–305.
———. *Galatians*. Hermeneia. Philadelphia: Fortress, 1979.
———, ed. *The Greek Magical Papyri in Translation Including the Demotic Spells*. Chicago: University of Chicago Press, 1986.
———. "The Problem of Apocalyptic Genre in Greek and Hellenistic Literature: The Case of the Oracle of Trophonius," Pages 577–97 in *Apocalypticism in the Mediterranean World and the Near East: Proceedings of the International Colloquium on Apocalypticism, Uppsala, August 12–17, 1979*. Edited by David Hellholm. 2nd ed. Tübingen: Mohr Siebeck, 1989.
Bieder, Werner. "Gebetswirklichkeit und Gebetsmöglichkeit bei Paulus." *TZ* 4 (1948): 22–40.
Bockmuehl, Markus N. A. "1 Thessalonians 2:14–16 and the Church in Jerusalem." *TynB* 52 (2001): 1–31.
———. "'The Form of God' (Phil 2:6): Variations on a Theme of Jewish Mysticism." *JTS* 48 (1997): 1–23.
———. *Revelation and Mystery in Ancient Judaism and Pauline Christianity*. WUNT 2/36. Tübingen: Mohr Siebeck, 1990. Repr., Eugene, OR: Wipf & Stock, 2009.
———. "Das Verb φανερόω im Neuen Testament." *BZ* 32 (1988): 87–99.
Boehringer, Sandra. "'Ces monstres de femmes': topique des *thaumata* dans les discours sur l'homosexualité féminine aux premiers siècles de notre ère." Pages 75–98 in *Conceptions et représentations de l'extraordinaire dans le monde antique: Actes du Colloque international, Lausanne, 20–22 mars 2003*. Edited by Olivier Bianchi and Olivier Thévenaz. Bern: Lang, 2004.
Boer, Martinus C. de. *Galatians: A Commentary*. NTL. Louisville: Westminster John Knox, 2011.
———. "Paul, Theologian of God's Apocalypse." *Interpretation* 56 (2002): 21–33.
Bonazzi, Mauro, and Jan Opsomer, eds. *The Origins of the Platonic System: Platonisms of the Early Empire and their Philosophical Contexts*. Leuven: Peeters, 2009.
Bonazzi, Mauro. "Pythagoreanising Aristotle: Eudorus and the Systematisation of Platonism." Pages 160–86 in *Aristotle, Plato and Pythagoreanism in the First Century BC: New Directions for Philosophy*. Edited by Malcolm Schofield. Cambridge: Cambridge University Press, 2013.
Bonner, Campbell. "Traces of Thaumaturgic Technique in the Miracles." *HTR* 20 (1927): 171–81.
Boring, M. Eugene. *Sayings of the Risen Jesus: Christian Prophecy in the Synoptic Tradition*. SNTSMS 46. Cambridge: Cambridge University Press, 1982.
———, Carsten Colpe, and Klaus Berger, eds. *Hellenistic Commentary to the New Testament*. Nashville: Abingdon, 1995.
Bornkamm, Günther. "The Revelation of God's Wrath (Romans 1–3)." Pages 47–64 in *Early Christian Experience*. Translated by Paul L. Hammer. London: SCM, 1969.
———. "μυστήριον, μυέω." *TDNT* 4:802–28.
Bouché-Leclercq, Auguste. *Histoire de la divination dans l'antiquité*. 4 vols. Paris: Leroux, 1879–1882.
Bousset, Wilhelm. "Die Himmelsreise der Seele." *AR* 4 (1901): 136–69, 229–73.
Braaten, Carl E. "The Current Controversy on Revelation: Pannenberg and His Critics." *JR* 45 (1965): 225–37.
Bremmer, Jan N. "Descents to Hell and Ascents to Heaven in Apocalyptic Literature." Pages 340–57 in *The Oxford Handbook of Apocalyptic Literature*. Edited by John J. Collins. Oxford: Oxford University Press, 2014.
———. *The Rise and Fall of the Afterlife*. London: Routledge, 2002.
———. "Romulus, Remus and the Foundation of Rome." Pages 25–48 in *Roman Myth and Mythography*. Edited by Jan N. Bremmer and Nicholas Horsfall. London: Institute of Classical Studies, 1987.
Brenk, Frederick E. "Genuine Greek Demons, 'In Mist Apparelled'? Hesiod and Plutarch." Pages 170–81 in *Relighting the Souls: Studies in Plutarch, in Greek Literature, Religion, and Philosophy, and in the New Testament Background*. Stuttgart: Steiner, 1998.

———. "Greek Epiphanies and Paul on the Road to Damaskos." Pages 415–24 in *The Notion of 'Religion' in Comparative Research: Selected Proceedings of the XVIth Congress of the International Association for the History of Religions*. Edited by Ugo Bianchi. Rome: Bretschneider, 1994.

———. "In the Light of the Moon: Demonology in the Early Imperial Period." *ANRW* 16.3:2068–145. Part 2, *Principat*, 16.3. Edited by Wolfgang Haase. Berlin: de Gruyter, 1986.

———. *In Mist Apparelled: Religious Themes in Plutarch's Moralia and Lives*. Mnemosyne 48. Leiden: Brill, 1977.

Brisson, Luc. *Sexual Ambivalence: Androgyny and Hermaphroditism in Graeco-Roman Antiquity*. Translated by Janet Lloyd. Berkeley: University of California Press, 2002.

Brooke, George John, Hindy Najman, and Loren T. Stuckenbruck, eds. *The Significance of Sinai: Traditions about Sinai and Divine Revelation in Judaism and Christianity*. Leiden: Brill, 2008.

Brooten, Bernadette J. *Love Between Women: Early Christian Responses to Female Homoeroticism*. Chicago: University of Chicago Press, 1996.

Brouwer, René. *The Stoic Sage: The Early Stoics on Wisdom, Sagehood and Socrates*. Cambridge Classical Studies. Cambridge: Cambridge University Press, 2014.

Brown, Raymond E. *The Semitic Background of the Term "Mystery" in the New Testament*. Philadelphia: Fortress, 1968.

Brownlee, William H. "The Wicked Priest, the Man of Lies, and the Righteous Teacher: The Problem of Identity." *JQR* 73 (1982): 1–37.

Bruce, F. F. *1 & 2 Corinthians*. London: Marshall, Morgan & Scott, 1971.

———. *1 & 2 Thessalonians*. WBC 45. Dallas: Word, 1982.

———. *The Epistle to the Galatians*. NIGTC. Grand Rapids: Eerdmans, 1982.

———. *Paul: Apostle of the Free Spirit*. Exeter: Paternoster, 1977.

Buchanan Wallace, James. *Snatched into Paradise (2 Cor 12:1–10): Paul's Heavenly Journey in the Context of Early Christian Experience*. BZNW 179. Berlin: de Gruyter, 2011.

Büchner, Dirk. "ἐξιλάσασθαι: Appeasing God in the Septuagint Pentateuch." *JBL* 129 (2010): 237–60.

Bultmann, Rudolf. "The Concept of Revelation in the New Testament." Pages 58–91 in *Existence and Faith: Shorter Writings of Rudolf Bultmann*. Translated by Schubert M. Ogden. London: Hodder & Stoughton, 1961. Translation of *Der Begriff der Offenbarung im Neuen Testament*. Tübingen: Mohr Siebeck, 1929.

———. *Theology of the New Testament*. Translated by Kendrick Grobel. 2 vols. London: SCM, 1952–1955.

Burkert, Walter. "Signs, Commands, and Knowledge: Ancient Divination Between Enigma and Epiphany." Pages 29–49 in *Mantikê: Studies in Ancient Divination*. Edited by Sarah Iles Johnston and Peter T. Struck. RGRW 155. Leiden: Brill, 2005.

Burton, Ernest de Witt. *A Critical and Exegetical Commentary on the Epistle to the Galatians*, ICC. Edinburgh: T&T Clark, 1921.

Caird, George B. *Principalities and Powers: A Study in Pauline Theology*. Oxford: Clarendon, 1956.

Callan, Terence. "Prophecy and Ecstasy in Greco-Roman Religion and in 1 Corinthians." *NovT* 27 (1985): 125–50.

Cameron, Ron, and Merrill P. Miller. "Introducing Paul and the Corinthians." Pages 1–15 in *Redescribing Paul and the Corinthians*. Edited by Ron Cameron and Merrill P. Miller. ECL 5. Atlanta: SBL Press, 2011.

Campanelli, Sara. "Eroizzazione e proprietà terriera nel 'Testamento di *Epikrates*': Per una proposta di lettura delle fondazioni cultuali di carattere familiare." *Hormos: Ricerche di storia antica* 4 (2012): 69–84.

Campbell, Douglas A. *The Deliverance of God: An Apocalyptic Rereading of Justification in Paul*. Grand Rapids: Eerdmans, 2009.

———. *Framing Paul: An Epistolary Biography*. Grand Rapids: Eerdmans, 2014.

———. *The Rhetoric of Righteousness in Romans 3:21–26.* JSNTSup 65. Sheffield: Sheffield Academic, 1992.
———. "Romans 1:17—A Crux Interpretum for the πίστις χριστοῦ Debate." *JBL* 113 (1994): 265–85.
Capes, David B. *Old Testament Yahweh Texts in Paul's Christology.* WUNT 2/47. Tübingen: Mohr Siebeck, 1992.
Carr, Wesley A. "The Rulers of this Age: 1 Cor 2:6–8," *NTS* 23 (1976): 20–35.
Cavallin, H. C. C. "The Righteous Shall Live by Faith: A Decisive Argument for the Traditional Interpretation." *ST* 32 (1978): 33–43.
Chester, Stephen. "Divine Madness? Speaking in Tongues in 1 Corinthians 14:23." *JSNT* 27 (2005): 417–46.
Chirassi Colombo, Ileana. "Teras ou les modalités du prodige dans le discours divinatoire grec: une perspective comparatiste." Pages 221–47 in *La Raison des signes: présages, rites, destin dans les sociétés de la Méditerranée ancienne.* Edited by Stella Georgoudi, Renée Koch Piettre, and Francis Schmidt. RGRW 174. Leiden: Brill, 2012.
Clivaz, Claire and Sara Schulthess. "On the Source and Rewriting of 1 Corinthians 2:9 in Christian, Jewish and Islamic Traditions." *NTS* 61 (2015): 183–200.
Collins, Derek. "Mapping the Entrails: The Practice of Greek Hepatoscopy." *AJP* 129 (2008): 319–45.
Collins, John J. "Before the Canon: Scriptures in Second Temple Judaism." Pages 225–41 in *Old Testament. Past, Present, and Future: Essays in Honor of Gene M. Tucker.* Edited by J. L. Mays, D. L. Petersen, and K. H. Richards. Nashville: Abingdon, 1995.
———. *Between Athens and Jerusalem: Jewish Identity in the Hellenistic Diaspora.* 2nd ed. Grand Rapids: Eerdmans, 2000.
———. "The Jewish Adaptation of Sibylline Oracles." Pages 181–97 in *Seers, Sibyls and Sages in Hellenistic-Roman Judaism.* JSJSup 54. Leiden: Brill, 1997.
Collins, Raymond F. *First Corinthians.* SP 7. Collegeville, MN: Liturgical Press, 1999.
———. "'It Was Indeed Written for Our Sake' (1 Cor 9:10): Paul's Use of Scripture in the First Letter to the Corinthians." *SNTSU* 20 (1995): 151–70.
Collman, Ryan D. "The Apostle to the Foreskin: Circumcision in the Letters of Paul." PhD diss., University of Edinburgh, 2021.
Conzelmann, Hans. *1 Corinthians: A Commentary on the First Epistle to the Corinthians.* Translated by James W. Leitch. Hermeneia. Philadelphia: Fortress, 1975.
Cook, John Granger. *Empty Tomb, Resurrection, Apotheosis.* WUNT 410. Tübingen: Mohr Siebeck, 2018.
Cornford, Francis M. *Plato's Cosmology: The Timaeus of Plato translated with a running commentary.* London: Kegan Paul, Trench, Trubner & Company, 1937.
Cothenet, Édouard. "Les prophètes chrétiens comme exégètes charismatiques de l'écriture." Pages 77–107 in *Prophetic Vocation in the New Testament and Today.* Edited by J. Panagopoulos. NovTSup 45. Leiden: Brill, 1977.
Cotter, Wendy. "Greco-Roman Apotheosis Traditions and the Resurrection Appearances in Matthew." Pages 127–53 in *The Gospel of Matthew in Current Study.* Edited by David E. Aune. Grand Rapids: Eerdmans, 2001.
Croy, N. C. "Religion, Personal." *DNTB*: 926–31.
Cullman, Oscar. *Christ and Time: The Primitive Christian Conception of Time and History.* Translated by Floyd V. Filson. London: SCM, 1951.
Dautzenberg, Gerhard. "Botschaft und Bedeutung der urchristlichen Prophetie nach dem ersten Korintherbrief (2:6–16; 12–14)." Pages 131–61 in *Prophetic Vocation in the New Testament and Today.* Edited by J. Panagopoulos. NovTSup 45. Leiden: Brill, 1977.
———. "Glossolalie." *RAC* 11:225–46.

———. *Urchristliche Prophetie: Ihre Erforschung, ihre Voraussetzungen im Judentum und ihre Struktur im ersten Korintherbrief.* BWA(N)T 10. Stuttgart: Kohlhammer, 1975.
———. "Zum religionsgeschichtlichen Hintergrund der διάκρισις πνευμάτων (1 Kor 12:10)." *BZ* 15 (1971): 93–104.
Davies, J. G. "The Genesis of Belief in an Imminent Parousia." *JTS* 14 (1963): 104–7.
Davies, J. P. *Paul Among the Apocalypses? An Evaluation of the 'Apocalyptic Paul' in the Context of Jewish and Christian Apocalyptic Literature.* LNTS 562. London: T&T Clark, 2016.
Davies, W. D. "Reflections about the Use of the Old Testament in the New in its Historical Context." *JQR* 74 (1983): 105–36.
Deissmann, Adolf. *Light from the Ancient East: The New Testament Illustrated by Recently Discovered Texts of the Graeco-Roman World.* Translated by Lionel R. M. Strachan. New York: Hodder & Stoughton, 1910.
———. "ἱλαστήριος und ἱλαστήριον: Eine lexikalische Studie." *ZNW* 4 (1903): 193–212.
Deming, Will. *Paul on Marriage and Celibacy: The Hellenistic Background of 1 Corinthians 7.* 2nd ed. Grand Rapids: Eerdmans, 2004.
Desto, Adriana, and Mauro Pesce. "The Heavenly Journey in Paul: Tradition of a Jewish Apocalyptic Literary Genre or Cultural Practice in a Hellenistic-Roman Context?" Pages 167–200 in *Paul's Jewish Matrix.* Edited by Thomas G. Casey and Justin Taylor. Rome: Gregorian & Biblical Press, 2011.
Dibelius, Martin. *From Tradition to Gospel.* Translated by Bertram Lee Woolf. Cambridge: James Clarke & Co., 1971.
———. *Die Geistwelt im Glauben des Paulus.* Göttingen: Vandenhoeck & Ruprecht, 1909.
Dillon, John. *The Middle Platonists: A Study of Platonism 80 BC to AD 220.* Rev. ed. London: Duckworth, 1996.
Dillon, Matthew. *Omens and Oracles: Divination in Ancient Greece.* London: Routledge, 2017.
Dodd, C. H. *According to the Scriptures: The Sub-Structure of New Testament Theology.* London: Collins, 1952.
———. *The Epistle of Paul to the Romans.* MNTC 6. London: Hodder & Stoughton, 1932.
———. "ΙΛΑΣΚΕΣΘΑΙ, Its Cognates, Derivatives and Synonyms in the Septuagint." *JTS* 32 (1931): 352–60.
Dodds, E. R. *The Greeks and the Irrational.* Sather Classical Lectures 25. Berkeley: University of California Press, 1959.
Dodson, Derek S. *Reading Dreams: An Audience-Critical Approach to the Dreams in the Gospel of Matthew.* LNTS 397. London: T&T Clark, 2009.
Dodson, Joseph R. "The Transcendence of Death and Heavenly Ascent in the Apocalyptic Paul and the Stoics." Pages 157–76 in *Paul and the Apocalyptic Imagination.* Edited by Ben C. Blackwell, John K. Goodrich, and Jason Maston. Minneapolis: Fortress, 2016.
Donaldson, Terence L. "Israelite, Convert, Apostle to the Gentiles: The Origin of Paul's Gentile Mission." Pages 62–84 in *The Road from Damascus: The Impact of Paul's Conversion on his Life, Thought, and Ministry.* Edited by Richard N. Longenecker. Grand Rapids: Eerdmans, 1997.
———. *Paul and the Gentiles: Remapping the Apostle's Convictional World.* Minneapolis: Fortress, 1997.
Downing, F. Gerald. *Has Christianity a Revelation?* London: SCM, 1964.
Driver, S. R. *A Critical and Exegetical Commentary on Deuteronomy.* 3rd ed. ICC. Edinburgh: T&T Clark, 1902.
Dungan, David L. *The Sayings of Jesus in the Churches of Paul.* Philadelphia: Fortress, 1971.
Dunn, James D. G. *Jesus and the Spirit: A Study of the Religious and Charismatic Experience of Jesus and the First Christians as Reflected in the New Testament.* Grand Rapids: Eerdmans, 1975.
———. *Jesus, Paul, and the Law: Studies in Mark and Galatians.* London: SPCK, 1990.

———. *Romans*. 2 vols. WBC 38. Dallas: Word, 1988.

Ehrensperger, Kathy. *Searching Paul: Conversations with the Jewish Apostle to the Nations*, WUNT 429. Tübingen: Mohr Siebeck, 2019.

Eidinow, Esther. "Oracles and Oracle-Sellers: An Ancient Market in Futures," Pages 55–95 in *Religion and Competition in Antiquity*. Edited by David Engels and Peter van Nuffelen. Collection Latomus 343. Brussels: Latomus, 2014.

———. *Oracles, Curses, and Risk Among the Ancient Greeks*. Oxford: Oxford University Press, 2007.

Ellis, E. Earle. *Paul's Use of the Old Testament*. Edinburgh: Oliver & Boyd, 1957.

———. *Prophecy and Hermeneutic in Early Christianity: New Testament Essays*. WUNT 18. Tübingen: Mohr Siebeck, 1978.

———. "Prophecy in the New Testament Church – and Today." 46–57 in *Prophetic Vocation in the New Testament and Today*. Edited by J. Panagopoulos. NovTSup 45. Leiden: Brill, 1977.

Engberg-Pedersen, Troels. "The Construction of Religious Experience in Paul." Pages 147–58 in *Experientia, Volume 1: Inquiry into Religious Experience in Early Judaism and Christianity*. Edited by Frances Flannery, Colleen Shantz, and Rodney A. Werline. SymS 40. Atlanta: SBL Press, 2008.

———. *Cosmology and Self in the Apostle Paul: The Material Spirit*. Oxford: Oxford University Press, 2010.

———. Foreword to *Paul and the Greco-Roman Philosophical Tradition*. Edited by Joseph R. Dodson and Andrew W. Pitts. LNTS 527. London: T&T Clark, 2017.

———. "The Past is a Foreign Country: On the Shape and Purposes of Comparison in New Testament Scholarship." Pages 41–61 in *The New Testament in Comparison: Validity, Method, and Purpose in Comparing Traditions*. Edited by John M. G. Barclay and Benjamin G. White. LNTS 600. London: T&T Clark, 2020.

———. *Paul and the Stoics*. Edinburgh: T&T Clark, 2000.

———, ed. *Paul Beyond the Judaism/Hellenism Divide*. Louisville: Westminster John Knox, 2001.

———, ed. *Paul in his Hellenistic Context*. Minneapolis: Fortress, 1995.

———. "Paul the Philosopher." In *The Oxford Handbook of Pauline Studies*. Edited by Matthew V. Novenson and R. Barry Matlock. Oxford: Oxford University Press, 2022.

Esler, Philip F. "Glossolalia and the Admission of Gentiles into the Early Christian Community." *BTB* 22 (1992): 136–42.

Eve, Eric. *Behind the Gospels: Understanding the Oral Tradition*. Minneapolis: Fortress, 2014.

Eyl, Jennifer. *Signs, Wonders, and Gifts: Divination in the Letters of Paul*. Oxford: Oxford University Press, 2019.

Fee, Gordon D. *The First Epistle to the Corinthians*. Rev. ed. NICNT. Grand Rapids: Eerdmans, 2014.

———. *God's Empowering Presence: The Holy Spirit in the Letters of Paul*. Peadbody, MA: Hendrickson, 1994.

Fishbane, Michael. "Through the Looking Glass: Reflections on Ezek 43:3, Num 12:8 and 1 Cor 13:8." *HAR* 10 (1986): 63–75.

Fitzmyer, Joseph A. *Romans: A New Translation with Introduction and Commentary*. AB 33. New York: Doubleday, 1993.

Flannery, Frances. *Dreamers, Scribes, and Priests: Jewish Dreams in the Hellenistic and Roman Eras*, JSJSup 90. Leiden: Brill, 2004.

———. "Dreams and Visions in Early Jewish and Early Christian Apocalypses and Apocalypticism." Pages 104–20 in *The Oxford Handbook of Apocalyptic Literature*. Edited by John J. Collins. Oxford: Oxford University Press, 2014.

Fletcher-Louis, Crispin. *All the Glory of Adam: Liturgical Anthropology in the Dead Sea Scrolls*. STDJ 42. Leiden: Brill, 2002.

Flood, Gavin. "Reflections on Tradition and Inquiry in the Study of Religion." *JAAR* 74 (2006): 47–58.
Flower, Michael Attyah. *The Seer in Ancient Greece*. Berkeley: University of California Press, 2008.
Fontenrose, Joseph. *The Delphic Oracle: Its Responses and Operations*. Berkeley: University of California Press, 1978.
———. *Didyma: Apollo's Oracle, Cult, and Companions*. Berkeley: University of California Press, 1988.
Forbes, Christopher. "Pauline Demonology and/or Cosmology? Principalities, Powers and the Elements of the World in their Hellenistic Context." *JSNT* 85 (2002): 51–73.
———. "Paul's Principalities and Powers: Demythologizing Apocalyptic?" *JSNT* 82 (2001): 61–88.
———. *Prophecy and Inspired Speech in Early Christianity and its Hellenistic Environment*. WUNT 2/75. Tübingen: Mohr Siebeck, 1995.
Foster, Paul. "Echoes without Resonance: Critiquing Certain Aspects of Recent Scholarly Trends in the Study of the Jewish Scriptures in the New Testament." *JSNT* 38 (2015): 96–111.
Fredriksen, Paula. "How Jewish is God? Divine Ethnicity in Paul's Theology." *JBL* 137 (2018): 193–212.
———. *Jesus of Nazareth, King of the Jews: A Jewish Life and the Emergence of Christianity*. New York: Knopf, 1999.
———. "Judaizing the Nations: The Ritual Demands of Paul's Gospel." *NTS* 56 (2010): 232–52.
———. "Paul and Augustine: Conversion Narratives, Orthodox Traditions, and the Retrospective Self." *JTS* 37 (1986): 3–34.
———. *Paul: The Pagans' Apostle*. New Haven: Yale University Press, 2017.
Fried, Lisbeth S. "Did Second Temple High Priests Possess the Urim and Thummim?" *JHebS* 7 (2007): 2–25.
Gamble, Harry. *Books and Readers in the Early Church: A History of Early Christian Texts*. New Haven: Yale University Press, 1995.
Garroway, Joshua D. *The Beginning of the Gospel: Paul, Philippi, and the Origins of Christianity*. Cham: Palgrave Macmillan, 2018.
———. "The Circumcision of Christ: Romans 15:7–13." *JSNT* 34 (2012): 303–13.
———. "Paul's Gentile Interlocutor in Romans 3:1–20." Pages 85–100 in *The So-Called Jew in Paul's Letter to the Romans*. Edited by Rafael Rodríguez and Matthew Thiessen. Minneapolis: Fortress, 2016.
———. *Paul's Gentile-Jews: Neither Jew nor Gentile, but Both*. New York: Palgrave Macmillan, 2012.
Gaston, Lloyd. "Angels and Gentiles in Early Judaism and in Paul." *SR* 11 (1982): 65–75.
Gathercole, Simon J. *Where is Boasting? Early Jewish Soteriology and Paul's Response in Romans 1–5*. Grand Rapids: Eerdmans, 2002.
Gaventa, Beverly Roberts. *From Darkness to Light: Aspects of Conversion in the New Testament*. OBT 20. Philadelphia: Fortress, 1986.
———. "On the Calling-Into-Being of Israel: Romans 9:6–29." Pages 255–70 in *Between Gospel and Election: Explorations in the Interpretation of Romans 9–11*. Edited by Florian Wilk and J. Ross Wagner. WUNT 257. Tübingen: Mohr Siebeck, 2010.
———. *Our Mother Saint Paul*. Louisville: Westminster John Knox, 2007.
Gerhardsson, Birger. *Memory and Manuscript: Oral Tradition and Written Transmission in Rabbinic Judaism and Early Christianity*. Translated by Eric J. Sharpe. ASNU 22. Lund: Gleerup, 1961.
Gill, David H. "Through a Glass Darkly: A Note on 1 Corinthians 13:12." *CBQ* 25 (1963): 427–29.

Gillespie, Thomas W. *The First Theologians: A Study in Early Christian Prophecy*. Grand Rapids: Eerdmans, 1994.
Gooder, Paula R. *Only the Third Heaven? 2 Corinthians 12:1–10 and Heavenly Ascent*. LNTS 313. London: T&T Clark, 2006.
Goulder, Michael. "Vision and Knowledge." *JSNT* 56 (1994): 53–71.
———. "Visions and Revelations of the Lord (2 Corinthians 12:1–10)." Pages 303–12 in *Paul and the Corinthians: Studies on a Community in Conflict, Essays in Honour of Margaret Thrall*. Edited by Trevor J. Burke and J. Keith Elliott. NovTSup 109. Leiden: Brill, 2003.
Grabbe, Lester L. *Priests, Prophets, Diviners, Sages: A Socio-Historical Study of Religious Specialists in Ancient Israel*. Valley Forge, PA: Trinity, 1995.
Graf, Fritz. *Apollo*. Abingdon: Routledge, 2009.
———. "Apollo, Possession, and Prophecy." Pages 587–605 in *Apolline Politics and Poetics: International Symposium*. Edited by Lucia Athanassaki, Richard P. Martin, and John F. Miller. Athens: European Cultural Centre of Delphi, 2009.
———. *Nordionische Kulte: Religionsgeschichtlich und Epigraphische Untersuchungen zu den Kulten von Chios, Erythrai, Klazomenai und Phokaia*. Rome: Schweizerisches Institut in Rom, 1985.
Gray, Rebecca. *Prophetic Figures in Late Second Temple Jewish Palestine: The Evidence from Josephus*. Oxford: Oxford University Press, 1993.
Green, Gene L. *The Letters to the Thessalonians*. PNTC. Grand Rapids, Eerdmans, 2002.
Grimes, Ronald L. "Ritual Criticism and Infelicitous Performances." Pages 191–209 in *Ritual Criticism: Case Studies in its Practice, Essays on its Theory*. Columbia: University of South Carolina Press, 1990.
Grudem, Wayne A. "1 Corinthians 14:20–25: Prophecy and Tongues as Signs of God's Attitude." *WTJ* 41 (1979): 381–96.
———. *The Gift of Prophecy in 1 Corinthians*. Lanham, MD: University Press of America, 1982. Repr. Eugene, OR: Wipf & Stock, 1999.
———. "A Response to Gerhard Dautzenberg on 1 Cor 12:10." *BZ* 22 (1978): 253–70.
Haacker, Klaus. "Exegetische Gesichtspunkte zum Thema Homosexualität." *TBei* 25 (1994): 173–80.
Hafemann, Scott. "Eschatology and Ethics: The Future of Israel and the Nations in Romans 15:1–13." *TynB* 51 (2000): 161–92.
Hallett, Judith P. "Female Homoeroticism and the Denial of Roman Reality in Latin Literature." Pages 255–73 in *Roman Sexualities*. Edited by Judith P. Hallett and Marilyn B. Skinner. Princeton: Princeton University Press, 1997.
Hamori, Esther J., and Jonathan Stökl, eds. *Perchance to Dream: Dream Divination in the Bible and the Ancient Near East*. ANEM 21. Atlanta: SBL Press, 2018.
Hamori, Esther J. *Women's Divination in Biblical Literature: Prophecy, Necromancy, and Other Arts of Knowledge*. AYBRL. New Haven: Yale University Press, 2015.
Hanges, James C. *Paul, Founder of Churches: A Study in Light of the Evidence for the Role of "Founder-Figures" in the Hellenistic-Roman Period*. WUNT 292. Tübingen: Mohr Siebeck, 2012.
Hankinson, R. J. "Stoicism and Medicine." Pages 295–309 in *The Cambridge Companion to the Stoics*. Edited by Brad Inwood. Cambridge: Cambridge University Press, 2003.
Hanson, A. T. *Jesus Christ in the Old Testament*. London: SPCK, 1965.
———. *Studies in Paul's Technique and Theology*. London: SPCK, 1974.
Hanson, John S. "Dreams and Visions in the Graeco-Roman World and Early Christianity." *ANRW* 23.1:1395–427. Part 2, *Principat*, 23.1. Edited by Wolfgang Haase. Berlin: de Gruyter, 1979.
Harnack, Adolf von. "The Old Testament in the Pauline Letters and in the Pauline Churches." Pages 27–49 in *Understanding Paul's Ethics: Twentieth Century Approaches*. Edited

by Brian S. Rosner. Translated by George S. Rosner and Brian S. Rosner. Grand Rapids: Eerdmans, 1995.

Harris, Murray J. *The Second Epistle to the Corinthians*. NIGTC. Grand Rapids: Eerdmans, 2005.

Harris, William V. *Dreams and Experience in Classical Antiquity*. Cambridge, MA: Harvard University Press, 2009.

Harrisson, Juliette. *Dreams and Dreaming in the Roman Empire: Cultural Memory and Imagination*. London: Bloomsbury, 2013.

Harvey, A. E. "The Use of Mystery Language in the Bible." *JTS* 31 (1980): 320–36.

Hayes, Christine. *What's Divine About Divine Law? Early Perspectives*. Princeton: Princeton University Press, 2015.

Hayes, Elizabeth R. "The Role of Visionary Experiences for Establishing Prophetic Authority in Isaiah, Jeremiah and Ezekiel: Same, Similar, or Different?" Pages 59–70 in *'I Lifted my Eyes and Saw': Reading Dream and Vision Reports in the Hebrew Bible*. Edited by Elizabeth R. Hayes and Lena-Sofia Tiemeyer. LHBOTS 584. London: T&T Clark, 2014.

Hays, Richard B. "Christ Prays the Psalms: Israel's Psalter as Matrix of Early Christology." Pages 101–18 in *The Conversion of the Imagination: Paul as Interpreter of Israel's Scripture*. Grand Rapids: Eerdmans, 2005.

———. *Echoes of Scripture in the Letters of Paul*. New Haven: Yale University Press, 1989.

———. *The Faith of Jesus Christ: The Narrative Substructure of Galatians 3:1–4:11*. 2nd ed. Grand Rapids: Eerdmans, 2002.

Heininger, Bernhard. *Paulus als Visionär: eine religionsgeschichtliche Studie*. Freiburg: Herder, 1996.

Hengel, Martin. *Judaism and Hellenism: Studies in their Encounter in Palestine during the Early Hellenistic Period*. Translated by John Bowden. London: SCM, 1974.

———. "Paul in Arabia." *BBR* 12 (2002): 47–66.

———. *The Zealots*. Translated by David Smith. Edinburgh: T&T Clark, 1989.

Heschel, Abraham J. *The Prophets*. New York: Harper & Row, 1962.

Hill, David. "Christian Prophets as Teachers or Instructors in the Church." Pages 108–30 in *Prophetic Vocation in the New Testament and Today*. Edited by J. Panagopoulos. NovTSup 45. Leiden: Brill, 1977.

———. *New Testament Prophecy*. London: Marshall, Morgan & Scott, 1979.

Himmelfarb, Martha. *Ascent to Heaven in Jewish and Christian Apocalypses*. Oxford: Oxford University Press, 1993.

———. *Tours of Hell: An Apocalyptic Form in Jewish and Christian Literature*. Philadelphia: University of Pennsylvania Press, 1983.

Holtz, Traugott. "Paul and the Oral Gospel Tradition." Pages 383–85 in *Jesus and the Oral Gospel Tradition*. Edited by Henry Wansbrough. JSNTSup 64. Sheffield: Sheffield Academic, 1991.

Horgan, Maurya P. *Pesharim: Qumran Interpretations of Biblical Books*. Washington DC: Catholic Biblical Association of America, 1979.

Horky, Phillip Sidney. "Cosmic Spiritualism among the Pythagoreans, Stoics, Jews and Early Christians." Pages 270–94 in *Cosmos in the Ancient World*. Edited by Phillip Sidney Horky. Cambridge: Cambridge University Press, 2019.

Horowitz, Wayne, and Victor Avigdor Hurowitz. "Urim and Thummim in Light of a Psephomancy Ritual from Assur (LKA 137)." *JNES* 21 (1992): 95–115.

Horsley, G. H. R. "χρηματισμός." *NewDocs* 4 (1987): 176.

———. "Answer from an Oracle." *NewDocs* 2 (1982): 37–44.

Horst, Pieter W. van der. "Sortes: Sacred Books as Instant Oracles in Late Antiquity." Pages 159–90 in *Japheth in the Tents of Shem: Studies on Jewish Hellenism in Antiquity*. CBET 32. Leuven: Peeters, 2002.

Hunt, Allen R. *The Inspired Body: Paul, the Corinthians, and Divine Inspiration.* Macon, GA: Mercer University Press, 1996.
Hurd, John C. *The Origin of 1 Corinthians.* London: SPCK, 1965.
———. "Paul Ahead of His Time: 1 Thess 2:13–16." Pages 21–36 in *Paul and the Gospels.* Vol 1 of *Anti-Judaism in Early Christianity.* Edited by Peter Richardson. SCJ 2. Waterloo, ON: Wilfred Laurier University Press, 1986.
Hurowitz, Victor Avigdor. "True Light on the Urim and Thummim." *JQR* 88 (1998): 263–74.
Hurtado, Larry W. *Destroyer of the Gods: Early Christian Distinctiveness in the Roman World.* Waco, TX: Baylor University Press, 2016.
———. *Lord Jesus Christ: Devotion to Jesus in Earliest Christianity.* Grand Rapids: Eerdmans, 2003.
———. "Religious Experience and Religious Innovation in the New Testament." Pages 179–204 in *How on Earth Did Jesus Become a God? Historical Questions About Earliest Devotion to Jesus.* Grand Rapids: Eerdmans, 2005.
———. "Revelatory Experiences and Religious Innovation in Earliest Christianity." *ExpTim* 125 (2014): 469–82.
Iles Johnston, Sarah. *Ancient Greek Divination.* Oxford: Wiley-Blackwell, 2008.
———. "Delphi and the Dead." Pages 283–306 in *Mantikē: Studies in Ancient Divination.* Edited by Sarah Iles Johnston and Peter T. Struck. RGRW 155. Leiden: Brill, 2005.
———. *Restless Dead: Encounters Between the Living and the Dead in Ancient Greece.* Berkeley: University of California Press, 1999.
Instone Brewer, David. "1 Corinthians 9:9–11: A Literal Interpretation of 'Do Not Muzzle the Ox'." *NTS* 38 (1992): 554–65.
Isaacs, Marie E. *The Concept of Spirit: A Study of Pneuma in Hellenistic Judaism and its Bearing on the New Testament.* HM 1. London: Heythrop College, 1976.
Jacobi, Christine. *Jesusüberlieferung bei Paulus? Analogien zwischen den echten Paulusbriefen und den synoptischen Evangelien.* BZNW 213. Berlin: de Gruyter, 2015.
Jassen, Alex P. *Mediating the Divine: Prophecy and Revelation in the Dead Sea Scrolls and Second Temple Judaism.* STDJ 68. Leiden: Brill, 2007.
Jeffers, Ann. *Magic and Divination in Ancient Palestine and Syria.* SHCANE 8. Leiden: Brill, 1996.
Jervell, Jacob. "The Signs of an Apostle: Paul's Miracles." Pages 77–95 in *The Unknown Paul: Essays on Luke-Acts and Early Christian History.* Minneapolis: Augsburg, 1984.
Jervis, L. Ann. "Promise and Purpose in Romans 9:1–13: Toward Understanding Paul's View of Time." Pages 1–26 in *God and Israel: Providence and Purpose in Romans 9–11.* Edited by Todd D. Still. Waco, TX: Baylor University Press, 2017.
Jewett, Robert. *Paul's Anthropological Terms: A Study of their Use in Conflict Settings.* AGJU 10. Leiden: Brill, 1971.
———. "The Question of the 'Apportioned Spirit' in Paul's Letters: Romans as a Case Study." Pages 193–206 in *The Holy Spirit and Christian Origins: Essays in Honor of James D. G. Dunn.* Edited by Graham N. Stanton, Bruce W. Longenecker and Stephen C. Barton. Grand Rapids: Eerdmans, 2004.
———. *Romans.* Hermeneia. Minneapolis: Fortress, 2007.
———. *The Thessalonian Correspondence: Pauline Rhetoric and Millenarian Piety.* Philadelphia: Fortress, 1986.
Jipp, Joshua. *Divine Visitations and Hospitality to Strangers in Luke-Acts: An Interpretation of the Malta Episode in Acts 28:1–10.* NovTSup 153. Leiden: Brill, 2013.
Johanson, B. C. "Tongues, A Sign for Unbelievers? A Structural and Exegetical Study of 1 Corinthians 14:20–25." *NTS* 25 (1979): 180–203.
Johnson Hodge, Caroline. *If Sons, Then Heirs: A Study of Kinship and Ethnicity in the Letters of Paul.* Oxford: Oxford University Press, 2007.

Johnson, Monte Ransome. "Aristotle on Kosmos and Kosmoi." Pages 74–107 in *Cosmos in the Ancient World*. Edited by Phillip Sidney Horky. Cambridge: Cambridge University Press, 2019.
Johnson, Sherman E. "Notes and Comments (1 Thess 2:16)." *AThR* 23 (1941): 173–76.
Johnston, Christopher N. *St Paul and His Mission to the Roman Empire*. London: A&C Black, 1911.
Jones, Christopher P. *New Heroes in Antiquity: From Achilles to Antinoos*. Cambridge, MA: Harvard University Press, 2010.
———. "Towards a Chronology of Plutarch's Works." *JRS* 56 (1966): 61–74.
Judge, Edwin. "St Paul and Classical Society." Pages 73–97 in *Social Distinctives of the Christians in the First Century: Pivotal Essays by E. A. Judge*. Edited by David M. Scholer. Peabody, MA: Hendrickson, 2008.
———. "St Paul and Socrates." Pages 670–83 in *The First Christians in the Roman World: Augustan and New Testament Essays*. Edited by James R. Harrison. WUNT 229. Tübingen: Mohr Siebeck, 2008.
Kamen, Deborah and Sarah Levin-Richardson. "Lusty Ladies in the Roman Imaginary." Pages 231–52 in *Ancient Sex: New Essays*. Edited by Ruby Blondell and Kirk Ormand. Columbus: Ohio State University Press, 2015.
Keck, Leander E. "Christology, Soteriology, and the Praise of God (Romans 15:7–13)." Pages 85–96 in *The Conversation Continues: Studies in Paul and John in Honor of J. Louis Martyn*. Edited by Robert T. Fortna and Beverly Roberts Gaventa. Nashville: Abingdon, 1990.
Keener, Craig S. *Acts: An Exegetical Commentary*. 4 vols. Grand Rapids: Baker Academic, 2012–2015.
———. *The Mind of the Spirit: Paul's Approach to Transformed Thinking*. Grand Rapids: Baker Academic, 2016.
Kertelge, Karl. "Apokalypsis Jesou Christou (Gal 1:12)." Pages 46–61 in *Grundthemen paulinischer Theologie*. Freiburg: Herder, 1991.
Kessels, A. H. M. "Ancient Systems of Dream-Classification." *Mnemosyne* 22 (1969): 389–424.
Kidner, Derek. "Isaiah." Pages 588–625 in *The New Bible Commentary, Revised*. Edited by Donald Guthrie and J. A. Motyer. London: InterVarsity, 1970.
Kim, Seyoon. "The Jesus Tradition in 1 Thess 4:13–5:11." *NTS* 48 (2002): 225–42.
———. *The Origin of Paul's Gospel*. WUNT 2/4. Tübingen: Mohr Siebeck, 1984.
———. *Paul and the New Perspective: Second Thoughts on the Origin of Paul's Gospel*. Grand Rapids: Eerdmans, 2002.
Kitz, Anne Marie. "The Plural Form of 'Ûrîm and Tummîm." *JBL* 116 (1997): 401–10.
———. "Prophecy as Divination." *CBQ* 65 (2003): 27–33.
Klauck, Hans-Josef. "With Paul through Heaven and Hell: Two Apocryphal Apocalypses." *BR* 52 (2007): 57–72.
Knox, Wilfred L. *St Paul and the Church of the Gentiles*. Cambridge: Cambridge University Press, 1939.
Koch, Dietrich-Alex. *Die Schrift als Zeuge des Evangeliums: Untersuchungen zur Verwendung und zum Verständnis der Schrift bei Paulus*. BHT 69. Tübingen: Mohr Siebeck, 1986.
Kooten, George H. van. "Ancestral, Oracular and Prophetic Authority: 'Scriptural Authority' According to Paul and Philo." Pages 267–308 in *Authoritative Scriptures in Ancient Judaism*. Edited by Mladen Popović. JSJSup 141. Leiden: Brill, 2010.
———. *Cosmic Christology in Paul and the Pauline School: Colossians and Ephesians in the Context of Graeco-Roman Cosmology, with a New Synopsis of the Greek Texts*. WUNT 2/171. Tübingen: Mohr Siebeck, 2003.
———. *Paul's Anthropology in Context: The Image of God, Assimilation to God, and Tripartite Man in Ancient Judaism, Ancient Philosophy, and Early Christianity*. WUNT 232. Tübingen: Mohr Siebeck, 2008.

———. "'Wrath Will Drip in the Plains of Macedonia': Expectations of Nero's Return in the Egyptian Sibylline Oracles (Book 5), 2 Thessalonians, and Ancient Historical Writings." Pages 177–215 in *The Wisdom of Egypt: Jewish, Early Christian, and Gnostic Essays in Honour of Gerard P. Luttikhuizen*. Edited by Anthony Hilhorst and George H. van Kooten. AGJU 59. Leiden: Brill, 2005.

Kovaks, Judith. "The Archons, the Spirit and the Death of Christ: Do We Need the Hypothesis of Gnostic Opponents to Explain 1 Cor 2:6–16?" Pages 217–36 in *Apocalyptic and the New Testament: Essays in Honor of J. Louis Martyn*. Edited by Joel Marcus and Marion L. Soards. JSNTSup 24. Sheffield: Sheffield Academic, 1989.

Lampe, Peter. "Die dämonologischen Implikationen von 1 Korinther 8 und 10 vor dem Hintergrund paganer Zeugnisse." Pages 584–99 in *Die Dämonen: Die Dämonologie der israelitisch-jüdischen und frühchristlichen Literatur im Kontext ihrer Umwelt*. Edited by Armin Lange, Hermann Lichtenberger, and K. F. Diethard Römheld. Tübingen: Mohr Siebeck, 2003.

Lane Fox, Robin, *Pagans and Christians*. New York: Knopf, 1986.

Lang, T. J. *Mystery and the Making of a Christian Historical Consciousness: From Paul to the Second Century*. BZNW 219. Berlin: de Gruyter, 2015.

———. "Trouble with Insiders: The Social Profile of the ἄπιστοι in Paul's Corinthian Correspondence." *JBL* 137 (2018): 981–1001.

Lange, Armin. "Interpretation als Offenbarung: zum Verhältnis von Schriftauslegung und Offenbarung." Pages 17–33 in *Wisdom and Apocalypticism in the Dead Sea Scrolls and in the Biblical Tradition*. Edited by Florentino García Martínez. BETL 168. Leuven: Peeters, 2003.

Lanier, David E. "With Stammering Lips and Another Tongue: 1 Cor 14:20–22 and Isa 28:11–12." *CTR* 5 (1991): 259–86.

Lee, Michelle V. *Paul, the Stoics, and the Body of Christ*. SNTSMS 137. Cambridge, Cambridge University Press, 2006.

Levene, David S. *Religion in Livy*. Mnemosyne 127. Leiden: Brill, 1993.

Levison, John R. *The Spirit in First-Century Judaism*. AGJU 29. Leiden: Brill, 1997.

Lightfoot, J. B. *Notes on the Epistles of St Paul from Unpublished Commentaries*. London: Macmillan, 1895.

———. *Saint Paul's Epistle to the Galatians*. 10th ed. London: Macmillan, 1890.

Lightfoot, Jane L. *The Sibylline Oracles: With Introduction, Translation, and Commentary on the First and Second Books*. Oxford: Oxford University Press, 2007.

Lim, Timothy H. *The Earliest Commentary on the Prophecy of Habakkuk*. Oxford: Oxford University Press, 2020.

———. *The Formation of the Jewish Canon*. New Haven: Yale University Press, 2013.

———. *Holy Scripture in the Qumran Commentaries and Pauline Letters*. Oxford: Oxford University Press, 1997.

Lincicum, David. "How Did Paul Read Scripture?" Pages 225–38 in *The New Cambridge Companion to St Paul*. Edited by Bruce W. Longenecker. Cambridge: Cambridge University Press, 2020.

Lincoln, Andrew T. "'Paul the Visionary': The Setting and Significance of the Rapture to Paradise in 2 Corinthians 12:1–10." *NTS* 25 (1979): 204–20.

Lindblom, Johannes. *Gesichte und Offenbarungen: Vorstellungen von göttlichen Weisungen und übernatürlichen Erscheinungen im ältesten Christentum*. Lund: Gleerup, 1968.

———. "Lot-Casting in the Old Testament." *VT* 12 (1962): 164–78.

Linderski, Jerzy. "Pax deorum (deum)." *BNP* 10:659.

———. "Quindecimviri sacris faciundis." *BNP* 11:346.

Linebaugh, Jonathan A. "Announcing the Human: Rethinking the Relationship Between Wisdom of Solomon 13–15 and Romans 1:18–2:11." *NTS* 57 (2011): 214–37.

———. *God, Grace, and Righteousness in Wisdom of Solomon and Paul's Letter to the Romans: Texts in Conversation.* NovTSup 152. Leiden: Brill, 2013.
———. "Not the End: The History and Hope of the Unfailing Word in Romans 9–11." Pages 141–64 in *God and Israel: Providence and Purpose in Romans 9–11.* Edited by Todd D. Still. Waco, TX: Baylor University Press, 2017.
Litwa, M. David. *Iesus Deus: The Early Christian Depiction of Jesus as a Mediterranean God.* Minneapolis: Fortress, 2014.
———. *Posthuman Transformation in Ancient Mediterranean Thought: Becoming Angels and Demons.* Cambridge: Cambridge University Press, 2021.
———. *We Are Being Transformed: Deification in Paul's Soteriology.* BZNW 187. Berlin: de Gruyter, 2012.
Lohse, Eduard. "'Kümmert sich Gott etwa um die Ochsen?' Zu 1 Kor 9:9." *ZNW* 88 (1997): 314–15.
Long, A. A. "Astrology: Arguments Pro and Contra." Pages 128–53 in *From Epicurus to Epictetus: Studies in Hellenistic and Roman Philosophy.* Oxford: Oxford University Press, 2006.
Long, Burke O. "Prophetic Call Traditions and Reports of Visions." *ZAW* 84 (1972): 494–500.
Long, Frederick J. "'The God of This Age' (2 Cor 4:4) and Paul's Empire-Resisting Gospel at Corinth." Pages 219–69 in *The First Urban Churches 2: Roman Corinth.* Edited by James R. Harrison and L. L. Welborn. WGRWSup 8. Atlanta: SBL Press, 2016.
Longenecker, Richard N. *Biblical Exegesis in the Apostolic Period.* Grand Rapids: Eerdmans, 1975.
———. *Galatians.* WBC 41. Dallas: Word, 1990.
Lührmann, Dieter. *Das Offenbarungsverständnis bei Paulus und in paulinischen Gemeinden.* WMANT 16. Neukirchen-Vluyn: Neukirchener Verlag, 1965.
Luz, Ulrich. "Stages of Early Christian Prophetism." Pages 57–75 in *Prophets and Prophecy in Jewish and Early Christian Literature.* Edited by Joseph Verheyden, Korinna Zamfir, and Tobias Nicklas. WUNT 2/286. Tübingen: Mohr Siebeck, 2010.
MacBain, Bruce. *Prodigy and Expiation: A Study in Religion and Politics in Republican Rome.* Collection Latomus 177. Brussels: Latomus, 1982.
Maier, Harry O. *New Testament Christianity in the Roman World.* Oxford: Oxford University Press, 2018.
Majercik, Ruth. *The Chaldean Oracles: Text, Translation, and Commentary.* Leiden: Brill, 1989.
Malherbe, Abraham J. *The Letters to the Thessalonians.* AB 32B. New York: Doubleday, 2000.
———. *Paul and the Popular Philosophers.* Minneapolis: Fortress, 1989.
Manetti, Giovanni. *Theories of the Sign in Classical Antiquity.* Translated by Christine Richardson. Bloomington: Indiana University Press, 1993.
Manson, T. W. "The Argument from Prophecy." *JTS* 46 (1945): 129–36.
Marshall, Jill E. *Women Praying and Prophesying in Corinth: Gender and Inspired Speech in First Corinthians.* WUNT 2/448. Tübingen: Mohr Siebeck, 2017.
Martin, Dale B. *Biblical Truths: The Meaning of Scripture in the Twenty-First Century.* New Haven: Yale University Press, 2017.
———. *The Corinthian Body.* New Haven: Yale University Press, 1995.
———. "Tongues of Angels and Other Status Indicators." *JAAR* 59 (1991): 547–89.
Martin, Troy W. "Paul's Pneumatological Statements and Ancient Medical Texts." Pages 105–26 in *The New Testament and Early Christian Literature in Greco-Roman Context: Studies in Honor of David E. Aune.* Edited by John Fotopoulos. NovTSup 122. Leiden: Brill, 2006.
Martyn, J. Louis. "Apocalyptic Antinomies in Paul's Letter to the Galatians." *NTS* 31 (1985): 410–24.
———. *Galatians.* AB 33A. New Haven: Yale University Press, 1997.

Matlock, R. Barry. *Unveiling the Apocalyptic Paul: Paul's Interpreters and the Rhetoric of Criticism.* JSNTSup 127. Sheffield: Sheffield Academic, 1996.
Maurizio, Lisa. "Anthropology and Spirit Possession: A Reconsideration of the Pythia's Role at Delphi." *JHS* 115 (1995): 69–86.
Mazurek, Tadeusz. "The decemviri sacris faciundis: supplication and prediction." Pages 151–68 in *Augusto augurio: Rerum humanarum et divinarum commentationes in honorem Jerzy Linderski.* Edited by C. F. Konrad. Stuttgart: Steiner, 2004.
Merklein, Helmut. "Der Theologe als Prophet: Zur Funktion prophetischen Redens im theologischen Diskurs des Paulus." Pages 377–404 in *Studien zu Jesus und Paulus II.* WUNT 105. Tübingen: Mohr Siebeck, 1998.
Metzger, Bruce M. *A Textual Commentary on the Greek New Testament,* 2nd ed. Stuttgart: Deutsche Bibelgesellschaft, 1994.
McCasland, S. Vernon. "Portents in Josephus and in the Gospels." *JBL* 51 (1932): 323–35.
———. "Signs and Wonders." *JBL* 76 (1957): 149–52.
McLean, B. Hudson. *The Cursed Christ: Mediterranean Expulsion Rituals and Pauline Soteriology.* JSNTSup 126. Sheffield: Sheffield Academic, 1996.
Michel, Otto. *Paulus und seine Bibel.* Gütersloh: Bertelsmann, 1929.
Miller, Gene. ΑΡΧΟΝΤΩΝ ΤΟΥ ΑΙΩΝΟΣ ΤΟΥΤΟΥ: A New Look at 1 Corinthians 2:6–8." *JBL* 91 (1972): 522–28.
Miller, James. "The Practices of Romans 1:26: Homosexual or Heterosexual?" *NovT* 37 (1995): 1–11.
Mininger, Marcus A. *Uncovering the Theme of Revelation in Romans 1:16–3:26.* WUNT 2/445. Tübingen: Mohr Siebeck, 2017.
Mitchell, Margaret M. "Concerning περὶ δέ in 1 Corinthians." *NovT* 31 (1989): 229–56.
———. *Paul and the Rhetoric of Reconciliation: An Exegetical Investigation of the Language and Composition of 1 Corinthians.* Louisville: Westminster John Knox, 1992.
Moody, R. M. "The Habakkuk Quotation in Romans 1:17." *ExpTim* 92 (1981): 204–8.
Morray-Jones, Christopher R. A. "Paradise Revisited (2 Cor 12:1–12): The Jewish Mystical Background of Paul's Apostolate: Part 2: Paul's Heavenly Ascent and its Significance." *HTR* 86 (1993): 265–92.
Morris, Leon. "The Meaning of ἱλαστήριον in Romans 3:25." *NTS* 2 (1955): 33–43.
———. "The Use of ἱλάσκεσθαι etc. in Biblical Greek." *ExpTim* 62 (1951): 227–33.
Mroczek, Eva. *The Literary Imagination in Jewish Antiquity.* Oxford: Oxford University Press, 2016.
Muir, Steven C. "Accessing Divine Power and Status." Pages 38–54 in *Early Christian Ritual Life.* Edited by Richard E. DeMaris, Jason T. Lamoreaux, and Steven C. Muir. Abingdon: Routledge, 2018.
Müller, Ulrich B. *Prophetie und Predigt im Neuen Testament: Formgeschichtliche Untersuchungen zur urchristlichen Prophetie.* SNT 10. Mohn: Gütersloh, 1975.
Munck, Johannes. *Paul and the Salvation of Mankind.* London: SCM, 1959.
Murphy-O'Connor, Jerome. "Paul in Arabia." *CBQ* 55 (1993): 732–37.
Myers, Jacob and Edwin Freed. "Is Paul Also Among the Prophets?" *Interpretation* 20 (1966): 40–53.
Najman, Hindy. "The Inheritance of Prophecy in Apocalypse." Pages 36–51 in *The Oxford Handbook of Apocalyptic Literature.* Edited by John J. Collins. Oxford: Oxford University Press, 2014.
Nagel, Peter. "1 Corinthians 14:21: Paul's Reflection on ΓΛΩΣΣΑ." *JECH* 3 (2013): 33–49.
Nanos, Mark D. "'The Gifts and the Calling of God Are Irrevocable' (Romans 11:29): If So, How Can Paul Declare That 'Not All Israelites Truly Belong to Israel' (9:6)?" *SCJR* 11 (2016): 1–17.

———, and Magnus Zetterholm, eds. *Paul Within Judaism: Restoring the First-Century Context to the Apostle*. Minneapolis: Fortress, 2015.
Nasrallah, Laura Salah. *An Ecstasy of Folly: Prophecy and Authority in Early Christianity*. HTS 52. Cambridge, MA: Harvard University Press, 2003.
Naveros Córdova, Nélida. *To Live in the Spirit: Paul and the Spirit of God*. Minneapolis: Fortress, 2018.
Neirynck, Frans. "Paul and the Sayings of Jesus." Pages 265–321 in *L'apôtre Paul: personalité, style et conception du ministère*. Edited by A. Vanhoye. Leuven: Leuven University Press, 1986.
Neutel, Karin B. "Circumcision Gone Wrong: Paul's Message as a Case of Ritual Disruption." *Neot* 50 (2016): 373–96.
Nicklas, Tobias. "Paulus – der Apostel als Prophet." Pages 77–104 in *Prophets and Prophecy in Jewish and Early Christian Literature*. Edited by Joseph Verheyden, Korinna Zamfir, and Tobias Nicklas. WUNT 2/286. Tübingen: Mohr Siebeck, 2010.
Nissinen, Martti. *Ancient Prophecy: Near Eastern, Biblical, and Greek Perspectives*. Oxford: Oxford University Press, 2017.
———. "The Socio-Religious Role of the Neo-Assyrian Prophets." Pages 103–26 in *Prophetic Divination: Essays in Ancient Near Eastern Prophecy*. BZAW 494. Berlin: de Gruyter, 2019.
Noack, Bent. "Current and Backwater in the Epistle to the Romans." *ST* 19 (1965): 155–66
Nock, Authur Darby. "Deification and Julian." Pages 833–46 in vol. 2 of *Essays on Religion and the Ancient World*. Edited by Zeph Stewart. Oxford: Clarendon, 1972.
Nongbri, Brent. *Before Religion: A History of a Modern Concept*. New Haven: Yale University Press, 2013.
North, John. "Diviners and Divination at Rome." Pages 51–71 in *Pagan Priests: Religion and Power in the Ancient World*. Edited by Mary Beard and John North. Ithaca, NY: Cornell University Press, 1990.
Novenson, Matthew V. *Christ Among the Messiahs: Christ Language in Paul and Messiah Language in Ancient Judaism*. Oxford: Oxford University Press, 2012.
———. "Did Paul Abandon either Judaism or Monotheism?" Pages 239–59 in *The New Cambridge Companion to St Paul*. Edited by Bruce W. Longenecker. Cambridge: Cambridge University Press, 2020.
———. "The Jewish Messiahs, the Pauline Christ, and the Gentile Question." *JBL* 128 (2009): 357–73.
———. "Messiahs and their Messengers." *STK* 95 (2019): 3–16.
———. "The Self-Styled Jew of Romans 2 and the Actual Jew of Romans 9–11." Pages 133–62 in *The So-Called Jew in Paul's Letter to the Romans*. Edited by Rafael Rodríguez and Matthew Thiessen. Minneapolis: Fortress, 2016.
O'Brien Wicker, Kathleen. "De defectu oraculorum (Moralia 409E–438E)." Pages 131–80 in *Plutarch's Theological Writings and Early Christian Literature*. Edited by Hans Dieter Betz. SCHNT. Leiden: Brill, 1975.
Obeng, E. A. "Abba, Father: The Prayer of the Sons of God." *ExpTim* 99 (1988): 363–66.
Oepke, Albrecht. "ἀποκαλύπτω, ἀποκάλυψις." *TDNT* 3:563–92.
Ogden, Daniel. *Magic, Witchcraft, and Ghosts in the Greek and Roman Worlds: A Sourcebook*. Oxford: Oxford University Press, 2002.
Oppenheim, A. Leo. "The Interpretation of Dreams in the Ancient Near East, with a Translation of an Assyrian Dream-Book." *TAPS* 46 (1956): 179–373.
Opsomer, Jan. "Plutarch and the Stoics." Pages 88–103 in *A Companion to Plutarch*. Edited by Mark Beck. Oxford: Blackwell, 2014.
Pahl, Michael W. *Discerning the 'Word of the Lord': The Word of the Lord in 1 Thessalonians 4:15*. LNTS 389. London: T&T Clark, 2009.

Paige, Terence. "Who Believes in 'Spirit'? Πνεῦμα in Pagan Usage and Implications for the Gentile Christian Mission." *HTR* 95 (2002): 426–33.
Pannenberg, Wolfhart. "Introduction." Pages 3–21 in *Revelation as History*. Edited by Wolfhart Pannenberg. Translated by David Granskou and Edward Quinn. London: Sheed & Ward, 1969.
Parke, H. W. *Sibyls and Sibylline Prophecy in Classical Antiquity*. London: Routledge, 1988.
———, and D. E. W. Wormell. *The Delphic Oracle*. 2 vols. Oxford: Blackwell, 1956.
Parker, Robert. "Divination, Greek." *OCD*: 469–70.
———. "Seeking Advice from Zeus at Dodona." *Greece & Rome* 63 (2016): 69–90.
Pearson, Birger. "1 Thessalonians 2:13–16: A Deutero-Pauline Interpolation." *HTR* 64 (1971): 79–94.
Penniman, John David. *Raised on Christian Milk: Food and the Formation of the Soul in Early Christianity*. Synkrisis. New Haven: Yale University Press, 2017.
Petridou, Georgia. *Divine Epiphany in Greek Literature and Culture*. Oxford: Oxford University Press, 2015.
Pfeffer, Friedrich. *Studien zur Mantik in der Philosophie der Antike*. Meisenheim am Glan: Hain, 1976.
Pfister, F. "Epiphanie." *PWSup* 4:277–323.
Poirier, John C. *The Tongues of Angels: The Concept of Angelic Languages in Classical Jewish and Christian Texts*. WUNT 2/287. Tübingen: Mohr Siebeck, 2010.
Popović, Mladen. "Reading the Human Body and Writing in Code: Physiognomic Divination and Astrology in the Dead Sea Scrolls." Pages 271–84 in *Flores Florentino: Dead Sea Scrolls and Other Early Jewish Studies in Honour of Florentino García Martínez*. Edited by Anthony Hilhorst, Émile Puech, and Eibert Tigchelaar. JSJSup 122. Leiden: Brill, 2007.
Porter, Stanley E. "Paul and His Use of Scripture: Further Considerations," Pages 7–30 in *Paul and Scripture*. Edited by Stanley E. Porter and Christopher D. Land. Pauline Studies 10. Leiden: Brill, 2019.
———. *When Paul Met Jesus: How an Idea Got Lost in History*. Cambridge: Cambridge University Press, 2016.
———, and Christopher D. Stanley, eds. *As It Is Written: Studying Paul's Use of Scripture*. SymS 50. Atlanta: SBL Press, 2008.
Rabens, Volker. *The Holy Spirit and Ethics in Paul: Transformation and Empowering for Religious-Ethical Life*. 2nd rev. ed. Minneapolis: Fortress, 2014.
Reinhardt, Karl. *Poseidonios*. Munich: Beck, 1921.
Reitzenstein, Richard. *Hellenistic Mystery-Religions: Their Basic Ideas and Significance*. Translated by John E. Steely. Pittsburgh: Pickwick, 1978.
Renberg, Gil H. "'Commanded by the Gods': An Epigraphical Study of Dreams and Visions in Greek and Roman Religious Life." PhD diss., Duke University, 2003.
———. "The Role of Dream-Interpreters in Greek and Roman Religion." Pages 233–62 in *Artemidor von Daldis und die antike Traumdeutung: Texte – Kontexte – Lektüren*. Edited by Gregor Weber. Colloquia Augustana 33. Berlin: de Gruyter, 2015.
———. *Where Dreams May Come: Incubation Sanctuaries in the Greco-Roman World*. 2 vols. RGRW 184. Leiden: Brill, 2017.
Rengstorf, K. H. "σημεῖον κτλ." *TDNT* 7:200–26.
———. "τέρας." *TDNT* 8:113–26.
Requena Jiménez, Miguel. "Prodigies in Republican Rome: The Absence of God." *Klio* 100 (2018): 480–500.
Roberts, P. "A Sign – Christian or Pagan?" *ExpTim* 90 (1979): 199–203.
Robertson, Archibald and Alfred Plummer. *A Critical and Exegetical Commentary on the First Epistle of St Paul to the Corinthians*. 2nd ed. ICC. Edinburgh: T&T Clark, 1914.

Robertson, Paul M. "De-Spiritualizing 'Pneuma': Modernity, Religion, and Anachronism in the Study of Paul." *MTSR* 26 (2014): 365–83.
Rodríguez, Rafael. *If You Call Yourself a Jew: Reappraising Paul's Letter to the Romans*. Eugene, OR: Wipf & Stock, 2014.
———, and Matthew Thiessen, eds. *The So-Called Jew in Paul's Letter to the Romans*. Minneapolis: Fortress, 2016.
Rollens, Sarah E. "The God Came to Me in a Dream: Epiphanies in Voluntary Associations as a Context for Paul's Vision of Christ." *HTR* 111 (2018): 41–65.
Roukema, Riemer. "Paul's Rapture to Paradise in Early Christian Literature." Pages 267–83 in *The Wisdom of Egypt: Jewish, Early Christian, and Gnostic Essays in Honour of Gerard P. Luttikhuizen*. Edited by Anthony Hilhorst and George H. van Kooten. AGJU 59. Leiden: Brill, 2005.
Rowland, Christopher. *The Open Heaven: A Study of Apocalyptic in Judaism and Early Christianity*. London: SPCK, 1982.
———. "Paul as an Apocalyptist." Pages 131–53 in *The Jewish Apocalyptic Tradition and the Shaping of New Testament Thought*. Edited by Benjamin E. Reynolds and Loren T. Stuckenbruck. Minneapolis: Fortress, 2017.
Sambursky, Samuel. *Physics of the Stoics*. London: Routledge & Kegan Paul, 1959.
Sanders, E. P. *Paul: The Apostle's Life, Letters, and Thought*. Minneapolis: Fortress, 2015.
———. *Paul, the Law, and the Jewish People*. Philadelphia: Fortress, 1983.
Sandnes, Karl Olav. *Paul – One of the Prophets? A Contribution to the Apostle's Self-Understanding*. WUNT 2/43. Tübingen: Mohr Siebeck, 1991.
Santangelo, Federico. *Divination, Prediction and the End of the Roman Republic*. Cambridge: Cambridge University Press, 2013.
———. "Pax Deorum and Pontiffs." Pages 161–86 in *Priests and State in the Roman World*. Edited by James H. Richardson and Federico Santangelo. Stuttgart: Steiner, 2011.
———. Review of *At the Temple Gates*, by Heidi Wendt. *HR* 58 (2019): 352–53.
Satlow, Michael L. "Disappearing Categories: Using Categories in the Study of Religion." *MTSR* 17 (2005): 287–98.
———. *How the Bible Became Holy*. New Haven: Yale University Press, 2014.
Satterfield, Susan. "Prodigies, the Pax Deum and the Ira Deum." *CJ* 110 (2015): 431–45.
Schäfer, Peter. "New Testament and Hekhalot Literature: The Journey into Heaven in Paul and Merkavah Mysticism." *JJS* 35 (1984): 19–35.
Schlatter, Adolf. *Paulus: der Bote Jesu: eine Deutung seiner Briefe an die Korinther*. Stuttgart: Calwer, 1934.
Schmidt, Francis. "Signes et prodiges chez Flavius Josèphe et Tacite (*Guerre des juifs* 6.288–315; *Histoires* 5.13)." Pages 253–89 in *La Raison des signes: présages, rites, destin dans les sociétés de la Méditerranée ancienne*. Edited by Stella Georgoudi, Renée Koch Piettre, and Francis Schmidt. RGRW 174. Leiden: Brill, 2012.
Schofield, Malcolm, ed. *Aristotle, Plato and Pythagoreanism in the First Century BC: New Directions for Philosophy*. Cambridge: Cambridge University Press, 2013.
Scholem, Gershom G. *Jewish Gnosticism, Merkabah Mysticism, and Talmudic Tradition*. New York: Jewish Theological Seminary of America, 1965.
Schrage, Wolfgang. "Zur Frontstellung der paulinischen Ehebewertung 1 Kor 7:1–7." *ZNW* 67 (1976): 214–34.
Schreiber, Stefan. "Das Weihegeschenk Gottes: eine Deutung des Todes Jesu in Röm 3:25." *ZNW* 97 (2006): 88–110.
———. "Weitergedacht: Das versöhnende Weihegeschenk Gottes in Röm 3:25." *ZNW* 106 (2015): 201–15.

Schulte, Hannelis. *Der Begriff der Offenbarung im Neuen Testament.* BEvT 13. Munich: Kaiser, 1949.
Schweitzer, Albert. *The Mysticism of Paul the Apostle.* Translated by William Montgomery. 2nd ed. London: Black, 1953. Repr. Baltimore: Johns Hopkins University Press, 1998.
Scott, Ernest F. *The New Testament Idea of Revelation.* London: Nicholson & Watson, 1935.
Seaford, Richard. *Dionysos.* London: Routledge, 2006.
Segal, Alan F. "Heavenly Ascent in Hellenistic Judaism, Early Christianity and their Environment." *ANRW* 23.1:1333–94. Part 2, *Principat,* 23.1. Edited by Wolfgang Haase. Berlin: de Gruyter, 1979.
———. *Paul the Convert: The Apostolate and Apostasy of Saul the Pharisee.* New Haven: Yale University Press, 1990.
Senft, Christophe. *La première Épître de Saint Paul aux Corinthiens.* Rev. ed. CNT 7. Geneva: Labor et Fides, 1990.
Seow, C. L. "The Syro-Palestinian Context of Solomon's Dream." *HTR* 77 (1984): 141–52.
Shantz, Colleen. *Paul in Ecstasy: The Neurobiology of the Apostle's Life and Thought.* Cambridge: Cambridge University Press, 2009.
Siegert, Folker. *Argumentation bei Paulus, gezeigt an Röm 9–11.* WUNT 34. Tübingen: Mohr Siebeck, 1985.
Simonetti, Elsa Giovanna. *A Perfect Medium? Oracular Divination in the Thought of Plutarch.* Leuven: Leuven University Press, 2017.
Smit, Joop F. M. "Tongues and Prophecy: Deciphering 1 Cor 14:22." *Biblica* 75 (1994): 175–90.
———. "'You Shall not Muzzle a Threshing Ox': Paul's Use of the Law of Moses in 1 Cor 9:8–12." *Estudios Bíblicos* 58 (2000): 239–63.
Smit, Peter-Ben. "In Search of Real Circumcision: Ritual Failure and Circumcision in Paul." *JSNT* 40 (2017): 73–100.
Smith, D. Moody. "Ο ΔΕ ΔΙΚΑΙΟΣ ΕΚ ΠΙΣΤΕΩΣ ΖΗΣΕΤΑΙ." Pages 13–25 in *Studies in the History and Text of the New Testament in Honor of Kenneth Willis Clark.* Edited by B. L. Daniels and M. J. Suggs. SD 29. Salt Lake City: University of Utah Press, 1967.
Smith, Jonathan Z. *Drudgery Divine: On the Comparison of Early Christianities and the Religions of Late Antiquity.* Chicago: University of Chicago Press, 1990.
———. "In Comparison a Magic Dwells." Pages 19–35 in *Imagining Religion: From Babylon to Jonestown.* Chicago: University of Chicago Press, 1982.
———. "When the Chips are Down." Pages 1–60 in *Relating Religion: Essays in the Study of Religion.* Chicago: University of Chicago Press, 2004.
Smith, Mark S. "The Three Bodies of God in the Hebrew Bible." *JBL* 134 (2015): 471–88.
Smith, Morton. "On the History of ΑΠΟΚΑΛΥΠΤΩ and ΑΠΟΚΑΛΥΨΙΣ." Pages 9–20 in *Apocalypticism in the Mediterranean World and the Near East: Proceedings of the International Colloquium on Apocalypticism, Uppsala, August 12–17, 1979.* Edited by David Hellholm. 2nd ed. Tübingen: Mohr Siebeck, 1989.
———. "Pauline Worship as Seen by Pagans." *HTR* 73 (1980): 241–49.
Sommer, Benjamin D. *The Bodies of God and the World of Ancient Israel.* Cambridge: Cambridge University Press, 2009.
Spittler, Russell P. "The Limits of Ecstasy: An Exegesis of 2 Corinthians 12:1–10." Pages 259–66 in *Current Issues in Biblical and Patristic Interpretation: Studies in Honor of Merrill C. Tenney Presented by His Former Students.* Edited by Gerald F. Hawthorne. Grand Rapids: Eerdmans, 1975.
Stanley, Christopher D. *Arguing with Scripture: The Rhetoric of Quotations in the Letters of Paul.* New York: T&T Clark, 2004.
———. "Paul and Homer: Greco-Roman Citation Practice in the First Century CE." *NovT* 32 (1990): 48–78.

———, ed. *Paul and Scripture: Extending the Conversation*. ECL 9. Atlanta: SBL Press, 2012.
———. *Paul and the Language of Scripture: Citation Technique in the Pauline Epistles and Contemporary Literature*. SNTSMS 74. Cambridge: Cambridge University Press, 1992.
Stendahl, Krister. *Paul Among Jews and Gentiles and Other Essays*. Philadelphia: Fortress, 1976.
Stettler, Christian. "The 'Command of the Lord' in 1 Cor 14:37 – A Saying of Jesus?" *Biblica* 87 (2006): 42–51.
Still, Todd D. *Conflict at Thessalonica: A Pauline Church and its Neighbours*. JSNTSup 183. Sheffield: Sheffield Academic, 1999.
Stökl, Jonathan. "Daniel and the 'Prophetization' of Dream Divination." Pages 133–55 in *Perchance to Dream: Dream Divination in the Bible and the Ancient Near East*. Edited by Esther J. Hamori and Jonathan Stökl. ANEM 21. Atlanta: SBL Press, 2018.
Stoneman, Richard. *The Ancient Oracles: Making the Gods Speak*. New Haven: Yale University Press, 2011.
Stowers, Stanley K. "The Dilemma of Paul's Physics: Features Stoic-Platonist or Platonist-Stoic?" Pages 231–53 in *From Stoicism to Platonism: The Development of Philosophy, 100 BCE–100 CE*. Edited by Troels Engberg-Pedersen. Cambridge: Cambridge University Press, 2017.
———. "Kinds of Myth, Meals, and Power: Paul and the Corinthians." Pages 105–49 in *Redescribing Paul and the Corinthians*. Edited by Ron Cameron and Merrill P. Miller. ECL 5. Atlanta: SBL Press, 2011.
———. "Paul and the Terrain of Philosophy." *EC* 6 (2015): 141–56.
———. "Paul's Four Discourses About Sin." Pages 100–27 in *Celebrating Paul: Festschrift in Honor of Jerome Murphy-O'Connor, O.P. and Joseph A. Fitzmyer, S.J.* Edited by Peter Spitaler. Washington, DC: Catholic Biblical Association of America, 2011.
———. "The Religion of Plant and Animal Offerings Versus the Religion of Meanings, Essences, and Textual Mysteries." Pages 35–56 in *Ancient Mediterranean Sacrifice*. Edited by Jennifer Wright Knust and Zsuzsanna Várhelyi. Oxford: Oxford University Press, 2011.
———. *A Rereading of Romans: Justice, Jews, and Gentiles*. New Haven: Yale University Press, 1994.
———. "What is 'Pauline Participation in Christ'?" Pages 352–71 in *Redefining First-Century Jewish and Christian Identities: Essays in Honor of Ed Parish Sanders*. Edited by Fabian E. Udoh. Notre Dame, IN: University of Notre Dame Press, 2008.
Struck, Peter T. *Birth of the Symbol: Ancient Readers at the Limits of their Texts*. Princeton: Princeton University Press, 2004.
———. *Divination and Human Nature: A Cognitive History of Intuition in Classical Antiquity*. Princeton: Princeton University Press, 2016.
Stuckenbruck, Loren T. "Overlapping Ages at Qumran and 'Apocalyptic' in Pauline Theology." Pages 309–26 in *The Dead Sea Scrolls and Pauline Literature*. Edited by Jean-Sébastien Rey. STDJ 102. Leiden: Brill, 2014.
———. "Some Reflections on Apocalyptic Thought and Time in Literature from the Second Temple Period." Pages 137–55 in *Paul and the Apocalyptic Imagination*. Edited by Ben C. Blackwell, John K. Goodrich, and Jason Maston. Minneapolis: Fortress, 2016.
Sturm, Richard E. "An Exegetical Study of the Apostle Paul's Use of the Words *Apokalyptō/Apokalypsis*: The Gospel as God's Apocalypse." PhD diss., Union Theological Seminary, 1983.
Swancutt, Diana M. "*Still* Before Sexuality: 'Greek' Androgyny, the Roman Imperial Politics of Masculinity and the Roman Invention of the *Tribas*." Pages 11–62 in *Mapping Gender in Ancient Religious Discourses*. Edited by Todd Penner and Caroline Vander Stichele. BibInt 84. Leiden: Brill, 2007.
Tabor, James D. *Things Unutterable: Paul's Ascent to Paradise in its Greco-Roman, Judaic, and Early Christian Contexts*. Lanham, MD: University Press of America, 1986.

Tervanotko, Hanna, and Kyle Schofield. "'Let us cast lots, so that we may know' (Jonah 1:7): Oracle of Lot as a Ritual-Like Activity in Ancient Jewish Texts." *BibInt* (2021): 1–22.

Tervanotko, Hanna. "Reading God's Will? Function and Status of Oracle Interpreters in Ancient Jewish and Greek Texts." *DSD* 24 (2017): 424–46.

———. "Searching the Book of Law: Jewish Divination in 1 Maccabees 3:48." Pages 121–37 in *The Early Reception of Torah*. Edited by Kristin de Troyer, Barbara Schmitz, Joshua Alfaro and Maximilian Häberlein. DCLS 39. Berlin: de Gruyter, 2020.

Theissen, Gerd. *Psychological Aspects of Pauline Theology*. Translated by John P. Galvin. Edinburgh: T&T Clark, 1987.

Thelle, Rannfrid I. *Ask God: Divine Consultation in the Literature of the Hebrew Bible*. BBET 30. Frankfurt: Lang, 2002.

Thiessen, Matthew. *Paul and the Gentile Problem*. Oxford: Oxford University Press, 2016.

———. "Paul's Argument Against Gentile Circumcision in Romans 2:17–29." *NovT* 56 (2014): 373–91.

Thiselton, Anthony C. *The First Epistle to the Corinthians*. NIGTC. Grand Rapids: Eerdmans, 2000.

Thompson, Michael B. *Clothed with Christ: The Example and Teaching of Jesus in Romans 12:1–15:13*. JSNTSup 59. Sheffield: Sheffield Academic, 1991.

Thorsteinsson, Runar M. *Paul's Interlocutor in Romans 2: Function and Identity in the Context of Ancient Epistolography*. ConBNT 40. Stockholm: Almqvist & Wiksell, 2003. Repr., Eugene, OR: Wipf & Stock, 2015.

Thrall, Margaret E. *2 Corinthians 8–13*. ICC. London: T&T Clark, 2000.

Tibbs, Clint. "Πνεῦμα as 'Spirit World' in Translation in the New Testament." *BT* 62 (2011): 172–84.

———. *Religious Experience of the Pneuma: Communication with the Spirit World in 1 Corinthians 12 and 14*. WUNT 2/230. Tübingen: Mohr Siebeck, 2007. Repr., Eugene, OR: Wipf & Stock, 2012.

Tieleman, Teun. "The Spirit of Stoicism." Pages 39–62 in *The Holy Spirit, Inspiration, and the Cultures of Antiquity: Multidisciplinary Perspectives*. Edited by Jörg Frey and John R. Levison. Ekstasis 5. Berlin: de Gruyter, 2014.

Tigay, Jeffrey H. *Deuteronomy*. JPS Torah Commentary. Philadelphia: Jewish Publication Society of America, 1996.

Tomasino, Anthony J. "Oracles of Insurrection: The Prophetic Catalyst of the Great Revolt." *JJS* 59 (2008): 86–111.

Trebilco, Paul. *Outsider Designations and Boundary Construction in the New Testament: Early Christian Communities and the Formation of Group Identity*. Cambridge: Cambridge University Press, 2017.

Twelftree, Graham H. *Paul and the Miraculous: A Historical Reconstruction*. Grand Rapids: Baker Academic, 2013.

———. "Signs, Wonders, Miracles." *DPL* 875–77.

Ustinova, Yulia. "Modes of Prophecy, or Modern Arguments in Support of the Ancient Approach." *Kernos* 26 (2013): 25–44.

Van Dam, Cornelis. *The Urim and Thummim: A Means of Revelation in Ancient Israel*. Winona Lake, IN: Eisenbrauns, 1997.

Verbeke, Gérard. *L'évolution de la doctrine du pneuma du stoïcisme à S. Augustin*. Paris: Descleé de Brouwer, 1945.

Verbruggen, Jan L. "Of Muzzles and Oxen: Deuteronomy 25:4 and 1 Corinthians 9:9." *JETS* 49 (2006): 699–711.

Versnel, Henk S. "What Did Ancient Man See When He Saw a God? Some Reflections on Greco-Roman Epiphany." Pages 42–55 in *Effigies Dei: Essays on the History of Religions*. Edited by Dirk van der Plas. SHR 51. Leiden: Brill, 1987.

Vollenweider, Samuel. "Der Geist Gottes als Selbst der Glaubenden," *ZThK* 93 (1996): 163–92.

Wagner, J. Ross. "The Christ, Servant of Jew and Gentile: A Fresh Approach to Romans 15:8–9." *JBL* 116 (1997): 473–85.
———. *Heralds of the Good News: Isaiah and Paul "in Concert" in the Letter to the Romans.* NovTSup 101. Leiden: Brill, 2002.
Walker Jr., William O. *Interpolations in the Pauline Letters.* JSNTSup 213. Sheffield: Sheffield Academic, 2001.
Walter, Nikolaus. "Paul and the Early Christian Jesus-Tradition." Pages 51–80 in *Paul and Jesus: Collected Essays.* Edited by A. J. M. Wedderburn. JSNTSup 37. Sheffield: Sheffield Academic, 1989.
Wanamaker, Charles A. *The Epistles to the Thessalonians.* NIGTC. Grand Rapids: Eerdmans, 1990.
Wardle, David. *Cicero: On Divination, Book 1, translated with introduction and commentary.* Oxford: Clarendon, 2006.
Wasserman, Emma. *Apocalypse as Holy War: Divine Politics and Polemics in the Letters of Paul.* AYBRL. New Haven: Yale University Press, 2018.
———. *The Death of the Soul in Romans 7: Sin, Death, and the Law in Light of Hellenistic Moral Psychology.* WUNT 2/256. Tübingen: Mohr Siebeck, 2008.
———. "Gentile Gods at the Eschaton: A Reconsideration of Paul's 'Principalities and Powers' in 1 Corinthians 15." *JBL* 136 (2017): 727–46.
Watson, Francis. "'I Received from the Lord . . .': Paul, Jesus, and the Last Supper." Pages 103–24 in *Jesus and Paul Reconnected: Fresh Pathways into an Old Debate.* Edited by Todd D. Still. Grand Rapids: Eerdmans, 2007.
———. *Paul and the Hermeneutics of Faith.* 2nd ed. London: T&T Clark, 2016.
Weber, Gregor. *Kaiser, Träume und Visionen in Prinzipat und Spätantike.* Stuttgart: Steiner, 2000.
Wells, Kyle B. *Grace and Agency in Paul and Second Temple Judaism: Interpreting the Transformation of the Heart.* NovTSup 157. Leiden: Brill, 2015.
Wendt, Heidi. *At the Temple Gates: The Religion of Freelance Experts in the Roman Empire.* Oxford: Oxford University Press, 2016.
———. "'Entrusted with the Oracles of God': The Fate of the Judean Writings in Flavian Rome." Pages 101–9 in *A Most Reliable Witness: Essays in Honor of Ross Shepard Kraemer.* Edited by Susan Ashbrook Harvey, Nathaniel P. DesRosiers, Shira L. Lander, Jacqueline Z. Pastis, and Daniel Ullucci. BJS 358. Providence, RI: Brown University, 2015.
———. "Galatians 3:1 as an Allusion to Textual Prophecy." *JBL* 135 (2016): 369–89.
Wenham, David. *Paul: Follower of Jesus or Founder of Christianity?* Grand Rapids: Eerdmans, 1995.
Wheeler-Reed, David, Jennifer W. Knust, and Dale B. Martin. "Can a Man Commit πορνεία with His Wife?" *JBL* 137 (2018): 383–98.
White, Joel. "Paul's Cosmology: The Witness of Romans, 1 and 2 Corinthians, and Galatians." Pages 90–106 in *Cosmology and New Testament Theology.* Edited by Jonathan T. Pennington and Sean M. Mcdonough. LNTS 355. London: T&T Clark, 2008.
White, L. Michael, and John T. Fitzgerald. "Quod Est Comparandum: The Problem of Parallels." Pages 13–29 in *Early Christianity and Classical Culture: Comparative Studies in Honor of Abraham J. Malherbe.* Edited by John T. Fitzgerald, Thomas H. Olbricht, and L. Michael White. NovTSup 110. Leiden: Brill, 2003.
Whittaker, Molly. "'Signs and Wonders': The Pagan Background." *SE* 5 (1968): 155–58.
Widmann, Martin. "1 Kor 2:6–16: ein Einspruch gegen Paulus." *ZNW* 70 (1979): 44–53.
Wilamowitz-Moellendorff, Ulrich von. *Der Glaube der Hellenen.* 2 vols. Berlin: Weidmannsche, 1931–32.
Wilckens, Ulrich. "The Understanding of Revelation within Primitive Christianity." Pages 57–121 in *Revelation as History.* Edited by Wolfhart Pannenberg. Translated by David Granskou and Edward Quinn. London: Sheed & Ward, 1969.

———. *Weisheit und Torheit: Eine exegetisch-religionsgeschichtliche Untersuchung zu 1 Kor. 1 und 2*. BHT 26. Tübingen: Mohr Siebeck, 1959.
Will, Ernest. "Sur la nature du pneuma delphique." *BCH* 66 (1942): 161–75.
Williams, Craig A. *Roman Homosexuality*. 2nd ed. Oxford: Oxford University Press, 2010.
Williams, Guy. *The Spirit World in the Letters of Paul the Apostle: A Critical Examination of the Role of Spiritual Beings in the Authentic Pauline Epistles*. FRLANT 231. Göttingen: Vandenhoeck & Ruprecht, 2009.
Williams, Ritva H. "Accessing Divine Knowledge." Pages 55–72 in *Early Christian Ritual Life*. Edited by Richard E. DeMaris, Jason T. Lamoreaux, and Steven C. Muir. Abingdon: Routledge, 2018.
Windsor, Lionel J. *Paul and the Vocation of Israel: How Paul's Jewish Identity Informs His Apostolic Ministry, with Special Reference to Romans*. BZNW 205. Berlin: de Gruyter, 2014.
Wire, Antoinette Clark. *The Corinthian Women Prophets: A Reconstruction Through Paul's Rhetoric*. Minneapolis: Fortress, 1990.
Wiśniewski, Robert. "Pagans, Jews, Christians, and a Type of Book Divination in Late Antiquity." *JECS* 24 (2016): 553–68.
Witherup, Ronald D. "'Functional Redundancy' in the Acts of the Apostles: A Case Study." *JSNT* 48 (1992): 67–86.
Wolter, Michael. "'It Is Not as Though the Word of God Has Failed': God's Faithfulness and God's Free Sovereignty in Romans 9:6–29." Pages 27–48 in *God and Israel: Providence and Purpose in Romans 9–11*. Edited by Todd D. Still. Waco, TX: Baylor University Press, 2017.
———. *Paul: An Outline of his Theology*. Translated by Robert L. Brawley. Waco, TX: Baylor University Press, 2015.
Wright, N. T. *The Climax of the Covenant: Christ and the Law in Pauline Theology*. London: T&T Clark, 1991.
———. *The New Testament and the People of God*. London: SPCK, 1992.
———. *Paul and the Faithfulness of God*. 2 vols. London: SPCK, 2013.
———. "Paul, Arabia and Elijah (Galatians 1:17)." *JBL* 115 (1996): 683–92.
Wynne, J. P. F. *Cicero on the Philosophy of Religion: On the Nature of the Gods and On Divination*. Cambridge: Cambridge University Press, 2019.
Yarbro Collins, Adela. "Ancient Notions of Transferal and Apotheosis in Relation to the Empty Tomb Story in Mark" Pages 41–58 in *Metamorphoses: Resurrection, Body and Transformative Practices in Early Christianity*. Edited by Turid Karlsen Seim and Jorunn Økland. Ekstasis 1. Berlin: de Gruyter, 2009.
———. "Apotheosis and Resurrection." Pages 88–100 in *The New Testament and Hellenistic Judaism*. Edited by Peder Borgen and Søren Giversen. Aarhus: Aarhus University Press, 1995.
———. "Ascents to Heaven in Antiquity: Toward a Typology." Pages 553–72 in vol. 2 of *A Teacher for All Generations: Essays in Honour of James C. VanderKam*. Edited by Eric F. Mason. JSJSup 153. Leiden: Brill, 2012.
———. *Mark*. Hermeneia. Minneapolis: Fortress, 2007.
———. "The Metaphorical Use of ἱλαστήριον in Romans 3:25." Pages 273–86 in *Sōtēria: Salvation in Early Christianity and Antiquity: Festschrift in Honour of Cilliers Breytenbach on the Occasion of his 65th Birthday*. Edited by David S. du Toit, Christine Gerber, and Christiane Zimmermann. NovTSup 175. Leiden: Brill, 2019.
Young, Stephen L. "Romans 1:1–5 and Paul's Christological Use of Hab 2:4 in Rom 1:17: An Underutilized Consideration in the Debate." *JSNT* 34 (2012): 277–85.

Index

Acts of the Apostles, 68, 79, 82, 107, 171n24
Alexander of Abonoteichus, 123–4
allegory, 134–5, 139n23, 161
angels, 39–40, 47–8, 49, 102–3
apocalypse, apocalyptic, 13–14, 75–6, 90–1, 168, 200
Apollo, 31–2, 36, 70, 86, 100, 111, 120, 123, 137, 138, 143–4, 151, 157, 191, 203–4
apostle, 18, 74, 115, 168
apotheosis, 70–3
Apuleius, 32–3, 203
Arabia, 84–5; *see also* Sinai
Aramaic, 98, 99–101
Aristeas, 70, 86
Aristotle, 28, 63, 180
Artemidorus, 63, 82, 87
Asclepius, 86, 94, 95, 123–4
Athena, 80, 142n33, 190
augury, 30, 80; *see also* ornithomancy
Aune, D. E., 14, 39, 95, 107, 131, 199n4

Bacis, 133, 143
baptism, 50, 99, 192
Barton, J., 90–1
Bates, M. W., 142
belly-talkers, 3n5, 107, 108, 123
Bethel, 125, 126
Betz, H. D., 71n40, 95
bibliomancy, 134
Bockmuehl, M. N. A., 12–13, 128n135, 193n120, 200
Boer, M. de, 76n58, 77n64, 88n109
Bultmann, R., 10, 201

Cassius Dio, 40, 72, 95, 131, 140, 148–9
categories, 1–2, 8–9, 14, 16–18, 22, 25–6, 133, 197, 199
Christianity, 15, 23–4, 68n25
Cicero
   De divinatione, 16, 29–1, 34, 37, 39, 40–1, 64n10, 100
   Dream of Scipio, 91, 129
circumcision, 81, 146n46, 186–8
cleromancy (lot divination), 5, 131
comparison in ancient religion, 7–9, 23, 25, 69
conversion, 68n25
creation, 46, 50, 54–5, 61, 69, 96, 98, 150, 201
crucifixion, 57, 105, 162, 192, 193–5, 196, 200
cult
   correct observance, 120, 123, 132, 179, 186–7, 195
   founding, 70, 71, 73, 78

daimons, 32–4, 37–8, 40, 45–7, 202–3
Daniel, 4, 57, 75, 130, 150n56
Dead Sea Scrolls, 5–6, 130, 144, 145–6, 167
dreams, 63–4
   and visions, 63–5, 198
   in the Hebrew Bible, 4, 64
   incubation, 4, 94
   interpretation, 82, 83
   of the dead, 69
   see also epiphanies
David, 136, 138, 143–4
Dio Chrysostom, 100, 113, 155, 156, 190

Diogenianus, 158
Dionysius of Halicarnassus, 66, 164
divination
    and magic, 9, 21
    as a means of social power, 21–2, 66–7, 78, 161
    as knowledge of the past, 138n20
    biblical prohibition, 3, 6–7
    definition, 2–3
    natural versus technical, 15–17, 57, 202
Dodson, J. R., 92n132
Dunn, J. D. G., 87n108, 100

ecstasy, 16, 40–1, 48, 55, 79, 89n111, 98, 99, 103, 108, 110–13, 175
Egypt, 83, 166–7
elements (of the cosmos), 46
Elijah, 85, 86–7, 127, 156–7
Engberg-Pedersen, T., 24–5, 171n25
ephod, 4–5
Epictetus, 29, 35, 121
Epicureanism, 28, 29
Epimenides, 143, 144, 191
epiphanies, 31, 63–5, 78–80
    Paul's vision of Christ, 43–4, 68–88
    see also dreams
eschatology, 11, 93, 114–15, 128–31, 159, 162, 168, 170, 199–200, 201–2
expiation, 178, 186, 189, 191, 195; *see also* hilastērion
Eyl, J., 19–21, 106, 134, 139n23
Ezekiel, 44n61, 78, 113n75, 128, 167

Fee, G. D., 119, 172n31
Flannery, F., 94
flesh (*sarx*), 58–9, 201–2
    thorn in the, 94
Forbes, C., 17–18, 102, 108n55
freelance religious experts, 18–19, 21, 83, 121, 123, 200

Garroway, J. D., 66n19, 81–2, 146n46, 188n101
Gentiles, 81, 84, 124, 131, 146–9, 162, 183, 184–9, 194
ghost *see* necromancy
glossolalia, 20–1, 101–5, 108–9, 170–5
God(s), 1, 203–4
    absence, 165
    and cosmos, 50, 54
    appearance, 27, 31, 44–5, 62–5, 78–80, 89, 95; *see also* epiphanies
    breath, 52–3
    character, 152–7, 199
    chthonic, 37, 94, 120, 192
    creator, 150
    "depths of God", 51–2
    discerning the right god, 16, 120, 166–7, 174–5, 183, 187
    Gentile gods, 16, 45, 124
    "God within", 35
    in relation to Jesus, 44–5, 69, 71, 86
    in modern theology, 10–11
    languages, 100–1, 173
    materiality, 42–3, 44
    of this age, 44, 45–6
    speaking oracles, 31–2, 109–10, 131, 136–8, 143–4, 150, 199
Gospels, 98, 121, 125
Greek Magical Papyri, 40, 65, 98, 123, 131n145
groans, 97–9, 103

Habbakuk, 159
Hafemann, S., 141
Hamori, E. J., 6
Hanges, J. C., 66n19, 78
Hanson, A. T., 142
Hays, R. B., 142, 147n47
healing, 94–5
heart, 44, 51, 55, 130, 174
heavenly ascent, 90–1, 93, 128–9, 198–9
Hellenism, 23–5
hepatoscopy (liver divination), 36, 163, 164
hermaphrodite births, 175, 180–2
hilastērion (propitiation), 189–93
Homer
    as an oracle, 131
    divination in, 17n59, 170
    exegesis of, 134, 142

idolatry, 24, 45, 120, 124, 177, 180, 184–5
impiety, 175–6, 177, 178–9, 183, 191
inspiration
    and *pneuma*, 38–41, 49–50, 54, 100
    as a category, 2, 9, 15–18, 26, 29, 57, 105, 163, 202
    of oracle collections, 133, 143
    of poets, 80, 134n6

of prophets, 27, 35–7, 38, 49–50, 65, 107–15, 128, 132, 137
of scripture, 1, 139, 142–3
Isaacs, M. E., 38–9, 57n108, 59n115
Isaiah, 78, 79, 90–1, 99, 116n86, 125n128, 135n10, 136, 138, 148, 160, 167, 173–4, 188

Jeremiah, 79, 85, 87n108, 137n18, 166n10
Jerusalem, 79, 84, 85, 86, 88, 124, 127, 176
Jesus Christ
  as healer, 94, 98
  as image of God, 44–5, 124
  as Messiah, 69, 142, 143, 148–9, 151, 162
  as *pneuma*, 50, 53, 60, 76–7, 100
  death as a sign, 162, 193–5
  death as propitiation *see hilastērion*
  in scripture, 141–4, 147–8, 203
  parousia, 13, 125, 128–31, 168; *see also* eschatology
  pre-existence, 71–2, 142
  resurrection, 43–4, 68–9, 71
Jesus-tradition, 121–2, 125
Jews, 15, 24, 83, 131, 184–9, 194
Judaism, 23–5, 68n25
John Chrysostom, 55–6
Josephus, 6n21, 83, 150–1, 167, 191
justice, 129, 179, 189, 192–3

Kitz, A. M., 163
Kooten, G. H. van, 53n93, 136–9
krasis, 41, 55

Lang, T. J., 105n37, 130
law (Torah), 48, 81, 84–5, 86n102, 136, 138, 158, 186–8, 189, 192, 203
Lightfoot, J. B., 84–5, 119
Lindblom, J., 12
Livy, 175, 192
Lührmann, D., 11–12, 75–6, 88n109, 200

Malachi, 154
Marcus Aurelius, 29, 35
Martial, 181, 182
Martin, D. B., 102, 103n29
Martyn, J. L., 76
Masoretic Text (MT), 126, 137n17, 173
merkabah, 90
Middle Platonism, 28, 30–1, 41, 60

mind (*nous*), 34, 36, 37–8, 44, 52, 93, 101, 108–10, 112–13, 115
  of Christ, 58, 60, 61, 93n132, 122
Moses, 29, 48, 85, 87n105, 136, 137–8, 154, 158, 166, 167
Musaeus, 133, 143, 144
mysteries, 93, 105, 129–31, 198–9
mysticism, 12, 90

necromancy, 6, 69
Neutel, K. B., 186
Novenson, M. V., 148, 188–9

Oepke, A., 10–11, 200
oneiromancy *see* dreams
oracle sanctuaries
  Claros, 120, 124
  Delphi, 17, 31, 38, 40, 41–2, 43, 72, 86, 87, 107, 123, 133, 138, 143, 157, 191, 203–4
  Dodona, 107n46, 117–20
  Trophonius, 37, 91
oracles
  as promises, 149–50
  as proverbs, 157–8
  enigmatic nature, 82, 114
  philosophical nature, 91n122, 120, 121, 151–2
  topics of inquiry, 83, 117, 119–20
  written collections, 133, 143–4, 151–2, 160–1
orders of discourse, 7–9, 17–8
Origen, 42–3, 45, 93n131, 192
ornithomancy (bird divination), 3, 17n59, 32, 163, 164, 170, 195; *see also* augury
Ovid, 181

Paul's letters
  1 Corinthians, 43–4, 45–7, 49–50, 51–9, 68–9, 71, 101–5, 112, 114–15, 117–24, 129–30, 158, 159–60, 169, 171–5, 176, 177, 193–5, 203
  2 Corinthians, 44–5, 88–95, 99, 116, 168
  Galatians, 48, 74, 76–7, 78, 81–2, 83–6, 88, 99–101, 116–17, 158, 169–70, 175
  Philippians, 71, 88, 178
  Romans, 86–7, 97–101, 130–1, 137–8, 141–51, 152–7, 158, 168, 175, 178–93
  1 Thessalonians, 116–17, 124–9, 165, 169, 176–7
  2 Thessalonians, 168, 170, 178

Pausanias, 91n122, 143, 144, 155–6, 157, 164
Pentateuch, 3, 4, 52–3, 64, 106, 135n10, 152–3, 158, 161, 177
Pharaoh, 154
Philo, 29, 39–40, 52–3, 108, 137, 183
philosophical schools, 28–30, 60
Plato, 16, 28–9, 32, 35–6, 57, 91, 108n53
Plutarch, 29–31
   De amicorum multitudine, 157–8
   De defectu oraculorum, 32, 34–5, 36–7, 41–2, 107, 151, 158
   De E apud Delphos, 117
   De genio Socratis, 16n57, 33–4, 37–8, 91
   De Pythiae oraculis, 109, 111, 113–14, 117
   De sera numinis vindicta, 191
   Lives, 66, 70, 71–2, 85–6, 150, 155, 156, 191
pneuma, 38–43, 50–9, 76–7, 97–103, 115, 122–3, 124, 169, 194–5, 201–2, 203
   at Delphi, 40–2, 43
   of the cosmos, 53–4, 60–1
   pneumata ("spirits"), 48–50
   see also Stoicism
Polybius, 65, 166, 190
Porphyry, 151–2
Posidonius, 27, 30, 34, 37, 39
possession (by a god or spirit), 31–2, 108–10
power (*dunamis, vis*), 19, 40–1, 46, 95, 168–71, 188, 194–5
priests, 4–5, 18, 31, 124, 125, 133, 139, 143, 173
prodigies, 139–40, 175, 180–2, 195
prophecy, 14–18, 106–8, 199
   as a sign, 171, 174–5
   Hebrew prophets, 6, 78–9, 90–1, 112, 125–7, 128, 138–9, 167
   versus divination, 15–17
   versus glossolalia, 104–5
Psalms, 135n10, 141–6, 147, 188, 203; *see also* David
Pythagoras, 28, 29
Pythia, 17, 100n15, 107n46, 109, 111, 123, 137, 138, 139, 143, 155; *see also* oracle sanctuaries

Qumran *see* Dead Sea Scrolls

redescription, 7
religious experience, 15n53, 66–7
Requena Jiménez, M., 165–6

revelation, 74–6
   and divination, 199–200
   in modern theology, 9–10
   see also apocalypse, apocalyptic
ritual, 98, 99, 140, 146, 176, 186–7, 192, 198
Romulus, 70–2

Sarapis, 83, 94
Satan, 94, 165, 202
Satlow, M., 8, 136n16
Satterfield, S., 140n25, 150n55, 175
Saul (king), 4, 6
scepticism, 28, 30, 100
Second Temple period, 5–6, 12, 67, 144
Septuagint (LXX), 3, 6n21, 8, 75, 126, 135n10, 166–7, 173, 179, 189n106, 190, 203
sexuality, 117–19, 181–3
scripture
   allusions, 135
   as oracle collection, 135–9, 160–1, 188, 199
   canon, 135–6
   charismatic exegesis, 15, 106, 107n44
   see also oracles
Sibyl, 91, 107, 111, 133, 137, 143, 144
   Sibylline Books, 139–40, 146, 148, 149, 150, 175, 191n113
   Sibylline Oracles, 143, 191n114
Sinai, 84–5, 86–7
Smit, P. B., 186–7
Smith, J. Z., 7, 8
Smith, M., 50, 103
soul, 33, 34–8, 39–42, 52–3, 55, 57, 58, 60, 72, 91, 109, 113, 201–2
spirit *see pneuma*
Stanley, C. D., 134n3
Stoicism, 28–9
   daimons, 34
   divination, 27, 29, 41, 54, 57–8, 60, 165
   pneuma, 39, 40–1, 49–50, 52
   sympathy, 34, 41, 57–8
   see also Posidonius
Stowers, S. K., 28–9, 168
Struck, P. T., 21–2, 60, 91, 134, 200
Suetonius, 170
Swancutt, D. M., 181

temple, 71n38, 157, 164, 176–7
Testament of Epicrates, 72–3

Tibbs, C., 49, 109n57
Theodotion, 75
Thiessen, M., 54n97, 55, 187–8
Thiselton, A. C., 102–3, 105
Thrall, M. E., 93
tongues *see* glossolalia

Urim and Thummim, 4–6

Virgil, 91

Wendt, H., 18–19, 20, 134, 161–2
Wilckens, U., 10
"word of the Lord", 124–9
wrath (of God), 140, 156, 175, 176, 178–80, 182–3, 189–91
Wright, N. T., 84, 85, 86, 183n84

Zenobius, 158
Zeus, 86, 117–20, 131, 155–6, 170, 204

EU representative:
Easy Access System Europe
Mustamäe tee 50, 10621 Tallinn, Estonia
Gpsr.requests@easproject.com